BREAKING NEWS

Alan Rusbridger was Editor-in-Chief of *Guardian* News & Media from 1995 to 2015. He launched the *Guardian* in the US and Australia as well as building a website which today attracts more than 100 million unique browsers a month. The paper's coverage of phone-hacking led to the Leveson Inquiry into press standards and ethics. *Guardian* US won the 2014 Pulitzer Prize for public service for its leading global coverage of the Snowden revelations. He is the author of *Play It Again*. He lives in London and Oxford, where he is the Principal of Lady Margaret Hall and chairs the Reuters Institute for the Study of Journalism.

@arusbridger | arusbridger.com

'Eloquent in its argument for well-resourced journalism, and never better than in its central narrative of how an old profession struggled to cope with a new technology that threatened it with obsolescence'
Guardian

'We love a good newspaper yarn, and Rusbridger provides a dandy'
Financial Times

'A fascinating book and an important one'
Scotsman

'Engaging, informed and readable . . . a right riveting read,
as we say in the trade'
Herald

'Alan Rusbridger is a quiet giant of modern British journalism. [*Breaking News*] is a cracking read as you would expect of a great writer . . . Buy this book, read it on any platform you can find. It is an important text'
Press Gazette

Also by Alan Rusbridger

Play It Again: An Amateur Against the Impossible

BREAKING NEWS

THE REMAKING OF JOURNALISM AND WHY IT MATTERS NOW

ALAN RUSBRIDGER

CANONGATE

This paperback edition published in Great Britain in 2019
by Canongate Books

First published in Great Britain in 2018 by Canongate Books Ltd,
14 High Street, Edinburgh EH1 1TE

canongate.co.uk

1

British Library Cataloguing-in-Publication Data
A catalogue record for this book is available on
request from the British Library

ISBN 978 1 78689 096 2

Printed and bound in Great Britain by Clays Ltd, Elcograf S.p.A.

To Lindsay and Georgina who, between them,
shared most of this journey

Contents

Introduction

By early 2017 the world had woken up to a problem that, with a mixture of impotence, incomprehension and dread, journalists had seen coming for some time. News – the thing that helped people understand their world; that oiled the wheels of society; that pollinated communities; that kept the powerful honest – news was broken.

The problem had many different names and diagnoses. Some thought we were drowning in too much news; others feared we were in danger of becoming newsless. Some believed we had too much free news: others, that paid-for news was leaving behind it a long caravan of ignorance.

No one could agree on one narrative. The old media were lazy and corrupt: and/or the new players were greedy and secretive. We were newly penned into filter bubbles: rubbish – they had always been there. There was a new democracy of information: bunkum – the mob were now in control. The old elites were dying: read your history – power simply changes shape.

On this most people could agree: we were now up to our necks in a seething, ever churning ocean of information; some of it true, much of it wrong. There was too much false news, not enough reliable news. There might soon be entire communities without news. Or without news they could trust.

There was a swamp of stuff we were learning to call 'fake news'. The recently elected 45th President of the United States, Donald Trump, used the term so indiscriminately it rapidly lost any meaning. The best that traditional journalism could offer was – or so he repeatedly told us – fake. We should believe him, not lying journalists.

Truth was fake; fake was true.

And that's when the problem suddenly snapped into focus.

Throughout recent centuries anyone growing up in a western democracy had believed that it was necessary to have facts. Without facts, societies could be extremely dark places. Facts were essential to informed debates, to progress, to coherence, to justice.

We took it for granted, perhaps, that facts were reasonably easy to obtain; and that, over time, we'd developed pretty effective methods of distinguishing truth from falsehood.

Suddenly it was not so easy to establish, or agree on, truths. The dawning realisation that we were in trouble coincided with the near-collapse of the broad economic model for journalism. People had – sort of – known that was happening, but in a world of too much news they had stopped noticing.

In a world of too much to absorb, and never enough time, people skipped the story.

And then people started noticing. For a brief period in January 2017 George Orwell's *1984* – 'How do we know two and two make four?' – went to the top of the Amazon bestseller list while Hannah Arendt's definitive guide to totalitarianism,[1] written just after the Second World War, sold out.

'The result of a consistent and total substitution of lies for factual truth is not that the lie will now be accepted as truth and truth be defamed as a lie,' Arendt had written in 1951, 'but that the sense by which we take our bearings in the real world – and the category of truth versus falsehood is among the mental means to this end – is being destroyed . . .'

Nearly 70 years later many of us may be surprised to be asking the most basic question imaginable: how do you know if something is true or not?

★

Here is just one small example of this new world of information chaos, playing out as I was writing this chapter. I could have chosen a thousand such illustrations, but this had most of the components of the unfolding problem.

In February 2017 Donald Trump used a rally in Melbourne, Florida, to draw attention to disturbing events he said were happening in Sweden.[2] 'You look at what's happening in Germany. You look at what's happening last night in Sweden.'

The President of the United States paused for the name to sink in and then repeated it.

'Sweden.'

'Who would believe this? Sweden. They took in large numbers and they're having problems like they never thought possible.'

Sweden was puzzled. The country, like others in Europe, was not without its tensions after the recent wave of migration from North Africa and the Middle East. There had been a widespread – but by no means universal – welcome to the 163,000 asylum seekers who arrived in the country that year.[3] But, amid a spate of really frightening terror attacks in Europe, it seemed curious to single out Sweden for a stump speech in Florida.

So little of note appeared to have happened in Sweden the previous evening – apart from a national singing competition – that social media regarded the intervention as a bit of a joke.

'Sweden? Terror Attack? What has he been smoking?' former Swedish prime minister Carl Bildt tweeted. There were spoof hashtags – #JeSuisIKEA and #IStandWithSweden – while other users questioned the safety of ABBA.

The following day Trump clarified his Sweden statement. He told his 40 million followers on Twitter that it had been 'in reference to a story that was broadcast on @FoxNews concerning immigrants & Sweden'.

And so began an anatomy of how Donald Trump arrived at his version of the truth. Which, given he was the most powerful man on earth, was quite important to understand.

The previous Friday night's *Tucker Carlson Tonight* had included an interview with someone we might call a media controversialist,

Ami Horowitz, about a documentary the latter was making about Sweden.

'There was an absolute surge in gun violence and rape in Sweden once they began this open-door policy,' Horowitz had told Carlson.

Who was Ami Horowitz? For 13 years he worked as an investment banker with Lehman Brothers before reinventing himself as a gonzo filmmaker. His website shows him engaged in a series of provocations ('Ami on the loose') where, for instance, he descends on the campus at the University of California, Berkeley, to alternate between waving an American flag and an Isis flag – and gauge the supposed difference in reaction from students. That, he says, was watched 15 million times across various platforms. In another, he retaliates at Palestinians lobbing stones at an Israeli checkpoint on the West Bank ('It was time to get stupid').[4] His work – inspired, he says, by Michael Moore – has been called 'docu-tainment' or 'mockumentaries'.

In 2017 anyone can be a 'journalist' and anyone can transmit their work to a global audience. It helps if a huge mainstream news channel amplifies your work. Horowitz has described Rupert Murdoch's Fox News as 'a partner' ('They've done a phenomenal job of disseminating the videos and my point of view'),[5] and they duly picked up on a YouTube video he'd published in December 2016 claiming that 'rape and violence has exploded across Sweden due it's [sic] immigration policies'.[6]

Within 15 seconds of the video, an alert viewer would see what kind of an exercise this was. Horowitz lingers on a BBC headline 'Sweden's rape rate under the spotlight'. In fact, that four-year-old, 1,200-word article – pegged to the extradition of WikiLeaks leader Julian Assange, rather than immigration – was a nuanced exploration of whether Sweden's apparently higher rates of rape were mainly down to changes in the way the police record incidents. But that was not how Horowitz used the headline.

Horowitz dealt in outrage, entertainment and provocation. It was central to his Unique Selling Point that he told uncomfortable home truths the despised Mainstream Media (MSM) ignored.[7] He was not a reliable source for the President of the United States. Or anyone else.

Following on from Trump's discovery of Horowitz's work the Swedish paper *Aftonbladet* analysed his film and found it 'contained many errors and exaggerations'.[8] Another newspaper, *Dagens Nyheter,* quoted two police officers interviewed by Horowitz as saying that the film-maker had selectively edited and distorted their comments to prove his thesis. 'We don't stand behind what he says,' said one of them, Anders Goranzon. 'He is a madman.'[9]

But the truth, or otherwise, of the film appears to have been of little concern to Fox, America's most-watched cable network – described as Murdoch's 'profit machine' by Bloomberg.[10] The programme, seen by as many as 2.5 million viewers, gave further exposure and credibility to the video, which had itself had half a million views on social media.

Enter the President of the United States.

It's doubtful that Donald Trump had any idea of who Horowitz was, or whether he had any journalistic credentials. In general, he appears predisposed to believe Fox News tells the truth and that the *New York Times* tells lies. So – after his stump speech in Florida – the President then broadcast the existence of Horowitz's gonzo docu-tainment to his 40 million-odd followers on Twitter.

Thus were half-truths blasted around the planet's new global information eco-system.

This horizontal transmission of news – from person to person – is virtually unmappable. But let us suppose that hundreds of millions of people around the world would by now have registered – at some level – this . . . germ.

I use the word 'germ' in the absence of another easy label. The exercise Horowitz was engaged in, and which the President and Fox News megaphoned, was not conventional journalism. These were not 'facts'. Deeply buried in some of the assertions in a ten-minute film there may even have been some semi-truths. I will not call the rest 'lies'. The point is that most of the hundreds of millions who will have been touched by the germ will not have registered the detail. They will not have researched the origins of Trump's Swedish intervention or looked into Horowitz's techniques or motivations.

The virus is likely to have lodged itself as little more than a perception, in those ready to believe, that Muslim immigration leads to unspeakable things such as mass rape – and that the west had better wake up. A couple of days after Trump spoke there was some rioting in the northern suburbs of the Swedish capital, Stockholm. No smoke without a fire? But which was the smoke, and which the fire?

The patient analysis and denials of Swedish newspapers counted for little as the virus spread. In the UK the former UKIP[11] leader (and friend of Donald Trump) Nigel Farage used his radio show on LBC to announce that Malmo, a city in southern Sweden, was now the 'rape capital of Europe and, some argue, perhaps even the rape capital of the world. And there is a Swedish media that just don't report it.'[12]

★

Months later I was browsing through my Twitter feed and saw someone I follow – Godfrey Bloom, a leading UKIP figure and former Member of the European Parliament – retweeting news of a horrific attack on a teenage girl in Malmo. Someone calling himself @PeterSweden7 tweeted about his 'blood being at boiling point . . . While she was being raped the rapists poured lighter fuel in her vagina and set it on fire. MSM is quiet. RETWEET.'[13]

This germ was so graphically specific and shocking that it caused understandable revulsion as it ricocheted around the internet. On the social media website Reddit there was a bitterly angry thread. The attack was said to be the fourth rape in two months. It was taken as read that the attackers were Muslim immigrants. If you let Muslims into your country – so many commenters raged – what do you expect?

This was war.

But did the incident – with the obscene barbarity alleged by @PeterSweden7 – actually happen? That was a more complicated question and would take more than a day of patient digging to get near any kind of truth.

A 17-year-old girl had undoubtedly been raped that evening in Malmo – and the attack had been widely reported in the press. But @PeterSweden7 was right to say that newspapers had made no mention of lighter fuel being poured into the victim's vagina and set on fire. Was this out of political correctness, or because it hadn't happened?

I tweeted an appeal for help in getting some facts. A couple of Swedish journalists sent me links to reports in the so-called MSM. I tried to read both . . . but, in each case, hit a paywall. One wanted me to commit to £9 a month before it would allow me to read the article; the other wanted nearly twice as much.

Chaotic information was free: good information was expensive.

In the horizontal world of twenty-first-century communications – where anyone can publish anything – the germs about rape in Malmo spread indiscriminately and freely. The virus was halfway round the world and the truth had barely even found its boots. Truth – if that's what journalism offered – was living in a gated community.

But the truth mattered. The idea that immigrants would reward a society's compassion by barbarically raping its women could – if true – profoundly shape popular attitudes and political responses to immigration in Sweden and beyond. That was especially true now Donald Trump – and numerous white nationalists and their fellow travellers – were using the country as a prime exhibit of the dangers of open borders.

I did my best, as a non-Swedish speaker, to establish some facts. For a start, who was @PeterSweden7? Many of those exploiting the horrific lighter fuel story belonged to far-right extremist groups around the world. @PeterSweden7's previous tweets gave some clue to his politics: 'I don't like fascism, but i think hitler had some good points. I am pretty certain that the holocaust actually never happened.'[14] Or another: 'The globalists (mainly Jews) are ones bringing in the Muslims to europe. They seem to work together.'[15] He had 81,000 followers on Twitter, growing at a rate of 10,000 a month.

I contacted @PeterSweden7, who appears in real life to be Peter Imanuelsen, a 22-year-old photographer born in Norway, but possibly living, at least some of the time, in North Yorkshire. He told a website called hopenothate.org.uk that his holocaust-denial was simply a phase brought about by realising that 'mainstream media was lying about everything'. Imanuelsen described this website as 'fake news'. His own website claims to be 'real independent journalism'.[16]

Via Twitter he repeated to me that Swedish media hadn't gone into detail 'on the horrible things the girl suffered'. I asked his source. He replied that 'word has gotten around in Malmo about the details and locals in Malmo have taken to social media to say what happened'.

So, a combination of local rumour and gossip, amplified instantly by horizontal transmission.

He later pointed me to a Facebook posting by a 37-year-old Chicago-educated researcher, Tino Sanandaji, who is considered to be the most prominent social media critic of Sweden's immigration policies, and also of the established media.

I tracked down Sanandaji. He had, indeed, blogged about the incident to his 76,000 followers. He said he had two sources, 'one citing the police investigation and one friend of the family . . . the same rumour was also on social media'. He was 'fairly sure' about his information, and he thought he had a duty to warn girls in the area after three rapes in Malmo in the space of seven weeks.

But here was the rub. Sanandaji claimed that the detail that had caused such revulsion and sent the germ around the world was not in his Facebook posting in its original Swedish, *'underliv'* – or so he claimed. He claimed to have written that a source had told him that the victim's 'abdomen' had been sprayed with fuel. By the time it had been picked up and redistributed by a Canadian-based British 'journalist' working for the alt-right website Breitbart, 'abdomen' had become 'vagina'.[17] Whether Sanandaji's finger-pointing at Breitbart was correct; or whether there had been inadequate automatic translation or distortion by Breitbart was difficult to establish. The Breitbart writer declined to comment.

In any event, it was untrue. Within days the police addressed the social media rumours and announced that – while the victim had other minor physical injuries – these did not include burns to the lower abdomen.[18] Within a few weeks police announced they had dropped another rape investigation after the woman admitted the attack had never happened.[19] Investigations into the 'lighter fuel' case were closed a few months later, with the police saying they could not show what actually happened, let alone who the offenders were.

Now, none of this is to minimise the severity of the attack, or attacks. The women of Malmo took to the streets to show how they refused to be intimidated. At the time of writing it was not known if Muslims were behind this, or other, rapes in Malmo. It was very difficult for an ordinary reader to reach a definitive conclusion about whether there was a link between increased immigration and increased rape reports in Sweden – though a painstaking investigation by Dagens Nyheter in May 2018 found no such correlation between them.

But if the facts were elusive, the digital world had transmitted half-truths and lies at a speed and scale that would have been unimaginable even a decade earlier. The patient work of journalists to take time to discover what actually happened was buried in the avalanche of rumour – and then invisible except to the relatively tiny minority who still cared enough for old-fashioned facts to pay for them.

When challenged about their own role in spreading unchecked information, most of the pollinators seemed unbothered. Godfrey Bloom told me his attitude was the same as all other users of Twitter: 'It is a lavatory wall.'

There were, if you looked hard enough, calm pieces to be found on the subject, some of them involving detailed work with available data. The BBC – freely available to all – investigated Farage's claim about Malmo being 'the rape capital of Europe' and concluded that the high level of reported rape was 'mainly due to the strictness of Swedish laws and how rape is recorded in the country'.[20] The Dagens Nyheter analysis agreed.

Bad information was everywhere: good information was increasingly for smaller elites. It was harder for good information to compete on equal terms with bad.

The more invisible decent journalists became, the easier it was to denigrate their work. They became part of the problem – an out of touch elite. *Lamestream media. Fake news. Failing. Lies. They're all the same. Enough of experts. Drain the swamp.*

It caught on.

★

By 2017 the newspaper industry in many parts of the world was a sickly thing. The advertising dollars that, for a century or more, had supported independent journalism were draining away and, in many communities, the local newspaper that once blazed a search beam now cast a flickering torchlight.

The *New York Times* still shone brightly – and it was the *New York Times* that the new president targeted: doing his obsessive best to denigrate and damn its reporting as fake. By the end of his first year in office, the new president had himself – in the eyes of dogged scorers – made nearly 2,000 false or misleading statements. He broke through the 3,000 barrier within 466 days, according to the *Washington Post* – a rate of 6.5 false claims a day. Americans had elected a liar, and now the liar turned his guns on the truth.

Within days of Trump's triumph questions were asked about the role of truth in the election. It transpired that many of the top-performing news stories on social media platforms such as Facebook were fake – generated by hoax sites and hyper-partisan blogs. Buzzfeed reporters identified more than 140 pro-Trump websites being run from a single town in the former Yugoslav republic of Macedonia.

The economic model for true news might have been failing, but there were numerous incentives – political and financial – for creating untrue news. Indeed, the market in sensationalist, conspiratorial and alarmist junk seemed to thrive in inverse proportion to the fortunes of the old media houses trying to plod the path of traditional reporting. The new automated distribution channels of social media turbo-charged the power of junk. Even before the election the World Economic Forum had identified the rapid spread of misinformation as one of the top ten perils to society – alongside cybercrime and climate change.

By 2017 social media had existed for barely a decade – a blink of the eye in the sweep of human communication, but long enough for a generation to grow up knowing no other world. Among those who had known another age there developed a kind of panic as they contemplated chaotic information systems that seemed to have emerged from nowhere.

Information chaos was, in itself, frightening enough. What made it truly alarming was that the chaos was enabled, shaped and distributed by a handful of gargantuan corporations, which – in that same blink of an eye – had become arguably the most powerful organisations the world had ever seen.

★

How did we get here? And how could we get back to where we once belonged?

For 20 years I edited a newspaper in the throes of this tumultuous revolution. The paper I took over in 1995 was composed of words printed on newsprint involving technologies that had changed little since Victorian times.

It was, in many ways, a vertically arranged world. We – the organs of information – owned printing presses and, with them, the exclusive power to hand down the news we had gathered. The readers handed up the money – and so did advertisers, who had few other ways of reaching our audience.

To be a journalist in these times was bliss – for us, anyway. I'm afraid we felt a bit superior to those without the same access to information that we enjoyed. It was easy to confuse our privileged access to information with 'authority' or 'expertise'. And when the floodgates opened – and billions of people also gained access to information and could publish themselves – journalism struggled to adjust.

Newspapers began to die in front of our eyes.

Societies may not have loved or admired journalists very much but they seemed to acknowledge that it was vital to have truthful and reliable sources of information. The fundamental importance to any community of reliable, unfettered news was one of the most important Enlightenment values.

It still is – or should be. But the significant money is – for the vast majority of news organisations – gone.

We are, for the first time in modern history, facing the prospect of how societies would exist without reliable news – at least as it used to be understood. There has never been more information in the world. We know infinitely more than ever before. There is a new democracy of knowledge that has swept over us so suddenly and so overwhelmingly that it is almost impossible to glimpse, let alone comprehend. Much of it is liberating, energising and transformative. It is a revolution to rival the invention of movable type in the fifteenth century. And much of it is poisonous and dangerous. Some of it – like the Swedish saga – is sort-of-slightly-true enough to be turned into toxic demagoguery.

In the new horizontal world people are no longer so dependent on the 'wisdom' of a few authority figures. The reach and speed of public connectedness is unbeatable by any media organisation on earth. Journalists, business and politicians are left looking out of touch and flat-footed.

'People in this country have had enough of experts,' said the (former *Times* of London journalist and Oxford-educated) Conservative politician Michael Gove, shortly before a referendum in which the British people defied expert opinion by voting to leave the European Union. In a way Gove was stating no more than the obvious at the end of an ugly, noisy campaign in which neither verifiable facts nor the opinion of Nobel-prize winning economists seemed any longer to count for much.

Old vertical media derided this new post-factual free-for-all. And, in a way, they were right. But much of the old media was itself biased, hectoring, blinkered and – it its own way – post-factual. Old journalism took it for granted that people would recognise its value – even, its necessity. But the denizens of new media found it too easy to pick holes in the processes and fallibilities of 'professional' news.

There were admirable, brave, serious, truthful journalists out there, some of them willing to die for their craft. But the commercial and ownership models of mass communication had also created oceans of rubbish which, in lazy shorthand, was also termed 'journalism'.

The new horizontal forms of digital connection were flawed, but – as with the rise of populist movements in the US and much of Europe – they were sometimes, and in some ways, closer to public opinion than conventional forms of media were capable of seeing, let alone articulating.

We can barely begin to glimpse the implications of this sea change in mass communications. Our language struggles to capture the enormity of what has been happening. 'Social media' is a pallid catch-all phrase which equates in most minds to the ephemeral postings on Twitter and Facebook. But 'social media' is also empowering people who were never heard, creating a new form of politics and turning traditional news corporations inside out.

It is impossible to think of Donald Trump; of Brexit; of Bernie Sanders; of Podemos; of the growth of the far right in Europe; of the spasms of hope and violent despair in the Middle East and North Africa without thinking also of the total inversion of how news is created, shared and distributed.

Much of it is liberating and inspiring. Some of it is ugly and dark. And something – the centuries-old craft of journalism – is in danger of being lost.

And all this has happened within 20 years – the blink of an eye. This is a problem for journalism, but it is an even bigger problem for society. The new news that is replacing 'journalism' is barely understood. But it is here to stay and is revolutionising not only systems of information but also the most basic concepts of authority and power.

The transformation precisely coincided with the time I was editing the *Guardian*.

This book describes what it felt like to be at the eye of this storm. A tornado can turn a house into toothpicks – and there was certainly a violent destructiveness to the forces that were being unleashed all around. But there was also exhilaration. Our generation had been handed the challenge of rethinking almost everything societies had, for centuries, taken for granted about journalism.

I had spent the past 40 years as a journalist and ended my career believing as strongly as ever that reliable, unpolluted information is as necessary to a community as a legal system, an army or a police force. But, at the moment of its greatest existential crisis, how much journalism lived up to the crying need for it? And were enough journalists alive to the need to rethink everything they did?

I became editor in 1995 – taking charge of a comparatively small British newspaper. We printed stories on newsprint, produced once a day. By the time I stepped down 20 years later that world had been turned upside down. By then, just 6 per cent of young (18- to 24-year-old) readers were getting their news from print; 65 per cent were relying on online sources, including social media, for their news. Nor was it just the young. Twice as many over-55-year-olds preferred online to print. In 1995 most journalists had just discovered they could use a phone to send text messages. By 2015 well over half their younger readers were using phones to read their news.

In 1995 it was given that (with the exception of television and radio) your readers expected to pay for news. By 2016, only 45 per cent of news consumers paid for a newspaper even once a week. A small minority (9 per cent in the US, less in the UK) was paying for any online news source.

The old order had, in the space of 20 years, been broken by this Force-12 hurricane of disruption. A new order was forming. The consequences for democracy were becoming all too apparent. We made choices without the benefit of hindsight. There was little data and no roadmap. We made plenty of mistakes; we got some things right. As the editorial floor reimagined journalism, so our commercial colleagues grappled with new business realities. The day-to-day work of news gathering went on as all of us tried to work out how on earth to steer a path into the future . . . not even knowing if there would be one, but determined to try. This was life at a sort of frontier.

In 2015 I stepped down from editing and moved to Oxford University. As well as heading a college, I became Chair of the Reuters Institute for the Study of Journalism. I belatedly discovered a considerable academic literature analysing the implications and fall-out of this revolution. But – oddly, for an industry of writers – there seemed to have been few attempts to describe what it felt like from the inside.

This is a universal story. Virtually every newsroom will have been confronted with the same dilemmas. The *Guardian*'s response is, in some ways, not typical. We were owned by a Trust, not shareholders. We did not have the quarter-by-quarter financial reporting pressures that led so many newspapers to, almost literally, decimate their journalistic resources. But nor were we a charity. The existence of a Trust – channelling money from other companies to subsidise the *Guardian*'s journalism where necessary – simply meant we were at least able to run on to the same playing field with what some called 'the billionaire press',[21] whose proprietors also took apparently expensive long-term decisions in order to grapple with a route to the future.

But that was the limit of our cushion. During the narrative of this book, the money very nearly ran out as the post-Lehman crash coincided with an advertising slump and the restructuring of the endowment which, for 75 years, had been there to keep the *Guardian* going. If the *Guardian* had taken the same risks as, say, Rupert Murdoch – they included buying MySpace, launching an iPad newspaper and unsuccessfully attempting to paywall the *Sun* – we would have been comprehensively wiped out. And, of course, our available funds were peanuts compared with the sums speculated to launch the West Coast tech giants who would ultimately pose an existential threat to all legacy news providers.

I have tried to capture the turbulence and challenges. And I have tried – while there is still a fresh collective memory – to describe what a news organisation felt like, and why its *institutional* quality mattered.

Great reporters are rightly celebrated. But they are – generally – only as good as the institution that supports them. If their reporting genuinely challenges power, they will need organisational courage behind them. They will need sharp-eyed text editors and ingenious lawyers. They may require people with sophisticated technological or security know-how. If they get into trouble they may need immediate logistical, medical, legal, financial or PR back-up. They need wise colleagues who have been in the same situations before. If they are lucky, they will have enlightened and strong commercial leaders to support and protect them; and gifted business minds who can bring in the money – but also observe the boundaries that preserve trust.

I was lucky enough to have worked for an institution that looked like that. In the middle of the turmoil I think we produced some great journalism that truly mattered. This is a record of those times.

The book also sets out the challenge for journalism. Journalists no longer have a near-monopoly on news and the means of distribution. The vertical world is gone for ever. Journalists no longer stand on a platform above their readers. They need to find a new voice. They have to regain trust. Journalism has to rethink its methods; reconfigure its relationship with the new kaleidoscope of other voices. It has to be more open about what it does and how it does it.

In a sense Donald Trump has done journalism a favour. In his cavalier disregard for truth he has reminded people why societies need to be able to distinguish fact from fiction. At their best, journalists do that job well. They can now harness almost infinite resources to help them.

But, at the same time, we have created the most prodigious capability for spreading lies the world has ever seen. And the economic system for supporting journalism looks dangerously unstable. The stakes for truth have never been higher.

I

Not Bowling Alone

In 2017, 40 years after joining my first newspaper, I find myself trying to describe the technology of those beginner times to a class of bright young students at Oxford.

I intended the class to be about 'digital' life. Within minutes it becomes obvious these 18-year-olds have little idea what I mean. All their lives have been 'digital'. What on earth is there to discuss?

They know of newspapers, of course. But they rarely read one in printed form or understand what, for 200 years or more, had been involved in the act of communicating news. Does it matter? I think perhaps it does. Otherwise how would you know that this present age is experimental, that there are other possibilities they may not have dreamed of?

I take a deep breath and start drawing little L.S. Lowry[1] stick figures on the whiteboard to show them what – even in recent history – was required for one person to communicate to more than a small group.

I describe the *Cambridge Evening News* of 1976. It was the paper I joined a week after graduating. It was where my own journey in journalism began.

First I draw a reporter – stick figure (SF) 1 – typing words on a manual typewriter (brief explanation necessary) onto a sandwich of paper and carbon paper (ditto) copies. Then I draw SF 1 handing the top sheet of paper to SF 2, the copy taster, and giving the carbon copy ('the black') to SF 3, the news editor. I show a copy taster assessing the stories, then bundling them up with pictures before passing each page plan to SF 4, the lay-out sub, who would then design the page and draw up a plan for the printers to follow, indicating the typographical instructions – type size, across what measure, the length required for each story to fit the allocated space, the size and typeface of the head-line needed, and so on.

SF 5, the sub-editor, would then take over and edit accordingly – cutting to length, correcting spelling or grammar and querying any facts. The copy would travel down the line to a revise sub, SF 6. The pages would then pass through a metaphorical curtain to another part of the building, to the composing room where a Linotype operator would key in the copy all over again.

By this stage of my drawing, my students are looking lost . . . and maybe a bit bored.

Deep breath, plough on: they need to know. Linotype machines, I explain, were squat dinosaurs of machinery, not much changed since Victorian times, used to compose metal lines of type. Thomas Edison, inventor of the light bulb, is said to have called these type-setting machines the Eighth Wonder of the World. An operator (SF 7) would sit in front of the clanking contraption – all cogs, chains, rods, wheels, plungers, pumps, moulds, matrices, crucibles, asbestos, pulleys, pistons and grease – and key in the text in front of him. The machinery included a tub of molten metal – a mix of lead, anti-mony and tin – heated to about 400 degrees Centigrade, which would produce a slug of type.

The students look mildly interested at the thought of foundries of boiling metal being in some way associated with communication.

Elsewhere in the composing room SF 8 would be sitting at a Ludlow machine – a heavy-duty version of the Linotype machine – casting a headline. Enter SF 9, who took all the type and arranged it into columns on a flat iron surface ('the stone') – adjusting it from time to time as readers elsewhere compared the original with the typeset print and sent through corrections. Then came SF 10, who, in a high-pressure press, would stamp a papier mâché mould of the metal-set page. SF 11 would place the mould, now curved, over a semi-circular casting box and pour more molten metal into it to create a semi-circular printing plate.

One of the students is surreptitiously consulting his mobile phone under the desk.

SF 12 placed the curved plate onto the vast rotary presses, capable of printing 50,000 copies an hour. In the belly of the cathedral-like printing hall, SF 13 would negotiate enormous rolls of newsprint onto the printing presses and gradually thread the paper through the presses' rollers. The presses would thunder into life and, in time, a printed newspaper emerged from the other end of the units and would be cut, folded and counted into bundles of 26 copies by SF 14. Then SF 15 stacked and sorted the bundles with the names and address of the wholesale and retail newsagents.

Not done yet.

It was the job of SF 16 to drive the papers in a van (or, once upon a time, a train for national newspapers) to the wholesale distribution points. SF 17 made sure they got into the hands of newsagents (SF 18) who would employ young children (SF 19) to cycle around the local streets delivering newspapers though people's front doors.

Nineteen stages (in reality, dozens – if not hundreds – of stick figures) needed for me to enable my act of communication with someone else.

'And, of course, now,' I say superfluously, because they already know this, 'if I want to communicate with any of you I just use this.' I wave my mobile phone in the air. 'And then I can communicate not only with you but, potentially, the whole world.'

'And so,' I add even more pointlessly, 'can you.'

The group look as if I have been relating how cave dwellers created fire by rubbing dry twigs together.

'But what if something happened just after deadline?' one of them asks.

'Well, we'd come back and update you the next day.'

The questioner doesn't look impressed.

★

In 1976 journalism was, by and large, something you did rather than studied.

There were very few postgraduate journalism schools. The common route into the business was being thrown into the newsroom of a local paper to learn on the job – with a few months at a local technological college to pick up shorthand along with the basics of law and administration.

A crash course in journalism included a single class on ethics and an awful lot of Pitman's or Teeline textbooks for shorthand. You were required to read two other books, one on libel and another explaining the mechanics and processes of local government written by a former member of Bolton County Borough Council. I was, in due course, to fail my shorthand exam. But I still 'qualified' to become a journalist. Sort of.

A week after finishing my finals paper on the dense modernist poetry of Ezra Pound, I swapped my university college – founded in 1428, all medieval courts, honeyed stone, velvet green lawns, punts and weeping willows – for the prosaic 1960s offices of the *Cambridge Evening News*, a mile to the east on the unlovely Newmarket Road. It was another education: three years spent in a different Cambridge, reporting on a world of factories, housing estates, petty crime and bustling community life.

There were not many graduates in the 20-strong reporting room of the *CEN*, a paper then selling just fewer than 50,000 copies a day. University types were – rightly – viewed with suspicion as arrogant interlopers who would trade the experience we gained in the provinces to secure a better-paid job in Fleet Street just as soon as we had even uncertificated proof of our ability to write quickly and of our familiarity with the finer points of the Local Government Act, 1972.

For the first week I wrote nothing but wedding reports – the journalistic training equivalent of intensive square-bashing or boot-polishing. It was a far cry from the *Cantos* of Pound. It was also more difficult than it looked: the mundane but essential ability to record every small detail with complete accuracy. The news editor took an ill-concealed pleasure in pointing out each and every error to arrogant young trainees with newly acquired degrees in English Literature.

The newspaper was owned by one Lord Iliffe of Yattendon, a largely absent figure who owned a 9,000-acre estate 100 miles away in Berkshire. More important to me was Fulton Gillespie, the chief reporter, known as Jock – a growling silver-haired Glaswegian with dark glasses and the stub of a cigar permanently lodged between bearded lips.

Jock became my new personal tutor. He was not a graduate, but a coal miner's son who had left school with no certificates of any kind and had started work at 14 as an apprentice printer at the *Falkirk Herald* in Scotland before crossing to the editorial side at 16.

He had cut his teeth recording market stock notes and prices in old pence and farthings along with shipping movements and cargoes from the nearby Grangemouth docks. From this he progressed to writing cinema synopses – A and B pictures with titles and stars' names. His equivalent of English Literature essays had consisted of funerals and lists of mourners; amateur dramatic societies' plays and musicals with cast lists; local antiquarian society meetings and debates; miners' welfare committee meetings; WI fêtes recording best cake and best jams. There had been farm shows to record, with their prize bulls and heifers to spell correctly, before turning up to report on local sports matches. And a quick change in the evenings for annual dinners of all kinds of local charities, sporting, civic and faith groups. The following morning back in courts, councils and other public bodies.

That was Jock's life in the mid-'50s. It would have been the same for any trainee reporter in the mid-'60s and it was – give or take – my life in Cambridge in the mid-'70s.

Early in my time as a trainee reporter Jock told us about the ritual for covering Scottish hangings. This involved befriending the murderer's soon-to-be widow by promising to write a sympathetic account, possibly hinting at a campaign to demand an 11th-hour reprieve. Once he'd extracted the quotes and purloined the family photographs the reporter would, on exit, shout at the distraught soon-to-be widow that her husband was an evil bastard who deserved to rot in hell.

'Why did you do that?'

'So that the next reporter to turn up wouldn't get through the door.'

That was what real reporting was about. Get the story, stuff the opposition. Jock saw it as his duty to school us in hard knocks. We would begin the day with the calls – a round trip to the police, ambulance and fire services. As we set off in the office Mini he would deliver one of a small repertoire of homilies about our craft. 'If you write for dukes, only dukes will understand, but if you write for the dustman, both will understand. Keep it short, keep it simple, write it in language you would use if you were telling your mum or dad.'

He explained that police work involved keeping one foot on the pavement and one in the gutter. You got their respect by kicking them in the balls at regular intervals, because, in the long run, they needed us more than we needed them. That, he emphasised, was a good rule applicable to all those in authority. It had been hammered into him by the old hacks on the *Falkirk Herald* and it would always be true. He repeated this homily often in case I had failed to grasp it. They needed us more than we needed them.

We owned the printing presses: they didn't. End of.

In time I was dispatched to a district office where the routine was the same, only with more alcohol. I drove the 20 miles to Saffron Walden in Essex on a clapped out old Lambretta scooter. There were three reporters for a town of fewer than 10,000 people. The chief reporter poured whisky into my morning coffee before we made the police calls. There were two or three pints at lunchtime, more Irish coffee in the afternoon and more pints in the evening before I wobbled my way back to Cambridge.

We covered all the local council committees and courts. There were golden weddings to record and local amateur dramatics to review. On Saturdays I would be packed off to cover 'The Bloods', Saffron Walden Town Football Club, who were forced to play in a modest Essex league because the sloping pitch at Catons Lane was deemed to have 'excessive undulations'. I knew little about football – just enough to be able to record the bare facts about the game on a telex machine in the corridor at the top of the stairs.

Above the telex – a machine that punched holes in paper tape to transmit the copy back to Cambridge for typesetting – was a list of footballing clichés. For every cliché that survived the attention of the subs back in head office and made it into print, we had to buy the other two colleagues in Saffron Walden a pint. They included describing the goalkeeper as 'the custodian of the woodwork'; 'a fleet-footed midfielder'; and (to describe a penalty) 'he made no mistake from the spot'. By 6 p.m. the match report was on the streets of Cambridge, along with all the other local and national football teams or in the special late Saturday afternoon 'pink 'un' sports edition.

Most of the news – back in Cambridge as well as the district offices – was pre-ordained, in the sense that the news editor in each newsroom kept an A4 diary on his desk in which he or she would record every upcoming council committee along with the relevant health, fire, ambulance, water and utilities boards. Late in the afternoon you would check the page to see what job had been assigned for the following day.

Often you would travel with a photographer. There was a strong demarcation between writers and snappers. A reporter would not dream of taking a photograph and a snapper would never dare to write a line of text. Indeed, union rules forbade it.

Around two thirds of the work was what you might call 'top down': the newspaper telling the citizens about the workings of the assorted institutions put in place to regulate or order local and civic life.

The other third of the news flowed the other way, bottom up. This was not a *Bowling Alone* world – the deracinated hollowed-out communities described by Robert Putnam 25 years later in America. There was bubbling social and institutional activity all around, and where we lacked the resources to cover it ourselves we recruited local stringers (today they might be called 'citizen journalists') to file accounts of discussion groups and scout sports days and charity baking mornings for the local hospital scanner. Every name sold a paper, as the news editor would remind us at regular intervals. We were duly encouraged to cram as many names as possible into our reports. Every picture sold a paper, too, so photographers knew to take group pictures and collect the names for the captions.

A typical week might include residents with damp problems who wanted to get on the radar of an unresponsive council. The petition about the dangerous pedestrian crossing. The man with the dog who'd made friends with an owl. A couple of times a day a reader would find their way to the Newmarket Road office and one of us would have to sit down in the reception area to debrief them. The representative of a group trying to stop the bulldozing of a few acres of Victorian cottages to make way for a shopping centre. The reader who has brought in a potato resembling Winston Churchill. Another is obsessed by an electricity junction box at the bottom of his garden. All our visitors want the local paper on their side.

The first edition of the paper hit the streets before lunchtime, with two or three more editions during the afternoon. A hinged door was all that separated the newsroom from the industrial machinery required to turn our words into type. Within a few yards of the sub-editors' desks were the Linotype and Ludlow machines. The smell of molten metal and grease would waft into the newsroom with each swing of the door. Around 11 a.m. the entire building would shudder as the rotary presses started to roll with the first edition.

It was impossible to forget that newspapers were as much light engineering as fine words.

★

There are many things we did not discuss back in 1976. We didn't talk about business models. The model for the *Cambridge Evening News* was relatively straightforward: nearly 50,000 people a day parted with money to buy a copy. There was display advertising – a local department store or car showroom promoting a special deal or sale. And then there was the lifeline of local newspapers: classified advertising. The vast majority of second-hand cars or houses in Cambridge and surrounding towns were offered for sale through the pages of the *Cambridge Evening News*. Every job vacancy was announced in the paper, along with every birth, marriage and death. Every official notification from the council or other public authority: they were all printed at the back of the newspaper between the news and the sport.

The profit margins on local papers at their peak – and the mid-'70s were as good a time as any – were in the 30 to 40 per cent range and would continue to be until the end of the century. Nearly 30 years later the regional press was still taking something like 20 per cent of the UK's advertising spend.

So, no, we didn't talk about business models; we didn't need to.

We didn't talk about ethics. And we didn't talk about technology. Not much had changed about the way our journalism reached the readers in a hundred years or more. Hot metal typesetting machines had been around since the 1880s. The presses had got faster over the years, but otherwise a journalist from the late nineteenth century would have found little to surprise him in the 1970s. We banged out stories on battered typewriters – the only technology we used apart from telephones. If we were out of the office on deadline we'd phone it in to copy takers who did their best to conceal their boredom. No intro more than 30 words. Get the salient facts into the top of the story so, in haste, it could be cut from the bottom. The production methods of a newspaper seemed timeless and immutable.

We met our readers out on stories and, by and large, we were welcomed and – apparently – trusted. Sometimes we deliberately intruded on grief. The 'death knock' was the name given to that heart-sinking moment when the news editor might send you to see the parents whose daughter had just died in a traffic accident. Oddly, we were rarely sent packing by devastated relatives. More often, the response was to welcome us in, even at this moment of unimaginable pain. For many, it seemed to be something of an honour for their relatives to be remembered in the pages of the paper.

★

Some 40 years after my stint in Cambridge I made contact with my old news editor, Christopher South, to check my memory of my local reporting days. South, now nearly 80, produced two cardboard boxes of old papers he'd stuffed into brown envelopes as he cleared his desk between roles. He was, he explained apologetically, a bit of a hoarder.

I had a Proustian moment as I unsealed the first box. The smell of the Newmarket Road office seeped out of the battered cardboard container as I sifted through the papers – mainly the smell of the cheap newsprint on which we typed. I found a story written by my old (now late) colleague John Gaskell on 27 April 1976. In the top right corner, his surname: in the top left, 'sweepers 1' – the catchline, or running head, given to the story so that it could be followed through the process from sub to compositor to printing press. The intro was tight, 23 words long. At the bottom of the page 'm.f.'. *More follows.*

On another piece of now-tattered copy paper – evidently intended for the staff newsletter – a call for any stamp-collecting enthusiasts who would like to 'pool their knowledge, contacts, exchange deals and ideas in order to enrich their hobby'. On another, a memo from the editor stressing the 'vital necessity for keeping costs down'. No reporter was to spend more than 75 pence on lunch, or £1.20 on dinner, without prior approval.

There was a memo from the agricultural correspondent on the state of the paper – presumably in response to some invitation for feedback. It suggested that the arts coverage should be 'more down to earth and more relevant to the readership we serve who aren't all intellectuals or artistic'. It ended: 'I would think twice before paying the new price of 4p but the basis is there for making it worth 5p if we all work at it.' And a randomly preserved copy of the *Times*, the crossword half-solved: Saturday 8 November 1975. There are 22 headlines on its front page, some of them over entire stories, some of them flagging up further news inside. The typography is busy, workmanlike, factual. There is one small picture. The page is densely informative. The pattern continues inside, with multiple stories and very small black and white pictures.

South had also clipped an article from the *New Statesman* of 21 March 1975 ('The Establishment and the Press'), which referred to the National Union of Journalists' rule, introduced in 1965, that no one could be recruited to Fleet Street without first having had three years' experience on a provincial newspaper. The author, Tom Baistow, reflected on why this rule had been introduced: 'This letter was forged in the heated resentment that developed as growing numbers of Oxbridge graduates were hired straight from university and in many cases given "direct commissions" without any pretence of putting them through the ranks. The anger of newspapermen who had been through the provincial mill wasn't based on the fact that these elite recruits had been to university but that they hadn't been anywhere else.'

And, finally, a staff list for 1973, recording that the company then employed more than 70 journalists, including two reporters in each of seven district offices. In the composing room there were 18 Linotype operators to work the old molten Linotype machines. There were eleven compositors, ten stone hands to assemble the type into pages, seven readers to check the typeset galleys against the original and five print apprentices. There were eight men in the foundries and 29 to run the pressroom, including cleaners and machine minders. Finally there were 16 mechanics – and drivers to drop off the papers at newsagents and street sellers throughout the county.

*

Back in 1976 there were, if we did ever pause to think about the finances, only two potential clouds on the horizon.

One was the advent of free newspapers, usually launched by small-scale entrepreneurs who imagined a much simpler model than traditional newspapers. They wanted to get the income (advertising) with almost none of the expense (journalism). But none of us really imagined that catching on because – well, people bought the paper for the stories to and read about their communities, schools and councils in a detail no free sheet could match.

The second was something rumbling away 90 miles northwest of Cambridge where a local newspaper, the *Nottingham Evening Post*, was locked in battles with its trade unions over the introduction of some-thing called new technology. This apparently involved journalists doing their own typesetting, thus abolishing the need for all the type hands on the other side of the newsroom swing door. Our journalists' union was against that. And, anyway, it all seemed a very distant prospect in 1976.

In a sense it was. It was another ten years before Rupert Murdoch would stage his bold confrontation with his national print workers, throwing 5,000 of them out of work and producing computer-set newspapers from behind barbed wire in Wapping, East London. And it was 13 years before the management at the *CEN* would sack all the pre-press workers and insist on full computer typesetting. After 124 years in independent ownership, the *Cambridge News*, by then renamed and a weekly paper, was sold in 2012 to a new consolidated company called Local World, backed by a hedge-fund manager intent on bringing together 110 titles and 4,300 employees in a 'one-stop shop' serving 'content' to local communities. Three years later the company was sold on to another newspaper group, Trinity Mirror, with the intention of delivering 'cost synergies' of around £12 million. The paper now sells fewer than 15,000 copies a week, reaching around 52,000 a day online.

*

The film of the year in 1976 was *All the President's Men*, in which Robert Redford and Dustin Hoffman gave us the journalist-as-hero role model, which would prove very resilient over the decades to come.

It is the narrative we have often told the world, and which a few journalists might even believe. It usually involves the word 'truth': we speak truth to power; we are truth-seekers; we tell uncomfortable truths in order to hold people accountable.

The truth about journalism, it's always seemed to me, is something messier and less perfect. Carl Bernstein, one of the twin begetters of Watergate, goes no further nowadays than 'the best obtainable version of the truth'.

When living in Washington in 1987 I read a new book by the *Washington Post*'s veteran political commentator David Broder,[2] which contained a passage that leaped off the page because it felt so much closer to what journalism actually does.

> The process of selecting what the reader reads involves not just objective facts but subjective judgments, personal values and, yes, prejudices. Instead of promising 'All the News That's Fit to Print', I would like to see us say over and over until the point has been made . . . that the newspaper that drops on your doorstep is a partial, hasty, incomplete, inevitably somewhat flawed and inaccurate rendering of some of the things we heard about in the past 24 hours . . . distorted despite our best efforts to eliminate gross bias by the very process of compression that makes it possible for you to

lift it from the doorstep and read it in about an hour. If we labelled the paper accurately then we would immediately add: 'But it's the best we could do under the circumstances, and we will be back tomorrow with a corrected updated version . . .'

'Partial, hasty, incomplete . . . somewhat flawed and inaccurate.' Most journalists I know recognise a kind of honesty in those words – as does anyone who has ever been written about by a journalist. That doesn't make journalism less valuable. But, as Broder argued, we might well earn more respect and trust if we acknowledged the reality of the activity we're engaged in.

As reporters and editors of the *Cambridge Evening News*, we lived among the people on whom we reported. We would meet the councillors and coppers the following morning in the queue for bread. Did that, on occasion, make us pull our punches? Probably. But that closeness and familiarity also bred respect and trust. We were on the brink of a new world in which a proprietor on the other side of the world could dictate his view of how a country should be run. Or when the chief executive of a giant newspaper conglomerate would have trouble finding some of his 'properties' on a map. Small was, in some ways, beautiful.

★

While a young reporter on the *CEN* I fell in love. The relationship lasted just under two years. It was between two consenting adults – one male, one female – and was perfectly legal, even if it did not accord with one of the commandments in the Book of Exodus, Chapter 20. The relationship caused some happiness; and some unhappiness to a few people – literally, no more than half-a-dozen either way.

One Friday night there was a knock on the door. A reporter and photographer from the *Sunday Mirror* wanted to tell the 'story of our love', as he put it, to the 4 million readers who then bought the newspaper every week. The reporter, a man called Richard, was charming.

I was a cub reporter, she was a university lecturer. Nobodies, end of story. Well, almost – for her late father had, some years earlier, been on the telly. So you could, at a stretch, make a consumable tale out of it: 'Daughter of quite famous man has affair.'

Our relationship really didn't seem to be anyone else's business and so we politely declined the opportunity to invite Richard and his photographer over the doorstep.

Richard's tone changed. 'We can do this nice or we can do it nasty,' he said abruptly, and then explained what nice and nasty looked like. Nice was for us to sit down on the sofa and tell the world about our love, and be portrayed in a sympathetic way that would warm the cockles of millions of *Sunday Mirror* readers all over Britain. Nasty meant they would start knocking on the doors of neighbours and contacting our relatives to put together a story that would be altogether less heart-warming.

It was a good pitch. How many people want their elderly parents, friends or neighbours telephoned or knocked up on a Friday night by a man preparing a self-confessed hatchet job? All the same, we felt this was – well, private. We were living together openly, and made no attempt to hide our relationship from friends or family. But we had no wish to tell the whole world. So we said no.

Richard and his photographer did not go away and sat outside the house for another 24 hours. From time to time he would lean on the doorbell – not to mention the neighbours' – to test whether we had changed our minds. They stayed until Saturday afternoon, reappearing the following Friday evening to try again. Eventually we asked them in for a cup of tea, and I – the trainee kid in the room compared with Richard – suggested I might ring his news editor to explain we wouldn't be talking. That seemed to do the trick. The story – nice or nasty – never saw the light of day.

My life at that point had been learning to report councils, courts, freak weather and flower shows. That was what I understood journalism to be – a record of public events of varying degrees of significance. The ring on the doorbell was my first, sharp realisation that 'journalism' meant many different things to many different people. And, also, of what it was like to have journalism done to you.

2

More Than a Business

It was a lovely time to be a local newspaper journalist. But after a couple of years I had – as my Cambridge colleagues knew I would – started to make my exit plans. I began using my days off doing reporting shifts at the *London Evening Standard*, where ancient typewriters were chained to dark green metal desks. I was turned down for a job there, and also by the *Times*. But my cuttings caught the eye of the news editor on the *Guardian*, Peter Cole. I bought a new suit and gave what Cole later described as the worst interview he could remember. But he was impressed by my scrapbook of stories and considered I had a modest facility with words. I feel I may have lied when asked about my shorthand speed.

There was another young reporter starting at the *Guardian* on my first day in July 1979 – fresh from the Mirror Group training scheme in the west country. His name was Nick Davies. He was extrovert; I was more introverted. He loved standing on doorsteps; I preferred polishing sentences. With his beaten leather jacket, he looked like a beatnik French philosopher. As has sometimes been remarked, I looked more like Harry Potter. We became lifelong friends . . . and got up to mischief.

The *Guardian* Nick and I joined had been around for 158 years.

The *Manchester Guardian* started life as a small start-up in 1821. Its intention was almost purely altruistic. Its founders had no ambition to reap huge profits from it. It was imagined as a piece of public service.

Somehow – amazingly, mystifyingly, staggeringly – it remained a venture devoted to that public service of news more than a century and a half later. It existed to ask questions, to bear witness and to offer forthright (and anonymous) opinion.

There was no great business model for serious, awkward, enquiring journalism in 1821, any more than there was in 2015 when I left the paper, 194 years into its existence. But most of the time – buttressed by advertising and subsidy from other companies within family or trust ownership – the paper struggled through, with occasional crises along the way.

Its founder, John Edward Taylor, was a Manchester businessman and advocate of parliamentary reform who had been present at what became known as the Peterloo Massacre. On 16 August 1819, in St Peter's Square, Manchester, a 60,000-strong unarmed crowd gathered to hear a speech by a great radical orator, Henry Hunt, who believed in some very dangerous things: equal rights, universal suffrage, parliamentary reform, an end to child labour and so forth.

Fearing that Hunt would stir the crowd to some form of insurrection, the city's magistrates ordered in the yeomanry, who literally cut their way to the platform on which Hunt was speaking in order to arrest him. Numerous men, women and children were treated for fractures, sabre cuts and gunshot wounds. More than 400 people were injured and 11 were killed. It was all over in ten minutes. The story of the day led to a great poem, 'The Masque of Anarchy', by Shelley ('Rise like lions after slumber . . . Ye are many – they are few').

The historian E.P. Thompson described the decision facing the authorities on that day in his 1963 book, *The Making of the English Working Class*: 'Old Corruption faced the alternatives of meeting the reforms with repression or concession. But concession, in 1819, would have meant concession to a largely working-class reform movement: the middle-class reformers were not yet strong enough (as they were in 1832) to offer a more moderate line of advance. This is why Peterloo took place.'

The term 'fake news' had not yet been invented. But Taylor, standing on the edge of the carnage, knew what to expect. The official authorities would tell lies about the day. They would claim they were acting in self-defence; they had been attacked by the mob and had drawn their swords as a desperate last measure.

The one national reporter on the scene, the *Times*'s John Tyas, ended the day in captivity (or sanctuary) and was unable to file a story. Knowing this, Taylor wrote his own report and got it swiftly to London. It was printed in the *Times* on the morning of 18 August, two days later. The story marked, in the words of one writer, the 'birth of the public reporter in English public life'.[1]

By the following day's edition Tyas was free to file his own eyewitness account and the *Times* went to town, filling more than two broadsheet pages.

In the volume of space devoted to the massacre you can feel the editor of the *Times*, Thomas Barnes, grappling with how anyone could establish the truth. Would people naturally trust the word of one reporter over that of the magistrates? Would readers be more convinced if there were multiple accounts broadly corroborating one version? In addition to its own reporting the paper went in for two techniques that became routine in the early twenty-first century – aggregation and crowdsourcing.

The aggregation took the form of excerpts from other local papers' reports of the day. The crowdsourcing came from a petition and from numerous 'private letters' similar to Taylor's. They painted a confusing picture, but the accumulation of evidence overwhelmingly demonstrated that the crowd had behaved peacefully and there was no possible justification for the violence meted out.

Taylor understood the importance of facts – and also predicted that the facts of the day would be contested, and litigated, for months, if not years. He wanted to place on record 'facts, undeniable and decisive . . . truths which are impossible to gainsay'.

He was entirely right. The authorities pushed back hard, creating a set of 'alternative facts' around the events of the day: they claimed to have witnessed pikes dipped in blood and torrents of stones and bricks thrown at the troops. The speakers on the day were later arrested and jailed by the same magistrates who had ordered the violence. Thanks to Taylor's quick response 'within two days all England knew of the event', says Thompson. 'Within a week every detail of the massacre was being canvassed in ale-houses, chapels, workshops, private houses.' And, thanks to the public reporting of the facts of the day, Thompson was able to write in 1963: 'Never since Peterloo has authority dared to used equal force against a peaceful British crowd.'

Peterloo is as good an illustration as any as to why good journalism is necessary. Nearly 200 years later, in the early days of the Trump presidency, the *Washington Post* expressed the same motivating ideal with the slogan: 'Democracy dies in darkness'. The *New York Times*, faced with an administration in 2017 that cared little for the distinction between facts and falsehoods, marketed itself with the words: 'Truth is hard to find. But easier with 1,000+ journalists looking.'

Power needs witnesses. Witnesses need to be able to speak freely to an audience. The truth can only follow on from agreed facts. Facts can only be agreed if they can be openly articulated, tested . . . and contested. That process of statement and challenge helps something like the truth to emerge. From truth can come progress. In the absence of this daylight, bad things will almost certainly happen. The acts of bearing witness and establishing facts can lead to positive reform. By the start of the twenty-first century these might – in relatively enlightened democracies – seem unremarkable statements, but 200 years ago these were comparatively new propositions.

Taylor decided to found his own paper. The first edition of the *Manchester Guardian* hit the streets about 18 months later – initially a weekly paper printed on machinery that could turn out 150 copies an hour. Its third edition reported on the House of Commons debate on the Peterloo massacre, over nine-and-a-half columns.

★

To compress a very long story into a very short narrative: the Taylor family married the Scott family. A young member of the latter tribe – C.P. Scott – became editor at the age of 25: by the time he died in 1932 he had not only edited the paper for 57 years, he also owned it. On the death, in rapid succession, of Scott and his son Edward, the family placed the paper into the care and ownership of the Scott Trust in 1936 to preserve and protect the *Guardian* 'in perpetuity'.

The Scotts could have made themselves very wealthy by selling the *Manchester Guardian* to Lord Beaverbrook or any other number of suitors: instead they gave away their inheritance in order to sustain decent, serious, liberal journalism. They were not in it for the money. The *Manchester Guardian* was a public service.

Pause and reflect on that very unusual moment – described by Winston Churchill's future lord chancellor, Gavin Simonds, as 'very repugnant' ('you are trying to divest yourself of a property right').[2] Sir William Hayley, later editor of the *Times*, said of John Scott's decision to, in effect, give away the *Guardian*: 'He could have been a rich man; he chose a Spartan existence. And when he made up his mind to divest himself of all beneficial interest in them he did so with as little display of emotion as if he had been solving an algebraical problem. Most men making so large a sacrifice would have exacted at least the price of an attitude.'[3]

On the paper's 100th birthday in 1921 Scott – who'd been editing for nearly 50 years – wrote perhaps the most famous short essay on journalism, with its pithy aphorism: 'Comment is free, but facts are sacred.'[4] He used the article to underscore his passionate belief that, while a newspaper was a business, it had little point unless it was *more than* a business. A newspaper could – then, as now – aim to be 'something of a monopoly'. Many business people might relish that. Scott felt the opposite. The *Guardian*, he thought, should 'shun its temptations'.

> A newspaper has two sides to it. It is a business, like any other, and has to pay in the material sense in order to live. But it is much more than a business; it is an institution; it reflects and it influences the life of a whole community; it may affect even wider destinies. It is, in its way, an instrument of government. It plays on the minds and consciences of men. It may educate, stimulate, assist, or it may do the opposite. It has, therefore, a moral as well as a material existence, and its character and influence are in the main determined by the balance of these two forces . . . It may make profit or power its first object, or it may conceive itself as fulfilling a higher and more

exacting function. I think I may honestly say that, from the day of its foundation, there has not been much doubt as to which way the balance tipped so far as regards the conduct of the paper whose fine tradition I inherited and which I have had the honour to serve through all my working life. Had it not been so, personally I could not have served it.

It is more or less inconceivable to imagine these words, or anything like them, from the lips of any newspaper owner today.

Since the predominant purpose of the *Guardian* lay in its influence, reporting, commentary and educative mission, it was obvious (to Scott's mind) that it had to be an editorially led venture. Scott wanted there to be a 'unity' between commercial and editorial – both driven by the same values. But he was absolutely clear that 'it is a mistake to suppose that the business side of a paper should dominate'. He had seen experiments to that effect tried elsewhere, and 'they have not met with success'.

> Between its two sides there should be a happy marriage, and editor and business manager should march hand in hand, the first, be it well understood, just an inch or two in advance.

The paper under Scott grew in influence far beyond Manchester. It was never afraid to be unpopular. At the end of the nineteenth century it was virtually alone in the UK press in opposing the Boer War and was excoriated for exposing the existence of British concentration camps – a moment when its reporters needed police guards as they turned up for work. In 1956, again, it stood virtually alone in condemning Britain's foolish adventure in Suez. It exposed labour conditions in apartheid South Africa and, under Peter Preston,[5] sleaze in parliament.

In 1961 it had taken an immense commercial risk by taking on an extra 500 staff to make the move from being a Manchester paper to one based in Fleet Street. The move nearly capsized the paper – but, with hindsight, it was a bold and visionary decision.

Some rivals in Fleet Street thought it was also self-regarding, prissy and politically correct. There was doubtless something in that. The early twentieth-century Tory politician Lord Robert Cecil once described the *Guardian* as 'righteousness made readable'. There was something in that, too. But the ethos of the paper was formed by its history and ownership. As we'll see by the end of this book, the correlation between ownership, profit, purpose and the quality of national conversation is a complex one.

The BBC was, in some ways, close in spirit – a publicly funded organisation dedicated to providing serious and trustworthy news. Large swathes of Fleet Street, of course, loathed the BBC and did all in their power to undermine or destroy it. The Murdoch family regarded it as a semi-socialist entity that affronted their view of how the free market was best placed to deliver what they regarded as independent news.

They didn't much like the *Guardian*, either.

★

That was the paper Nick and I joined in 1979. The paper still had the feeling of a family newspaper. The generation in their late 50s or early 60s who were in charge had begun their careers in Manchester and seen the newspaper transition to being a London title. The Trust was then chaired by Richard Scott, a former Washington correspondent and grandson of C.P. Scott. Peter Preston, our editor, had been on the paper since 1963 and was four years into a 20-year spell as editor. His predecessor, Alistair Hetherington, had also done 20 years. People tended to spend their entire lives at the paper.

For much of its existence the paper teetered on the borderlines of profit or loss – supported, when it went severely into the red, by the profits of the *Manchester Evening News*. In terms of circulation it was ninth in the league of national newspapers. Gradually, in the early '80s, the financial position of the *Guardian* improved. Preston was restless in modernising the paper and, in conjunction with the business managers, building up the classified advertising. By the late '80s the paper had fat, extremely profitable print sections on Monday to Wednesday carrying hundreds of jobs in media, education and public service.[6]

Our day began around 10 a.m., by which time we were expected to have read most of the other papers. The paper's first edition went to bed around 9 p.m. in the evening, though the flow of copy meant that, if you weren't writing for the front page, they appreciated copy by about 6 p.m.

On most days you wrote one story, maximum two. So the day had a shape to it. Reporters were encouraged to be out of the office as much as possible. If you were in the newsroom there was time to read yourself in to the subject you'd been assigned, to make calls. A break for lunch. Some more calls. You might be writing a backgrounder – the context and analysis – in which case you'd start writing about 3 p.m. Otherwise you might have five or six hours on a story before you threaded your first sheet of carbon paper into the scuffed old typewriter.

Fleet Street, where most of the UK's national papers were based, was both a community and a battleground. Before Murdoch's great confrontation with the doomed print unions at his new plant at Wapping in 1986,[7] most of the newspapers – nearly 20 of them, including Sunday editions, which mostly had separate staffs and editors – were gathered along or around Fleet Street, which runs from St Paul's Cathedral and the Old Bailey in the east to the Royal Courts of Justice in the west.

To walk that half mile from Ludgate Circus to the High Court takes no longer than ten minutes. But – before Wapping – you would pass the glass, stone and marble-front edifices of the *Express*, the *Telegraph*, Reuters, Press Association. Down the eighteenth-century Bouverie Street – once home to William Hazlitt and Charles Dickens' *Daily News* – lay the cathedral-sized press hall of the *News of the World* and the *Sun*, capable of thundering out 4 million copies in a night from presses weighing hundreds of tons, with print lorries and delivery trucks lined up along the narrow street to restock newsprint or race to the night trains.

The outliers on this map in the early '80s were the *Financial Times* – a little to the east – and the *Times* and the *Sunday Times*, half a mile to the north. The *Guardian*, which only began to establish a significant London presence in the 1960s, shared printing facilities with the *Times* but its newsroom was in an unlovely '70s converted light-engineering building in Farringdon Road, ten minutes' walk from Fleet Street. It was always the slight outsider.

There was a demarcation between broadsheet, mid-market and red-tops in which supposed quality was in inverse proportion to proven popularity. Arguably the most serious broadsheet – the *FT* – sold the fewest: around 200,000 copies a day – followed in unpopularity by the *Times*, the *Guardian* and the *Telegraph*, which led the 'serious papers' with daily sales of around 1.5 million.

Then came the mid-markets – the *Mail* and the *Express*, each selling around 2 million copies – and finally the really popular red-tops, the *Sun* and the *Mirror* edging towards 4 million.[8]

*

My career took a traditional enough path. A few years reporting; four years writing a daily diary column; a stint as a feature writer – home and abroad. In 1986 I left the *Guardian* to be the *Observer*'s television critic – then a plum chair that had been occupied by Clive James and Julian Barnes. But I discovered I didn't have the right temperament to sit at home watching video-tapes all day, and it was a relief when I was approached to be the Washington correspondent of a new paper to be launched by Robert Maxwell.[9]

The *London Daily News* was a brief adventure: Maxwell ran out of patience within six months of starting it and closed it even more suddenly than he had opened it. But I was in the US long enough to develop a life-long respect for American journalism's methods, serious-ness and traditions. If Fleet Street sometimes felt like a knowing game, American newspapers were soberly earnest. Back in the UK, I rejoined the *Guardian* and was diverted towards a route of editing – launch-ing the paper's Saturday magazine followed by a daily tabloid features section (named G2) and moving to be deputy editor in 1993.

I had developed a love of gadgets. During my stint as diary writer in the mid-'80s I had bought a battery-powered Tandy 100 computer, which displayed a few lines of text. On assignment in Australia I learned how to unscrew a hotel phone and, with crocodile clips, squirt copy back to London using packet-switching technology in the middle of the night.

It felt like landing a man on the moon. I had no idea what was to come.

3

The New World

In 1993 some journalists began to be dimly aware of something clunk-ily referred to as 'the information superhighway' but few had ever had reason to see it in action. At the start of 1995 only 491 newspapers were online worldwide: by June 1997 that had grown to some 3,600.

In the basement of the *Guardian* was a small team created by Peter Preston – the Product Development Unit, or PDU. The inhabitants were young and enthusiastic. None of them were conventional journal-ists: I think the label might be 'creatives'. Their job was to think of new things that would never occur to the (largely middle-aged) reporters and editors three floors up.

The team – eventually rebranding itself as the New Media Lab – started casting around for the next big thing. They decided it was the internet. The creatives had a PC actually capable of accessing the world wide web. They moved in hipper circles. And they started importing copies of a new magazine, *Wired* – the so-called *Rolling Stone* of tech-nology – which had started publishing in San Francisco in 1993, along with the HotWired website. 'Wired described the revolution,' it boasted. 'HotWired was the revolution.' It was launched in the same month the Netscape team was beginning to assemble. Only 18 months later Netscape was worth billions of dollars. Things were moving that fast.

In time, the team in PDU made friends with three of the people associated with *Wired*. They were the founders, Louis Rossetto and Jane

Metcalfe; and the columnist, Nicholas Negroponte, who was based at the Massachusetts Institute of Technology and who wrote mindblowing columns predicting such preposterous things as wristwatches which would 'migrate from a mere timepiece today to a mobile command-and-control centre tomorrow . . . an all-in-one, wrist-mounted TV, computer, and telephone.'[1]

As if.

Both Rossetto and Negroponte were, in their different ways, prophets. Rossetto was a hot booking for TV talk shows, where he would explain to baffled hosts what the information superhighway meant. He'd tell them how smart the internet was, and how ethical. Sure, it was a 'dissonance amplifier'. But it was also a 'driver of the discussion' towards the real. You couldn't mask the truth in this new world, because someone out there would weigh in with equal force. Mass media was one-way communication. The guy with the antenna could broadcast to billions, with no feedback loop. He could dominate. But on the internet every voice was going to be equal to every other voice.

'Everything you know is wrong,' he liked to say. 'If you have a preconceived idea of how the world works, you'd better reconsider it.'

Negroponte, 50-something, East Coast gravitas to Rossetto's Californian drawl, and altogether more buttoned up, was working on a book, *Being Digital*, and was equally passionate in his evangelism. His mantra was to explain the difference between atoms – which make up the physical artefacts of the past – and bits, which travel at the speed of light and would be the future. 'We are so unprepared for the world of bits . . . We're going to be forced to think differently about everything.'

I bought the drinks and listened.

Over dinner in a North London restaurant Negroponte started with convergence – the melting of all boundaries between TV, newspapers, magazines and the internet into a single media experience – and moved on to the death of copyright, possibly the nation state itself. There would be virtual reality, speech recognition, personal computers with inbuilt cameras, personalised news. The entire economic model of information was about to fall apart. The audience would pull rather than wait for old media to push things as at present. Information and entertainment would be on demand. Overly hierarchical and status-conscious societies would rapidly erode. Time as we knew it would become meaningless – five hours of music would be delivered to you in less than five seconds. Distance would become irrelevant. A UK paper would be as accessible in New York as it was in London.

I decided I should go to America and see the internet for myself.

★

It was easy, in 1993, to be only dimly aware of what the internet did. The kids in the basement might have a PC capable of accessing the web, but most of us had only read about it.

Writing 15 years later in the *Observer*,[2] the critic John Naughton compared the begetter of the world wide web, Sir Tim Berners-Lee, with the seismic disruption five centuries earlier caused by the invention of movable type. Just as Gutenberg had no conception of his invention's eventual influence on religion, science, systems of ideas and democracy, so – in 2008 – 'it will be decades before we have any real understanding of what Berners-Lee hath wrought'.

And so I set off to find the internet with the leader of the PDU team, Tony Ageh, a 33-year-old 'creative'. He had had exactly one year's experience in media – as an advertising copy chaser for *The Home Organist* magazine – before joining the *Guardian*. I took with me a copy of *The Internet for Dummies*. Thus armed, we set off to America for a four-day, four-city tour.

In Atlanta, we found the *Atlanta Journal-Constitution* (*AJC*), which was considered a thought leader in internet matters, having joined the Prodigy Internet Service, an online service offering subscribers information over dial-up 1,200 bit/second modems. After four months the internet service had 14,000 members, paying 10 cents a minute to access online banking, messaging, full webpage hosting and live share prices.

The *AJC* business plan envisaged building to 35,000 or 40,000 by year three. But that time, they calculated, they would be earning $3.3 million in subscription fees and $250,000 a year in advertising. 'If it all goes to plan,' David Scott, the publisher, Electronic Information Service, told us, 'it'll be making good money. If it goes any faster, this is a real business.'

We also met Michael Gordon, the managing editor. 'The appeal to the management is, crudely, that it is so much cheaper than publishing a newspaper,' he said.

We wrote it down.

'We know there are around 100,000 people in Atlanta with PCs. There are, we think, about 1 million people wealthy enough to own them. Guys see them as a toy; women see them as a tool. The goldmine is going to be the content, which is why newspapers are so strongly placed to take advantage of this revolution. We're out to maximise our revenue by selling our content any way we can. If we can sell it on CD-ROM or TV as well, so much the better.'

'Papers? People will go on wanting to read them, though it's obviously much better for us if we can persuade them to print them in their own homes. They might come in customised editions. Edition 14B might be for females living with a certain income.'

It was heady stuff.

From Atlanta we hopped up to New York to see the *Times*'s online service, @Times. We found an operation consisting of an editor plus three staffers and four freelancers.[3] The team had two PCs, costing around $4,000 each. The operation was confident, but small.

The @Times content was weighted heavily towards arts and leisure. The opening menus offered a panel with about 15 reviews of the latest films, theatre, music and books – plus book reviews going back two years. The site offered the top 15 stories of the day, plus some sports news and business.

There was a discussion forum about movies, with 47 different subjects being debated by 235 individual subscribers. There was no archive due to the fact that – in one of the most notorious newspaper licensing cock-ups in history – the *NYT* in 1983 had given away all rights to its electronic archive (for all material more than 24 hours old) in perpetuity to Mead/Lexis.[4]

That deal alone told you how nobody had any clue what was to come.

We sat down with Henry E. Scott, the group director of @Times.⁵ 'Sound and moving pictures will be next. You can get them now. I thought about it the other day, when I wondered about seeing 30 seconds of *The Age of Innocence*. But then I realised it would take 90 minutes to download that and I could have seen more or less the whole movie in that time. That's going to change.'

But Scott was doubtful about the lasting value of what they were doing – at least, in terms of news. 'I can't see this replacing the newspaper,' he said confidently. 'People don't read computers unless it pays them to, or there is some other pressing reason. I don't think anyone reads a computer for pleasure. The *San Jose Mercury* has put the whole newspaper online. We don't think that's very sensible. It doesn't make sense to offer the entire newspaper electronically.'

We wrote it all down.

'I can't see the point of news on screen. If I want to know about a breaking story I turn on the TV or the radio. I think we should only do what we can do better than in print. If it's inferior than the print version there's no point in doing it.'

Was there a business plan? Not in Scott's mind. 'There's no way you can make money out of it if you are using someone else's server. I think the *LA Times* expects to start making money in about three years' time. We're treating it more as an R & D project.'

This approach became known as 'reach before revenue'. It was the business model for much of the internet.

From New York we flitted over to Chicago to see what the *Tribune* was up to. In its 36-storey Art Deco building – a spectacular monument to institutional self-esteem – we found a team of four editorial and four marketing people working on a digital service, with the digital unit situated in the middle of the newsroom. The marketeers were beyond excited about the prospect of being able to show houses or cars for sale and arranged a demonstration. We were excited, too, even if the pictures were slow and cumbersome to download.

We met Joe Leonard, associate editor. 'We're not looking at Chicago Online as a money maker. We've no plans even to break even at this stage. My view is simply that I'm not yet sure where I'm going, but I'm on the boat, in the water – and I'm ahead of the guy who is still standing on the pier.'

Reach before revenue.

Finally we headed off to Boulder, Colorado, in the foothills of the Rockies, where Knight Ridder had a team working on their vision of the newspaper of tomorrow. The big idea was, essentially, what would become the iPad – only the team in Boulder hadn't got much further than making an A4 block of wood with a 'front page' stuck on it. The 50-something director of the research centre, Roger Fidler, thought the technology capable of realising his dream of a 'personal information appliance' was a couple of years off.[6]

Tony and I had filled several notebooks. We were by now beyond tired and talked little over a final meal in an Italian restaurant beneath the Rocky Mountains.

We had come. We had seen the internet. We were conquered.

★

Looking back from the safe distance of nearly 25 years it's easy to mock the fumbling, wildly wrong predictions about where this new beast was going to take the news industry. We had met navigators and pioneers. They could dimly glimpse where the future lay. Not one of them had any idea how to make a dime out of it, but at the same time they intuitively sensed that it would be more reckless not to experiment. It seemed reasonable to assume that – if they could be persuaded to take the internet seriously – their companies would dominate in this new world, as they had in the old world.

We were no different. After just four days it seemed blindingly obvious that the future of information would be mainly digital. Plain old words on paper – delivered expensively by essentially Victorian production and distribution methods – couldn't, in the end, compete. The future would be more interactive, more image-driven, more immediate. That was clear. But how on earth could you graft a digital mindset and processes onto the stately ocean liner of print? How could you convince anyone that this should be a priority when no one had yet worked out how to make any money out of it? The change, and therefore the threat, was likely to happen rapidly and maybe violently. How quickly could we make a start? Or was this something that would be done to us?

In a note for Peter Preston on our return I wrote, 'The internet is fascinating, intoxicating . . . it is also crowded out with bores, nutters, fanatics and middle managers from Minnesota who want the world to see their home page and CV. It's a cacophony, a jungle. There's too much information out there. We're all overloaded. You want someone you trust to fillet it, edit it and make sense of it for you. That's what we do. It's an opportunity.'

I spent the next year trying to learn more and then the calendar clicked on to 1995 – *The Year the Future Began*, at least according to a recent book by the cultural historian W. Joseph Campbell, who used the phrase as his book title twenty years later. It was the year of O.J. Simpson, the Dayton Ohio peace accord and the entanglement of Bill Clinton and Monica Lewinsky. It was the year Amazon.com, eBay, Craigslist and Match.com established their presence online. Microsoft spent $300m launching Windows 95 with weeks of marketing hype, spending millions for the rights to the Rolling Stones hit 'Start Me Up', which became the anthem for the Windows 95 launch.

Cyberspace – as the cyber dystopian Evgeny Morozov recalled, looking back on that period – felt like space itself.[7] 'The idea of exploring cyberspace as virgin territory, not yet colonised by governments and corporations, was romantic; that romanticism was even reflected in the names of early browsers ("Internet Explorer," "Netscape Navigator").'

But, as Campbell was to reflect, 'no industry in 1995 was as ill-prepared for the digital age, or more inclined to pooh-pooh the disruptive potential of the Internet and World Wide Web, than the news business'. It suffered from what he called 'innovation blindness' – 'an inability, or a disinclination to anticipate and understand the consequences of new media technology'.

1995 was, then, the year the future began. It happened also to be the year in which I became editor of the *Guardian*.

4

Editor

I was 41 and had not, until very recently, really imagined this turn of events. Peter Preston – unshowy, grittily obstinate, brilliantly strategic – looked as if he would carry on editing for years to come. It was a complete surprise when he took me to the basement of the resolutely unfashionable Italian restaurant in Clerkenwell he favoured, to tell me he had decided to call it a day.

On most papers the proprietor or chief executive would find an editor, take him/her out to lunch and do the deal. On the *Guardian* – at least according to tradition dating back to the mid-'70s – the Scott Trust made the decision after balloting the staff, a process that involved manifestos, pub hustings and even (by some candidates) a little frowned-on campaigning.

I supposed I should run for the job. My mission statement said I wanted to boost investigative reporting and get serious about digital. It was, I fear, a bit Utopian. I doubt much of it impressed the would-be electorate. British journalists are programmed to scepticism about idealistic statements concerning their trade. Nevertheless, I won the popular vote and was confirmed by the Scott Trust after an interview in which I failed to impress at least one Trustee with my sketchy knowledge of European politics. We all went off for a drink in the pub round the back of the office. A month later I was editing.

'Fleet Street', as the UK press was collectively called, was having a torrid time, not least because the biggest beast in the jungle, Rupert

Murdoch, had launched a prolonged price war that was playing havoc with the economics of publishing. His pockets were so deep he could afford to slash the price of the *Times* almost indefinitely – especially if it forced others out of business.

Reach before revenue – as it wasn't known then.

The newest kid on the block, the *Independent*, was suffering the most. To their eyes, Murdoch was behaving in a predatory way. We calculated the *Independent* titles were losing around £42 million (nearly £80 million in today's money). Murdoch's *Times*, by contrast, had seen its sales rocket 80 per cent by cutting its cover prices to below what it cost to print and distribute. The circulation gains had come at a cost – about £38 million in lost sales revenue. But Murdoch's TV business, BSkyB, was making booming profits and the *Sun* continued to throw off huge amounts of cash. He could be patient.

The *Telegraph* had been hit hard – losing £45 million in circulation revenues through cutting the cover price by 18 pence. The end of the price war left it slowly clawing back lost momentum, but it was still £23 million adrift of where it had been the previous year. Murdoch – as so often – had done something bold and aggressive. Good for him, not so good for the rest of us. Everyone was tightening their belts in different ways. The *Independent* effectively gave up on Scotland. The *Guardian* saved a million a year in newsprint costs by shaving half an inch off the width of the paper.

The *Guardian*, by not getting into the price war, had 'saved' around £37 million it would otherwise have lost. But its circulation had been dented by about 10,000 readers a day. Moreover, the average age of the *Guardian* reader was 43 – something that pre-occupied us rather a lot. We were in danger of having a readership too old for the job advertisements we carried.

Though the *Guardian* itself was profitable, the newspaper division was losing nearly £12 million (north of £21 million today). The losses were mainly due to the sister Sunday title, the *Observer*, which the Scott Trust had purchased as a defensive move (against the *Independent*) in 1993. The Sunday title had a distinguished history, but was haemorrhaging cash: £11 million losses.

Everything we had seen in America had to be put on hold for a while. The commercial side of the business never stopped reminding us that only 3 per cent of households owned a PC and a modem.

★

But the digital germ was there. My love of gadgets had not extended to understanding how computers actually worked, so I commissioned a colleague to write a report telling me, in language I could understand, how our computers measured up against what the future would demand. The Atex system we had installed in 1987 gave everyone a dumb terminal on their desk – little more than a basic word processor. It couldn't connect to the internet, though there was a rudimentary internal messaging system. There was no word count or spellchecker and storage space was limited. It could not be used with floppy disks or CD-ROMs. Within eight years of purchase it was already a dinosaur.

There was one internet connection in the newsroom, though most reporters were unaware of it. It was rumoured that downstairs a bloke called Paul in IT had a Mac connected to the internet through a dial-up modem. Otherwise we were sealed off from the outside world.

Some of these journalist geeks began to invent Heath Robinson solutions to make the inadequate kit in Farringdon Road to do the things we wanted in order to produce a technology website online. Tom Standage – he later became deputy editor of the *Economist*, but then was a freelance tech writer – wrote some scripts to take articles out of Atex and format them into HTML so they could be moved onto the modest Mac web server – our first content management system, if you like. If too many people wanted to read this tech system at once the system crashed. So Standage and the site's editor, Azeem Azhar, would take it in turns sitting in the server room in the basement of the building rebooting the machines by hand – unplugging them and physically moving the internet cables from one machine to another.

What would the future look like? We imagined personalised editions, even if we had not the faintest clue how to produce them. We guessed that readers might print off copies of the *Guardian* in their homes – and even toyed with the idea of buying every reader a printer. There were glimmers of financial hope. Our readers were spending £56 million a year buying the *Guardian* but we retained none of it: the money went on paper and distribution. In the back of our minds we ran calculations about how the economics of newspapers would change if we could save ourselves the £56 million a year 'old world' cost.

★

It would be nice to claim that I had seen the future and would urgently toil night and day to make it happen. But an editor's life isn't like that, as I was discovering. For one thing, we were never out of court.

The English defamation law in the late 1990s had not developed from its eighteenth-century roots in seditious libel as much as one might imagine. Britain had no first amendment enshrining the importance, never mind the supremacy, of free speech. If someone rich or powerful sued you, a) the onus was on you to prove the facts and b) you had to be prepared to risk very large sums of money – often, millions of pounds – in the defence of your reporting. As a country we paid lip service to Milton, Hazlitt, Wilkes, Junius, Delane, Barnes, C.P. Scott and others who – over three centuries – had helped the press gain its comparative freedom. But, in reiterating the importance of a free press, people usually manage to insinuate a qualifier. As in, 'I stand second to none in my belief in the Freedom of the Press, but . . .'

Libel confrontations were a spectator sport. They ended up as pitched gladiatorial battles in the gothic revival splendour of the Royal Courts of Justice at one end of Fleet Street. Each side would be represented by ranks of lawyers. The press benches would be packed. These were fights to the reputational death.

I knew little about media law at the time beyond what I had studied at Harlow Technical College as a cub reporter. In 1995 the *Guardian* did not employ a single in-house lawyer: complaints were handled by a retired foreign editor, and farmed out to external solicitors if they became unwieldy.

So serious investigative journalism in London – the so-called 'libel capital of the world' – was never easy. For an editor, these confrontations

34

took up vast amounts of time and nervous energy. I inherited what was to turn into a marathon case over allegations that Neil Hamilton, the MP for Tatton, together with another MP, Tim Smith, had accepted cash from the owner of Harrods department store, Mohamed Al-Fayed, in return for asking questions in the House of Commons. Smith didn't contest the charges and eventually left politics. Hamilton claimed it was all lies and – together with a prominent political lobbyist, Ian Greer – launched a protracted libel suit against the paper.

There was an obstacle: parliamentary privilege prevented MPs from suing. But Hamilton succeeded in changing the British constitution, amending the 1688 Bill of Rights in order to be free to fight his action. There was a scarcely concealed fury among many MPs that a newspaper should vigorously attack corruption in parliament – just as they vented their wrath on the *Sunday Times* (and, later, the *Daily Telegraph*) for their own work in the same area.

In September 1996 – on the eve of the High Court hearing which could have cost the *Guardian* several million pounds – the Hamilton/Greer case collapsed with nine minutes to spare. 'A Liar and a Cheat' was our blunt front-page headline the following morning. There followed another five years of inquiries, committees, further libel actions (thankfully, not directly against the *Guardian*) and appeals. At one stage we were almost certainly in contempt of parliament, for publishing an embargoed copy of the official report into the allegations of parliamentary sleaze we had uncovered.

*

The Hamilton action coincided with another marathon successful defence of a case brought by five police officers based at Stoke Newington police station in North London, who were caught up in a corruption inquiry and could have been awarded £125,000 each if they had won.[1] The point was this: robust, inquiring journalism was time consuming, difficult and expensive. It was knotty, hard and often exhausting to do; and usually laborious, labyrinthine and prohibitively costly to defend. A single journalist on their own could be picked off and silenced. A journalist doing brave work needed to know their organisation would defend their reporting. In the absence of that defence, journalism meant nothing. The institutional strength of the media was all.

The next gargantuan battle – with the Cabinet minister and Conservative MP Jonathan Aitken – was hardly typical. But within three months of becoming editor I was plunged into yet another drawn-out gladiatorial battle over a series of articles questioning the minister's involvement with assorted figures, including arms dealers, in the Middle East. There were unanswered questions about who had paid his hotel bill when staying at the Ritz hotel in Paris while a government minister. Was it the Saudi businessmen who were also staying there or was it, as Aitken claimed, his wife?

We had taken up this questioning where my predecessor, Peter Preston, had left off. One day in April 1995 a colleague rushed into my office and told me to switch on the television. There was Aitken broadcasting live to the nation: 'If it now falls to me to start a fight to cut out the cancer of bent and twisted journalism in our country with the simple sword of truth and the trusty shield of traditional British fair play, so be it.'

He was going to sue us – and, in an act of supreme bravado, had announced the fact live on television to the nation. I experienced a sensation that had previously just been a figure of speech: my stomach turned over. This was going to be an unforgivingly public fight. Alongside us in the dock would be Granada TV, who had made a parallel programme, *Jonathan of Arabia*. They were insured for costs. We weren't.

We had – as in previous trials – the solicitor Geraldine Proudler and the QC George Carman running our case. Carman – a diminutive, chain-smoking, by then semi-alcoholic in his late 60s – was perhaps the most famous barrister in Britain, with a reputation for pulling legal rabbits out of the hat at the last minute.[2] We were going to need one. The requirement that a defendant has to prove the truth of everything they have written (the opposite of the law in most parts of the world)[3] meant the onus was on us to determine who had been where, when; and who had paid what.

That was only possible by exhaustive and expensive disclosure of Aitken's financial records, which was never going to be easy. In the run-up to the trial Aitken's supporters in the media anticipated with lip-smacking relish the impending humbling of the *Guardian*. Political loyalties – with some notable exceptions – trumped journalistic solidarity.[4] At this point Aitken was still seen as a future prime minister – handsome, charming, intelligent and well-connected. His £8 million,[5] six-bedroomed house at 8 Lord North Street – barely five minutes' walk from the House of Commons – had a private ballroom and was the perfect venue for political soirées and intrigues. His only serious mistake to date had supposedly been to break the heart of Margaret Thatcher's daughter – a romantic crime for which he had to serve considerable time in the political wilderness.

A newspaper article, once it ends up as an exhibit in a High Court action, becomes cadaver for repeated dissection. Every sentence – every word – is excised and held up to the light. Was it precisely right? What did it mean? Was it balanced by other words or sentences? By this stage it is useless for the journalist to argue what they intended by their words. A judge will decide the meaning. You may end up having to defend a judge's decision about what a sentence meant, rather than what you actually meant.

The case was multi-pronged. On some prongs, we knew we were right but would struggle to prove it. Sources will sometimes tell you things they know to be true, but would run a mile rather than appear as a witness on oath in court in the full glare of the world's press. On some allegations we knew we were right, but – without full access to the movements and financial records of Aitken and his family – we lacked the killer proof. With other prongs we could defend our meaning of our words, but not a judge's view of what he thought we meant to say.

Aitken's subsequent autobiography showed that he, too, had internal turmoil about the ordeal ahead. But, as he observed our exhaustive and expensive attempts at discovery of paperwork, he shrewdly, if recklessly, deduced that we were far from home and dry.

About a month before we were due to lock horns in the High Court I tried a last-ditch effort at resolving the case through Aitken's friend, the advertising magnate Maurice Saatchi, who duly suggested a lunch with Aitken at Wilton's, an old-world fish restaurant near Piccadilly. Saatchi was optimistic he could broker a deal that would save face all round. I turned up at the agreed time: Aitken didn't. He was out campaigning for the impending general election and obviously felt sufficiently confident he was going to trounce us.

The trial paperwork was mounting up. Aitken's witness statement alone ran to 280 pages. He had 80 witness statements to bolster his case: we had 70. Between them, they ran to 1,800 pages. On top of that there were a further 1,450 documents that might be needed during the course of the High Court hearing. Over the months the 255 pages of pleadings were (in legal jargon) amended, re-amended, re-re-amended and even re-re-re-amended. Every amendment took time. Time was money, and this case was already becoming eye-wateringly expensive for whoever lost.

Every hour I spent locked away with lawyers was an hour away from learning the ropes of editing; or from thinking about the digital future; or from planning the *Guardian* I wanted to shape.

Aitken's QC, Charles Gray, secured a trial without a jury. This was a blow. In the police federation case, the common sense of 12 fellow citizens had saved us from defeat. Trial by jury was the norm for libel actions, and we'd hoped that the Aitken case would be heard by one, too.

But our fate now rested in the hands of Sir Oliver Popplewell, a 70-year-old patrician figure whose own attitude to journalists was perhaps betrayed by his memoirs, which appeared to dismiss them as 'scribblers'. Doubtless, Popplewell would have put his feelings to one side but one reason we had chosen Carman was because he was a supreme jury advocate. His down-to-earth mix of bluntness and twinkly charm might not be so effective in a trial by a judge alone.

Two days before the case started Proudler had suggested a mission so apparently desperate I was at first disinclined to take it seriously. She suggested sending a reporter to Switzerland to see if they could obtain the relevant hotel records to show the whereabouts of Lolicia Aitken at the time the Ritz hotel bill in Paris had been settled. I had little faith that a reporter would be able to gain access to individual client records, but eventually agreed to send Owen Bowcott, a reliable and experienced journalist, on the trail.

The trial opened to a packed court 10 on 4 June 1997 – more than two years after the action had been launched. Gray told the court how the *Guardian* had 'butchered' Aitken's personal, political and professional reputation. In addition to claiming Aitken had lied about who had paid the Ritz bill, he listed the other prongs of the case: we'd said that he was in the pockets of the Saudi royal family; had been dabbling in the arms trade; and had been pimping for prostitutes to entertain rich Arabs on their visits to the UK.

There followed eight days of Aitken in the witness box. I popped in from time to time to watch him, my heart sinking as (it seemed to me and others in court) he established an easy-going rapport with Popplewell. The judge later wrote that he found Aitken a 'very convincing witness' even though he had simultaneously seen through his lies. He concealed his scepticism about Aitken's story well, perhaps because the plaintiff was a consummate master of detail. He was understated, but confident. He had an attractive self-deprecatory wit. He told convincingly of his 'pole-axing' pain and sleepless nights at reading some of the *Guardian* allegations – the equivalent, he said, of a heart attack. The coverage, he said, had had a devastating impact on his wife, Lolicia, and their three children. Carman later said he was the best-prepared witness he had ever encountered in court.

Carman had Aitken on the stand for five days of cross-examination. Aitken was evasive about the precise details of how or when his wife (rather than the Saudis) had paid his hotel bill in Paris ('I can't even now grip it – exactly who did what where – I wasn't there') but Carman struggled to lay a knock-out blow. The onus was on us to demonstrate exactly what had happened. All we knew was what Aitken *said* had happened: that his wife had been staying at the Hotel Bristol in Villars, Switzerland, before travelling to Paris on the Sunday morning, whereupon she had paid the Ritz bill in cash.

Aitken's story felt impossible. Everything about the supposed Ritz payment pointed to the fact that he was lying, but we still lacked the documentary evidence to prove it. From Aitken's point of view the case was going very nicely indeed. He and Popplewell were both cricket lovers, and Aitken would later deploy the game's imagery, saying: 'I was on a good wicket, finding myself largely untroubled by Carman's bowling.' He heard distant trumpets of victory.

In the course of one slightly gloomy meeting in Carman's chambers off Gray's Inn Road to discuss the fact that we had been forced to withdraw part of our pleas on grounds of 'meaning', we learned that Granada TV's insurers were pulling the plug. If the TV executives didn't settle now, they would refuse to be liable for any subsequent costs. The TV executives themselves wanted to hang in.

All eyes were on me: would the *Guardian* also fold?

The answer was no. To have said otherwise would have been a terrible betrayal of the reporting that had gone into this story. The journalism had, we felt, been overwhelmingly right, even if we were struggling to defend every single sentence in court under the arcane procedures of English libel cases. I knew I had the backing of our managing director, Caroline Marland, and of the Scott Trust under Hugo Young. But we had to prepare for the possibility that this trial could end in expensive disaster. Unless, unless . . .

. . . unless Carman could, for one last time in his long career, produce a legal rabbit out of the hat. The only chance now was a forlorn one – Bowcott's mission impossible. And, yet, with that doomed adventure, there was a twist. Bowcott had arrived at the Hotel Bristol and – what were the chances? – found it had recently gone into receivership. He was granted permission to descend into the deserted hotel's basement to sleuth his way through thousands of shoeboxes containing the old records. And . . . he eventually found something that could conceivably look like a rabbit – Lolicia Aitken's reservation. It meant little to him so he faxed the paperwork back to Proudler in London.

Proudler began her own forensic examination of what these newly acquired records showed. They seemed to suggest that Lolicia – at the very time when Aitken had said she was having a bath in their room in Paris – had in fact been tucking into a breakfast of cornflakes and apple juice 570 kilometres away in Villars. Proudler was even more interested to see that Lolicia had settled her Bristol bill with an American Express card that had never been disclosed to the defence in the libel trial. Proudler began an investigative journey of her own, demanding all the relevant financial statements from Aitken's solicitors. We were not to get sight of them until 12 June, more than a week into the hearing.

From those records – car rental, airline tickets, etc. – Proudler was able painstakingly to piece together Lolicia's movements. It took time. British Airways' own microfilm archive was held in a warehouse near Heathrow. The airline estimated it could take more than a month to provide the clinching evidence. Proudler offered them help. The detective trail was moving agonisingly slowly.

Back in court, Aitken was by now so confident of success he played one last daring card. Thursday 19 June was so-called 'Ladies' Day' at Ascot races – the day punters dress up to the nines to watch the Gold Cup. In a break in court proceedings the previous day Aitken's solicitor, Richard Sykes, tipped off the press that it would also be Ladies' Day in court. Aitken was putting Lolicia and his 17-year-old daughter, Victoria, into the witness box to confirm his story once and for all.

Victoria, then studying for her A levels in Switzerland, had signed a witness statement supporting her father's version of events with an entirely fabricated story he had drafted for her. Aitken later described this as his 'worst and most shameful mistake' but, as he typed out the document of lies, his only thought was: 'That will do nicely.' This, surely, would destroy our case and leave his path clear for re-entry into politics . . . and maybe, one day, Downing Street. The humiliation of the *Guardian* would be complete. My editorship could have been a very short one.

The two women were saved from having to perjure themselves in court.

Shortly before adjournment on 18 June, Carman produced his rabbit. And what an extraordinary rabbit it was. I sat at the back of the court, heart racing, as our QC handed the judge a sworn witness statement from a British Airways investigator, Wendy Harris, showing that Lolicia had never been anywhere near Paris on the relevant dates. She had flown in and out of Geneva. The entire story had therefore been invented by Aitken. Even I (who knew in my heart that his story couldn't possibly be true) found it barely credible that he would have risked so much – his career, his marriage, his home, his freedom – on such a bare-faced lie.

Popplewell took a moment to absorb the significance of the documents before handing them to Aitken's QC suggesting, in mild but deadly legal shorthand, that he might wish to consider his position overnight.[6] I watched Aitken's features as the realisation sunk in that the case was lost and his life ruined. But his face was a testament to a privileged upbringing of masks, concealment and reserve – the same semi-amused insouciant smile on his lips. In reality, he later admitted, his head was pounding, his confidence was 'exploding into tiny pieces like flying shrapnel'.[7] He had, as he put it, 'been caught red-handed' and in that moment of disaster knew he had lost his whole world. He had unsheathed the 'simple sword of truth' only to be impaled upon it.

For Carman, it was the most sensational ending to any trial in his 44 years at the Bar. In Popplewell's judgement, it had been one of the bitterest and most enthralling libel actions ever heard in an English court.

We adjourned to Proudler's office for an overnight negotiation of the terms of the settlement. In the middle of the evening the Press Association published a brief story announcing that Aitken and his wife had separated.

Word leaked out that, in place of Ladies' Day, there would be surrender in Court 10. Both inside and outside the gothic cathedral of justice there were jostling throngs of reporters and camera crews. Aitken was nowhere to be seen: he had donned a Washington Redskins baseball cap and slipped out of the country before dawn – flying to New York via Paris in an attempt to avoid the press.

The hearing was brief, almost anti-climactic. Popplewell – shocked by Aitken's behaviour, if not (he said in his memoirs) surprised – took the rest of the day off at Lord's cricket ground, discussing the case with the former prime minister John Major. Peter Preston and I emerged blinking into a wall of flashbulbs to pronounce on the verdict. Barely two years earlier I would have been on the other side of the cameras, notebook in hand. I had unwittingly, and to some extent unwillingly, become a public figure.

The emotions were feverish on all sides. There was, for us, relief, exhaustion, exhilaration: for Aitken, hollow emptiness and remorse. He knew he now faced the wreck of a marriage and career as well as jail for perjury and probable bankruptcy,[8] with costs nudging £2 million.

Win, lose or draw, there was nothing remotely enjoyable about fighting libel actions. Ben Bradlee, editor of the *Washington Post* at the time of Watergate, said he would rather be publicly whipped than lose one.

He added, of one battle fought on behalf of two reporters, that if he'd known in advance what would be involved: 'I would have told them both to go piss up a rope.' He wouldn't, of course.

We drew some criticism for reporting Aitken's perjury to the Attorney General, though the judge would almost certainly have been bound to do so himself. For us, it was a matter of principle that libel shouldn't be seen as some sort of high-stakes gamble. I didn't rejoice at Aitken's subsequent downfall, but the defence of a free press did require the law to defend the truth and punish lies. I was unable to shrug the past two years of slog and anxiety off and behave as if it had all been a game.

Aitken subsequently served six months of an 18-month prison sentence, and was released in January 2000. The following year another prominent Conservative politician, (Lord) Jeffrey Archer, was jailed for four years for an even more egregious act of perjury in successfully suing the *Daily Star* in 1987.

The two cases signalled that libel cases had extremely serious consequences. Together, they were the high-water mark of defamation. The number of high-profile contested cases fell off over the next decade and – after some brilliant lobbying by human rights groups and lawyers – the law was eventually reformed.

★

Aitken found God, or God found him. His book, *Pride and Perjury*, is the story of a religious journey as well as a public downfall. In 2005 he was invited to talk at the Hay Festival, a jamboree of books and ideas in a little town on the Welsh borders, then sponsored by the *Guardian*. By mischievous design or accident he had been booked to stay in the same bed and breakfast as me, and we found ourselves sharing a polite cup of tea in the garden of our slightly discombobulated hosts. All bitterness and passion had, on both sides, melted away. I had great respect for the way he rebuilt his life with considerable humility and integrity. He remained very active in the cause of prison reform. When I eventually stepped down as editor in 2015 he came to the farewell party.

5

Shedding Power

The legal entanglements sometimes felt like a full-time job on their own, on top of editing. Trying to engineer a digital future for the *Guardian* felt like a third job. There were somehow always more urgent issues – including printing; international circulation; and the *Guardian*'s sister Sunday paper, the *Observer*, which continued to drain away cash at an alarming rate.

The *Observer* had the most wonderful, romantic history – a paper of principle, humanity and cultural distinction. But, commercially, the paper was struggling to an extent that would exhaust vast amounts of editorial, management and commercial time for the best part of the next decade. The paper had had two editors between 1948 and 1993. Within five years of buying the Sunday title, we were on our fourth.

We struggled to bring the two titles together under one roof and with a broadly common culture. The paper was proudly independent – perhaps even defined by a wish to be seen as quite distinct from the *Guardian*. That was understandable, but the economics of purchasing the paper had been predicated on a large degree of co-operation, if not integration. Without some degree of collaboration it was difficult to see how the Scott Trust coffers – intended to be just about sufficient as rainy day money for the *Guardian* – weren't going to be siphoned away by the newly acquired sister paper.

If it was this difficult to integrate even two newspapers, how much more difficult would it be to graft on an entirely different medium?

By March 1996 ideas we'd hatched in the summer of 1995 were already out of date. That was a harbinger of the future. No plans in the new world lasted very long.

It was now apparent that we couldn't get away with publishing selective parts of the *Guardian* online. Other newspapers had shot that fox by pushing out everything. We were learning about the connectedness of the web – and the IT team tentatively suggested that we might use some 'offsite links' to other versions of the same story to save ourselves the need to write our own version of everything. This later became the mantra of the City University of New York (CUNY) digital guru Jeff Jarvis – 'Do what you do best, and link to the rest.'[1]

We began to grapple with numerous basic questions about the new waters into which we were gingerly dipping our toes.

Important question: should we charge?

The *Times* and the *Telegraph* were both free online. A March 1996 memo from Bill Thompson, a developer who had joined the *Guardian* from Pipex, ruled it out:

> I do not believe the UK internet community would pay to read an online edition of a UK newspaper. They may pay to look at an archive, but I would not support any attempt to make the *Guardian* a subscription service online . . . It would take us down a dangerous path.
>
> In fact, I believe that the real value from an online edition will come from the increased contact it brings with our readers: online newspapers can track their readership in a way that print products never can, and the online reader can be a valuable commodity in their own right, even if they pay nothing for the privilege.

Thompson was prescient about how the overall digital economy would work – at least for players with infinitely larger scale and vastly more sophisticated technology.

What time of day should we publish?

The electronic *Telegraph* was published at 8 a.m. each day – mainly because of its print production methods. The *Times*, more automated, was available as soon as the presses started rolling. The *Guardian* started making some copy available from first edition through to the early hours. It would, we were advised, be fraught with difficulties to publish stories at the same time they were ready for the press.

Why were we doing it anyway?

Thompson saw the dangers of cannibalisation; that readers would stop buying the paper if they could read it for free online. It could be seen as a form of marketing. His memo seemed ambivalent as to whether we should venture into this new world at all:

> The *Guardian* excels in presenting information in an attractive easy to use and easy to navigate form. It is called a 'broadsheet newspaper'. If we try to put the newspaper on-line (as the *Times* has done) then we will just end up using a new medium to do badly what an old medium does well. The key question is whether to make the *Guardian* a website, with all that entails in terms of production, links, structure, navigational aids etc. In summer 1995 we decided that we would not do this.

But was that still right a year later? By now we had the innovation team – PDU – still in the basement of one building in Farringdon Road, and another team in a Victorian loft building across the way in Ray Street. We were, at the margins, beginning to pick up some interesting fringe figures who knew something about computers, if not journalism. But none of this was yet pulling together into a coherent picture of what a digital *Guardian* might look like.

*

An 89-page business plan drawn up in October 1996 made it plain where the priorities lay: print.

We wanted to keep growing the *Guardian* circulation – aiming a modest increase to 415,000 by March 2000 – which would make us the ninth-biggest paper in the UK – with the *Observer* aiming for 560,000 with the aid of additional sections. A modest investment of £200,000 a year in digital was dwarfed by an additional £6 million cash injection into the *Observer*, spread over three years.

As for 'on-line services' (we were still hyphenating it) we did want 'a leading-edge presence' (whatever that meant), but essentially we thought we had to be there because we had to be there. By being there we would learn and innovate and – surely? – there were bound to be commercial opportunities along the road. It wasn't clear what.

We decided we might usefully take broadcasting, rather than print, as a model – emulating its 'immediacy, movement searchability and layering'.

If this sounded as if we were a bit at sea, we were. We hadn't published much digitally to this point. We had taken half a dozen meaty issues – including parliamentary sleaze, and a feature on how we had continued to publish on the night our printing presses had been blown up by the IRA – and turned them into special reports.

It is a tribute to our commercial colleagues that they managed to pull in the thick end of half a million pounds to build these websites. Other companies' marketing directors were presumably like ours – anxious about the youth market and keen for their brands to feel 'cool'. In corporate Britain in 1996, there was nothing much cooler than the internet, even if not many people had it, knew where to find it or understood what to do with it.

★

I found the sheer power of an editor frightening – but temptingly enjoyable. I hope I had just about enough self-awareness early on for the unease to trump the heady, head-turning possibilities of gripping the megaphone. Prime ministers, generals, spies, archbishops, princesses, ambassadors, bankers, film directors, presidents, rabbis, oligarchs and business leaders would come to lunch at the drop of an invitation. There was often deference in their voices. They wanted to be liked by newspapers.

Over the years I watched many fellow editors at close quarters. Several of them visibly enjoyed the deference. Among the ranks of editors some were reserved, shy, almost scholarly. Some were humane, sane and straightforward. Some were brash, extrovert, larger than life. A very few were fully fledged bullies – self-important, thin-skinned, mean-eyed and aggressive individuals. These characteristics didn't necessarily bar them from being very capable editors.

There was nothing in the job description of an editor that said they had to be well-rounded, compassionate and lovable. Some of the 'best' editors were none of the above. Some pounded through long days (it was rumoured) on a cocktail of alcohol, adrenalin or cocaine. Some had (to me) quite strange ideas about class, race, immigration, gender, politics or sex, which dominated their worldview. Some editors kept these opinions, beliefs or prejudices to themselves. Others let rip with them in their newspapers.

Here's the paradox: sometimes the most demotic figures produced 'brilliant' newspapers of raucous energy and flair. They were regarded as 'great' editors, in touch with popular opinion, their finger on the pulse. They could write the killer headline, crop a picture and lay out a page like no one else. They were true 'professionals'.

There was little to stop them behaving like unfettered autocrats: within their newsrooms they enjoyed absolute power, sometimes verging on the despotic. In some cases, their internal control was mirrored by an apparent craving for external dominance.

James Graham's 2017 play about the birth of the Murdoch Sun, titled Ink,[2] portrays one such (real-life) character in its editor, Larry Lamb[3] – so ruthlessly driven that even the 'Murdoch' character is visibly alarmed by the monster he has unleashed on the world.

Lamb's successor, Kelvin MacKenzie,[4] was even more over the top, with a gift for sugaring lethal aggression with a quite winning seaside humour.

MacKenzie pushed the sales of the Sun to well over 4 million with a mix of bonk journalism and populist politics. The more odium he attracted from the despised bien pensant Establishment (as he saw them), the more he felt encouraged to be increasingly outrageous in exposing homosexuals, adulterers, hypocrites . . . and anyone else qualifying for the category of general scumbag.

Complaining readers were treated with contempt. According to the authors Peter Chippendale and Chris Horrie in their book about the *Sun*, 'He would pick up their letters and say: "What a wank. What a complete fucking wank," spitting the words out and holding their letter at arm's length between finger and thumb as though it were made of some particularly repellent substance.'[5]

But no one put a check on MacKenzie, even when his notoriously offensive front-page 'The Truth' headline about the supposed behaviour of fans at the Hillsborough tragedy in 1989 was shown to be a travesty – and led to an entire city, Liverpool, boycotting the paper in perpetuity.

In 2004 – 15 years later – the *Sun* admitted the treatment of this story had been 'the most terrible mistake in our history'. That did not stop MacKenzie's return to the paper as a columnist in 2006; or being hired as an opinion writer by the *Daily Mail* in 2011; or by the *Telegraph* in 2013; or returning to the *Sun* in 2014. He was eventually sacked by the *Sun* in April 2017 after comparing a mixed-race footballer with a 'dim-witted' gorilla. It was all good fun until it wasn't.

Today, MacKenzie's 13-year dominance at the paper seems an era of considerable bigotry, cruelty and prejudice rather than wit, brio and much-envied (and imitated) professionalism. There are editors, then and now, whose behaviour would – in any other context – seem borderline unhinged. They appear, to an outsider, worryingly aggressive and obsessive. They seem to derive pleasure from threatening, humiliating, harassing or intimidating their targets.

A newspaper is probably the last institution or organisation in the democratic world where such people would be allowed to operate with quite so little scrutiny or redress. Anyone who tried to run a government, school, public company, hospital, charity or prison in such a monocratic way would not survive in the modern age. And they would be savaged by the press.

I also knew that no newspaper could be edited by committee. In the end someone has to call the shots and take responsibility for the multiple decisions, small and large, involved in daily editing. One editor of the *Daily Mail*, Mike Randall, once counted 200 decisions he took in a single day. If you got 50 per cent right, he reckoned, you were doing well.[6]

★

The absence of a controlling owner meant we could run the *Guardian* in a slightly different way from some papers. Each day began with a morning conference open to anyone on the staff. In the old Farringdon Road office, it was held around two long narrow tables in the editor's office – perhaps 30 or 40 people sitting or standing. When we moved to our new offices at Kings Place, near Kings Cross in North London, we created a room that was, at least theoretically, less hierarchical: a horseshoe of low yellow sofas with a further row of stools at the back. In this room would assemble a group of journalists, tech developers and some visitors from the commercial departments every morning at about 10 a.m. If it was a quiet news day we might expect 30 or so. On big news days, or with an invited guest, we could host anything up to 100.[7]

A former *Daily Mail* journalist, attending his first morning conference, muttered to a colleague in the newsroom that it was like *Start the Week* – a Monday morning BBC radio discussion programme. All talk and no instructions. In a way, he was right: it was difficult, in conventional financial or efficiency terms, to justify 50 to 60 employees stopping work to gather together each morning for anything between 25 and 50 minutes. No stories were written during this period, no content generated.

But something else happened at these daily gatherings. Ideas emerged and were kicked around. Commissioning editors would pounce on contributors and ask them to write the thing they'd just voiced. The editorial line of the paper was heavily influenced, and sometimes changed, by the arguments we had. The youngest member of staff would be in the same room as the oldest: they would be part of a common discussion around news. By a form of accretion and osmosis an idea of the *Guardian* was jointly nourished, shared, handed down and crafted day by day.

It led to a very strong culture. You might love the *Guardian* or despise it, but it had a definite sense of what it believed in and what its journalism was. It could sometimes feel an intimidating meeting – even for (or *especially* for) the editor. The culture was intended to be one of challenge: if we'd made a wrong decision, or slipped up factually or tonally, someone would speak up and demand an answer. But challenge was different from blame: it was not a meeting for dressing downs or bollockings. If someone had made an error the previous day we'd have a post-mortem or unpleasant conversation outside the room. We'd encourage people to *want* to contribute to this forum, not make them fear disapproval or denunciation.

There was a downside to this. It could, and sometimes did, lead to a form of group-think. However herbivorous the culture we tried to nurture, I was conscious of some members of staff who felt awkward about expressing views outside a (we hoped, fairly broad) consensus. But, more often, there would be a good discussion on two or three of the main issues of the day. We encouraged specialists (or outside visitors) to come in and discuss breaking stories. Leader writers could gauge the temperature of the paper before penning an editorial. And, from time to time, there would be the opposite of consensus: individuals, factions or groups would come and demand we change our line on Russia, bombing in Bosnia; intervention in Syria; Israel, blood sports or the Labour leadership.

The point was this: that the *Guardian* was not one editor's plaything or megaphone. It emerged from a common conversation – and was open to internal challenge when editorial staff felt uneasy about aspects of our journalism or culture.

*

Within two years – slightly uncomfortable at the power I had acquired as editor – I gave some away. I wanted to make correction a natural part of the journalistic process, not a bitterly contested post-publication battleground designed to be as difficult as possible.

We created a new role on the *Guardian*: a readers' editor. He/she would be the first port of call for anyone wanting to complain about anything we did or wrote. The readers' editor would have daily space in the paper – off-limits to the editor – to correct or clarify anything and would also have a weekly column to raise broader issues of concern. It was written into the job description that the editor could not interfere. And the readers' editor was given the security that he/she could not be removed by the editor, only by the Scott Trust.

On most papers editors had sat in judgement on themselves. They commissioned pieces, edited and published them – and then were supposed neutrally to assess whether their coverage had, in fact, been truthful, fair and accurate. An editor might ask a colleague – usually a managing editor – to handle a complaint, but he/she was in charge from beginning to end. It was an autocracy. That mattered even more in an age when some journalism was moving away from mere reportage and observation to something closer to advocacy or, in some cases, outright pursuit.

Allowing even a few inches of your own newspaper to be beyond your direct command meant that your own judgements, actions, ethical standards and editorial decisions could be held up to scrutiny beyond your control. That, over time, was bound to change your journalism. Sunlight is the best disinfectant: that was the journalist-as-hero story we told about what we do. So why wouldn't a bit of sunlight be good for us, too?

The first readers' editor was Ian Mayes, a former arts and obituaries editor then in his late 50s. We felt the first person in the role needed to have been a journalist – and one who would command instant respect from a newsroom which otherwise might be somewhat resistant to having their work publicly critiqued or rebutted. There were tensions and some resentment, but Ian's experience, fairness and flashes of humour eventually won most people round.

One or two of his early corrections convinced staff and readers alike that he had a light touch about the fallibility of journalists:

> In our interview with Sir Jack Hayward, the chairman of Wolverhampton Wanderers, page 20, Sport, yesterday, we mistakenly attributed to him the following comment: 'Our team was the worst in the First Division and I'm sure it'll be the worst in the

Premier League.' Sir Jack had just declined the offer of a hot drink. What he actually said was: 'Our tea was the worst in the First Division and I'm sure it'll be the worst in the Premier League.' Profuse apologies.

In an article about the adverse health effects of certain kinds of clothing, pages 8 and 9, G2, August 5, we omitted a decimal point when quoting a doctor on the optimum temperature of testicles. They should be 2.2 degrees Celsius below core body temperature, not 22 degrees lower.

But in his columns he was capable of asking tough questions about our editorial decisions – often prompted by readers who had been unsettled by something we had done. Why had we used a shocking picture which included a corpse? Were we careful enough in our language around mental health or disability? Why so much bad language in the *Guardian*? Were we balanced in our views of the Kosovo conflict? Why were *Guardian* journalists so innumerate? Were we right to link to controversial websites?

In most cases Mayes didn't come down on one side or another. He would often take readers' concerns to the journalist involved and question them – sometimes doggedly – about their reasoning. We learned more about our readers through these interactions; and we hoped that Mayes's writings, candidly explaining the workings of a newsroom, helped readers better understand our thinking and processes.

It was, I felt, good for us to be challenged in this way. Mayes was invaluable in helping devise systems for the 'proper' way to correct the record. A world in which – to coin a phrase – you were 'never wrong for long' posed the question of whether you went in for what Mayes termed 'invisible mending'. Some news organisations would quietly amend whatever it was that they had published in error, no questions asked. Mayes felt differently: the act of publication was something on the record. If you wished to correct the record the correction should be visible.

We were some years off the advent of social media, in which any error was likely to be pounced on in a thousand hostile tweets. But we had some inkling that the iron grip of centralised control that a news-paper represented was not going to last.

I found liberation in having created this new role. There were few things editors can enjoy less than the furious early morning phone call or email from the irate subject of their journalism. Either the complainant is wrong – in which case there is time wasted in heated self-justification; or they're right, wholly or partially. Immediately you're into remorse-ful calculations about saving face. If readers knew we honestly and rapidly – even immediately – owned up to our mistakes they should, in theory, trust us more. That was the David Broder theory, and I bought it. Readers certainly made full use of the readers' editor's existence. Within five years Mayes was dealing with around 10,000 calls, emails and letters a year – leading to around 1,200 corrections, big and small. It's not, I think, that we were any more error-prone than other papers. But if you win a reputation for openness, you'd better be ready to take it as seriously as your readers will.

Our journalism became better. If, as a journalist, you know there are a million sleuth-eyed editors out there waiting to leap on your tiniest mistake, it makes you more careful. It changes the tone of your writing. *Our readers often know more than we do.* That became a mantra of the new world, coined by the blogger and academic Dan Gillmor, in his 2004 book *We the Media*[8] but it was already becoming evident in the late 1990s.

The act of creating a readers' editor[9] felt like a profound recognition of the changing nature of what we were engaged in. Journalism was not an infallible method guaranteed to result in something we would proclaim as The Truth – but a more flawed, tentative, iterative and interactive way of getting towards something truthful.

Admitting that felt both revolutionary and releasing.

6

Guardian . . . Unlimited

Perpetuity is a very long time. If your job is to make consistent margins now, or keep the dividends healthy, you run your business accordingly. If your mandate is, in theory, to make your organisation future-proof for eternity you gaze at more distant horizons.

A habitual doodler, I got in the habit in the late nineties of drawing two lines which, it seemed to me, were a pretty unexceptional prediction of what would happen to our business, even if the drawing had no scale to suggest meaningful time or quantum.

One was a red downward line, inclining at about 45 degrees. That seemed, over the years, to be the inevitable fate of print: a story of gentle but persistent decline. Circulation, sales, readership, advertising, revenues – they would all diminish over the years. If we did nothing, the *Guardian* would one day cease to exist.

The other, blue, line went upwards – at about the same incline. That was digital growth: users, audience . . . and, maybe, even revenues.

It was impossible to draw anything more sophisticated at the time. There was no data, it was all hunch.

The two lines did cross, but in the intersection I would draw a big green bubble – a visual representation of the anticipated losses as we transitioned from one medium/technology to the other. I couldn't see how it could be otherwise. We couldn't bail out of print – that's where all the revenues were – so we had to keep that (costly) show on the road. At the same time we would have to invest – perhaps heavily? – in digital. At some point the blue would begin to cannibalise the red line. We were only just keeping our heads above water as it was. So it was difficult to imagine how we weren't entering a period of considerable losses. The question was: could we sustain the losses until (to mix metaphors) we were safely on the other bank of the river?

Next question: how to take a 175-year-old newspaper and reinvent it as something else? If that's what we were trying to do. Some newspaper companies evidently regarded the internet as a different kind of distribution channel: *we can squirt the thing down phone lines instead of trucking it to you.* But what if the medium dictated the content? Then we would have to create something sufficiently '*Guardian*' to be true to the name; but sufficiently different to be true to the medium.

The *Guardian*, like all newspapers, was currently a random bundle of information held together by the glue of appearing in the same printed package. On the face of it the cricket scores, the weather, the ballet review, the fashion advice and the parliamentary report had little in common – but they hung together as a coherent package. It seemed likely that, over time, someone would come and do each of those areas better than a general newspaper could do. And then what would happen? Would the physical brand of the *Guardian* be sufficient glue to hold it all together in a world of bits and bytes?

One thing that was plain by early 1997 was that the five-year strategy agreed by the Board and the Trust less than a year earlier was not remotely digital enough. We would need smart technologists to help us think about the problems and possibilities. But web developers might know nothing about the news – or even the *Guardian*, for that matter. There was some feeling that the PDU, while brilliantly innovative, had become something of a 'state within a state' – not attuned enough to the culture of a newspaper to take people with them. I decided we needed one of the best younger journalists on the paper to lead the reinvention of the *Guardian*. Ian Katz,[1] our 29-year-old New York correspondent, did not sound thrilled to be asked. I wanted him to give up one of the plum jobs in journalism to come back to London and start a website?

The role, as described, had very little appeal. 'I thought it was a fucking bonkers idea,' Katz was to observe to me later.

★

The London office Katz returned to may have been one where some key individuals appreciated the size of the revolution around the corner. But, in most other respects, it was woefully unready for digital. Some visiting academics did a case study of the *Guardian* in 1998 and discovered that 'the *Guardian* gives the impression of being a newspaper on the brink of a sudden explosion in Internet use' but that actually not more than one in ten journalists were actively using the world wide web.

The academics reported that the editor ('a strong proponent') would hold regular lunches to explain what was going on out there, ending each lunch by telling them 'You are all bonkers if you are not using it. It ought to be an absolutely standard tool.' But it was not clear it was yet having much effect.

The authors quoted former *Times* editor (and future *Guardian* columnist) Simon Jenkins, predicting that the effect of the internet would be both minimal and short-lived: 'The Internet will strut an hour upon the stage, and then take its place in the ranks of the lesser media' – including Ceefax, Prestel, touch screen and CD-ROM.

'Jenkins sees red over the much-lauded two-way communication characteristics of the Internet . . . to those who claim "the advent of digital hypertext will liberate the reader from the tyranny of the writer" he retorts that this is the "freedom of the brain-dead".'

Jenkins was not alone.

★

Katz, by now barely 30 and with almost no editing experience, set himself up over the road in the Ray Street loft and started to assemble a team. They had no idea who they were looking for, or how much to pay them. One of the first through the door was Robin Houston, a 21-year-old Etonian, Oxford-educated computer scientist who had spent just one year as a web programmer and was, according to Katz, 'the cleverest human being that ever walked through the *Guardian*'s doors'. He had one bag of clothes, long hair and brightly painted fingernails.

Houston was originally hesitant about taking the job because he thought the *Guardian* was 'too commercial'. Katz sent his recently hired business lead, Justin Walter, round to convince him that the *Guardian* was completely uncommercial and that we were destined to lose vast amounts of money. That did the trick and Houston, along with a 'hippy guy called Danny', built the first content management system. No one else understood how the system worked.

Katz – young, impatient, ambitious, contrarian, mischievous – also knew very little about the internet, but he had no intention of simply replicating what we did already in print. He wanted it to look, feel and behave differently from its text-and-paper parent. He settled on the – slightly – enfant terrible graphic designer Neville Brody,[2] who ignored the newspaper's typography and gave the website a different identity – all bold modular blocks of colour, white space and sans serif fonts.

Not only did the emerging site look different: so, too, did the name. Katz settled on 'Guardian Unlimited'[3] – an umbrella for deeper wells of specific subjects. They focused on things they thought would be big on the web – news unlimited, film unlimited, cricket, football, politics, books and arts, along with work, jobs and skills. These channels later became known as 'verticals'. At one point Katz drew it as a series of rectangles, at another as a spider – with the body as the news hub and the legs special subject nodes.

The little team over the road, all trainers and t-shirts, understood that a shirt-and-tie newspaper was a broad, shallow thing – with many subjects covered in not much depth because of constraints of space. A website was, literally, unlimited. You could go as deep as you liked into anything you chose. There would be a network of sites, rather than just one. And each site would have to be the best of its kind, because that was how the internet worked.

'That level of ambition was, looking back, quite insane,' reflected one of the core team in later life.

As we started spending on digital, we had to find other areas to cut. In 1995 we'd had a protracted debate about whether we could ever use colour pictures for news. Eamonn McCabe, picture editor since 1988, argued vehemently that colour was a distraction for the eye – that black and white was the proper medium for news. In 1998 we closed the darkroom. Pictures came in pixels now. And in colour.

The closure of the darkroom was to save money. But the production of the newspaper itself was Byzantine – and, with the introduction of more colour and (with more advertising) more pages, was about to get more complex.

To some of the older print journalists across the road – the ones paying attention, anyway, since most still didn't have access to the internet in the newsroom – the digital operation was a distraction which would damage the reputation of the *Guardian*: stuff being thrown together at speed by so-called 'web monkeys' with no experience of real journalism. Noses were put out of joint by one of the Ray Street team visiting morning conference and uttering the phrase 'dead-tree journalism'. To the older hands the 'electronic operation' didn't have the authority or real depth of print.[4]

But 'depth' was relative. Within a short time the newcomers were posting (or linking to) verbatim chunks of the Hansard parliamentary record; or publishing Clinton's entire State of the Union speech. This was journalism of record few broadsheet newspapers had attempted in years.

Ray Street was frontier living, an experimental sandbox (or, pejoratively – to the cynical older eyes in the main newspaper – 'the sandpit' or 'playpen'). There were basic technological decisions to take – commonplace now, but not at all obvious then – such as making sure that every web page address, or URL, stayed the same. The aim was that everything should be permanent, addressable, discoverable. That meant it stayed where it was; that it could be linked to by other systems and was findable by search.

At the time everyone spoke the language of feeds: you fed your stuff to Yahoo or Drudge and, if you were lucky, they would like it and post a link. But the uniformity of URLs was even more essential when, within a couple of years, Google could find your journalism if it was in the right format. Suddenly a kind of consistency began to emerge about how everyone described their 'content' (as it was unavoidably becoming known) and made it available. Soon, the audience would be numbered in millions rather than thousands and even the sceptics began to wonder if there might, after all, be a business in it somewhere.

The death of Diana, Princess of Wales, in the early hours of Sunday 31 August 1997 taught them an early lesson about demand – with numerous *Guardian* readers ringing up all day to ask where the coverage was. It was a good question. I'd woken to the news at 4 a.m. and had roused the obituaries editor and deputy editor, realising we had nothing at all pre-prepared. I was completely focused on the next day's paper. My aim was to get a seasoned pro – Charles Nevin, a feature writer, was my first choice – and give him all day and 4,500 words to play with.

The Ray Street team managed to get something up and running by mid-morning, much of it agency copy, but with additional newspaper pieces as they became available. They also opened a talkboard for people to comment. By lunchtime there were hundreds of comments. The readers were teaching us: big news couldn't wait until the following breakfast time. If the *Guardian* didn't provide it, people would just look elsewhere.

The Guardian Unlimited site was finally up and running in July 1998 with six sites, which would grow by another dozen over the following 18 months. Within two weeks around 100,000 readers had registered for access – about a quarter of the number buying the physical product. But digital managing editor Simon Waldman later decided to remove registration: 'because it was actually killing the site, it was one of the things that was pulling us down, just the extra load. Once we did that, obviously, things started to rocket. The idea that we'd one day be bigger than the electronic *Telegraph* was a pretty fanciful idea in 1999.'

Ian Mayes, in his weekly column, in early 1999, did his best to explain to readers the nature of the dramatic changes under way.

'There will be an increasing number of occasions when *Guardian* scoops appear first on our electronic pages and we shall all learn to brag about it,' he announced, sounding not entirely convinced.[5]

By October 1999 Mayes was reporting to readers on progress: there were now more than half a million registered users. Nearly 60 people were by then working on the website, of whom about 20 were journalists.[6] We briefly experimented with producing a 24-page tabloid to be printed on A3 paper for distribution to luxury hotels around the world.

There were still companies who thought print, however delivered, was the future.

*

This new world of interconnectivity was baffling and uncomfortable in equal measure. The New York correspondent of any British newspaper would feel safe in buying the *New York Times*; creatively rewriting and adding to it; and then filing a version of it back to London. Then the penny dropped that, in this new world, their editors back in London could also read the *New York Times*; indeed, they'd read it five hours ahead of you. Moreover, American readers of your website wouldn't tolerate warmed-up *NYT* copy a day late. You either filed original material on the day or you were irrelevant.

We were woefully ignorant of how those of our readers who were now online were consuming the news. We did gradually come to understand that the new world was one of information promiscuity: readers who had been loyal to one newspaper all their lives could now browse and graze to their hearts' content.

In the summer of 1997 the *Guardian* editorial executives had descended on a country-house hotel for an annual awayday. Katz had presented on our progress so far and showed the *NYT* website, which at the time had an Associated Press (AP) wire on the front page. Research showed, to general dismay, that the AP feed was the most-read thing on the website. We were just learning the new buzz phrase 'commodity news' – news available to everyone and therefore not distinctive and (in commercial terms) not valuable. Yet here was the *NYT* letting their readers have access to the firehose – the source material, used by all papers, out of which many of our correspondents used to fashion their own work.

A (print) news editor stared at the slide in horror. 'They've put their wires on the internet? People can see the wires on the internet?'

It was our sausage-factory moment.

7

The Conversation

At the end of one millennium and the beginning of the next, the media world was divided between those who still shrugged and those who were panicking.

This thing had come from nowhere and now CEOs were demanding urgent primers on what the internet was and what could be done about it.

The big consultancy firms did good business flying around the world telling media companies how to get with the act. In January 1999 two McKinsey principals, John Hagel and Marc Singer, published a book about 'the merging role of the Infomediary'. 'The truth is that very few of today's companies have what it takes to become an infomediary,' they warned. 'Most lack either the customer relationships that will be necessary to get started or the risk-taking culture that will be necessary to succeed.'[1]

They foresaw a rapid period of alliance between internet-based and more traditional businesses – a marriage of speed-driven decision making and deep pockets. Success in future would depend on a business's ability to capture information about customers and use this for commercial purposes. In the two years from early 1998 to February 2000 the internet sector earned over 1,000 per cent returns on its public equity.[2] By the end of 2000 those returns had completely disappeared, but for a while the world went a little bit mad.

Our problem was, if anything, the reverse. We were spending modest amounts on the website and – probably – going too slowly rather than too quickly. The current rate of spend was around £3.8 million on staff costs by 2000/1, rising to £5.6 million in 2002. The total expenditure over the first five years of digital experimentation was around £18 million. Ian Katz, having launched the original Guardian Unlimited website and assembled a team of brilliant mavericks, was needed back on the paper. For the next few years the web operation was in the hands of two formidably talented and visionary journalists, Simon Waldman and then Emily Bell.[3]

The business model was looking as though it would involve a combination of recruitment revenue; business-to-business advertising and sponsorship; the licensing or syndication of content; as well as traditional advertising. The forecast for annual revenues in two or three years' time was £7.4 million. Peanuts compared with what we were taking in print – but then we were planning for a world in which print might itself be taking peanuts.

Advertising was actually healthy enough at this stage, but we had launched a stand-alone website, Workthing, designed to replace, and even grow, the classified print revenues. It was promoted as a 'complete employment network' aimed at younger junior or middle managers. Everything in recruitment was moving online: digital was quicker and more comprehensive: the internet had better reach and could save 80 to 90 per cent of costs. The market was going to be worth $7 billion by 2005, and we wanted a large chunk of it.

Consultants crawled all over the projections and estimated that by March 2005 we could be making anything between £8 and £30 million a year in profits – but only after sinking £30 million of losses to get it airborne. Sales in 2000/1 were, at £5 million, still modest – but the team had high hopes of building that to more than £60 million within a few years.

Reach before revenue.

We were in the green bubble all right. The newspaper division would go on losing money – but, as the other parts of the organisation were highly profitable, this level of investment felt manageable to the Scott Trust. Long term meant long term. We could be patient.

★

Our investment on the main *Guardian* website was still modest – a drop in the water compared to frenzied activity over at News International. Around mid-1999, according to a semi-authorised book[4] about Murdoch's business at this point by Wendy Goldman Rohm, he was convinced by his sons that he was 'missing the internet boat' and, within nine months, had allocated more than \$2 billion in resources to online projects. 'The market was going wild, there was money to be made and he decided to jump on the bandwagon.'

While on honeymoon in Tuscany with his second wife, Wendi, he and some executives (evidently joining the honeymoon) planned a new UK internet division, to be called News Network, according to Rohm. This would be the digital arm of News International, the UK newspaper division which published the *Times*, *Sunday Times*, *News of the World* and *Sun*.

But the bubble in internet ventures was about to burst in the summer of 2000 and – less than a year after announcing he'd 'got it' – Murdoch ordered a retreat. According to Rohm, in a Los Angeles bar in July 2000 his top internet gurus were told there was to be no more spending on internet businesses. A few months later News Corp formally announced it was folding all its online businesses that had operated under News Digital Media back into their respective company divisions.[5]

Murdoch was not alone in struggling to make quick returns on digital investments. Nearly everything was failing. In September 2000 everyone was trying to create women's portals with names like Handbag, iCircle, Beme and uk.women.com. They all petered out. Emap, a trade magazine company, splashed out £50 million, only to announce a wave of site closures as they failed to work. Pearson were scaling back after lavishing more than £100 million in investment on the *FT* (£30 million on marketing alone). Trinity Mirror decided £10 million a year was more appropriate than the £42 million pre-bubble rate of spend. Associated had launched Charlotte Street, a 'women's portal' in October 1999 and then relaunched it a year later, concentrating on 29- to 40-year-olds. It lasted another year before being quietly put out of its misery.

Success in this new world was proving even more uncertain and expensive than anyone had imagined.

*

What was a newspaper becoming? The old newspaper model could be sketched as a tablet of stone – something handed down from on high. Our talented Polish-born illustrator Andre Krauze once drew the old world of newspaper production as journalists throwing newspapers over a high wall at readers on the other side.

Newspapers encouraged letters from readers. Hundreds would arrive every day – a tiny number to be selected for publication by the letters editor. As with nearly everything in the old world, we were in control. Who gets a voice, who doesn't? We chose.

But this new world in which we were now playing didn't feel like a tablet of stone. It became fashionable to start using the term 'a conversation'. It wasn't really, but there was much more two-way traffic. An early idea was to set up talkboards where the readers could congregate virtually and chat. They are, of course, ubiquitous now but were then in their infancy: it took a while for us to get our heads around them. It began around 1999, with a version of what was then a football bulletin board, and grew rapidly.

We were – mostly – pleased to host them. They were very lightly moderated and the user interface was rudimentary. Occasionally the users would rebel if we changed something in a way not to their taste, and there would be periodic desertions: it was relatively easy for a number of disgruntled users to clone the site and take it elsewhere – an early reminder, if we needed one, that we were no longer in control.

Over time readers started their own threads on multiple issues a day – including media, film, books, international news. The best and worst of humanity was on display. At their most unpleasant they were scrappy, almost wild – with bullying, stalking, trolling and name-calling. Some of them were, in the words of one poster, 'utterly batshit'. The Israel/Palestine discussions were good ones to steer clear of if looking for rational, calm discussion.

At their most obsessive they were a place where lonely pseudony-mous souls would argue for days about the relative merits of tinned or dried chickpeas, or whether different flavoured crisps projected a range of sexual orientations. As one former contributor wrote: 'They could give expert guidance on everything from the structure and formation of PCTs,[6] to the best laptop to buy, via a debate about God and the true meaning of existence, interspersed with a spat about who would win in a fight, a caveman or an astronaut.'[7]

There was (to old newspaper eyes) a kind of anarchy in play, much to the despair of the occasional moderator who would vainly plead: 'this is a board to discuss current affairs – there are countless chat sites on the web if you want to chat'. The moderators (or 'mods') would soon retire hurt. Yes, the *Guardian* had created this space, but it was, in the users' eyes, 'their' space and they'd do what they liked with it. If they wanted to spend Christmas creating a Thread to Talk Like the King James Bible – where you had to write about boring everyday matters in the style of a sixteenth-century biblical scholar – that was their business. Rarely did any thread stay on topic for more than three posts.

And then there would be threads that endlessly warmed, sustained, amused, diverted, educated and enthralled. People met their partners there. Friendships were forged, relationships were incubated: several marriages and children followed. One couple live-posted the home birth of their baby. Another still remembers the support she received when receiving treatment for cancer. There was not one porn post.

One of the most popular shared activities was watching televi-sion in the virtual company of others. The talkboarders would chat away to each other throughout the first series of *Big Brother* – the C4 reality show, aired in 2000, which spied on 'housemates' marooned inside a custom-built home. There would always be a gaggle on hand to discuss anything David Attenborough was doing. One poster reflected later: 'That couldn't happen now as there isn't a social media that really allows it (Twitter is too huge) and everyone is On Demand so not watching at the same time.' We learned from the behaviour of the users. Live coverage of big television 'events' became a staple of later coverage on the main site.

The community of regular, active contributors was never huge – maybe only a few thousand. Over time their space became overtaken by larger experiments and the talkboards became a bit of a forgotten backwater, untended by moderators.[8] Untended spaces tend to become unkempt, and some areas of the talkboards ended up almost feral.

But the users were, to some extent, pioneers: they formed their own basic grammar, or (what become known as) netiquette. There were symbols for (((hugs))) and ////Horror!\\\\ The Exclamation Marks!!!!!!!!!!!!!!!!!. Most talkboard users adopted the conventions that spontaneously developed: italics for quotes from earlier posts in the discussion, bold for emphasis, indented paragraphs for blockquotes. There was usually a form of self-correction, if not exactly self-policing.

Light moderation was not unusual on small technology blogs or Usenet discussion groups, but really rare on a national news brand. It was considered by many onlookers elsewhere in Fleet Street, not to mention within the building, as slightly crazy. A newspaper had so many layers of editing around everything. It was a huge philosophical leap for an organisation full of people dedicated to refining everything before it was allowed into the outside world to enable anybody to post anything.

Why allow it, anyway? It had nothing to do with journalism, did it? We had managed for 200 years to produce newspapers without giving much thought to whether readers wanted to meet each other or hold conversations. Weren't we losing sight of our main function: to find stuff out and publish it? Anything else was a distraction.

That was always possible. But it seemed to me then – and still does now – that technology had to drive behaviour. If, for centuries, technology only allowed one-way communication then – of course – that's what your journalism would look like. If it suddenly opened up two- or multiple-way communication then it was probably a mistake to carry on as though the world hadn't changed.

Plenty of people disagreed, some quite vehemently. The argument went to the heart of how we regarded journalism in the coming century. Were readers a mob, best ignored while we got on with what we always did? Or were they part of what we did – part of our club? They were now beginning to connect in ever-growing numbers to the most mind-blowing network anyone in history could ever have imagined. Should a newspaper become part of that network, or would its chances of survival be greatest by remaining separate, and distinct, from it?

The talkboards were certainly ahead of their time. Someone later described them as 'Web 2.0 social networking before Zuckerberg was a Harvard freshman'. It was when Mark Zuckerberg was a sophomore at Harvard in September 2003 that he started playing around with ways of linking up communities of students – four years after the first stumbling efforts on the *Guardian* and elsewhere. Reddit – with an equally unso-phisticated interface – started five years after the *Guardian* talkboards as 'the front page of the internet' and, with 250 million unique monthly users, was by 2017 the ninth-biggest website in the world. Mumsnet was launched by Ian Katz's wife, Justine Roberts, around the same time as the *Guardian* talkboards and has 12 million unique monthly users today.

Was it an accident that the *Guardian* led the experimentation with reader participation in this way? It's difficult to imagine a company more driven by the bottom line seeing the immediate point of creating these spaces. There was no obvious way of monetising them. In the absence of a proprietor our main relationships were horizontal – with the readers, and with sources. *Guardian* readers were, by and large, a bright crowd with much in common. Why not put them in touch with each other? We might discover the commercial value in time.

But meanwhile we were learning how people behaved in this new space. The driving principle found articulation in a new mantra: '*Of* the Web not just *on* the Web.' It was a small thing to say, but a huge thing to imagine, let alone do. But it became a useful way of testing anything we proposed to do. 'Is this really something that we would do if we were purely digital?' became the key question.

*

The division (including the *Observer* losses) was due to lose £9 million in 2000/1. Circulation was still over 400,000 but all papers were begin-ning to pad out their figures by distributing 'bulk' copies either abroad, or in hotel chains, airlines and trains. Advertisers, it seemed, were none too fussy about whether a reader had parted with cash for a newspaper or whether the copy 'sale' had, in effect, been 'subsidised' by the publisher.

Headline numbers seemed fine. It was the dying light of the broad-brush world. Within a decade advertisers would want scrutiny of figures down to the level of individual users.

Buying circulation, through whatever marketing wizardry, was expensive but, if it kept the ABC figure up,[9] it was generally considered worth it. In 2000 we were generously distributing copies of the *Guardian* to French hotels and on KLM. The *Independent* were price-cutting regionally and offering two-for-one cinema tickets and flights to Australia from £20. The *Times* had two-for-one flights and cut-price vouchers for the paper. If you were a *Telegraph* reader, you could benefit from short-break offers, receive a week of papers for £1.50 and collect a 'free' Mark Knopfler CD from the newsagent by presenting vouchers clipped from the newspaper (20 per cent off at Debenhams for Sunday readers).

The full price sales were not wonderfully healthy for anyone – 95 per cent of *Guardian*s sold for full price. Over at the *Indie* it was 75 per cent, the *Times* 65 per cent, the *Telegraph* 59 per cent and the *FT* 39 per cent. A casual glance at the headline figures showed a barely perceptible annual decline across the broadsheet market of 0.66 per cent. The real figures were more alarming, but less visible. There was a cloud of nostalgic dismay when the *Express*, which had at its peak in the early 1960s sold 4 million copies a day,[10] was passed on to Richard Desmond,[11] then the publisher of *Asian Babes* and other 'adult' titles.

Along with everyone else, we did from time to time consider whether we should be charging readers to pay for our journalism online. It would be five years before a major general newspaper – the *New York Times* – would make a determined stab at extracting money directly from online readers. Around the turn of the millennium virtually all newspapers held out little hope of persuading their users to part with cash. Almost everyone who had tried to charge had abandoned it. In the US there were only two newspapers – the *Wall Street Journal* and the *Champaign News Gazette* charging.[12] The *NYT* originally tried to charge $35 for readers outside the US, but abandoned that. Even the *Financial Times*, at that point, wasn't convinced it could make people pay.[13] Instead there was much talk of the 'attention economy'.

We were with the consensus. We were a very small newspaper (still the ninth-biggest) in a very small pond: Britain. If we could break onto the world stage, the commercial managers figured, we might stand a chance of acquiring a big enough audience to attract significant advertisers. The market of English-speaking, college-educated potential readers was possibly 500 million. The BBC would, in time, reach 150 million of them.[14] If the *Guardian* could get launched, even modestly, on that global ocean it could stand a chance of survival. Overseas expansion couldn't work if you asked non-Brits to pay. But trying to move into the digital age with a tiny, mainly British, not notably wealthy readership did not strike anyone as a recipe for long-term survival.

Editorially, the paper was making waves. We'd just been named newspaper of the year four years running. We were breaking stories. We brought a £2 million fine down on the heads of Carlton TV (corporate affairs chief, one David Cameron) by proving they had faked key scenes in a documentary about drug running. We had devoted ten pages over five days to examining the science and commerce behind genetically modified food. We forced the resignation of two government ministers – Peter Mandelson and Geoffrey Robinson – over our revelations of the unusual mortgage agreement they'd entered into for buying the former a house. We had first-rate reporting from Kosovo, Libya and Iraq by veteran correspondents Jonathan Steele and Ian Black. We'd opened an archive and readers' centre across the road for debates around our work – another extension of our journalism. And there was a little schoolroom where a class of kids a day came to put together a 'newspaper' of their own.

And then, on 11 September 2001, four passenger airliners were hijacked by al-Qaeda terrorists and the world shook.

8

Global

It was quite possibly the biggest news story of all time – watched in real time by maybe a third of the world's population. Even as the raw, horrific drama played out on the screen, billions of people began calculating the appalling geo-political consequences. Sites all over the globe – including the BBC – fell over as the world tried to follow every heart-stopping moment. The internet couldn't cope.

It was an object lesson in how news knew no national boundaries. Many of those coming to the *Guardian* site that day were American, unable to find news from domestic sources with less robust technology. Some of them went onto the talkboards to update the rest of the planet with what they knew. The same was happening through thousands of weblogs. Those days in Manhattan were captured not only by newsrooms but also in a multitude of disparate voices able to speak to virtually all humanity.

We'd recently refurbished our servers to allow a million page impressions in a day. On 9/11 we served two and a half million. At one point there were 146 page impressions a second. The *Guardian* – with anxious tech developers sitting up all night – didn't go dark.

Something about the *Guardian* audience changed dramatically in the period immediately following 9/11. Page views for September were 42 million (up from 29 million), October 51 million. A decade later the comparable figures would be more than 400 million. The realisation dawned that these new readers might be here to stay. Was it that hundreds of thousands of Americans had suddenly woken up to the fact that their own security was irrevocably bound up with things happening halfway across the globe? Was there something about the less objective style of British journalism that caught hold? Were there not enough liberal non-consensus voices back home? Whatever it was, we had to get serious about finding out – and to get better at, well, everything.

Guardian Unlimited relaunched at the end of 2001 with a big marketing push – just as advertising growth went into reverse after the political shocks of 9/11 and its aftermath. Break-even was pushed back again. But we were now the market leader in the UK, tabloid or broadsheet. Carolyn McCall, the managing director, was completely clear with the staff about her appetite for patient planning: 'We have always seen this as a long-term investment and a fundamental part of where we see our brands and our business in the future – not a get-rich-quick scheme.'

That was just as well because it was plain the future was about to get expensive. It had cost £3.5 million to junk the old dumb terminals and get the newsroom onto terminals which could actually see the internet, but it was clear we'd need to spend much, much more to create a modern content management system that could take an early-twentieth-century process of editing and make it reasonably fit for at least the first decade of the twenty-first century.

New people with new skills started appearing on the commercial and tech development floors. The word 'monetise' was in the air. They called journalism 'content'. 'How are we going to monetise the content?' they asked. Or, sometimes, 'How can we monetise the reader?'

When would we see the end of print? It was the most often-asked question and it was impossible to answer. My stock response was that it was completely out of our control. People would keep inventing ever-cleverer, ever-faster, ever-lighter devices. We couldn't stop that from happening, even if we wanted to. At some point, I assumed, the old Victorian production chain of newsprint – light manufacturing; lorries driving through the night; wholesalers and newsagents taking their cut; and (if you were lucky) news delivery boys on their bikes before school – would no longer work economically. I had no idea when that would be, but the prudent course was to be ready for it.

Many colleagues were binary – understandably suspicious. If you loved digital then you must hate print, right? What was wrong with print? It still paid our wages – unlike digital pipe dreams. It had serendipity and portability – and generated cash. What was not to like?

I would patiently explain that I loved print. I had spent my life in print. I still thought of myself as a writing journalist who liked words. But I was also overwhelmed by the possibilities of the emerging digital world. Loving one didn't mean hating the other. In the end the choice would be out of our hands.

No one, to paraphrase William Goldman,[1] knew anything.

*

Even before 9/11 the pain of disruption was being felt throughout the industry. '2001' said a forlorn internal note by a senior commercial director, 'was the most miserable year for newspaper publishers in living memory.' A hike in the price of newsprint had been the last straw. Each week there were rumours that national titles would have to close. Every newspaper responded by raising the cover price; slashing marketing; cutting headcount; dumping internet investment; freezing wages and abandoning product development.

This was a familiar pattern in the American newspaper market – the so-called death spiral. Circulation decline led to advertising decline. Managements cut back editorial employees to stem declining margins while, at the same time, asking them to work harder and adding new digital requirements to their roles. Newspapers shrank and became less compelling. Readers found less of interest and stopped buying them. With few readers came fewer advertisers. The margins declined further. Managements made further cuts . . .

The consultants were back at the *Guardian*, this time looking at each individual day of the week to work out its contribution to the bottom line. The greatest immediate worry was still over the anticipated flight of classified advertising from print. Companies were beginning to do their own recruitment through their own corporate sites. There were numerous new competitors on the block. Finally, there was a shift to CV searching rather than advertising.

The good news was that we were no longer the minnow in UK terms. For its entire history the *Guardian* had languished at or near the bottom of every league table of readership. In February 2002 the Nielsen NetRatings survey placed the *Guardian* at number one. It measured us at 934,000 users against 286,000 for the *Telegraph*, and 249,000 for both the *Times* and the *Sun*.

That was cheering, but had to be seen in a wider context. We ranked at only 50 in the same rankings of the UK's 100 biggest domains. We were the only newspaper in the ranking, but we were well outside the premier league of big sites and advertising networks. Price Waterhouse Cooper reckoned 80 per cent of all digital spending was going to the top ten sites. We were still nowhere near.

The areas that had previously been profitable for newspapers – such as IT, motoring and finance – were now in competition with specialist portals on niche websites. In the old world, advertisers – like journalists – had only a rough sense of who was reading what. In the new world, every advertisement was measured on the effectiveness of its response. 'We have a problem,' wrote the forlorn commercial director, 'that people come to our sites to read stories – not click on ads. Our response rates are very, very low – particularly on our news site, where we have most inventory. This means we often find ourselves falling off schedules after advertisers evaluate their performance on our sites.'

It was a prescient note. But we were not alone at the time in not divining what Plan B was.

Still, none of the British competitors were serious about charging – not least because there was so much good, free, English language content available, including the public broadcasters, the BBC and ITV News, and numerous American portals (MSN, Yahoo, AOL, etc.) and news sites. The *Irish Times* had recently tried a paywall, found they ended up with an audience of just 6,000, and promptly dropped it. Peter Chernin, the President of News Corporation, had recently admitted that they could see 'no viable business model that works' for the internet. The

UK newspaper websites were, he said, nothing more than adjunct, promotional vehicles for the newspapers.

We had further debates about long-term reach or short-term revenue. The Board didn't think too long about which route to take. The revenue route involved the *Guardian* probably having a readership not much bigger than the *New Statesman* magazine.[2] It was impossible to imagine breaking further into the American market with a paywall or to hope that younger readers would contribute. The advertising revenues were speculative, at best. So a revenue strategy looked like a route to a niche UK-only publication for older readers.[3] The fact that, at this stage, virtually no other general news publisher in the UK or US was prepared to go for revenue over reach suggested that their boards were all looking at a similar dilemma and coming to the same conclusion.

In time future commentators would describe this period as the moment of 'original sin'. The phrase was coined by Alan Mutter, an expert in media economics and management, who blogged in February 2009: 'the Original Sin among most (but not all) publishers was permitting their content be consumed for free on the web'.[4] He made comparisons with the 'far more proactive' music industry, though that was hardly a happy example, with ten songs downloaded illegally for every song purchased lawfully.

'By the end of the decade,' wrote the Spanish academic Ángel Arrese, 'the general consensus in the world of the press was that free online news content would attract massive readerships, whose accumulated attention could be sold efficiently to advertisers.' He went on to describe a period (2001–7) of what he calls 'the frenzy of failed trials' following the bursting of the so-called dot.com bubble.[5]

Newspaper executives, seeing the bubble burst and the old model teetering, returned to insisting on payment – including subscriptions, e-paper, pdf formats, premium content, and micropayment. Some (including the *Guardian*) tried charging for particular features (in our case, the crossword). Others 'closed' their websites completely: *El País* in Spain was an early pioneer and managed to attract 45,000 paying subscribers. It dropped the barrier within three years: there was no business that worked on such low numbers. The *NYT* abandoned a similar attempt at charging for access to columnists and the archive.

'By the end of 2007,' wrote Arrese, 'a general consensus existed that free content would remain the standard way of commercial exploitation of digital news.'

★

In October 2002 one or two colleagues stumbled across a new service called Google News. One self-mockingly responded by slumping across his desk in a pose that suggested there was little point in carrying on. How could one compete with this all-seeing eye on the world, hoovering up anything that happens, anywhere on the planet and alerting users within minutes in a remorseless *perpetuum mobile* of breaking information?

The most sinister thing from the point of view of the average desk editor sitting in Farringdon Road or Wapping or Canary Wharf was the little line at the bottom of the site: *The selection and placement of stories on this page were determined automatically by a computer program.*

That's right: it was produced entirely by machines. Not one human being was involved in the generation of this modern, news version of the Doomsday Book. It was all produced by a cyber spider which whisked its way around the world filtering news sites and linking to them. Quite how it was done was a mystery as closely guarded as the recipe for Marmite or Coca-Cola.

I discussed it with a colleague working on the *Washington Post* website. He shrugged: 'None of us can predict anything more than six months out. This is TV in 1948.'

We began to debate what it meant to run both print and digital alongside each other in a way that acknowledged the qualities of each. If the net was so much better at handling large amounts of text, why try to compete? What was the point of a verbatim parliamentary report if the whole thing was online the following morning in Hansard? Why not just link to it? Why publish long official reports, speeches or inquiries? We can digest them, explain them, contextualise them and analyse them in print. But aren't there better uses of space than to print them?

Similarly, with the online version, why simply replicate the paper, as if we were putting radio on television? Wasn't our strategy right of

77

building deeper, richer sites around specific subjects? You can cater for fragments of the paper readership who want more of the feature, issue or individual they most treasure. There were people who wanted more football or news from Brussels than we could ever serve in a newspaper. There were writers with individual followings that, we suspected, could dwarf departments. All the talk was of the *Wall Street Journal* technology blogger, Walt Mossberg, and how the *Journal* had upped his salary to nearly $1 million a year to stop him taking his blog elsewhere. Another high-profile blogger, Andrew Sullivan, set himself up as a blogging brand – launching the Daily Dish in 2000. It was said to be more profitable than Amazon.[6]

But this idea of seamlessly linking the paper and the website to exploit the best of both did rather depend on newspaper readers having access to broadband computers and vice versa. Every time we told paying newspaper customers that they could get more detailed, better material online we alienated a significant proportion of them. They would write politely angry letters explaining that they knew about the internet, thank you, but had no wish to use it. What they wanted was a proper newspaper. Which they were happy to pay for.

*

A small last-days-of-Fleet Street vignette . . .

On 9 March 2003 I give the after-dinner speech at the Thirty Club – a members-only gathering of big commercial cheeses in the advertising and media worlds. There are a hundred or so guests at Claridge's hotel in London, all black tie and gowns. I wish I was better at the mix of badinage and homily that the best after-dinner speakers manage. As I stand to speak I'm very conscious of the contingent from News International across the table. Les Hinton, the amiable if faintly menacing executive chairman of Murdoch's newspapers, is sitting right opposite me, flanked by Rebekah Brooks, editor of the *Sun*, and Andy Coulson, editor of the *News of the World*.

I'm talking about trust – and the truly abysmal ratings for newspapers. Depending on the poll and the year, we were lucky if 13 to 18 per cent of the population trusted newspapers. I try to avoid catching my colleagues' eyes as I add that the red-tops sold most, but were trusted least.

I liken British journalists to fans of the London football club Millwall – official chant: *No one likes us, we don't care*. I know what Andy and Rebekah are thinking: *We're in for a pious sermon from someone who can barely make a profit and whose sales are embarrassingly small*. I can hear the ritual jibe from Piers Morgan, editor of the *Mirror*, every time he sees me: 'I sell more copies in Cornwall than you do in the entire country.'

I waffle on more about trust; how we'd lost it; how to earn it back; why it would matter so much more in the digital world. It is worthy stuff.

Afterwards the three Murdoch colleagues are very friendly. They suggest we go on to a club. We end up drinking in the Soho House till the early hours. The champagne's on them. The speech is not mentioned. The evening is fun. Rebekah and Andy are good company. Les is full of seen-it-all bonhomie. Deep down, we're all hacks together.

Cut to 11 years later: Coulson was in jail, Hinton had resigned and Brooks had suffered the ordeal of a nerve-shredding trial at the Old Bailey – all because of reporting in the *Guardian*. That night in the Soho House feels like a lost world of Fleet Street innocence. A funny word – 'innocence' – to use about Fleet Street. But we were certainly all innocent of what was to come – in virtually every way possible.

9

Format Wars

'Simplify, then exaggerate' was the advice to young journalists from the former editor of the *Economist*, Geoffrey Crowther.[1] All good journalism has, to some extent, to simplify difficult material. But, in most countries, you will find one or more newspapers that do not shy away from complexity. Complexity, more than anything, was what distinguished a broadsheet paper.

The term referred to the physical size of the newspaper. But the shape mattered less than the mindset behind it. 'Broadsheet' was a style of journalism that – as well as relishing complexity – endeavoured to separate news from comment; was sober in tone; operated to a high, if unwritten, ethical code; took policy and politics seriously; responded to 'high' culture as well as popular entertainment; was independent – of party, government, advertising or ownership; and was considered to speak with authority on a broad range of serious issues.

What 'authority' did it have?

Any authority derived from what it covered, and who got to cover it. At the end of the twentieth century it was still assumed that any broadsheet would have full-time specialists with considerable knowledge of such areas as defence, education, religion, politics, social policy, science, home affairs, law, diplomacy, economics, industry, technology, culture, business, finance, industry, the environment, sport, crime, health and so on. All those areas would be staffed by one correspondent – and in some cases several.

The specialists who covered these areas were, at their best, knowledgeable, experienced – and trusted. They often knew their patches better than the ministers they were writing about, having, in many cases, covered the turf for much longer than here-today, gone-tomorrow politicians. Alan Travis, for instance, had been assiduously covering Home Affairs – police, prisons, immigration, justice, etc. – since 1992. During that time he saw 11 home secretaries, eight justice ministers, eight lord chancellors and countless prison ministers come and go.

Science coverage was, as good as any, an illustration of the broadsheet mindset. Around the turn of the century it was hard not to feel an immense sense of excitement at what was soon to be possible, and soon to be discovered – from microscope technology; gene sequencing tools; image sensors on telescopes; ways to tag cells in living organisms; superconducting magnet technology; computing power and tools for handling massive datasets. The Human Genome Project had laid the foundations for a genuine understanding of how humans work on the molecular scale. The Large Hadron Collider was under construction at CERN. We were seeing for the first time the afterglow of the big bang, that relic radiation from the birth of the universe, imprinted on the sky. All this was on the cards at the start of the twenty-first century: we knew it was coming.

There was an awful lot to tell people about.

But it was complex. It is not easy for a humanities graduate to sit down with an academic paper on astrophysics, neurophysiology or oceanography and to spot the news value, let alone render the contents accurately and accessibly into English that an average reader would comprehend.

At one point we had a team of at least six covering science and the environment. Between them their qualifications included PhDs in chemical engineering, evolutionary genetics, biomaterials and earth sciences; and a BSc in physics. They understood what they were writing about. They could talk on trusted terms with the best scientists who, in return, felt safe with them writing reliably about their work.

They were not idle. In the age of print-alone it was just about imaginable for one person to keep up with the news across all science and deliver three or four pieces a week. But the new beast had to be fed constantly, seven days a week. Science articles were well-read and appreciated.[2]

How did they see the role of the broadsheet over at the *Telegraph*, then being edited by Charles Moore, a libertarian Conservative Old Etonian who subsequently wrote a three-volume biography of Margaret Thatcher?

He and I did not see eye to eye on many political and social issues – and, from time to time, our two papers would snipe at each other. But at the heart of what we did there was a similar idea of what a serious newspaper's job was in this age of peak broadsheet.

I recently asked him to describe it from his end of the telescope.

> Well, I suppose, because there was no alternative edited source of serious information other than the BBC, we considered ourselves to have a duty to tell the readers everything that was important that had happened in the country and, to a lesser extent, in the world the day before – and, indeed, more broadly.
>
> I took it to mean, for example, reporting parliament, and law reports. So this would mean that quite a lot of things would go in that you were perfectly well aware might be quite boring, but you still thought you should put them in – and that you would be failing if you didn't.
>
> If there was a White Paper on reform of Higher Education or something, you had to do a story on it. It meant employing specialist correspondents, of whom we had a great many, and who have disappeared to a remarkable degree now. The paper I inherited had this very strict way of doing news with a huge number of small stories, a vast number of facts thrown in and very little analysis, and no comment. We had masses of foreign correspondents.
>
> It was a fundamentally, much more deliberately, self-constrained framework in which our basic thing was to keep on telling people what we thought mattered and what had happened. Which is quite a simple aim to state and a difficult thing to achieve.

He was describing different priorities and obsessions, but an equal seriousness about doing justice to complex subjects. Some of our coverage might even be 'boring', but there was some sense of duty about covering things we felt important. This was sometimes mocked as 'eat your peas' journalism.

The mindset was fine. But the reality was difficult to sustain. Specialists and foreign correspondents were expensive, and, on some titles, the first to go when a finance director scrutinised the payroll. One business manager on another (then) broadsheet explained to me they had done research that showed that almost no one – barring the journalist's friends and family – ever noticed the byline on a story. The broad inference he drew from this was that – with the exception of a few high-profile columnists – journalists were pretty interchangeable.

Printed newspapers were in a remorseless slide to eventual oblivion: that much seemed overwhelmingly probable. The pointers to the future were there in every developed country, with circulations of serious European papers falling at anything between 7 and 10 per cent a year. End-of-print obituaries were now routine. Redundancies were mounting – more than 2,000 press jobs lost in the US (4 per cent of the total workforce) between 2000 and 2004. Epitaphs for a dying idea of journalism were already in book form.

'In the old model, monopoly made publishers wealthy and secure enough to indulge in personal pleasure, and some found pleasure in producing good journalism well beyond what was needed to keep the business functioning,' wrote Philip Meyer, professor of journalism at the University of North Carolina, in his 2004 book *The Vanishing Newspaper*. 'These philosopher-kings of journalism cared about results beyond their own career spans. They wanted to protect the long-term wealth of both their businesses and the communities they served. They recognized that a community is defined by both economic and social forces, and that a good newspaper is a meeting place where those elements come together to form a public sphere.'

As ownership has shifted to investor-owned corporations, that long-term orientation is rare. If your expectation as an investor is based on an industry's history of easy money, you feel justified in doing whatever it takes to keep the cash flowing.

A breakdown of our revenues in spring of 2003 showed a roughly equal three-way split between classified advertising (£75 million), print display advertising (£69 million) and copy sales (£75 million). If the pace of change stayed steady, we felt the transition might just be manageable. At the same time we felt a sense of management fatigue. The advent of the BlackBerry meant that we were all now available 18 hours a day, seven days a week. There were endless strategy meetings, position papers, budget spreadsheets and marketing plans. You could easily attend six hours of meetings a day to consider those . . . and then have to produce a newspaper and website on top.

At this point the *Guardian* itself was actually profitable to the tune of about £8 million, though that was more than off-written by a £13 million loss on the *Observer*. Guardian Unlimited was losing nearly £4 million – slightly outperforming the budgeted loss of £6 million. In all, the division was losing around £8 million – £6 million better than originally budgeted. These were considered by the Boards to be comfortable losses, given the £40 million-odd profits we were making elsewhere in the Guardian Media Group.[3]

Revenues were flat, but projected to start growing again – and at some point we had to spend a lot to improve the ageing presses on which we printed, probably building new towers to print more colour advertising and installing inserting machinery to handle the classified advertising sections that otherwise had to be hand-inserted by newsagents. We also faced having to move out of the network of offices we had in Clerkenwell, which were hopelessly unintegrated and quietly decaying.[4]

And then – in the last week of September 2003 – the *Independent* announced that, with immediate effect, the paper would be printed in two sizes, broadsheet and tabloid, 'becoming the world's first newspaper to give readers a choice'.

It seemed a minor development in the great scheme of things. Perhaps. But Fleet Street tilted a little on its axis.

★

The *Independent* had been born in the mid-1980s at the height of the furious struggle over computer-setting, which saw 13 months of pitched battles and picketing around the fortress Rupert Murdoch had secretly constructed at the newsroom and printing plant he had – astonishingly – built barely two miles east of Fleet Street on a brownfield site at Wapping. His aim in January 1986 was, in the words of one *Sunday Times* journalist, to move 'from steam to microchip in a week'.

Three former *Telegraph* journalists, led by Andreas Whittam Smith, responded quickly to the new opportunities of printing with much lower production costs. They launched a new broadsheet paper, the *Independent*, in October 1986. The original founders mainly had the *Telegraph* in their sights, but the paper was soon damaging the *Telegraph*, *Guardian* and *Times* equally. It was instantly elegant, authoritative, well-written and fresh. The *Guardian* immediately felt staid, predictable and stale. By the late 1980s the *Independent* had overtaken the *Times* and had come within inches of eclipsing the *Guardian*.

There followed a ruthless Fleet Street fight – the last of the great newspaper battles.

As the *Indie* raided both its star staff and readers, the *Guardian* relaunched first with a modernist redesign; and then by funding a new Sunday title, the *Correspondent*, aimed at discouraging Whittam Smith from launching his own Sunday title. In the latter ambition it failed, but the distraction of launching a Sunday newspaper so early in its life is generally thought to have led to substantial managerial and financial torments for the new upstart.

The Murdoch price war had also had a devastating effect on the fledgling *Independent*. By 1995 the bulk of the shares were jointly owned by Mirror Group Newspapers and Tony O'Reilly, the owner of the Irish Independent newspapers. In a dozen years the daily and Sunday papers ran through 12 editors. The paper was struggling for cash, had started vigorous cost-cutting and had lost the sureness of tone it had enjoyed in its earlier years. The veteran former foreign editor Godfrey Hodgson wrote a piece in 1994 lamenting the plunge downmarket, trying 'to second-guess the professionals in that Bermuda Triangle of British journalism, the "middle market" . . . The tragedy of the *Independent* is that it started as something special, something to which good people would give their best shot. Now it is – to use management-speak – just a product.'

In the autumn of 2002 the *Independent* – by now losing around £7 million a year – had found another editor, Simon Kelner,[5] who said he had enjoyed a eureka moment while in a supermarket. He later described the moment, using the language of consumer products. 'I was buying toothpaste, and I noticed that the paste comes in a tube, a pump thing, in various sizes – but they are the same quality product,' he recalled. If newspapers were just consumer products, he thought, why couldn't they do two sizes, but keep the content the same?

By the end of September 2003 – Kelner was producing the *Independent* in two sizes. Within two months the *Times* had followed suit with its own 'compact' version.

By the spring of 2004 both titles had jumped to being tabloid-only: the toothpaste analogy only worked so far.

The move presented the three remaining broadsheet papers (the *Guardian*, *FT* and *Telegraph*) with a dilemma. It was rumoured the *Telegraph* had its own tabloid dummy ready to go. Our marketing team had periodically looked at the question of formats and were convinced that Hodgson's Bermuda triangle of the middle market was, indeed, the place to aim for.

The *Daily Mail*'s gravitational pull was immensely strong: what if a left-wing competitor to the *Mail* moved into the middle-ish market? The marketing team felt sure we could end up vastly boosting our circulation. There was heady talk of doubling our circulation – perhaps even selling three-quarters of a million. Simon Kelner's equivalents at the *Independent* had doubtless been telling him the same.

The research kept coming in: broadsheets were masculine, old-fashioned and – especially on public transport – difficult to read and inconvenient to handle. They came from a different age. The editor of the *Times*, Robert Thompson, considered the length of arms required to handle a broadsheet and even pondered whether it wasn't 'an act of misogyny' to publish one. The consensus was clear: if we didn't move we were doomed. By December the *Guardian*'s circulation was 14,000 below forecasts – partly also due to the new free tabloid *Metro*. We dummied up another tabloid, to no great enthusiasm from the majority of those who saw it.

★

What's in a size?

Compared with almost any other issue the British press was facing at the time, the dilemma of whether to print on a large or small sheet of paper was hardly in the top five, or even top ten. The word 'tabloid' was often taken to mean lurid, sensational, downmarket journalism, but there were serious European tabloid papers, which proved that small and serious could be done.

The decision about size was strangely frustrating, because it was so complicated, important and – possibly – pointless. The internet was surely a much bigger problem – or prize – than print. Changing formats was – on any long-term view – a distraction.

I knew Simon Kelner saw things differently because a couple of times a year we'd meet for a game of golf, and he'd gently rib me about what he saw as my obsession with digital. 'Tell me when it starts making money and I'll start taking it seriously.' That wasn't just a flippant aside on the fairways. Interviewed a couple of years later by the *American Journalism Review*,[6] he confessed he had no idea how many people worked on his website. 'My only job is to sell copies of my newspaper.'

He had a point, of course. He had two shareholders wanting – if not quick returns – at least smaller losses, and fast. Copies sold was money in. We needed money in, too – but the Scott Trust was there to preserve the *Guardian* in perpetuity. I was pretty sure that perpetuity wouldn't feature a daily newspaper, of whatever format.

Meanwhile we had built up 13 million unique users a month on our website (the *Times*, by comparison, was at 4.7 million – itself 150 per cent up on the previous year) and were bringing in seven-figure sums in digital advertising. What a moment to have to take the foot off the online accelerator and go back to thinking full-time about print again.

Two things held us back from following suit to tabloid – one practical, one journalistic.

The practical objection – ironic now – was that in 2002/3 we still published a staggering number of classified advertising on Mondays, Tuesdays and Wednesdays, which brought in £74 million a year. We calculated that in order to print all those ads in tabloid format we would sometimes have to publish editions of up to 220 pages. Any gain from the smaller page size would be wiped out by the reader having to juggling a multi-section paper – sandwiches within sandwiches – which could fall apart in their hands.[7]

In short, producing a tabloid looked – for the *Guardian* in 2004 – pretty impossible.

But what if staying broadsheet was, as we kept being told, a short-cut to oblivion? We consulted the editorial staff – with a hundred or so colleagues convening to debate the issue. The meeting ended with a 60 to 40 per cent vote against going tabloid. But, even if we did stay broadsheet, we would still have to re-press within four years when our printing contract expired. For eight years – since our own print plant had been terminally damaged by the IRA in a 1996 Canary Wharf bomb blast – we had been printed in London on an ageing, mainly black-and-white press owned by Richard Desmond.

To make it more complicated I thought the Kelner 'compact' *Independent* was actually quite successful in its own terms. The paper, which had lost its identity as a broadsheet, had recovered some confidence and found a new voice as a tabloid. But it had come at a cost: it had sacrificed a consistency of tone for something more strident, politically unsubtle and obsessed with single issues.

Similarly, the *Times* had gained something in focus and sharpness. Story lengths were certainly down. There were some early slips of voice as the venerable sub-editors tried to mimic a tabloid style. The paper had become a tighter read; it had also lost something in elegance, consistency and tone. The paper's former veteran Middle East correspondent, Christopher Walker, wrote in the *British Journalism Review*: 'The move down from heavyweight to the welterweight division has arisen not only from the new emphasis on the trivial in the choice of stories, but also an aggravating habit by the home and foreign desks to demand that stories be tailored to suit the angle emerging from the morning and afternoon conferences.'[8]

This led to my second reservation: I didn't think the *Guardian* would necessarily succeed in a war against the revitalised tabloid *Independent*, in particular. Nor did I want to change the paper in ways that would have been necessary to be in with a chance.

Simon Kelner was pioneering a profoundly different kind of journalism from the restrained, original broadsheet *Independent* – with its small Century headlines; its artful pictures; its seven or eight stories separated by horizontal Oxford rules. Broadsheet papers tended to sell on their long-established identity and judgement. Tabloid newspapers relied much more on day-to-day impact, at least in Britain, with most sales on the news stand rather than home delivery. A brilliant tabloid front-page image and headline – and Kelner produced many – would shift copies. But the reverse was also true: a page that mundanely relayed the news of the day in quiet headlines could not stand out. Charles Moore's 'boring but important' stories would not fare well in tabloid.

Kelner realised this and produced ever more powerful single-issue front pages – often quite unrelated to the news of the day. They were distinctive and often shouty. They got the *Independent* talked about. They halted the slide in circulation, even if the figures never soared anywhere near the peaks our marketing teams had whispered. But this was a new form of journalism in the UK: a broadsheet in tabloid clothing.

Kelner was quite frank about what he was up to. His front pages, he confessed, were 'an elision of marketing and journalism'. In other interviews, he went still further: he was moving from a newspaper to what he called 'a viewspaper'.

Newspaper–viewspaper? Hold on a moment. Was Kelner not just changing shape and style – but also bailing out of the primacy of facts? It seemed so. 'Why pay 70p for something you've heard on the radio?' Kelner demanded in his 2006 *AJR* interview. 'We've got to provide something of value.' The *AJR* writer, Frances Stead Sellers, continued: 'The added value he promises is attitude. Pages of it. Right from the word go – on A1.'[9]

At least the *AJR* noticed that something had changed. In the UK, there was a kind of collective shrug, as if 'a viewspaper' was simply a play on words, or a cool piece of rebranding, as opposed to a completely different concept of editorial endeavour. Throughout all this time I can't remember a single discussion in the mainstream press, radio or television about whether the greater public good would be improved or damaged by having nine tabloid newspapers in Britain, all using more or less the same techniques to sell copies.

In the office we'd start comparing each day's *Independent* with the mid-market tabloids. There was no question: Kelner knew how to produce a *Mail*-style front page dominated by a powerful picture or headline. When the Butler report into the uses of intelligence before the Iraq war appeared in July 2004, the *Mail* and *Independent* had strikingly similar front pages mocking his conclusion: 'No one to Blame!' in one paper, 'Who was to Blame? – No one!' in the other. When the Hutton report into the BBC's alleged failings of reporting was published, the *Independent*'s front-page headline read simply 'Whitewash?' The *Daily Mail*'s read 'Justice?'

Views first, news later.

More strikingly still, the paper started ignoring news stories which shouted to be splattered all over the front page. In September 2004 the world was captivated by Chechen rebels holding 1,000 people hostages in a school in Beslan – a siege that led to hundreds of children dying. Front-page news around the world. The *Independent* decided otherwise: it had commissioned the editor of *Vanity Fair*, Graydon Carter, to mark George W. Bush's 'four years of double standards' by compiling 'Bush by Numbers'. So, no report on Beslan for *Independent* readers – just a graphic showing Bush's failings. Asked to defend the front page Simon shrugged and said a newspaper couldn't compete with television.

The *Times* settled down into a more even-toned newspaper. But there were still moments for years to come when the front page would make you blink at what had happened to a particular style of journalism. To take one random example: in 2012, the European Court of Human Rights halted attempts by the British government to deport a radical Islamist cleric, Abu Qatada. The case was a complex one, involving deadlines arguably missed by the UK Home Office and ambiguities in the law and translations of it. The tabloid *Times* devoted its front page to a photo of 11 of the ECHR judges under the headline 'Europe's Court Jesters'.[10]

Now, the *Times* has excellent and pretty comprehensive legal coverage. It is probably the paper most senior lawyers and judges read. But this was pure *Daily Mail* – a foreshadow of that paper's infamous 'Enemies of the People' front page in 2017, which used a similar device to put judges in the dock.

The more I watched such shifts in presentation – especially in the hands of Kelner – the more dangerous it seemed to me to allow the *Guardian* to be lured into competition with this new kind of journalistic animal. The *Guardian* had comprehensively seen off the *Independent* after a period in which the newcomer had appeared to pose a mortal risk. We had, so to speak, 'won' at being a serious, broadsheet newspaper. And now here was a very talented editor luring us into a different game: *Okay, so you were better at news, but can you beat us at views?*

This seemed like a seminal moment for newspapers: an ongoing concern for complexity, facts and nuance versus a drift towards impact, opinion and simplicity.

I thought back to the occasions when I had sat in on the Page One meeting of the *New York Times* under a succession of executive editors – Joseph Lelyveld, Howell Raines, Bill Keller. As many as 30 senior editors would meet solemnly every day at 4 p.m. around a table with lengthy summaries of the main stories of the day. With a concentration and high-mindedness which wouldn't have been out of place in a cathedral, the editors would pitch their offerings to a figure as magisterial as a cardinal. The executive editor – fingers steepled at the head of the table – would consider the world as presented to him and make decisions about the relative importance of each story.

A senior executive called Allan M. Siegal would, as the room emptied, draw up the agreed front page with a pencil and ruler. Geometry and typography were the *NYT*'s way of imposing a hierarchy of order on the otherwise random torrent of information pouring across its newsroom desks every minute of the day. Wasn't that needed more than ever in an age when the ocean of information threatened to engulf us all?

But doubt kept creeping in. What if not enough citizens/readers wanted to be informed? Or, rather, that there was a level of surface news-grazing which was just fine for most people? You could argue Kelner was right: news was all around – the radio headlines in the morning, a ten-minute scan of *Metro* on the way to work, text alerts for breaking headlines, the internet, numerous 24-hour news TV channels. That was, arguably, all most people wanted.

The competition was gnawing away on all sides. The dent that the give-away *Metro* made in all our circulations was particularly baffling. The free newspaper owned by the Daily Mail & General Trust – skimming the surface and with little original reporting – was reaching more than a million people.[11] It seemed to have little overlap with a newspaper like the *Guardian*, but thousands of readers began substituting it on their morning commute.

'*How much more do I honestly need to read to be informed enough?*' these people might be asking. '*It's all very well to talk about the compact between citizen and legislator, but voting doesn't seem to change much. And the real power in the modern world – and the real problems – lie way beyond my ability to do anything about them. Why do I need to know all this detail?*'

The apathetic reader – if that's what these people were – might not be apathetic about everything. They'd have their own passions, obsessions and causes. But it seemed just possible that the internet did passions, obsessions and causes better than newspapers. People could burrow deeply into their own subjects, engage with communities of other equally engaged people. And, as for the rest, well, maybe a ten-minute skim would do.

What, we debated over long sessions in 2003/4/5, should a news organisation do, faced with legions of apathetic readers? Give them what they want? If they don't want difficult stuff, perhaps we shouldn't give them difficult stuff. Or the (apocryphal?) BBC dictum: 'Don't give the public what they want. They deserve much better than that.'

Maybe we needed to be smarter in differentiating what print and digital could do? We argued it both ways: keep print for a comprehensive but shallow summary, with the depth to be found online? Or (as an equal number of colleagues wanted it) that print was the medium for depth, with the internet giving you constant, but shallow, updates.

Turn the volume up? Make the news seem more exciting, striking, pumped up? Try to shock and energise them out of their apathy?

Was there still some notion of duty that went with the privilege of mediating the news and the argument? Did we have any kind of responsibility to tell our readers things they might not think they wanted to know? Would it matter if all newspapers started turning up the volume . . . to shout, rather than talk? Would public debate be improved, or become impossible?

Would a move to less complexity end up reinforcing a pattern of ignorance, or carelessness about things that ultimately do matter to us all? What would be the impact on politics? At its mildest it might simply frustrate politicians, unable to get their message across. Or it might create a breed of politicians who felt they could get away with more or less anything because the main medium of political communication had abandoned the territory.[12]

From the distance of 2018 maybe the world is a bit more attuned to the dangers of creating a monoculture of simplicity. The politicians who succeed in it are sometimes the ones with the simplest messages. Populism is a denial of complexity.

Here was the dilemma. It looked increasingly questionable whether, for a decent paper like the *Independent*, there was going to be a commercial model which could sustain the dogged, fact-by-fact, nuanced recording of news. But a world without such reporting would surely favour a new, cruder, kind of politics and discourse.

Most of public life was not faithfully representable in either black or white. Somebody – surely – had the duty to paint in the greys. We could not have predicted, within 15 years, the degree to which complexity had been squeezed out of public discourse. Who could have anticipated a President of the United States communicating with his 50 million followers in bursts of a few words? The average length of a political soundbite in broadcast news had shrunk from 43 seconds in 1968 to nine seconds in 1988. By 2012 it hovered between seven and nine seconds.[13] The immense complexity of a decision on Britain's place in the world would be settled by a simply yes or no answer. An ever-more polarised public – favouring either black or white answers to complicated problems – had lost either interest or trust in a world of greys.

We could not see all that happening so swiftly in 2003. But it didn't take a soothsayer to see that a simplified media could lead to a simplified politics.

Our period of reflection at the *Guardian* coincided with the publication of two provocative books about journalism: John Lloyd's 2004 polemic *What the Media Are Doing to Our Politics* and a 2003 book, *The Elements of Journalism*, by two veteran American journalists, Bill Kovach and Tom Rosenstiel – the culmination of much similar soul-searching among American editors.

Lloyd's central hypothesis was that the world, as described by British journalists, existed in a kind of parallel universe to the world as it's actually experienced by doctors, public administrators, soldiers, politicians, judges, teachers, bishops and so forth.

The Kovach/Rosenstiel book about the basics of our craft did make waves in America. We invited Kovach over to lead some internal discussions about the sort of journalism that – in his words – 'provided citizens with the information they need to be free and self-governing'.

But the British debate around these two books was extremely limited. In particular, the former *FT* writer John Lloyd, where he was noticed at all, was almost universally rubbished by other journalists. *Whose side are you on?* they wanted to know.

We tried an exercise to test Lloyd's argument. We devoted twenty pages of Media Guardian over two weeks to the unedited responses of a cross-section of leaders in public life, prefaced by the late Anthony Sampson's last essay. As Sampson, the author of the iconic 1962 book *Anatomy of Britain*, recognised, the respondents overwhelmingly agreed with Lloyd. 'There can be no doubt,' he wrote, 'about the genuine anguish of many distinguished people who feel aggrieved or simply resigned to the misrepresentations of the press.'

Once again, what was notable was the almost complete absence of any response to this exercise. One or two media commentators dismissed the 50 writers – more or less asking, *What do they know?*

Not one of the 50 was asked on to any radio or TV programme to discuss the subject. I tried imagining something similar happening in any other walk of life. What if 50 distinguished leaders in the community united to suggest something close to crisis in the police; or in the army; or in medicine; or in the universities or the nuclear industry. Would such an intervention be greeted by a weary shrug by newspapers and current affairs programmes?

The former editor of the *FT*, Richard Lambert, made a similar point in a speech in December 2004: 'If this were any other business, especially one with as strong a consumer interface as the media, we would be talking about a crisis of trust and demanding different behaviours on the part of the protagonists. Consumers would be boycotting the products to demonstrate their feelings . . . The oil and the chemical industries have not been able to get away with behaviour like this. Why should the media be different?'

He continued: 'I believe that a series of market failures runs through the process – meaning that this is a case where competition and quality products do not go hand in hand. The result is a media which in some extreme cases is more of a threat to our democracy than its guarantor . . . Half a dozen powerful characters shape the personality of the British print media, and the regional press carries little clout. As a result, no politician, from any of the parties, is willing to take the press barons head on. Rather the opposite.'[14]

He was right. But no one was listening.

★

This (largely absent) debate about media and politics played out at the margins as we weighed up limited options for future printing formats. If tabloid was undo-able and broadsheet was unsustainable, then what?

By now we knew that, come what may, we would have to change our printing arrangements. The industry was moving to full colour on every page – advertisers would settle for no less – and the ageing Richard Desmond presses we printed on could only offer eight pages on any night. We knew News International were contemplating spending £600 million on new all-colour presses.[15] The options boiled down to paying someone else to print us indefinitely – or operating our own. Financially, we were advised there was not a huge difference.

Many serious European newspapers favoured the Berliner format[16] – the so-called Goldilocks option: neither too small nor too big. It could cope with the unusual demands we then required in terms of classified advertising. In a world of – potentially – nine or ten tabloids fighting for attention on the news stands, it was distinctive. And, most importantly, we could continue with the journalism we believed in.[17]

Five years later – as classified advertising drained out of all news-papers – we might have made a different decision. The practical objections would have disappeared, even if the journalistic anxieties lingered. In 2018 – with virtually no classified advertising left in print – the *Guardian* did finally switch to tabloid.

Even as we ordered the Berliner presses we knew these would be the last we would ever own.[18]

★

The great format wars – which had eaten up so much time, resources, energy, noise and marketing – seemed, ten years later, to be – at best – a footnote. But the obsession with print sales was hard to shrug off. Within a year of the size battles, the entire UK national press was in wholesale panic about the startling rate of overall print decline. It was an age of fewer metrics – and the key metric for advertisers and press commentators was circulation. Up: good. Down: bad.

In order to maintain, never mind grow, national circulations, most publishers – including the *Guardian* – were forced to spend larger and larger sums on bulk sales (the copies you find on trains, planes and in hotels),[19] foreign sales, cut-price subscriptions and promotions involving CDs, wall charts, books, dream cottages and DVDs. We became an industry of freebie junkies.

According to a piece in the *Independent* in July 2005, a total of 20 million DVDs were given away across Fleet Street *in just one weekend* as executives desperately tried to bribe readers to stay loyal to print. The *Times*'s giveaway of *The African Queen* reportedly saw the paper rewarded with more than a million customers – its highest full-price sale ever. But the sales did not stick.

The DVDs may have been 'free' to the reader, but they were massively expensive to the newspapers – around 30p a disc plus the cost of buying the rights. The *Independent* article claimed that the *Daily Mail* was lavishing £80 million a year simply on promotions – a budget considerably larger than the entire sum the *Guardian* and *Observer* spent on their journalism.

Success didn't look like anything anyone planned when the format wars broke out in 2003.

Just over a dozen years later the *Independent* had died – at least in printed format.[20] The promises of huge circulation gains had proved illusory. The poster front pages – as Kelner later admitted – were difficult to sustain. The *Times* bundled up digital and print subscriptions and restructured itself so that the *Times* and *Sunday Times* corporate entities could contract everything except editorial to other parts of the Murdoch empire.

And the *Guardian*? Some critics claimed the Berliner was a waste of time and money. Given the huge complications of printing in tabloid in 2004, it's probable that, had we simply contracted out our printing, we'd have been forced to remain a broadsheet for a few years. Who can say what that would have meant in terms of circulation?

In pure profit and loss terms the big winner was, ironically, the broadsheet *Telegraph*, still delivering an operating profit of £32 million in 2016/7. Chapter 21 examines the price the company separately paid in terms of editorial reputation.

The *Independent* started planning its tabloid in early 2003. We went Berliner on 5 September 2005. That period saw the launches of LinkedIn, Skype, MySpace, Facebook, Flickr, Bebo and YouTube.

Historians might well argue that, for two years, Fleet Street had had its collective head buried in the sand.

10

Dog, Meet Dog

A newspaper never sleeps. This book is concerned with the backstage of institutional life as well as the play itself. But there is one ineffaceable truth you know being an editor: you're the one whose head is on the block.

An editor today is expected to take the credit, or blame, for the business as much as the editorial mission. In most companies he/she will find themselves increasingly required to attend strategy days; think about dramatic organisational restructuring; be an expert in HR issues; contribute to board meetings; attend finance or marketing sessions; understand technology; stay on top of metrics; be nice to advertisers.

All these are necessary parts of the job. You have talented colleagues who, round the clock, keep the show on the road. But there will still be regular moments when the editor will have to drop everything to concentrate on one particular thing. It might be a single sentence. A contested word. A disturbing image. An inflammatory cartoon. A powerful person or entity you're about to unmask.

Writers still need talking to. Furious politicians or business leaders need a calm hearing.

Get any of it wrong and you're the one whose head is on the block.

One day in mid-March 2005 Nick Davies came in for lunch. Our journalistic paths had taken very different routes. I'd ended up editing. He still stood on doorsteps and reported.

98

Some brilliant reporters can't write. Some brilliant writers can't report. Some very able reporters report, but don't break news. Some news-breaking reporters can't see the bigger picture. Many thinking journalists aren't interested in reporting.

Nick was one of the very few journalists I'd ever worked with who could do it all. He just loved reporting: he'd even started lecturing to journalism students about the art of a 'doorstep' (approaching someone cold with a knock on the door). 'You have about ten seconds before they slam the door in your face. What you say, how you look, what you wear . . . it's all crucial.'

But he could invariably see the larger picture and fit individual human stories into a larger intellectual framework. Sometimes it was the other way round: he'd have an idea and then find a way of bringing it to life through narrative detail.

Since I'd hired him back on the *Guardian*, he'd increasingly worked off-diary. He'd moved to Lewes, a seaside town 70 miles outside London, and rarely appeared in the office. He relished long projects and, over the years, produced some powerful work on drugs, prisons, the police and crime. I then asked him to spend a year looking at schools and Britain's public education system. He'd produced four books along the way.

He worked on a long leash, dropping in for occasional meetings to update me on where he'd got to; how many libel lawyers we'd need to brief for his next series; or to alert me to expect an angry phone call from someone he was investigating.

On this day he looked tired and out of sorts. He was thinking of retiring. He was 52. He'd spent his life interrogating power – who had it, who used it, who abused it. But he'd said all he wanted to say about the police and the judicial system. He wanted to fit out a camper van and drive across Eastern Europe. There was something of the hippy about Nick.

But before he retired he wanted to do one last big series about power. The last truly unexamined centre of power in Britain – unexamined, because no one had the interest, or the guts, to investigate it.

The press.

I may well have shifted uncomfortably in my seat. Nick was a heat-seeking missile. If he spent the next year digging into the press you could guarantee he would come up with something extraordinary. He always did.

Power was the subject that obsessed him most: the misuse of power. 'For various reasons, I got hit a lot by adults when I was a child,' he once told me in a reflective moment. 'And I deeply hate people who abuse power because of that. So, deep down under all those layers, that's what drives me. I want to get my own back on people who abuse power and by good chance that's what a good journalist should do.'

The germ of the idea had come from the Iraq war and the press's role in aiding and abetting a conflict based on what now we would call fake news.

He had no idea where it would end, nor, obviously, did I. But I suspected it could lead somewhere difficult. There would come a day when I would be getting threats from editors or publishers. *We don't wash our dirty linen in public, Alan. You do this and see what we do to you.* Or words to that effect.

But for 20 or more years I'd supported Nick in what he decided to investigate. What would it mean if I told him the press itself was off limits? Everyone – including the press – thought the media had a really significant impact on public life. How could the press demand that it, alone, should be exempt from the scrutiny of the press?

The lunch with Nick caught me at a lonely moment in thinking about our trade. There was a marked lack of discussion – in the UK mainstream media at least – about the way news was changing and about journalism itself.

Viewspaper–newspaper? Meh.

On the *Guardian* we had long published a Monday media section – and, latterly, a media website. In the dog-politely-ignores-dog world of Fleet Street that was never going to lead to a comfortable life, and it didn't. Over time I was threatened by not quite every publisher or editor in London . . . but a good many of them.

Editor 1: '*I'll always retaliate. We should be sticking together, not writing about each other.*'

Editor 2: '*My circulation is three times yours. You write about me, I'll write about you. In the end you'll stop.*'

Editor 3: '*I hate writing about the media, but I make an exception for the* Guardian.'

Publisher 1: '*We've both got ink wells, Alan. Remember that.*'

Publisher 2: '*I'll release the hounds of hell on you. You have to stop writing about us.*'

Some tried for bilateral deals: '*You don't write about us, we won't write about you.*' In general, they were as good as their word. If the *Guardian* upset a rival editor or publisher you could guarantee a form of retribution within days. It could be a snide diary paragraph or a threat to dig up dirt on *Guardian* employees' private lives – including mine. It could be a hatchet job about 'troubles' at the paper. Sometimes these stories had a grain of truth, at other times they were simply invented. At first I was shocked that even broadsheet rivals would knowingly run untrue stories about us in 'revenge'. After a while I understood we were all supposed to see this as the great game.

One or two Fleet Street elders were in deadly earnest about preserving the *omertà*. One softly spoken executive took me to breakfast at the Savoy and, after the poached eggs, pushed an envelope across the table. It contained photocopies of stories we had run about his titles.

He tapped the envelope. 'It has to stop.'

'I can't promise you that.'

His amiability drained away. 'I don't think you understand. It has to stop.'

'But I can't publish a media section having done a private deal with one executive not to cover his particular titles.'

'It has to stop.'

Another lunch, another senior figure in the industry:

'Why do you do this, Alan? We should be fighting our enemies all around, sticking together, not digging up dirt.'

Again, he wanted no coverage of his own title.

'Surely you think it's a good thing to have a media section, writing about the media?'

He didn't.

Having failed to get their reassurances both publisher and editor found numerous excuses over the years to keep their promises. An eye for an eye.

★

I agreed to Nick having a deep dive into the press. I had no idea what he would discover, but nor did it feel right that the Fleet Street elders should get their wish that their journalism should be a coverage-free zone.

It was a *Sliding Doors* decision.

11

The Future Is Mutual

In journalism school they teach you how to write. A classic story is supposed to be constructed like an inverted pyramid, with the lead paragraph summarising the story's most important facts as concisely and interestingly as possible.

Readers logging in to the *Guardian* website on 13 March 2003 to follow the cricket world cup match between New Zealand and India were confronted with something very different – a Joycean stream of consciousness. The match report began as follows:

> Preamble
>
> It's really simple: India are already through, New Zealand has to win.
>
> Meanwhile, have you ever thought WHAT SORT OF LIFE IS THIS AND WHAT THE HELL AM I DOING BOARDING A TRAIN FOR MOORGATE AT 6.30 IN THE MORNING AND THEN STANDING AROUND FOR AGES WAITING FOR A TUBE WHILE STARING AT A SIGN TELLING YOU THAT IF YOU WAIT FOR FOUR MINUTES YOU CAN BOARD A TRAIN TO UXBRIDGE I'D RATHER WAIT FOUR HOURS FOR A JOURNEY WITH THE GRIM REAPER QUITE FRANKLY AND THEN YOU GET TO WORK AND THEN THERE'S THIS AND I KNOW THE CRICKET'S

GOOD AND ALL THAT BUT I'VE GOT OUT OF THE
WRONG SIDE OF BED THIS MORNING AND IN ANY
CASE IT'S NOT AS IF I'LL WRITE A CRACKING MATCH
REPORT AND THEN GET REWARDED BY BEING SENT
ON A WONDERFUL ASSIGNMENT AROUND THE
WORLD BECAUSE I'LL BE VERY SURPRISED IF ANY OF
MY BOSSES WILL READ ANY OF THIS LET'S BE HONEST
THEY WON'T ALTHOUGH ON THE OTHER HAND
THAT'S PROBABLY JUST AS WELL HEY I WOULDN'T
BE ABLE TO GET AWAY WITH TYPING THINGS LIKE
THIS KIqL!UYS^%$DFLI ZSDSAFC SFE4O92)(^(*^o'$ bBLKU
E875O3 96*&^%o*'$ogb LOOK I'M SORRY THIS ISN'T
EXACTLY THE SORT OF QUALITY EDITORIAL COPY
YOU EXPECT FROM THE GUARDIAN BUT LOOK AT
THE FACTS I'M ADRIFT IN THE MIDDLE OF ONE OF
THE WORST CITIES IN THE WORLD SITTING IN FRONT
OF THE SAME COMPUTER SCREEN I FACE DAY AFTER
INTERMINABLE DAY HELL I COULD BE WAKING UP
IN SAY THE MALDIVES OR SYDNEY OR COPENHAGEN
OR A CROFTER'S COTTAGE IN SKYE AND GOING FOR
A WALK IN THE CRISP MORNING AIR?

No? Only me then. Good.

This was not how newspaper reporting was done. Nothing like it
had ever appeared under the *Guardian* banner. Several readers – not
to mention some colleagues – thought the writer, Scott Murray, must
have been under a lot of strain recently. But then the report – an over-
by-over account of the match – was picked up by Popbitch, a celebrity
website, and it went a bit viral. Some rival newspapers speculated about
whether Murray had been hacked. Others offered him jobs.

★

While so many of us had spent two years with our heads in print, the
world elsewhere had been changing fast.

We were now a two-speed organisation.

As a company we were very unintegrated – with digital either in a different building or (later) at the same address but on an entirely separate floor. That, in time, led to all kinds of organisational problems. But, for now, one advantage was that there was a sizeable group of people who had less-than-zero interest in printed artefacts and were keeping their minds focused on the way the digital world was moving.

Some of what they did was what we all did. At the irreducible core, there are things that all journalism aspires to: speed and accuracy, to name but two. Some of the print journalists worried about how you combined them. We'd point out that the entire business model of news agencies such as AP or Reuters was to beat everyone to a story – *and* also to get it right. You stuck to what you knew.

But how fast? On the print floors – whatever the shape or size of the newspaper that eventually rolled off the presses at 10.30 in the evening – the day was built around one deadline early in the evening. A whole set of internal processes flowed from that central assumption.

Most obviously, if you were a reporter and you had to submit your copy by 6 p.m. you knew you had to start writing, say, at 4.30 p.m. That might (depending on how many other stories you had to write during the day) leave you with two or three hours to read a report; go to a press conference; make a few calls to people for comment or to gain deeper understanding; consult the library of cuttings; and then write 'your story'.

I can't now remember exactly when Emily Bell wandered into my office and said, 'I'm beginning to wonder if "the story" is actually going to be the main form of journalism any longer.'

Call them Emily's Mad Pronouncements. They came regularly – a profound utterance that upended a fundamental tenet of what we'd taken for granted all our lives. You would dismiss them as ridiculous. *These guys are drinking way too much Kool-Aid on the fifth floor.* And then – days, weeks, months later – you'd revisit the conversation because something would have happened to make you understand what she was getting at.

'Explain how it's the end of the story?'

I mean, I sort of knew what she was talking about, but she was usually a year or two ahead of me.

Well, she said, the story had been the natural vehicle for a printed newspaper. It had a narrative shape that began with the most interesting/ grabby/new/salient fact and packed in information in a set of paragraphs that could be cut from the bottom if there was not enough space.

'But in our world,' she added, pointing to the fifth floor, 'there are no deadlines. We can't wait until tonight: our readers want the information now – and if we don't give it to them, someone else will.'

So?

So therefore it might not make sense to build the traditional architecture of a story. We might:

A) want to release it in sections, as and when we know stuff

B) link to alternative sources who had newer, or better, or different relevant information

C) include responses from readers, who might be in a position to supply other viewpoints or material.

This was not a story so much as a live form of blogging, or a live-blog. Familiar now, crazy then.

We had, in fact, been experimenting with live-blogs for some time.[1] We had an early experiment with the 1997 Ashes tour. Football followed, then tech writers who, as printed newspapers shrank following the 2001 advertising recession, simply wrote things online they couldn't get into print.

There were all kinds of reasons why live-blogging a sporting event was a terrible idea. Proper journalism involved sending a seasoned reporter to the ground to report on a match. Live-blogging was done, sometimes from home, by a bloke in an armchair watching the television.

But what made both work was the chemistry between the commentators and the audience.

After the Scott Murray blog, and subsequent experiments, the live-blog grew into a kind of maturity during that summer of 2005.

The cricket Ashes of 2005 between England and Australia was a sporting marathon, tensely played out over 61 sessions in five test matches. The whole series went down to the last day of the last game. We had our 'expert' correspondents – Mike Selvey and Vic Marks – at the grounds. And then we had four bloggers,[2] taking it in turns to keep up the running commentary which readers would follow all day on their desktops while pretending to be working.

Both forms of journalism were 'valid'. Both Marks and Selvey had themselves played test cricket for England. They were 'experts'. They could see things in a match that even the most knowledgeable sporting journalist might miss. But the audience for the bloke-in-front-of-the-telly dwarfed not only the professional verdict of the cricket correspondents: it also dwarfed anything else we might be doing on the website that day.

In time we started live-blogging more and more. Same story. It almost didn't matter what you live-blogged. The audience, in the new medium, found this form of storytelling compelling.

Suddenly we had a return channel. For 200 years journalism had been about pushing stuff out at readers. And now, here they were – not in a letter arriving a day or two later which might (possibly) find its way to a writer via the letters desk some time thereafter. Here were real live readers – sometimes thousands of them – responding instantly to things you were telling them.

It wasn't quite a conversation: it wasn't one-to-one. Nor was it one-to-many. This was many-to-many. There were multiple witnesses to, and participants in, every 'conversation'.

Some writers immediately took to it. It felt, somehow, lighter, less portentous. It was a place of humour and running gags. It was a place where you could ask questions rather than simply tell. You could opine – or you could listen. And you could link. You could send readers off elsewhere to catch up on things that had been well-reported or which looked authoritative. Your tone changed.

Not everyone welcomed it and not everyone was good at it. Many couldn't see the point of it. Not everyone had the time for it. Some tried it, and found themselves overwhelmed. Some had an early encounter with a rude or aggressive reader and retired hurt. A few persevered.

★

Emily's Mad Pronouncements. The age of the first internet was over. It was big. But this was the age of Web 2.0 and – guess what? – it was even bigger.

Again, I stared at her, unconvinced. What could be bigger than what we'd done so far – take a print business and publish it in an entirely different way: different medium, different deadlines, different everything.

She agreed it had been big, but insisted that what was to come was bigger.

She shared a chart,[3] showing the difference between Web 1.0 and Web 2.0

Web 1.0		Web 2.0
DoubleClick	-->	Google AdSense
Ofoto	-->	Flickr
Akamai	-->	BitTorrent
mp3.com	-->	Napster
Britannica Online	-->	Wikipedia
personal websites	-->	blogging
evite	-->	upcoming.org and EVDB
domain name speculation	-->	search engine optimization
page views	-->	cost per click
screen scraping	-->	web services
publishing	-->	participation
content management systems	-->	wikis
directories (taxonomy)	-->	tagging ("folksonomy")
stickiness	-->	syndication

If a story was a linear piece of narrative, we were moving into something that looked entirely different. You might think of it as a spine and spokes, or as a tree and branches. A reader might not want to start at the beginning and finish at the pre-ordained end. They might want to branch off here to explore this tributary. They might want to dig deeper here and follow those links, because that's the angle that really interested them. They might want to check the source for this or the original document for that. They might want to chip in with their own thoughts here.

Whatever this new form was, it wasn't a story. Emily's Mad Pronouncement was possibly not so mad after all.

★

The 'Guardian reader' had, in the minds of some, been something of a stereotype. You might draw the stereotype as a worthy, earnest sort. The male Guardian reader typecast might have a wispy beard and a tweed jacket with leather elbow patches and sandals. His female counterpart – lank hair and forbidding glasses – would be drizzling olive oil over sun-dried tomatoes.

Some were, indeed, like that still – and fine people they often were, doing essential, unsung, not very well-cherished or remunerated jobs in public services. But, as the global taste for the Guardian grew, there developed a community of 'Guardian readers' who shared a similar outlook on life – we can shorthand it as intelligent liberals – and who fell on the company of others of the same ilk, no matter where they lived. They didn't wear sandals or drive Citroën deux chevaux, but they were part of a tribe, or tribes. For the most part they were a pretty nice, interesting, amusing, knowledgeable bunch. Inviting them in wasn't a faddish experiment or chore. They contributed.

We began to wonder: how could we use them better?

We looked elsewhere around the internet. We thought about how our own habits when not at work had changed. We observed our children and how they behaved. Increasingly, they turned to each other rather than seek out established sources of authority. They went peer-to-peer. They wanted the opinions of their friends, people who thought like them.

We started with something easy: travel writing. Some of us still used newspaper travel pages for ideas about holidays or weekend breaks. More of us had begun to use websites such as Lonely Planet, i-escape or TripAdvisor, which had started five years previously as a site to swap reviews – people exchanging 'official' reviews of places from newspapers or guidebooks. The TripAdvisor founders allowed users to add their own comments – and, in the words of Stephen Kaufer, one of the original developers, 'Boy, did that just take off.'[4]

So why not ask Guardian readers to mimic the behaviour of the web rather than the behaviour of newspapers? Why not create a space for their own recommendations?

We created a section of the travel site called Been There and watched it fill up with thousands of recommendations about hotels, bars, markets, beaches, restaurants, shops, museums, and so on. We segmented the recommendations by city and activity, so that, before travelling to Barcelona, you could look to see where other *Guardian* readers had been and what they'd done. The premise was that *Guardian* readership was, in some sense, a community. You would more readily seek out holiday recommendations from a fellow *Guardian* reader than you would from a *Daily Express* reader or even a TripAdvisor user. A *New York Times* reader might feel the same about her own paper as distinct from the *New York Post* or *Wall Street Journal* . . . and vice versa.

The objection was the obvious one: what's to stop the hotelier's sister from bigging up the joint? Or the restaurateur's brother from slagging off a rival? Where, in other words, is the quality control you'd expect from a newspaper?[5] Which was a fair point, but which presupposed that newspaper travel writing was purer than pure.

In truth, travel writing was, on most papers, an – how should one put it? – unusual journalistic form. A few papers – the early days of the *Independent* were a notable example – refused to accept any 'free' holidays. Its correspondent, Simon Calder, had exposed what he called 'Freebieland' in an article in 2000.[6] The strapline read: 'These days, virtually all newspaper and magazine travel pages are filled with features by journalists who have been on all-expenses-paid press trips, so how objective, let alone useful are they?'

Calder found it difficult to measure exactly how the figures stacked up, but found that the Scottish Tourist Board was willing to admit that the average value of the hundreds of free trips it organised for journalists each year was over £10,000 each in equivalent advertising spend. 'Coverage in a newspaper or magazine also buys something that advertising cannot: the appearance of objectivity. As a marketing executive from Australia's biggest airline once told me bluntly: "If a journalist recommends Qantas, the consumer is going to believe that more than our advertising."'[7]

Then there was scale. A typical travel section in print might have four or five holiday articles a week at most – no more than 250 a year. But in an age of search, an internet user could access hundreds of thousands of ideas at the click of a mouse.

Finally, the quality issue. Yes, the Been There section was gameable – just like Amazon reviews, or TripAdvisor recommendations or anything else on the internet which allowed people a voice. There were, no doubt, 'corrupt-ish' contributions.

But others were written by people with a considerable expertise in a place. They hadn't dropped in for a few days – acquiring instant expertise on the bars of Berlin or the street markets of Merida. Some of the most enthusiastic contributors actually lived in the places they wrote about!

Our readers know more than we do. Sometimes. Quite often.

None of this was to disparage the genuinely insightful travel writing by professional journalists that we, and others, continued to run. Some of it was textured, sensitive . . . and, of course, independent. But only the binary-minded argued that it had to be one thing or the other. In the digital world you could have the best of both.

Both sport and travel worked in terms of readers not simply passively consuming the *Guardian*, but positively contributing to it.

We gave this a name. We called it mutualisation. It wasn't a very good name, but it sort of hinted at what we thought we were doing. It would do for now.

*

On 9 May 2005 – as we had our heads deep in thinking about the typography of the Berliner title piece (should it stay Garamond/Helvetica? Or switch to Egyptian?) – the *Huffington Post* was launched to a fair amount of sniggering. Arianna Huffington – the most upwardly mobile Greek since Icarus, as my colleague Michael White brilliantly described her when she married the multi-millionaire Republican congressman Michael Huffington in 1986 – had appeared to reinvent her life several times. She had moved from left to right and back again without batting a socialite eyelid. It was easy to sneer at an eponymous website that had all the trappings of a vanity project.

That was the ridiculous bit. The even more laughable proposition: she would be getting her celebrity friends to write – wait for it – for no payment! If you were a journalist from the pre-internet age this was more than risible. It was offensive.

Journalists had mortgages: we were professionals. How dare some Californian hostess imagine she could undercut the work of proper paid commentaries by publishing the work of writers who were doing it for nothing?

Those who believed this had contempt for large parts of what Web 2.0 represented. They would curl their lip as they spat out the phrase 'citizen journalist'.

'Would you like a "citizen brain surgeon" for a tumour?' they sneered. 'How about a "citizen dentist"?' As if reading two books plus-a-bit-of-shorthand to 'qualify' as a journalist was the equivalent of six years of a neurosurgical residency on top of a four-year medical degree to be a brain surgeon.

In any event, the *Huffington Post* was not widely expected to succeed.

Emily, typically, was not so sure. Nor were the other web watchers whose word I respected. Why wait for Arianna to roll her tanks onto your lawn in the UK? Start your own version now.

I turned to Georgina Henry, my friend and deputy editor who had so stoically kept the newspaper ticking over while our heads were buried in redesigning the Berliner. Georgina – universally known as George – had never worked in comment or online, but she had prodigious energy, was an inspiring editor and had the sort of political instincts that instantly saw the point of broadening debate to the widest number of participants.

She set herself 12 weeks to get our own opinion site launched. Like *HuffPost* it would encourage a far wider range of voices than were to be found in traditional print sections. This would be nothing like the old talkboards, where readers chatted away on any subject of their choosing. This would be a pro–am meeting place of journalists, experts and readers. She moved upstairs to be with the tech dev team on the fifth floor. They decided to name their endeavour after C.P. Scott's famous dictum in the *Manchester Guardian* centenary essay of 1921: 'Comment is free, but facts are sacred.'

Comment is Free, it was. CiF for short.

The site launched on a propriety word-processing platform, Movable Type. Later in her life (she died, tragically early, from cancer at 53) George recalled that period of almost manic activity: 'I literally just emailed everybody. I talked to all the existing columnists, who were all really suspicious. I remember one said to me, "How can we have all those voices? I'm your authority on this." We had no comment policy, we initially had no moderators, we just had nothing at all in place. It was a bloody nightmare, practically gave me a heart attack.'

Internally, it was not an overwhelmingly popular move – at least on the first four floors. Some thought it would dilute the brand to have any old Tom, Dick or Harriet writing commentary pieces for the *Guardian*. And not all existing commentators were thrilled to learn there would be comments underneath all opinion pieces.

The start was anarchic. The site launched on 14 March 2006. Initial quality control was low; the moderation team was not prepared for the level or response; the editors commissioned far too much; the site had obsessions and flaws. We hadn't quite worked out how best to display the everyday 'amateur' columnists in relation to the 'professionals'. How could we coax internal voices to engage with the responses 'below the line'?

But something radical was happening – yet another lesson about the nature of the great disruption.

In the traditional world of commentary a few preached to the many. I looked at the *NYT* commentary team with envy: nearly every one of them wrote like a dream and had interesting things to say. Most of them were middle-aged, white, middle-class journalists living in the same place, it was true; but any newspaper would have been pleased to employ any one of them. Had the internet not happened life would have gone on.

But the internet did happen and the old ways were not the only ways. For example, Thomas Friedman was – still is – the *NYT*'s foreign affairs commentator, and very good he is, too. He'll write at a moment's notice about China, the Middle East, Europe, Korea, Castro, Rwanda, Japan, Beirut, Iceland, India, Putin or Venezuela. He can do climate change, energy, water, genocide, hunger, disease,

war, globalisation, labour, transport, trade or security without changing into second gear.

HuffPost – and now the *Guardian* – were trying something different.
They said: wouldn't it be nice to hear a variety of voices instead of just
one? What about an Indian writing about India? A Palestinian and an
Israeli instead of the view from 8th Avenue, New York, or Farringdon
Road, London? Make that more nuanced still: a Palestinian from the
West Bank and a Hamas sympathiser from Gaza; and perhaps add in a
settler, a Peace Now activist or a Likudnik from West Jerusalem or
Tel Aviv.

Print couldn't do that, of course: not enough space. And, by and
large, print didn't want to do that. Mostly, big newspapers employed a
small cadre of columnists to opine. Good writers almost became mini-
brands themselves, with devoted followings. Many of them – especially
political writers – tended to be 'top down' most of the time: that is, they
would explain the thinking, intrigues, schemes, dreams and problems
of leading politicians to their readers.

CiF was intended to complement that approach with more diffuse
voices, some of them more bottom-up. The key word was 'complement'. There was a lot of time spent reassuring colleagues we weren't
trying to abandon columns by paid (sometimes highly paid) professionals. It didn't have to be either/or. It could be both.

Everyone knew there was a problem with diversity in newspapers. The
'white, middle-class, middle-age' thing at the *NYT* was no worse than
the commentary teams – never mind the newsrooms – at the *Washington
Post*, or *Wall Street Journal* or the *Guardian* or *Times* or *Telegraph*.

It was quite a difficult problem to fix at a time of declining head-
counts, especially with a union-enforced, no-compulsory-redundancy
agreement. Clearing out dead wood to hire large numbers of people
from differing backgrounds was not then an option. But creating a new
website for multiple voices was a quick and highly effective way of
giving a mainstream platform for voices who were seldom heard.

An early example was encouraging a variety of Muslim voices to be
published in CiF. Mainstream papers in the UK had, off the top of my
head, just one regular Muslim opinion writer – Yasmin Alibhai-Brown,

who described herself as a Ugandan-born 'leftie liberal, anti-racist, feminist, Shia Muslim'.

CiF was launched just eight months after the 7 July suicide bomb attacks in London which had killed 52 people and injured 700. Three of the bombers had been the British-born children of Pakistani immigrants. The attacks were followed by a prolonged period of soul searching as to what could explain such dreadful murderous intent within the minds of young British men.

George and another columnist, Madeleine Bunting, had assembled a group of young Muslims to try to answer the questions that followed. What were the consequences of an increasingly assertive Muslim political identity in Britain? If multiculturalism was no longer an appropriate term to describe Britain's increasing diversity – discredited with key constituencies – then what could be put in its place? How do you develop habits of belonging and national identity – the essential lubricant of modern societies – alongside diversity? What is to be the relationship between religious and ethnic identity?

This was a debate which was not really happening in the media at the time – at least not involving Muslims themselves. It was complex: it didn't lend itself to soundbites. It had become too stratified: some of it was in the language of academia, which could, at its most abstruse, have little wider resonance. Who was listening carefully to the voices on the streets, in homes, in mosques and schools?

Who got to mediate those voices was important. Some on the British left had deeply ingrained secularist instincts which did not always make them the best interpreters of the signals from Muslim communities. The uglier manifestations of an isolationist right wing were no more help.

We received some funding from the Barrow Cadbury Trust to give a platform to 100 young Muslims to debate these issues – which we covered extensively in the paper. That also gave us a database of voices to whom we could turn over subsequent months and years.

In time George launched microsites within CiF, one of which, CiF Belief, explored issues of faith in even more depth. For a year we had one writer, Ziauddin Sardar, a London-based writer and scholar, blogging the Qur'an.[8] He introduced it like this:

These blogs are a continuation of my struggle with the meaning
of the Qur'an. They explore what the Qur'an means to me – here
and now. I want to share what I understand and think of the
Qur'an as a dynamic text, of whose relevance and implications
for our time we have hardly scratched the surface. And, of course,
that means reflecting on the thinking and ideas of other Muslims
and non-Muslims as well.

What Muslims make of the Qur'an, the meaning and significance they derive from it, is important not just for Muslims but
for everyone. Look around you. Notice just how many conflicts,
how much strife, is generated around the world based on what
Muslims think they are reading in the Qur'an. Everyone is
affected, directly or indirectly, by how the Qur'an is read and
understood.[9]

The Qur'an – the understanding of which, as Sardar, said was so crucial –
had never been dissected or discussed in such subtlety and depth in a
mainstream publication in Britain before.

George hit the ground running, with the exuberance and energy of
someone who spent their downtime doing black skiing runs in the Swiss
Alps. The quality in the early days was variable. She acknowledged
after a few months that she was commissioning far too much – 2,800
pieces and 72,000 comments in three months. But, within a year, there
had been a few thousand voices on the *Guardian* site who would never
have been heard before. It was a lively, buzzing, disputatious, sometimes anarchic, sometimes worrying, often uplifting space.

The site covered sexual politics, gender, identity, socialism, the
Middle East – perhaps too exhaustively – food security, civil liberties (a microsite edited by Henry Porter)[10] and much more. Some of
the below-the-line responses were middling-to-ugly. Others were
marvellous. At one point Madeleine Bunting started a thread about
the Enlightenment – something that preoccupied her as she thought
about the place of faith in society. It was difficult to think of another
public space where you could have so many startlingly well-informed people arguing in such an engaged and civilised way about

such an important subject. One American web expert, familiar with the general tone of blogging in his own country, said: 'Believe me, your site is like the Oxford Union.' He meant that nicely.

For every piece above the line there would be dozens, sometimes hundreds – occasionally thousands – of comments below the line. This felt like what the web was destined to be: the polar opposite of the old world in which a reader would compose a letter in the hope it might catch an editor's eye. This was the democratisation of opinion.

Or was it? The resident writers couldn't decide. The CiF editing team would urge them into the comment threads. Some dipped their toes in. Some plunged straight in the deep end. Others stood suspiciously by the side not sure they wanted to take part.

For some it was philosophical. 'The world has always been divided between the Club and the Mob,' one veteran columnist, channelling de Tocqueville, said over lunch one day. 'I'm afraid I'm on the side of the Club.'

For others there was simply no time. How could they possibly do their research, read and talk to people – let alone write – if they had to spend half a day in not-very-fruitful conversations with readers?

Some loved it. They found a new, easy tone of voice – the opposite of the conventional 'columnar' timbre – and would spend hours in their threads chatting away.

Some were put off by the aggression, ignorance and spite they encountered in the threads. We might have wished for an elegant Socratic dialogue, but the responses could sometimes feel more like graffiti.

'Think about your own tone of voice,' Emily or George would sometimes tell disheartened or dismayed columnists. 'Can you see how you yourself sound? Your own stridency or aggression is bound to provoke an equal and opposite response.'

Some listened, and moderated their voice – writing a little less as if from the secular pulpit. If this was supposed to be a more conversational medium then maybe they themselves should find a more conversational tone. That often worked. Those who did go into threads with the 'right' voice often found that the comments immediately calmed down and improved.

That led to thoughts about the form of the column. In print, columnists usually wanted to write long: there was much turf warfare over who got 1,100 words to play with rather than 700 words down page. On screen the positioning mattered less. In an age of search and social, the readers would find you. And long was rarely an advantage over short. Wikipedia dates the coining of the acronym tl;dr ('too long; didn't read') to 2003.[11]

Enter a new skill into newsrooms: the moderator − usually a young person, not long out of college, who had aspirations to work in journalism. To begin with, one 'mod' could just about read every word both above and below the line, to keep it legal, more or less decent and more or less truthful.

But as the site prospered so the number of comments multiplied to the extent it became impossible for one person to read them all. We tripled the number of mods, but still they couldn't keep up. The larger the site got, the less it felt like a coherent community.

The rise of search and social was one factor. Fewer and fewer people came to the *Guardian* front page and navigated their way through the website to the comment section. They were more likely to come straight to the article page, referred by someone or something else. Some barely registered they were on the *Guardian*; even if they did, they might not know much about the paper's politics or traditions. Some knew all too well and − at least, it felt this way − came along deliberately to troll the liberals.

We did a very rough analysis of the quality of comments across ten different threads early on. We scored two thirds of them as four star, only 2 per cent as five star (out of five). A further 6 per cent were no stars, 17 per cent three stars, and the rest were ones and twos.

But the quality varied from subject to subject. If you were writing about economics, culture or science you might have quite a reasonable discussion. If it was about feminism, or Israel/Palestine or Islam or immigration then the threads could soon turn ugly. As with the earlier experiment in talkboards, it didn't take long for *Guardian* readers to believe this was 'their' space. Anything that looked like interference or editing was denounced as 'censorship'.

Some of the readers tried to coach us in the way the new world worked. We were (they said) still hung up on control, because that's where we came from – 200 years of being in charge. The internet wasn't about control. If you don't like the new rules, don't play.

Soon, even three mods couldn't hope to read everything, so we switched to a flagging system whereby any reader could refer anything that looked offensive or libellous. The mods' job became firefighting – whacking trolls wherever they cropped up.

These problems weren't unique to the *Guardian*, but the nature of CiF placed us at the sharp end of what everyone was having to learn – and quickly. No one had previously tried anything like this on a mainstream newspaper website at this scale. The more we grew – and we were growing quickly on both sides of the Atlantic and elsewhere – the more pressing the questions became.

Should we demand real names? Possibly, but how could you ever be sure that you had truly determined someone's true identity? And what about the valuable contributions from people who might, for perfectly good reasons, prefer anonymity?

A lot of commenters were blogging from work. We were already surfacing numerous telling first-person accounts from people who would be in deep trouble personally or with their employers if they used their real names. There were, for instance, doctors or nurses who were forbidden from talking about their work, but who gave fascinating insights into the running of the NHS.

I was open to persuasion on anonymity. I didn't think of it as a 'right' in the way some digital evangelists did. It was difficult to think of many other areas of public discourse in democracies where people demanded the right to take part in public debate anonymously. If we (the hated mainstream media) were so often blasted for lack of transparency, why didn't the same standards apply to the online brigade?

I also had some sympathy with my colleagues who were reluctant to take part in asymmetrical debates with external critics, nearly all of whom – whether out of shyness, cowardice or convention – wouldn't themselves break cover.

If we were gently nudging some writers to adopt a different tone in online conversations, shouldn't the reverse be true, too? Wouldn't some commenters speak in a different way if they knew they would be held accountable for what they said?

Should we make them pay to comment? We considered it, but rejected it because at that point we feared it would limit the debate.

Should we ban repeat offenders permanently? We began with a yellow/red card system (from soccer) in which someone breaking the community rules would be warned, and then banned for a while. But determined trolls could game this by re-registering with an alternative identity. We would need more sophisticated technology to make this work.

Should we move to pre-moderation? We did with some threads, but this involved a huge workload for the mods and raised new legal issues. The law, as it was developing, gave a publisher some protection if they moved quickly to amend or remove a comment that had been drawn to their attention. If you vetted material in advance of publication you assumed a greater legal responsibility for the posting because it implied some sort of endorsement. Did we trust 23-year-old mods to make fine judgements about defamation or to be sufficiently attuned to language around Israel/Palestine?

It seemed inevitable that we would have to hire more moderators – maybe many of them. At one point – inspired by talking to Jimmy Wales, the founder of Wikipedia – we toyed with the idea of training an army of *Guardian* readers to be volunteer (or even paid) moderators. The union wrinkled their noses.

There still seemed mileage in a 'traffic light' system of ranking users by quality or, alternatively, nuisance value. Reddit had devised a system of notional 'rewards' granting greater or lesser visibility. On Reddit offensive or pointless posts became hard to find, but didn't disappear altogether.

We moved on to a new proprietary commenting system, Pluck, and tried 'staff picks' whereby a writer, mod or editor could indicate some kind of endorsement. We also tried allowing anyone registered on the site to 'pick' or share any posting. Some of it had some effect . . . at the margins.

From time to time our own columnists would write critically about this experiment in democratising comment. After five months Jackie Ashley, a political writer, bemoaned the lack of civility, and continued:

When it comes to blurring the lines between amateurs and professionals, I'm beginning to feel like one of a dying generation. When I grew up, eminent columnists like Bernard Levin or T.E. Utley[12] would hand down their views on tablets of stone before heading off to their club for lunch. They rarely, I imagine, had to defend those views to scores or even hundreds of correspondents. Inevitably, that journalistic elite, like other elites, has crumbled, and a good thing too. It's a huge advance that, thanks to the internet, columnists can now engage immediately with a large community of correspondents.

What I will say in defence of professional columnists is that most of us have years of experience covering, say, politics, social policy or international affairs. We listen to the speeches, we attend the seminars, we read the paperwork and we talk to the experts . . . at length. There will always be those who know much more about a subject than a columnist. And equally there will always be those who think they know much more. I'm delighted to hear from both: just so long as you make proper arguments and don't call me a fucking stupid cow.

Jonathan Freedland, a marvellous columnist who sometimes suffered anti-semitic abuse in the comment threads, was also among those disturbed. He wrote a private note to me:

There are four key worries about this stuff.

First, no one wants to give a mainstream platform to ideas which used to surface only in the inky newsletters of the far right.

Second, this is bad for our staff and contributors. I'm told that the regular columnists are almost unanimous in their feelings about writing for CiF: they don't enjoy it, even dread it, gritting their teeth as they brace themselves for the bruising that follows. This is one reason why so few writers join the threads on their own pieces. (Few writers like to say this out loud, but most admit privately that the constant barrage of personal attacks – describing journalists' work as crap, demanding they be sacked, etc. – does, after a while, erode their self-confidence, to the point when many avoid even reading the comment threads, lest it bring their spirits down.)

Third, this can't be good for our readers. Many are surely put off entering what seems an unpleasant space to be, the very opposite of our goal in this new, social era of the Web. Not many people, and still fewer *Guardian* types, want to hang out in a place where angry, white guys – and, while this may well change in due course, that seems to be the profile of much of the blogosphere just now – hurl invective at each other and anyone who strays before them.

Fourth, and perhaps most seriously, I worry that this stuff, even if statistically only a small portion of the material on the site, is badly contaminating the *Guardian* brand, linking our good name and liberal history to attitudes of which we would want no part and which can only damage our reputation.

Another columnist, Andrew Brown, wrote to me, also privately, in 2010, when the problem of trolling was getting worse, not better. He alluded to Teresa Nielsen Hayden, an American science fiction editor who had had some experience as a moderator:

> You know the theory that one of the things you have to do to keep communities from falling into crime is to fix the broken windows? The same thing happens on a website. When people first come into it, they look around and they see what's happening there, and if they have any sensitivity at all, they will moderate their behaviour to suit what's going on. If you let things get started in such a way that it looks like an uncivilized frontier, then people will feel justified in behaving badly. That will drive off exactly the people you'd rather have around, while it encourages more bad behaviour.

Brown wasn't arguing against mutualisation – he thought it probably essential to the *Guardian*'s long-term survival. He just didn't think we were doing it particularly well.

Then there was the perpetual fear of new kids on the block, ready to take bleeding chunks out of what we were doing. They were certainly doing it commercially . . . and editorially. New players were springing up to cover sport, arts, finance, listings, travel, food and drink, fashion – all essential parts of the newspaper bundle.

The unbundling was happening, and it felt quite urgent to make sure that we defended the core of what we did – even if it was also the least remunerative bit. We had to make sure commentary and politics weren't similarly carved out by others. We watched it happen in Washington the following year, when two *Washington Post* executives walked out to start Politico – a website specialising in politics, both nationally and internationally. At the last count it employed 500 staff, including 350 reporters in the US and Europe. It had 26 million unique visitors to its US website and a further 1.5 million to Politico.eu.

As a deterrent we largely succeeded. CiF may have been scrappy and raw to begin with. It never quite grappled the issues of community moderation to the ground; it was hardly alone in that. But it was successful enough to make sure that no one – to date – has successfully managed to move in on the political commentary space in the UK in a threatening way.

There have been many determined attempts at the UK market, including really good websites such as Open Democracy, the *New Statesman*, Buzzfeed and Politics.co.uk. Any of those could have established themselves as one of the main commentary forums in the UK. The *Huffington Post* did not launch *HuffPost* UK until July 2011 – perhaps, in part, because we had occupied the space they had pencilled in for themselves. By then we had a much better idea of what we were doing.

As for the *Huffington Post*, by then owned by AOL, it comfortably overtook the *NYT* in terms of traffic in June 2011 – just six years after launch. A provocative tweet from an AOL executive crowed: 'Six years to disrupt 100 years.'[13]

12

The Money Question

Deathwatch or powderpost beetles infest hardwood, where, barely detectable, they can remain for years. The structures look sound – but have been hollowed out from within and, if you're really unlucky, turn to dust.

Around 2005 Simon Waldman came back from one of his regular trips to the West Coast to tell the Guardian Media Group Board about deathwatch beetle. He told them about Craig Newmark, a 52-year-old web enthusiast and Leonard Cohen fan from San Francisco, who was, he said, singlehandedly destroying the American newspaper industry.

The Board listened attentively. Simon flashed up a slide of Newmark – an affable-looking geek. The website looked like nothing. Newmark hadn't employed expensive typographers or designers. There was no editorial content at all. It grew and grew as a site that did one simple thing well: a place to exchange information. You could buy or sell a house, a boat, a guitar. You could find a job, a babysitter, a boyfriend or a motorcycle.

It's what newspaper classified advertising sections did. That's what kept the lights on.

The difference with Craig Newmark was that – for the vast majority of advertisements – his noticeboard was completely free. That's free to both sides – buyer and seller. This, as a business model, was hard to beat. But for Newmark, it had proved so successful he was now operating in 190 cities and carried 6 million advertisements at any one time.

Newmark (continued Simon) did charge a few people a small amount of money. In New York he charged 25 bucks for a job ad that would cost between $672 and $954 in the *New York Times*. He was slowly spreading his operation around the world. Simon showed the Board the basic site for Craigslist, Manchester, England.

One or two Board members sat up. The *Manchester Evening News* (*MEN*) had – since back in the days of C.P. Scott – helped support the *Manchester Guardian* – and still did. The classified advertising ensured the evening paper produced healthy profits – even in the early part of the twenty-first century.

How did Craigslist survive? Here was Simon's killer slide – a picture of the Craigslist HQ in San Francisco, a little, battered nineteenth-century clapboard house just big enough to accommodate 18 desks – i.e. the entire staff.

Newmark had turned down many offers to sell his stock or float the company. He was not interested. His two aims in his professional life were to use the internet to provide a public space for others to use – and to pay the salaries of his 18 members of staff.

The model was, in every way, the opposite of the *New York Times*, which the previous September had announced it was cutting 500 jobs – or 4 per cent of its overall payroll. Simon's next slide: Newmark's modest little office side by side with the *New York Times*'s new Renzo Piano-designed 52-storey skyscraper headquarters opening soon on Eighth Avenue.

Some journalists estimated Newmark's annual turnover was little more than $10 million. But then, $10 million went quite a long way between 18 people.

I looked at my fellow Board members. Were they thinking what I was thinking? Shouldn't we sell the *Manchester Evening News*? Immediately?

Intuitively we – or some of us – had known this was going to happen for the past ten years – ever since I had been in the *Chicago Tribune* newsroom watching classified advertising photos of house interiors download agonisingly slowly. It was obvious it was going to happen. But maybe we thought we would do it in our own time and in our own way. Now, we had our very own deathwatch beetle hollowing out our company from the inside.

But the GMG Board was not in the mood to sell. The *MEN* was still producing a decent cashflow and, in their collective opinion, would continue to do so. Somehow, we persuaded ourselves, there was life in print yet. The *MEN* was then selling 140,000 copies;[1] we experimented with giving away 50,000 free copies into the city centre to boost circulation. That didn't work. We launched – and closed – Channel M, a local TV operation based in the newsroom. That didn't work either. We tried launching a classified advertising site, Fish4jobs, in collaboration with other local newspaper publishers. That didn't do the trick either.

We were not alone in not cashing in while we could. Around the same time similar conversations would have been happening in the boardroom at Associated News – publisher of the *Daily Mail*, but also the owner of the Northcliffe chain of local newspapers. Like us, they refused to believe the problem was as bad as the doom-mongers were saying. In 2006 they turned down £1 billion for Northcliffe Media – eventually selling it six years later for £53 million in cash and a 39 per cent stake in another (doomed to decline) local newspaper company, Local World Ltd.[2]

By the time GMG finally got round to selling the Manchester paper – plus assorted weeklies in the region – in 2010 it got just £7.4 million in cash. Trinity Mirror, the purchaser, also agreed to waive GMG from a £37.4 million print contract.[3]

It was sad eventually to sever ties with the *MEN*. Many great *Guardian* figures had cut their teeth there and there was a strong sentimental link. But this new world didn't encourage sentiment. The *Guardian* was in a small life raft of its own. If (as seemed probable) the *MEN* was going to struggle to make a living in future it would be better off with a larger mother ship – and Trinity Mirror was a much, much larger ship than the *Guardian*.

*

If readers wouldn't pay and advertisers wouldn't advertise where did that leave us? There were always siren voices insisting that paywalls were a universal panacea. One or two notable newspapers were, in time, to reap benefits from closing off their journalism to all except those willing to pay. Similarly, there were multiple examples of others trying them and failing. One GMG director, John Paton, was not a fan, having been CEO of media companies in four different countries and run the number two newspaper group in the US. He tried putting up 75 paywalls across the US and came to the conclusion that – at least then – they didn't work. They collected less than $1 million in revenue on newspaper sales/subscription revenues approaching $300 million. Some of those companies that were – in his view – running 'paywalls' were in fact running them as a way of increasing the subscription price of the home-delivery option. The price of news went up X per cent to the punter but 'included' unlimited access to the website. For that to be valid there had to be a paywall. Paton found that this kind of packaging did add substantial revenue for about 18 months . . . until it cycled upon itself and then decline continued.

His conclusion: 'Short-term thinking and zero planning for the future.' The GMG Board agreed.

People kept making comparisons with the music industry. People would pay for news, they insisted. But people had never paid for news – in the sense that their contributions had never been sufficient to fund a fully staffed broadsheet news operation.

Until the early nineteenth century news had been subsidised by politics. The newspaper historian Francis Williams traced how – in the wake of John Wilkes's victory for press freedom in the 1740s – newspapers found a new independence through taking advertising. 'The daily press would never have come into existence as a force in public and social life if it had not been for the need of men of commerce to advertise,' he wrote in *Dangerous Estate*.[4] 'Only through the growth of advertising did the press achieve independence.' A newspaper in the early nineteenth century had to derive at least half its income from advertising in order to survive.

It was the same in the US. Paul Starr, the historian of newspapers' development, put it like this: 'For the past three hundred years, newspapers have been able to develop and flourish partly because their readers have almost never paid the full cost of production. From the eighteenth century to the middle of the nineteenth century, many newspapers were politically subsidized, directly by governments or through political parties. Then, as consumer markets expanded, newspapers increasingly sold not just news to readers, but also readers to advertisers. And the more advertisers they gained, the less dependent they were on any single one.[5]

It was a qualified form of independence, as George Orwell acknowledged in his 1946 essay, 'Why I Write': 'All the papers that matter live off their advertisements, and the advertisers exercise an indirect censorship over news.' Noam Chomsky couldn't have put it better.

One of the hidden influences of advertising was that newspapers went in search of wealthier readers who would be of more interest to advertisers. Two economists, Fred Hirsch and David Gordon, explored how this worked in their 1975 book *Newspaper Money*: 'Newspapers are among the few products for which one buyer's money is not as good as another's in the eyes of the seller: 8p a day from a reader earning £5,000 a year is worth much more than 8p from a reader earning £2,000 a year, because a newspaper is not just selling its editorial product to its readers, but is selling its readers' incomes to advertisers.'

This created a pressure on newspaper managements to 'upgrade' the readership.[6] 'Safety today lies in the appeal to a cohesive socio-economic group, the more well-heeled the better.'

It was a type of filter bubble.

'Minorities with high spending power find themselves excellently catered for,' wrote Hirsch and Gordon (who, lest he sounds a trifle Marxist, later went on to run the *Economist*). 'Minorities who have less pull on advertisers find themselves neglected.'[7]

The *Guardian*'s problem in 1975, in the eyes of Hirsch and Gordon, was that it didn't have the advantages of high-income readers – the opposite of the *Financial Times*, which could print a tiny number of copies to a very select readership . . . and still make healthy profits.

More than 40 years later the position described by Hirsch and Gordon remained essentially true. If you had high-income readers your sums looked different. There was no one-size-fits-all economic model for news.

If you run the *NYT*, the *WSJ*, *FT* or *Times* today, you can – just as in the 1960s – create a 'club' of people who are mouth-wateringly desirable to advertisers.

One Saturday before Christmas 2016 I read the advertising in the *Times* and *FT* rather than journalism. Britain's political classes were still reeling from the vote to leave Europe – and the parallel decision of American electors to choose Donald Trump. There was much hand-wringing about the have-nots, the left-behinds and the one-percenters.

I turned the pages slowly to absorb the staggering value of the gifts that the *Times* and *FT* readers were being urged to buy for their loved ones, or, possibly, themselves. Some of the suggested potential merchandise came in the form of identifiable advertising, but there was a significant volume of accompanying editorial that carried the same message: splash out vast amounts of cash on these treats. And then there was the in-between content: stuff that, even to a reasonably experienced eye, could have been advertising or editorial.

If the *FT*'s *How to Spend It* magazine is a guide, the paper has readers who would not think twice before buying an £87,000 diamond-encrusted Richard Mille watch; or a Chopard Happy Diamonds timepiece for £36,000. The fashion writers suggest a Ganryu polyester dress for £2,275, or a Molly Goddard cowhide jacket for £3,000. La Perla handbags start at £3,600. Fendi mink jackets – this appears to be editorial, but could be an advertising feature – will set you back £9,850; a Gucci sequinned dress £5,000. The laminated plywood chair on which one model is sitting comes in at £14,500. There are yachts to charter for £8,500 a night.

Denim jackets for these *FT* readers are not your average denim jacket. This one – again it is not quite clear if this is an advertisement or editorial – will cost you £2,400. It's laminated, too.

Still stuck for an idea for the man in your life? A regular *FT* writer suggests buying him a Linley eucalyptus cocktail bar, finished off in rose and white gold leaf. Yours for £130,000 (Linley advertises later in the magazine). Another *FT* writer tries out a new breed of road-going 'super bike' which is said to marry exceptional performance with exotic materials. If you're tempted by the Honda RC213V-S you will have to heat your garage to prevent it from corroding – and fork out £150,000 to buy it. The writer quotes one UK-based manufacturer of high-end bikes: 'This level of clientele is recession-proof.'

The *Times Luxx* magazine is in the same recession-proof league. Before reaching the index page you wade through adverts for Vuitton and Fendi handbags, Cartier watches, Gucci shoes, Tiffany bracelets, Tom Ford perfumes and Bulgari rings.

There are 11 named commercial staff listed as working for the magazine, along with 24 contributors and *Luxx* specialists covering beauty, boats, books, design, fashion, food, gardens, grooming, interiors, jewellery, men's style, motoring, property, technology, travel, watches and wine (two writers).

The editor's letter acknowledges that 2016 has been an 'unpredictable and unsettling year' – but that makes it 'all the more essential to celebrate what's good about the world today'. What unites the recommendations in this issue, he says, is 'passion, perseverance and pricelessness – pricelessness in the context of the price being irrelevant'. These are the sort of readers, it transpires, who regularly take their faces to the 'face gym' at lunchtime for a 'skin-tightening and brightening 24 karat workout' at £150 a go.

The fashion expert recommends ostrich-feather adorned jeans ('top of my lust list this season') for £1,200. The jewellery specialist has gasped when the chairman of a diamond company shows her a £70 million stone he has recently bought. The watch specialist recommends eight watches, average price about £20,000. The property writer praises a new apartment block in Mayfair, London, for UHNWI ('ultra-high net-worth individuals'). They are likely to sell at £25 million each.

The motoring writer contemplates buying a Bugatti Chiron – prices start at £2.08 million – and test drives a £575,000 Aston Martin ('there is a healthy queue of eager buyers'). At the other end of the magazine from the Gucci adverts is a gentle interview with the 'fashion world's favourite CEO' – Marco Bizzarri of Gucci.

To be clear – the *Guardian* would have loved such advertising, and did its best to take some crumbs off the table. But the average annual income of a *Guardian* reader in 2016 was £24,000 – three nights on a luxury yacht or considerably less than most of the watches advertised in either the *Times* or the *FT*. Creating a similar small, select 'club' of *Guardian* readers couldn't possibly work, either for the revenues they could afford to pay or in terms of the advertising they could attract.

There was not going to be one business model for all newspapers. We were each going to have to find our own – in our case, probably unsupported by Bulgari or Bugatti.

★

So this was what we thought we knew around the middle of 2006.

- Newspapers were going to find their traditional revenues – particularly in classified advertising and, probably, in cover price – eaten into over coming years.
- Many newspaper managements would naturally respond by cutting costs. At the same time they would need to invest significantly in the digital future against the day when new technologies might determine future reading habits; and when significant amounts of advertising might well migrate to the internet.
- None of this would happen smoothly. There would be profound jolts along the way. We – and others – could expect to lose lots of money in the coming years if we had any chance of making the transition.
- In a rapidly converged world, newspapers would have to ask themselves whether they remained a purely text medium. And they were going to have to face the fact that younger readers, especially, were questioning previously accepted notions of journalistic authority.
- We would have to get used to the idea that audiences were fragmenting and that many people were increasingly finding non-conventional news sources a valuable addition, if not a ready substitute, for mainstream media.
- Newspapers had to decide how much they embraced these new forms of discourse and dissemination or whether they stood apart

from them. Should we be *of* the web, or simply on it?

- Thousands of websites would aggregate what we do, syndicate it, link it, comment on it, sneer at it, mash it up, trash it, monetise it, praise it and attempt to discredit it – in some cases all at once. We were going to have to be more transparent about what we did and earn trust in this new world.

- But it was hard to see that many would actually go to the risk and the expense of setting up a global network of people whose only aim was to find things out, establish if they're true, and write about them quickly, accurately and comprehensibly. The blogosphere, which was frequently parasitical on the mainstream media it so remorselessly critiqued, couldn't ever hope to replicate that. That – assuming people remained interested in serious news – should give us a huge advantage.

- Against that, the digital world could do many things much better than we could currently do – including niche fragmentation, multimedia, voice, diversity, connectivity, range, scale, speed, responsiveness and community.

- Our cost base was simultaneously our best protection and a mill stone around our necks. Between them the *Guardian*, *Observer* and Guardian Unlimited employed well over 600 journalists, more than two dozen of them based around the world. That was half the size of the *NYT* and a tenth the size of the BBC, but still a significant investment in serious journalism. We could be sunk by our cost base, or it could make what we did difficult for others to replicate.

- No internet start-up on earth would ever contemplate such an investment in expensive, non-commercially productive people. The Yahoos and Googles of this world were explicit: they had no interest in creating content. They did, however, want to do interesting things with other people's content. That could be good for us. Or it might not. Google could be our friend or our enemy. Or both.

- We could not survive into a newspaperless future as a UK-only news company. The audience simply wasn't rich enough or large enough to support us – and an advertising-supported operation could only work if we could deliver much larger numbers.

- That meant taking our non-British readers more seriously. We would, in particular, have to expand our North American operation.
- There could be no hope of trying to build a US audience with a paywall.

It wasn't the most hopeful snapshot of the future, but by now we had enough people in the building who more or less agreed on the same vision of where we were heading.

The new managing director, Tim Brooks, took to quoting Charles Dickens in his internal presentations: 'It was the best of times, it was the worst of times.'

And then came Facebook.

13

Bee Information

Facebook had started life in 2004 while some of us we were deeply mired in rethinking print: it was opened up to general users on 26 September 2006. At that point it had about 10 million regular users – a seventh the size of the more successful MySpace. The launch made a few hundred words in the *Guardian*.

Looking back now I hear the words of Clay Shirky, the NYU academic and economist who has consistently and incisively blogged about the disruption of news.

'That is what real revolutions are like. The old stuff gets broken faster than the new stuff is put in its place. The importance of any given experiment isn't apparent at the moment it appears; big changes stall, small changes spread. Even the revolutionaries can't predict what will happen.'[1]

A few months after Facebook moved up a gear I found myself on a platform with Mark Zuckerberg[2] in Davos, with the biggest cheeses from venerable old-world media companies. All the chatter was about Murdoch, who was also there, and his purchase for $580 million of MySpace.[3] Tom Glocer, CEO of Reuters, talked about Murdoch's acquisition as the tipping point when the business world finally woke up and took notice. They thought: 'This isn't just my kids any more, this is real business.'

Murdoch's big 'I get it' speech to the American Society of Newspaper Editors in 2005 had been, in some ways, touchingly honest. It admitted he had to try to apply a digital mindset 'with no first-hand experience dealing with [it]'. He now realised that younger generations 'don't want to rely on the morning paper for their up-to-date information. They don't want to rely on a God-like figure from above to tell them what's important.'

Also on the panel was Arthur Sulzberger Jr, the publisher of the *NYT*. He looked a little in awe of Zuckerberg, who said not very much and looked generally bemused to be there. He was 22.

A few months later Facebook was still with us, growing at 3 per cent a week, with a commentator on Mashable predicting on 10 June that Facebook would win out over MySpace: 'Facebook is just starting to become popular (well, popular with those who were not on it when it was limited to schools). So, you might want to check it out, while it's still cool.'

Who didn't want to be cool? I joined Facebook nine days later, with four initial friends. I couldn't see that it had anything to do with the news business; but if we were to try to understand the eco-system of information all around us, it seemed important to hang out there a bit.

Many employers were banning social media at work, complaining about the distraction and time wasted. We decided to do the opposite: we made it compulsory for all heads of department to sign up. With various degrees of reluctance they complied. We bombarded them with messages and links. My daughter messaged me at the end of the first month: 'You are a Facebook bore.'

It was true.

Shirky would describe much more coherently the scale of what was happening in his 2008 book, *Here Comes Everybody*: 'When we change the way we communicate, we change society. The tools that a society uses to create and maintain itself are as central to human life as a hive is to bee life . . . The hive is a social device, a piece of bee information technology that provides a platform, literally, for the communication and co-ordination that keeps the colony viable. Individual bees can't be understood separately from the colony or from their shared, co-created environment. So it is with human networks.'

Fine, but what had that got to do with journalism?

Shirky's book would have a few pointers. 'For people with a professional outlook,' he wrote in Chapter 3 ('Everyone is a Media Outlet'), 'it's hard to understand how something that isn't professionally produced could affect them – not only is the internet not a newspaper, it isn't a business, or even an institution.'

'There was a kind of narcissistic bias in the profession; the only threats they tend to take seriously were from other professional media outlets, whether newspapers, TV or radio stations.' Professions existed, he said, because there was a scarce resource – one that required specialisation; but 'the professionals are often the last ones to see it when that scarcity goes away. It is easier to understand that you face competition than obsolescence.'

He had a deadly phrase to describe a printed newspaper – 'a merely provisional solution'. He spelled the problem out bluntly: 'The Web didn't introduce a new competitor into the old eco-system, as *USA Today* had done. The Web created a new eco-system.'

He termed the new system 'mass amateurization'. The question media companies were going to have to answer was: 'What happens when the cost of reproduction and distribution go away? What happens when there's nothing unique about publishing anymore, because users can do it for themselves?'[4]

Shirky's book had little to say about Facebook: it was too new. He was more impressed by the 'wildly successful' MySpace.

Editorially, our own writers were far from convinced that Facebook would work.

One leading technology columnist was pretty dismissive about the very thing we were trying to get on the radar of our senior editorial team: 'Facebook . . . looks like the triumph of hope over experience. If I were Facebook's owners, I'd try and flog it to Yahoo while there's still time. Then I'll cancel my membership and move on to something more interesting.'[5]

Rupert Murdoch obviously thought the same. Asked if he might consider buying it in October 2007 he said, 'We're going in slightly different ways. They [Facebook] are more of a utility – I won't say a phone book – for friends to connect with each other,' and described MySpace as more 'cultural'.

Asked to comment on speculation that Facebook might already be worth $10 billion he was dismissive: 'What it really does is it tells you that News Corp is totally under-priced.'[6]

By October 2007 Ofcom, the British media regulator, declared that a quarter of Britons were on social media 23 times a month – and were the most avid users in the world: 0.96 per cent of young people were using a social media account regularly. The front page of Technorati – the Google of the blogosphere – told us that it was now tracking 24.5 million blogs and 1.8 billion links.

Web 2.0 – the thing Emily had warned was going to take over the world – was now called social media.

The GMG CEO Carolyn McCall and I took another swing to the West Coast to see what was on the horizon. We dropped in on Flickr, the picture-sharing platform; on Yahoo; on Google; on Topix. net, a content aggregator in Palo Alto. We had drinks with the founders of Digg, a social recommendation platform; tea with Knight Ridder in San Jose; coffee with Real Networks and then on to Microsoft in Seattle.

So many people trying so many different things; vast sums of money in play; the speed of development; the seeming impossibility of picking who would be the next big thing and who, in a couple of months, would have shut up shop or sold out.

What we were doing had got us noticed on the West Coast: everywhere Carolyn and I went people wanted to know when we would do more in America and whether we could partner with them in any way. Of all the so-called dead-tree world, they felt the *Guardian* was doing more things right than wrong.

The Pulitzer prizes of the internet were called Webbies – devoted to rewarding the best of the 51 million websites now in existence. We'd won the 2005 Webby for the best newspaper website in the world – beating the *NYT* into second place. By 2006 there were 105 million websites to choose from. Once again, we won – this time beating the *Washington Post*. The pattern continued: in 2007, 155 million websites: we won again, *NYT* second. The *NYT* took it in 2008. We took it back in 2009, by which time there were 234 million websites in the world.

By 2018 there were more than 4 billion internet users and a billion and a half websites. That was the scale of the explosion in the parallel world.

The Webby trophies – supersized metal spring coils – were brought back from glamorous award evenings in New York. Upstairs on the digital floor they were greeted with champagne, cake and bunting. Down on the 'proper' newsroom floor it didn't count for much that we were apparently running the best newspaper website in the world. Their form of recognition came each year at a drunken evening at a West End hotel when the 'real' British Press awards were handed out. They were evenings of bitter rivalries; of tribal raucousness; of punches and epic hangovers.

We were, in effect, building two cultures under one roof and, as long as one didn't unduly threaten or impinge on the other, we could muddle through. For now.

Emily had been right about Web 2.0 – as no one was now calling it. It was all anyone in the US was interested in. The social web, social media. None of the terms being used to name or describe it captured the dramatic upheaval of the revolution we were now entering. It was as if someone had tried to summarise the effects of Gutenberg as 'distributed publishing'.

Social media was where the users, the money, the technology and the energy were swarming. And it left us quite confused about where a newspaper fitted in. Web 1.0 was 'I look'. Web 2.0 was 'I participate'. Newspapers were comfortable with 'I look'. They got that. It was new, but it was old.

But 'I participate' was something entirely different.

Most editors wanted to be in control. The one obvious thing about the social web was that no one was in control. Anyone could do, or say, anything. That might please free speech fundamentalists or anarchists, but was hardly cheering news to most journalists.

If you had assembled a hundred journalists back in the office and discussed with them the nature of the social web. It might have looked a little like this:

- 10 per cent: Habitual users in their personal and professional lives. *'It's so obviously the future, why can't we go faster?'*

- 30 per cent: Know a little about it and have played with it a bit personally, or have children who do. '*I'm quite excited about the possibilities, but can't really see the relevance to what we do.*'
- 20 per cent: Aware of it, but have not personally tried it much. '*Open to persuasion, but can't see where the money's going to come from.*'
- 30 per cent: Hostile to the idea. '*It's stupid, dumbing down. Have you seen the shit they write? Can we get back to doing what we do?*'
- 10 per cent: The world's gone mad. '*The editor's lost his marbles. We should get back to basics – and the sooner we charge people for everything we do online the better. Anything else is a waste of time.*'

How to bridge these two worlds: the white heat of West Coast innovation that would, very likely, sweep through our little patch and possibly overwhelm us – and the decent common sense of good colleagues who just wanted to go on producing their best work, paying their mortgages and bringing out a bloody good newspaper?

Conventional leadership might involve a charismatic figure raising a banner and inviting the troops to fall in line. That was never going to work here. These were journalists, ffs (as we didn't say then) – the most sceptical, independent-minded, professionally mistrustful, cynical and unimpressible group of individuals you could possibly assemble in any one room.

If you could persuade even half of them that a vision was worth trying you would be doing well. But even that half would be riven with doubts. Of course they would. I was riven with doubts, so was Carolyn.

We were a tiny media organisation trying to play in a massive league. We had peanuts to invest compared with most of the other players, new or old. We couldn't splash out half a million quid on something that, as it might or might not transpire, failed. Pocket money to Murdoch or the *NYT* or Associated News, but it would wipe us out. The *NYT* had, famously, bought the *Boston Globe* for $1.1 billion just as the internet began to catch on in 1993. Just 20 years later the paper was worth $70 million. That kind of misjudgement would have finished off the *Guardian*.

We would be wrong about some things, albeit necessarily on a much smaller monetary scale. How could it be otherwise?

You might, if you were lucky, persuade the newsroom to follow your instincts for a while. But what would they feel when, a few months later, you had to go back to them to admit things weren't quite how you'd seen them? In the West Coast culture of permanent revolution that was the new normal. In the old Fleet Street that was ball-aching incompetence.

There were some decisions that could not be dodged for much longer. Bluntly, which had priority: print or digital? To the digital sceptics it was a no-brainer. We might not have a huge readership, but there were still a few hundred thousand people prepared to part with money to read a newspaper over breakfast tomorrow morning. In what realm of twisted insanity would you give them – give them! – the story this afternoon? The lunatics were running the asylum.

To the digital evangelists it was also blindingly obvious – but for precisely opposite reasoning. Print was going to die, so you either had a digital future or you didn't. If a reader could read something this afternoon – on the BBC, on any other English language news site, or on the numerous websites springing up to cover the particular niche that interested them – why make them wait until tomorrow morning? You couldn't stop them reading other things. This was simply a strategy for making the *Guardian* totally irrelevant in the digital world. And since, one day, there would be no print world, you would slowly die of irrelevance.

★

Around this time a group of big shot West Coast entrepreneurs and angel investors announced they wanted to meet us. The Said Business School in Oxford had started something called Silicon Valley comes to Oxford (SVCO). The twenty or so entrepreneurs arrived in private jets: we caught the train from Paddington. We walked into a room with some legendary figures worth billions. They included Reid Hoffman, who'd started PayPal and LinkedIn and whose investments (Facebook, Airbnb, Flickr, Last.fm, etc.) would make him a billionaire several times over; and Biz Stone, fresh from starting Twitter with Jack Dorsey.

These people knew everything there was to know about machine data, crowdfunding, accelerators, acquisitions, digital cultures, systems and software. Google any of them and you'd be prompted 'net worth'. Some of them were rich enough to absorb the *Guardian*'s losses from their loose change.

We presented to them for 20 minutes or so in a private room under the signature ziggurat that jostles with the nearby supposedly dreaming spires on the Oxford skyline.

There was a pause. 'So why don't you close the newspaper?' one of them asked.

'Um, because lots of people still buy it? It brings in lots of cash. We wouldn't have a cashflow without it.'

One of them mentioned Kodak. This was the kind of conversation they would have been having when it was obvious digital was going to be the future of images. There would always have been the guy in the room saying, *But there's still money in film.*

'We can't do it,' we said. Certain we were right, and wondering if we were wrong.

One of them sighed, as if to say, *These people can't be helped.*

'Okay, then, what you have to do is give the digital team a clear instruction: their job is to kill the newspaper. You must tell them to do everything in their power to finish off the printed product as soon as possible.'

We shuffled in our seats. There was more sighing their side of the table. We had disappointed them. They liked reading the *Guardian*, but was this the best we could offer? We had a polite sandwich lunch.

We could tell they thought we were doomed.

★

Emily's Mad Pronouncements – mid-2007. Twitter would soon be one of the most significant news organisations in the world.

What?

She repeated herself. We could never compete with the scale, reach and immediacy of Twitter. We had better get used to it.

Twitter had been launched in June 2006. Emily Bell was on it by March 2007. It would be two-and-a-half years before I joined. It was just one more damn thing. There would be more. In ten years we had, or would, come to terms with Google (2002); YouTube (2006); Wikipedia (2001); the BBC iPlayer (2007); the iPhone (2007); Facebook (2006); Spotify (2009) and much more. There didn't feel like a gap in one's life for keeping track of millions of people giving tiny little updates on their lives.

Like Facebook, Twitter looked like a place for irritating people to share irritating things with other irritating people. The fact that X wanted to tell Y what film they'd seen that evening or what a delicious osso bucco they'd enjoyed afterwards didn't interest me and didn't, on the face of it, have much to do with news.

That's how weird this time was. You could intellectually understand some of what was happening. You could grasp that this was huge and transformative and would affect everything we did. And yet you could shrug when the latest new, new thing came along because . . . Because you still hadn't quite internalised it properly? Because half your head was still in the print world? Because there weren't enough hours in the day? Because a small part of you was still in denial?

Gradually the truth dawned that Twitter was, in some respects, a smarter version of Google, applying human intelligence, discernment and recommendation to the ordering of information in real time. The 18 million users (nearly 340 million active users in early 2018) created a network of people who would, in many cases, see things and report them. They would share, discuss, analyse, debunk, challenge and expose before most reporters had got their boots on.

Twitter would become an astonishing tool in a reporter's armoury. Formidable at distribution, aggregation and immediacy, it would greatly help the process of verification as well as spread falsehoods. It would be an indispensable marketing weapon. It would change the tone of public engagement and conversation, level the playing field between the voiced and the previously voiceless.

It would create a flatter society. There would be common conversations across geographies where none existed previously. It would speed the world up. It would have different news values from the agendas set by mainstream media. The power of hundreds of thousands of people articulating their own news values would wash back into newsrooms.

It would be used numerous times a day by the most powerful man on earth to speak directly to more than 50 million people.

It would change accepted notions of authority – who was an 'expert'; and of the value of the 'expert' in relation to the power of peer-to-peer authority.

It would prove to have a long attention span – the opposite of the received opinion. Once Tweetdeck became a standard window on reporters' desktops, journalists often discovered that their readers' appetite for a story lasted long after the moving searchlight of a newsroom had swept on.

It would become an agent of change. Companies and politicians rapidly learned to respect, even fear, the challenge of collaborative media. Increasingly, social media would disrupt conventional politics and transform the speed at which it happened. Twitter was bound to confront differing laws and practices relating to expression and speech.

All that became apparent the more it began to go mainstream.

As did the downsides. It was, obviously, not necessarily good at complexity – though it could link to complexity. It could be frustratingly reductive. It didn't patiently and painstakingly report, in the way a good news organisation still did. It was to some extent parasitical.

Wrongly used, it could create 'filter bubbles' in which those users who wanted to narrow their minds could simply reinforce their own echoing prejudices. It could be used by autocrats to undermine the truth as readily as it could be used to publish it. The full glare of the world's attention could focus on a single unstable piece of information. It could be distracting, indiscriminate and overwhelming. At its worst, it gave a megaphone to the mad, the bad, the haters, racists, trolls and misogynists. At its best it elevated and combined voices of real knowledge, humanity and wisdom.

Within six years of Emily's Mad Pronouncement that one day we would find it hard to rival Twitter, the *Times* of London announced that it could not possibly compete with the BBC and 'Twitter's 340 million correspondents around the world' – and would back off rolling news in favour of three digital updates a day.

Business model? Like everyone else in this new space it was reach before revenue. It was 12 years before Twitter[7] managed to post its first quarterly profit – $91 million (£65 million) – in the fourth quarter of 2017. By then it had lost more than $2 billion in total since its launch.[8]

Any legacy player with those kinds of figures and that sort of patience would long ago have been denounced as a basket case.

*

We had survived one advertising recession. The next one was just around the corner. The interlude between the two wasn't long . . . and it wasn't particularly sunny. In November 2006 Enders Analysis, the consulting firm used by many of the big corporates in the UK and beyond, issued a note on the decline of classified advertising in print and online. It began: 'The UK newspaper industry is engulfed in a perfect storm . . . Their only chance for survival, in our view, resides in a new operational model for the physical product, with new formats to sustain circulation and far lower costs.'[9]

Classified advertising in print was now in permanent decline: but there looked to be big opportunities online. News would have to become cheaper to produce. There would have to be less emphasis on 'hard news' and more on entertainment and syndicated features. An Enders chart showed newspaper circulations declining steadily through to 2028, by which time some of them were close to hitting the ground.

Enders noted that newspapers had been on a frantic buying spree trying to snap up ready-made websites that could make up for the decline in print advertising. Regional newspapers alone had splashed out £400 million in 18 months trying to get new footholds in car, property or jobs advertising. But they were ambivalent about the new opportunities – simultaneously reluctant to let go of a world in which they could charge £5,000 a page in favour of the £400 equivalent online.

In the US eBay had started in the classified advert business, publishing twice as many ads as 1,500 newspapers by 2001; five times as many by 2003 and 90 times as many three years later. Many newspapers were doing what the *Guardian* had tried with Workthing (by now deceased) – offering an additional range of services, including CV creation and curation.

Just as many newspapers were moving inexorably towards 'free' models, so Enders expected inexorable movement towards free-to-advertise models.

Scale was the issue. Only by going for reach could you make up for what Enders called the 'frightening disparity' between the yields in traditional and online media. It was still difficult to see how you could build a big enough online audience while simultaneously asking them to pay for the privilege. Quite a bit of print would follow that logic – with a mushrooming of give-away titles. For the moment, for general news, the online future looked as though it was bound to be free.

So many consultants, so much to keep abreast of.

The social web was the focus of the 2006 report by Mary Meeker, a Morgan Stanley venture capitalist whose annual pronouncements on digital media were treated as close to holy writ.

Murdoch's MySpace was singled out as a company of extraordinary growth. Mobile was a glimmer in the eye (8 per cent of global phone subscribers were on 3G). The fastest growing companies were the Web 2.0 websites. Wikipedia was up 100 per cent year on year; YouTube up more than 2,000 per cent. Companies with UGC – user-generated content – were moving to the top of the internet pack.

Penultimate slide: Facebook gets a small mention. One to watch.

★

Over at the *Telegraph* their political correspondent, Andrew Sparrow, wrote a perceptive memo to his bosses at the end of 2006 to tell them why journalism didn't get the net and how the *Telegraph* could regain its reputation for being a fair and comprehensive 'newspaper' of record.

Sparrow was a classic *Telegraph* reporter – at least as that role used to be defined: straightforward, quick, accurate, fair. He looked as old-school as they came: short back and sides; wore a suit and tie to work; had trained on a local paper in Wales and done his hard miles as a political reporter on the *Mail*. But he was, also, in his late thirties, something of an internet evangelist.

'Most of the stories that appear on newspaper websites read as if they have been written for a newspaper – which, of course, most of them have,' he wrote to his bosses. 'I don't think anyone has developed a perfect model for internet news reporting yet. But I think it is already obvious that internet users want their news delivered in a more personal and discursive manner.'

By contrast, Sparrow preferred political blogs, 'because they read as if they were written by someone passionately interested in politics, whereas most stories in newspapers don't'. But the *Telegraph* website was organised to give the impression that blogging was something journalists did as a sideline. Blogging would, he thought, eventually become the model for all internet reporting. Like Emily, he glimpsed the end of 'the story'.

He acknowledged his colleagues were reluctant to include links in their stories. 'Why reveal that the story, quotes and all, has been given to you on a plate?' The answer was simple: in the age of the internet any motivated reader was going to find that out anyway. In fact, if you were not adding value to the press release, why not just leave it at that: it's not like journalists haven't got enough stories to write in a day. Use links – including links to rivals. The *Guardian*, he noted, was the only paper that routinely told readers what's in the other papers.

The *Telegraph* should allow readers to respond to stories, not be herded into a separate 'Your View' section. 'One advantage is that it would make the paper fairer. Any individual or organisation wanting to "correct" a story would be able to do so . . . I would go further. I think *Telegraph* journalists should be encouraged to post comments on each others' articles if they have constructive criticism to make.'

It was an excellent memo[10], full of shrewd instincts about the way journalism was going. We poached him a year later to write a political blog for the *Guardian*, which soon became the essential one-stop-shop record of the day in Westminster.

I had never met Sparrow back in 2006, but his memo coincided with most of the things I felt about the way journalism was going to have to adapt.

But it was going to be very hard with the existing editing structures.

I was playing around with a new doodle.

The traditional newspaper production chain could be drawn like a funnel – a huge amount of material at the top of the drawing sifted and winnowed down to a relatively small and digestible trickle at the bottom.

The killer job on a newspaper was the news editor – the narrowest part of the funnel. Everything had to go past him/her. News editors worked ridiculously long hours, were hollow-eyed and – unless temperamentally quite unusually resilient – burned out worryingly rapidly.

But what Sparrow was describing – and what we were also imagining – was something in which individual journalists would be liberated to publish much more material much more often. Their copy couldn't, therefore, sit in a funnel waiting to pass through the single choke point of a news desk.

My doodle tried to imagine a different structure for a newsroom. I drew it as a number of circles. You might have a politics circle; a science/tech/environment circle; a media and culture circle; and so on. For newspaper stories, copy would go through the traditional funnel. But – as they filed repeatedly throughout the day – they could 'desk' their own copy.

Easy enough to draw. But what would it entail?

Would we allow anyone to publish directly to the web with no editing at all? Andrew Sparrow – if we were to be lucky enough to hire him – was wise, professional and accurate enough to be trusted to behave like a blogger and file directly. Wasn't he? In an age of speed and unparalleled competition were we going to insist on layers of copy-editing before Andrew could file his 20 or more blogged 'stories' in a day?

But if we allowed someone like Andrew to file directly, wouldn't they all want to do that? And then what would happen to quality control? Some of the best reporters were, to be brutal, not very good writers. Most reporters would concede that copy-editors had often saved them from embarrassment, small and large. What about legal issues?

Could we try a more dispersed newsroom, perhaps with a copy-editor per desk? Could we have more blogs, some of them using material written by outsiders? It was only going to be a matter of time before our commercial colleagues started wanting more video: that would, presumably, be centrally organised. We'd need a content management system that could juggle, track and co-ordinate all these multiple publishing events. We couldn't carry on living four floors apart.

But we didn't have enough physical space inside our cramped assortment of buildings up and down Farringdon Road to allow for any kind of logical re-arrangement of our copy-editing processes. How did we harmonise these two different models – centralised funnel and dispersed networks? And how did our sister Sunday paper fit into all this?

Was 'harmonise' even the right word? We didn't want to lose the raw edges of digital. Was 'integrate' a better word? Was it possible to fold digital into print, or vice versa? 'Converge'? That captured the ambition to bring together text, video, audio, graphics and interaction to create different style of narrative.

We had – by accident or design – ended up with a semi-integrated model. The *Washington Post* had far bigger headaches, having originally set up their online operation in an entirely different state – Virginia – largely for reasons of employment law.

But we had begun to create a 'mirror' news operation on the fifth floor – one that looked more like the Sparrow blueprint. Increasingly, they wanted to hire people who could file at the time and in the style they needed.

Four floors beneath them there were pockets of experimentation and pockets of resistance. One reporter called a union meeting because she had been asked to tweet the verdict of a trial she was covering. It was the thin end of the wedge.

The Guardian Unlimited team was unhindered by any of the trappings of legacy media – which was, doubtless, why we were growing enormously fast and winning global accolades. The bad thing was that costs were mounting as we replicated all the old roles on the fifth floor.

It was worse than that. We'd tried our best to shower the *Observer* with sufficient resources to build the level of circulation the Board felt would bring it to break-even. But, after a period of growth, the circulation stubbornly refused to budge against the much-better resourced *Sunday Times*. It was now haemorrhaging money.

So we had, in effect, three editorial teams. On a Saturday it wasn't unusual for a *Guardian*, *Observer* and Guardian Unlimited writer all to be covering the same football match. We would have three versions of a film review, three political commentaries, three takes on a running news story. A Sunday paper had little resource available for, or interest in, the digital world.

Two separately edited and proudly independent newspapers under one digital brand made for confusion among readers. Many readers were extremely puzzled to see wildly divergent views under the common Guardian Unlimited brand.

'Brand' was the sort of marketing-speak that made most journalists want to retch. But, stripped of jargon, it mattered. Some papers created an entirely different voice online – usually downmarket. The *Sydney Morning Herald* was one, the *Independent* (in latter incarnations) another. Mail Online – which was to become the biggest newspaper website in the world – had such a downmarket feel to it that the editor of the printed paper was forced to pretend it had nothing at all to do with him.

If you believed that, one day, the digital *Guardian* would be the *Guardian* for most, if not all, readers then – given the Scott Trust mandate – it was vital for the voice, spirit and values to remain the same.

But at the moment we were trying to do that with three different teams in three different locations and not enough money.

Something would have to give.

14

Creaking at the Seams

The *Guardian* had teetered on the brink between profit and loss for as long as anyone could remember. It had never been in its DNA to aim for huge margins. Every editor and business manager since Scott had instinctively understood this subtle balance between the mission and the money.

For much of its history there had had to be a form of subsidy available to the paper in case of rainy days, of which there were many. It was not unique in this. The *Times* could, in lean times, depend on the almost infinitely deep pockets of Murdoch. The *Independent* had a variety of sugar daddies. The *FT* would, at times, have struggled without Pearson and the *Economist*. Great swathes of the French press are now alive because of the profits of luxury goods, defence sales or finance deals.[1] The *Washington Post*, which now has the support of Amazon's Jeff Bezos, was, for many years, buoyed up by the Graham family's investments in the Kaplan Educational publishing business.

For decades, the *Guardian* had the *Manchester Evening News*. Now a new life raft for the *Guardian* developed in the most unlikely form: a second-hand car magazine.

AutoTrader had been founded in 1975 by a man called John Medejski, who subsequently bought Reading Football Club. Over 30 years it flipped in and out of ownership by assorted private equity and venture capital partners . . . and the Guardian Media Group.

The success of *AutoTrader* was based on proprietary software which sat on the computer terminals of most car dealers in the UK, giving them an easy-to-use system for creating advertisements to sell their stock. By the end of the twentieth century it was such a cash-generating beast that I sometimes felt every morning conference at the *Guardian* should begin with a quiet prayer to the gods of the used car dealer.

The more successful the company was, the more nervous we became. It would have to transition to digital, obviously: and it did. With a ruthless efficiency any newspaper would have envied, the magazine transformed from an entirely print business to an entirely digital business without losing a penny in revenue.[2]

But surely this would be its Achilles heel? Numerous online players eyed up its annual tide of profits and did their best to steal them. New entrants had managed it with property, travel and jobs. What was to stop them destroying *AutoTrader*? Over the years Murdoch, eBay, Google and others all had a go – and failed. By 2016 it was still making a clean £170 million profit on turnover of £281 million.

But by then we had exited in stages. Paul Myners, the larger-than-life former investment banker now chairing the GMG Board, devised the vision that would see us gradually wind down our interest in *AutoTrader* and use the consequent endowment to support the *Guardian*.

He called it the 'Wellcome Trust model' after the biomedical research charity created out of the profits of pharmaceuticals. Myners anticipated that we would, eventually, have a fund of around £1 billion. A sensible drawdown on that investment might be around 4 per cent a year. So GMG would be relaxed about a world in which the *Guardian* could 'lose' up to £40 million a year. It would be the ongoing Scott legacy to public-service journalism.

The Myners plan eventually created just that – a £1 billion endowment. But the intricacies of the ownership structure meant that it wouldn't be quite that simple in the short term. For the time being we'd have to keep some funds invested. We'd have to invest some other funds in another operating business in order to avoid huge tax charges. We'd need a modest cash sum to keep us going in the interim. All would (probably) be well, assuming the economy didn't completely tank.

The problem was that there was no cheap way of transitioning the newspaper business if nearly all the moving parts had to change. Someone compared the task of digital transformation to rebuilding a plane in mid-flight.

Most urgently, there was America to think about. Since 9/11 – without spending a cent on marketing – we had acquired 4 million unique users there: in June 2006 the US overtook the UK in terms of audience. Jupiter Research found Fox News and the *Guardian* were the fastest-growing news websites in the US.

Our total revenues from these 4 million users in 2005/6 had been precisely £73,000.

The message from the finance and advertising executives was clear: that we absolutely had to try to monetise these readers. Indeed, it was now clear that, without America, we couldn't make it in anything like the form that we existed today.

The market was so huge. The advertising budgets were so vast – $12 billion online in 2005 compared with $2.5 billion in the UK. Huge marketing resources would be shifting online over the next few years. If we could present agencies and clients with impressive enough numbers the money would surely follow. It was a big decision and was discussed at length, and agreed, by both operational Boards and the Scott Trust.[3]

The editorial pitch was that liberal America was not feeling well-served by its media at this point. The soul-searching of the domestic media after the Iraq war had not yet dissipated a widespread mistrust in the methods, ownership and views of many major American newspapers. There was a sense that the coastal progressives were on a keen look-out for like-minded spirits in the world.

At the time we had an editorial team of half a dozen in the US and virtually no commercial presence. The commercial team reckoned it was realistic to double the audience fairly quickly – and expected significant revenues to follow after a period of sunk investment. More losses short term: the prospects of significant gains long term.

Reach before revenue. Virtually the entire digital ecosphere was being constructed on this premise. If legacy businesses were going to insist on revenues before reach they would lose every time.

That was the theory.

Editorially it took a while to find our feet. Did we want an American who could learn what the *Guardian* stood for, or a *Guardian* person who could interpret the paper's values for America? The former *New Republic* editor Michael Kinsley and the political writer Michael Tomasky had got the site up and running, but the latter was continually frustrated that we weren't doing it with enough of a fanfare or enough resources.

He was probably right. But – though we would eventually have a certain cushion, thanks to our used car revenues – it was still nothing like the sums others could speculate. It would be some time before Guardian America found its voice, with a new editor sent from London, Janine Gibson.

The need for investment in newer, better, faster technology was never ending. We couldn't begin to monetise the American website without being able to geo-target users with the right stories and advertisements.

The developers in the building were intent on moving from a world where we were building web pages to a world where we were creating journalism which could then be distributed, via the web, on different platforms – including mobile, which we could distantly see coming over the horizon.

The plan was to build a content management system nicknamed R2, which eventually consumed 110 developers working in so-called agile teams in the basement of Farringdon Road.

The reporters two floors above them had little idea they were there. They didn't know that, currently, the website was hosted on (in the words of one developer) 'a pretty unpleasant bit of middleware' called Vignette. They didn't think about content management systems or APIs or taxonomy – how their stuff would be ordered or found or labelled.

Many of the best developers who wanted to work at the *Guardian* were attracted by the journalistic work we did; they could certainly earn better money elsewhere. They were, often, more idealistic about the nature of the enterprise than some of the journalists themselves. They truly believed in reporting as public service and wanted to find new tools to tell stories better.

They worked long hours and treasured any time snatched over beers with any reporters they could befriend. Some of the smarter journalists eventually began to see the point of them. I will never forget the look on a City reporter's face when a 22-year-old digital trainee built a widget that, in a couple of hours, completed a task for which he'd set aside three weeks.

Most journalists' curiosity about technology went little further than wanting systems that worked straight out of the box: their lives were complicated enough already. If they had to work with new software to build web front pages then please just make it simple.

To the developers it was anything but simple. No one had ever built this kind of ambitious content management system before – one that could combine words, video, audio, graphics and advertising in ways which worked in print, on our own website, and on other platforms. Just creating a front-page editor was – in the words of one developer – 'probably one of the most difficult engineering media projects anybody's done'.

★

We could put it off no longer. If we were to make the *Guardian* truly ready for a digital future we could no longer stumble on across three newsrooms with a writing, editing and production system held together by string and Sellotape.

By the end of 2006 we had nearly 14 million unique users a month – two thirds of them outside the UK. We were attracting around 4.5 million page views a day and around 300,000 audio downloads a week. There was a slump at weekends, partly because we didn't have the resources to run a seven-day operation (the *Observer* was busy on a Sunday edition on the Saturday and didn't want to think about the web, and the *Guardian* had virtually no one around on a Sunday except for those preparing the Monday print edition).

We needed to move buildings: the main office was now near the end of its useful life and it was hopeless running an organisation scattered among different floors in different buildings up and down Farringdon Road.

Fleet Street was now a wasteland of banks and anonymous offices. Many newspapers had moved to the new skyscrapers of steel and glass in Canary Wharf to the east. Some were in the fashionable shopping thoroughfares of Kensington. The *Telegraph* was near the heart of political power in Victoria. We settled on Kings Cross – then an area of drug-dealing, prostitution and derelict land earmarked for development. Not glamorous, but Kings Place, a new building designed by the architect Jeremy Dixon,[4] was to have large enough floor plates that we could get the editorial operation onto one and a half floors.

We ended up designing a news desk that looked like a pair of handcuffs – three groups of home/foreign/business editors across print and digital. Everyone could at least see each other.

Next decision: how much of the future would be about text and how much about other forms of media? In Farringdon Road we had taken a disused windowless space and nailed egg boxes to the walls to create something soundproofed enough to call an audio studio. How many sound/video studios should we create in Kings Place?

Crystal balls to the ready.

But the really difficult bit was taking three different parts of the organisation and deciding how we would work together. At present, just 14 people were officially working across platforms.

No one really wanted it.

If you worked 'in print' on the *Guardian* (increasingly, few people did print alone – but many thought of themselves still as primarily *of* print) then you rather dreaded the thought of joining a news sausage machine.

If you worked in digital (and there were now about 100 of them, editorially – plus developers) then you had a terror that the dinosaurs of print would now flex their muscles and push you out of the way. A radical, ground-breaking team producing the best newspaper website in the world was about to be subsumed into people who didn't understand it.

If you worked for the *Observer* you didn't want to merge with either team. Sunday journalism was about being left in peace and quiet to come up with something special at the end of the week. The last thing you wanted was to be pooled with everyone else.

So no one thought this was a good idea. But *not* integrating was a really bad idea, too.

Just a year or so after all the debates we'd had internally about 'Berliner' journalism we regrouped to start new discussions about web journalism.

The 'long tail' for instance. The phrase had been popularised by Chris Anderson, editor-in-chief of *Wired*, in a book of that name published in July 2006.[5] Print journalism had a very short tail: the effective life of a newspaper was 24 hours. Sure, you could go down to the library and seek out old copies. But, for most readers, the editorial value lasted no longer than a day.

The same was true of the commercial value. Within 24 hours you had exhausted all the cover price and advertising revenues from the artefact that would soon be lining the bottom of the parrot cage or being used to light fires.

In the new world you would still usually attract most attention for a story on day one. But it would live for ever and would (if properly tagged) remain findable and (if appropriately written or edited) relevant. Commercially, its audience (and therefore value) over time could be greater than its value on day one. That was the theory of the long tail.

What did an editorial long tail look like? We came to shorthand this as the 'Nick Clegg' problem. Nick Clegg was the rising star of the (centre-left) UK Liberal Democrat party. An MP in 2005, leader of his party by 2007 and (centre-right) deputy prime minister by 2010. Suppose you wanted to know all about Clegg and came to the *Guardian* (via Google) to find out.

At least 90 per cent of what you'd find on the *Guardian* would be the daily ticktock of incremental news. Clegg said this in Sheffield; opened that in Birmingham; criticised this in Westminster. Interesting for a few hours, but of very little substance in the longer term.

Go to the Nick Clegg Wikipedia page – edited by amateurs – and, by contrast, you found something which made more structural sense, even if you couldn't vouch for the accuracy of the information. This was information that had been edited for the long tail.

Was there a way of 'long-tailing' newspaper journalism so that it remained useful, well-organised and relevant for the future? Was it best done by humans? Too resource intensive and expensive. Could it be done by algorithms? The tech devs were gagging to have a go, but there was never enough time or money.

One interim solution was to develop 'keyword pages' which gathered together material on particular issues. Maybe we could have a hundred 'top of the page' subjects to which we could devote extra editing care. But it was a weak answer to a searching question.

Here was another long-tail related question we'd already stubbed our toe on. A story didn't 'end' just because it had 'gone to bed' (in print parlance). The newspaper cycle climaxed in the evening. The next day you would regroup and decide whether a particular story was 'over' or whether you revisited it – with a fresh angle.

In the parallel world of social media a story had a life independent of the news organisation which created it. The reporter might have gone home, or to the pub or cinema. But her story was now a living thing – being shared, critiqued, rubbished, celebrated, clarified, responded to, rendered irrelevant, added to, challenged – maybe all of the above – while she was trying to take a well-earned break.

How could any news organisation possibly cope with that? More blogs, fewer stories, was one answer. But that pulled in the opposite direction to print.

Every time we thought about video we felt slight panic. Some newspapers simply bought packages from television or agencies, sometimes augmenting them with in-house voice-over. Some built mock TV studios, others used their newsrooms as a kind of set. We tried a little bit of each.

The commercial team wanted more and more video – especially of 'softer' lifestyle subjects. The value of a video advert was exponentially greater than any display panel on a webpage. But the best solution then on offer was a 'pre-roll' advert which forced the user to sit through 10 to 30 seconds of advertising before getting to a short video clip. Most people didn't bother.

What skills would be required in an integrated world? Newspaper sub-editors were, to state the obvious, skilled at dealing with text and images on a page. Web editors thought about web architecture, search, community, engagement, social media, databases, audio, video, Flash (when to use, when not to use) and web design. They were becoming practised at using and interpreting the static about who was reading what in real time.

We needed more people (editorial, commercial, marketing, audience development) who understood data. We needed product managers who could look after specific areas (fashion, travel, culture, etc.) as 'publishers' co-ordinating editorial, technology and commercial. We therefore developed a sub-set of executive producers who, for instance, understood the best time to launch particular stories and how they would behave once launched.

★

So began the Great Integration. The thing almost nobody wanted but couldn't be avoided any longer.

Like it or not, this was the moment of no going back. The arguments over details would rumble away for years to come – but this was now one workforce under one roof pointing in roughly the same direction. Some years later Marty Baron, executive editor of the *Washington Post*, told me one of the key attributes he looked for when hiring was optimism. I felt the same: if we were to have a chance of making it we had to be surrounded by enough people who really believed it was possible.

With the help of external organisational consultants, we sat for hours, days, weeks in a converted Georgian house in Canonbury, North London, working out how to create the future processes and teams that would deliver the digital journalism that – probably – a majority still didn't really believe in. If all the discussions about the re-invention of journalism were absorbing, intellectually fascinating and rich, so the deliberations about welding three operations into one were slow, awkward and painful. They involved workflows, floor plans, HR consultants and lawyers.[6]

Fairly late in the day Emily Bell threw a spanner in the works. She was no longer convinced this was the right model for the future. Maybe we should just be dividing the organisation into Fast and Slow? We should have a live production desk which would pick up any story and quickly turn it into a properly produced web package, findable on search engines as well as through navigational pages. And then we'd have a slower unit producing more journalism with more background and context as well as softer features.

Possibly she was right, but it was too late in the day to go into reverse. In time, a number of web start-ups saw 'slow' as a business model and attempted to do exactly what Emily was groping towards.

If 'follow my leader' wouldn't work as a leadership style, what would? We devised three or four hypothetical situations which we were likely to face – a high-profile sports event on a Saturday, a big breaking news story on a Thursday night, and so on – and crowdsourced solutions among editorial employees.

For instance, they might consider a major prison report being published on, say, a Tuesday. The desk might want the home affairs correspondent on the *Guardian* to write a snap story, with the most important news line; they would then want a gut of the report, some analysis and maybe some audio or video. Comment might commission a piece. The newspaper would want a front-page story with reaction for later in the day. That's a lot on the shoulders of one writer. It being Tuesday, the *Observer*'s home affairs correspondent elsewhere in the building might be having a lighter day. The website might have a much less experienced reporter to hand. Should the *Observer* correspondent chip in to help, or did that cross a sacred line?

We asked reporters to lead these sessions, in groups of about 20 at a time. I would sit at the back of the room playing no part as journalists from the *Observer*, *Guardian* and Guardian Unlimited tried to find the best solutions to the dilemma the reporter/moderator gave them. We sat through enough of these sessions to expose more than 250 journalists to the four-dimensional chess in our heads.

More often than not the sessions ended up with the unavoidable logic: that we had to move to some form of integrated model. Everything else was too messy, complicated or expensive. Even those who disagreed had at least spent two hours facing the same issues we were grappling with.

They might not agree: but they might understand why someone might reasonably come to a different conclusion.

That was probably the best we could hope for.

*

There was very fast journalism, fast journalism, slow journalism . . . and very slow journalism.

Much investigative journalism is in the last category. Reporters are not policemen: they can't produce a subpoena or a search warrant. They can't interview witnesses under caution. They can just plug away following leads, asking questions, unearthing documents, finding sources.

Take, for example, David Leigh's tireless and brilliant work on the controversial al-Yamanah deal, which he pursued for more than 20 years.[7] The deal was Britain's biggest ever arms deal, keeping British Aerospace (BAE) afloat for 20 years and bringing in £40 billion of revenue.

Within weeks of the deal being signed in 1985 allegations of corruption surfaced – and never went away, not least because Leigh never lost interest. His original stories concentrated on huge commission payments and the involvement – tangential or otherwise – of the then prime minister's son, Mark Thatcher (who has always denied any wrongdoing in connection with the deal).

The Serious Fraud Office (SFO) began investigating the deal in 2004 after another Leigh story about a £20 million slush fund. Astonishingly, the SFO was ordered to drop the inquiry in December 2006 after the government made 'representations' about the need to safeguard national security. It transpired that Saudi Arabia had given Britain ten days to halt the probe or lose a contract for 72 Eurofighter Typhoon combat jets.

The following year the US Department of Justice began its own investigation into BAE's compliance with US anti-bribery laws. The US government compelled BAE to pay $400 million (£260 million) in penalties.

In June 2007 Leigh, still on the case with his colleague Rob Evans, wrote a story claiming that BAE secretly paid Prince Bandar of Saudi Arabia more than £1 billion in connection with the contract.[8]

On all kinds of grounds this sort of journalism was difficult to defend. There was no consultant on earth who, looking at Leigh's productivity over the years on the BAE story, would conclude that this was a sensible investment of time or resource.

A newsroom run strictly on metrics would, like the British government and the SFO, order the investigation to be closed. Big investigations (see Watergate) often work by the incremental disclosures of sometimes not very headline-grabbing material. The readership for each of the smaller numerous stories along the way would be barely measurable. Even the news desk sometimes had a haunted look in its eyes as Leigh approached with yet another piece of the jigsaw.

The great editor Harold Evans used to say that an investigation only really began to count once the readers and even the journalists were bored with it. He knew a thing or two about great campaigns – proving that Timothy Evans was innocent of the 1949 murder of his wife,[9] and pursuing – over decades – a campaign to secure justice for the victims of the Thalidomide scandal.[10]

So how to justify an obsession, like Leigh's, which has no apparent financial return and, for most of the time, is of little interest to the readers?[11]

The answer to that was central to the idea of a newspaper. If journalism is, in some sense, a public service then an editor has to understand the ethos of public service – something which is of value to a society without necessarily making a direct financial return. This means thinking of this kind of journalism in the same way you might think of a police, ambulance or fire service. You would, as a citizen, expect such services to be run efficiently, but you would not expect them to have to justify themselves on grounds of profit.

There is actually a financial benefit to a newspaper of such investigations, but it is a long-term one. Readers, on some level, want their newspapers to be brave, serious, campaigning and dogged. They like corruption to be exposed, overweening power to be challenged, and serious scandals to be unearthed. It reminds them what journalism is for. They admire it. They are even willing to pay for it – see the so-called Trump Bump, when the more the *NYT* challenged the newly elected president and the more Trump denounced the paper, the more subscriptions soared. A newspaper that consistently breaks investigative stories will (with apologies to those who hate the word) build a brand. The Evans *Sunday Times* was certainly a 'brand'. To this day it is regarded as one of the high-water marks of challenging twentieth-century journalism. The Bradlee *Washington Post* – most recently immortalised by Steven Spielberg – was the same. The Ingrams/Hislop[12] *Private Eye* is a brand, so was Granada TV's *World in Action*. Brands stand for something. Brands have value. A paper that stands for nothing will soon lose its sheen; and then its point; and then its readers.

'If I was running a news organisation,' Nick Davies would lecture me, 'first of all, I would run masses of agency copy. I would have a rule that no staff member is allowed to rewrite agency copy, the agencies will cover the news for us. Then we're going to sit back and make those crucial judgements about what really matters and we're going to throw our resources into investigating, understanding and commenting – unique stuff. If somebody else wants to write about a cat that's got flushed down the toilet, a train that crashed in Poland, any of what we call "news", fine. We can no longer afford to do that, so we let the agencies do it. We're not going to touch it.'

But the bleaker the financial figures, the tougher the immediate argument for investigative journalism became to sustain.

And it was about to become even harder.

15

Crash

We produced the first edition from our new home in Kings Cross on 15 December 2008. Precisely two months earlier – on 15 September – Lehman Brothers had filed for bankruptcy, provoking the biggest financial crisis and deepest recession since the 1930s. The GMG chairman, Paul Myners, had abruptly resigned – urgently asked by the then prime minister, Gordon Brown, to move into government to help save the banking system.

The party – such as it was – was well and truly over.

Ten days before we moved, the Tribune chain of newspapers filed for Chapter 11 bankruptcy protection. Its worth had essentially halved since 2007, when Chicago billionaire Sam Zell took it private in an $8.2 billion leveraged buyout. Zell blamed the bankruptcy on a 'perfect storm' – declining revenues, a tanking economy and a credit crisis.

Several smaller chains and newspapers in Minneapolis and Philadelphia followed suit. In Denver, Seattle and Tucson – still two-newspaper towns in 2008 – longstanding metropolitan dailies would stop printing newspapers. More than one hundred daily papers eliminated print publication on Saturdays or other days each week.[1]

The financial cutbacks were savage. Many US newspapers cut their reporting staff by half. The *Baltimore Sun* newsroom shrank from 400 to 250; the *LA Times* from 1,100 to 600. The number of American journalists had fallen from 60,000 in 1992 to 40,000 in 2009. In America, the huge historic profits of news had long since dried up.

Everywhere, confusion. Over here was the Enders consultancy team predicting that newspaper advertising would halve in the next five years. But over there was Les Hinton, Murdoch's right-hand man, predicting a 'long and prosperous life ahead' for printed newspapers.

Fleet Street turned on the new West Coast competitors. Hinton complained that the internet had unleashed 'an epidemic of amplified ignorance' and blamed search engines for 'sucking the lifeblood out of the newspaper industry, nourishing themselves off the journalism we spent hundreds of millions to produce'. He claimed Google threatened to 'make newspapers road-kills along what we once called the information superhighway'.[2]

Within months of moving into Kings Place there were cost-cutting groups poring over every line of expenditure. At least three firms of external consultants, including McKinsey, were wandering through the commercial and news floors at various points over a two-year period.

Internally, there was a divide which mirrored the Enders–Hinton split. Some read the tea leaves as an incentive to accelerate the journey to digital. As many thought it was mad to sacrifice print. The less we made the paper worth reading, the fewer people would buy it. By stopping bulk and international sales we'd invite headlines about our plummeting ABC sales. Any rival could write about the 'failing *Guardian*'. It didn't matter that we'd overtaken everyone else digitally. That wouldn't, at least in their telling, count. And that could damage confidence among advertising agencies, still mostly run by middle-aged executives who feared Google was about to dismember their own business model as aggressively as it had disrupted news.

One day – who knew? – we might be able to persuade readers to pay for online content. But that time still seemed far off, with two thirds of our audience still abroad. An Enders note by their respected senior analyst Douglas McCabe, in early 2009, could find no easy solution to the universal problem: the need to sustain traffic in order to increase advertising rates. '[That] makes it virtually impossible for publishers to simply put "pay here" walls around their content and expect consumers to pay for the content they previously enjoyed for free: the industry is past the point of no return.'

One problem was an over-supply of general news. 'It is not just that the websites of the UK's 13 national dailies (and the same on Sundays) are offering variations on the same themes,' wrote McCabe. 'It is that for the first time they are doing so in direct competition with broadcasters, bloggers and also international versions of all these. These services are free, at least at the point of access. Free news is ubiquitous . . .'

It got worse, warned McCabe. Just over the horizon was the 'larger threat' from wireless handheld devices. 'Assuming at least one wireless handheld reader takes off, picking up news headlines for free will take off with it. No publisher is suggesting that they would literally put all their content behind a payment wall . . . In any case, digital "leakage" of content from all news providers is an insurmountable barrier . . .'

The one thing he was certain about was this: 'An already intolerably volatile transition period is about to become even more difficult to manage.'[3]

Reading McCabe's note nine years later gives a jolt of recognition – and some modest balm of relief. McCabe was a really good analyst: Enders were used, at one time or another, by all the major media companies in the UK. Yet here he was in May 2009 thrashing around as blindly as the rest of us.

It's not that he was wrong on the big picture – but, in a sense, we all intuitively felt most of that. It's just that his tarot pack was no better than anyone else's. Wireless handheld devices would, indeed, be a huge part of the future, but his note doesn't mention the iPhone, introduced nearly two years earlier, or foresee the iPad, due out the following April. There's no mention of apps because his crystal ball couldn't yet imagine them. Sony and Plastic Logic never made it into this space. He spotted Apple's potential to play in the news environment, but didn't mention Facebook.

None of this is a criticism of McCabe. As he candidly said, it was near impossible for anyone to peer through the fog into the future.

His phrase, 'intolerably volatile' did some justice to the jittery atmosphere of the times. We – Fleet Street – had been big fishes in the UK pool. Governments used to bow down before us. Corporations would bend to our will. Now we were at the mercy of whatever would come next from a handful of tech giants 5,000 miles away. We were living incarnations of the impotence of those at the receiving end of globalisation.

There is a university thesis to be written on the deep psychological consequences of this new powerlessness and how, within a decade, it would lead a large swathe of British newspapers passionately to advocate Brexit – departure from the European Union – in the 2016 referendum. It was as if, at some subterranean level, we understood what it was like to live or work in a place that had been stiffed by far-away forces beyond our comprehension or power. This was what it was like to have been a Manchester cotton mill owner, or a Yorkshire pitman.

Discuss.

*

A year into this savage recession the *Guardian* was feeling the pain as much as anyone, if not more – because, in the old world, we had been so dominant in classified advertising. That was now voting with its feet – straight out of the front door. The operating loss was £36.8 million, of which the *Observer* losses were around a third. Our overall revenues had peaked at £262 million in 2007/8. The bleak truth was that nearly £40 million in revenue had simply disappeared in two years. To lose 15 per cent of income from just one revenue stream in short order was the kind of body blow that would make any company shudder.

We had now invested £20 million in digital since 2002, including capital expenditure – which the Board described as 'appropriate and relatively modest'. It certainly came nowhere near the BBC, which had spent £177 million on digital in just one year, 2008/9. How could we compete with that, let alone the best brains in California as well?

Digital revenues were giving some hope: from £4 million in 2001 to £25 million that year, and forecast to be £36 million by 2012/13. They now accounted for 11 per cent of total revenues and were predicted to rise to 15 per cent within four years.

But there was more gloomy Enders news. The consultants were predicting that no fewer than seven national newspapers would close by

2014 – with the assumption that 80 per cent of that readership and ad revenue would effectively disappear from the market.

The doomsday scenario would not happen, at least in that timescale. They were right that there was a simple over-supply of news. But there had never been a shortage of billionaires and oligarchs to keep the show on the road. There was no escaping the general economic outlook: no return to growth predicted for two or three years, depending on who you listened to.

We shared all our figures with the unions as we looked for savings across the business. One area for examination was the amount of resource and money we were lavishing on weekend publishing – 16 sections across both days on Saturday and Sunday, quite a lot of which was effectively repetitive (two travel sections, two lots of fashion, food, gardening, culture, etc.).

The *Observer* had now notched up nearly £200 million of losses over the years we'd owned it, including the original purchase price. Its head-count had risen to 170 at its peak as we had increased sections and resource. But everything now was out of kilter. The *Observer* was losing £7 for every pound lost on the *Guardian* and Guardian Unlimited. It was predicted to lose another £36 million over the next four years.

Cash was now the problem. However substantial the eventual 'Wellcome Trust' model might be, we only had set aside £200 million liquid in hand as GMG restructured the 50 per cent ownership of AutoTrader. That had looked comfortable before the economic crash: now it looked worryingly small. If the recession was deeper than antic-ipated, the money would simply run out.

The most alarming Enders slide showed the entire business hitting the ground around 2012/13 – i.e. we had just three years in which to turn things round.

This (as we kept reminding colleagues) was a crisis for all publishers, particularly those exposed to classified advertising. The *Sunday Times*, which at one point had made £1 million a week in profit, was rumoured to be losing £15 million a year as it, too, watched the classifieds vanish into the ether.

My predecessor Peter Preston, who had done so much to help build up the classified advertising sections, wrote in his *Observer* column on

9 August 2009: 'I lived, on the *Guardian*, through the peril of 1966, when merger threatened obliteration . . . I've been there and run things, and it wasn't at all simple. And that was a doddle compared to now. Believe me.'

Long hours and weeks were spent modelling different scenarios. The weekend at first looked the obvious place to start – and we spent much time locked in joyless rooms with the editor of the *Observer* and the *Guardian* weekend sections to see if there was a better way of reconfiguring the printed papers over Saturday and Sunday. A paper like the *New York Times* had a relatively thin paper on Saturday and a bumper paper on Sunday. Our problem was having to produce two thick newspapers – with different titles – on two consecutive days. Logically, it made no sense. But, in the end, all other options under contemplation – including a seven-day *Guardian* – made the cashflow worse. We did eventually manage to stop the Sunday title haemorrhaging cash, though at some cost to the ability of the *Observer* to sail as a fully independent vessel.

If you were an *Observer* journalist, the chances were that you felt you'd been sacrificed on the high altar of digital. Keeping the internal culture wars from boiling over was never easy.

★

In any business, periods of drastic cost-cutting lead to introspection. Before the fall of Lehman Brothers we had been looking at the *Guardian*'s emerging position on the global stage: for a while the marketing team had dabbled with the idea of 'the world's leading liberal voice'. Many American papers had become more parochial at precisely the time when it was difficult to understand many things except in global terms. Foreign bureaux were being closed all over the world: too expensive. The *Washington Post*, once international in renown as well as outlook, had retreated into being more of a local paper once more. But there was no local way of explaining the economy, security, the environment, science, immigration, energy or technology. These were all global stories. 9/11 taught Americans to be interested in faith and the Middle East. The Lehman crash taught the British that when Wall Street caught a sub-prime cold we developed pneumonia.

There was no such thing as 'abroad' any more – at least in media terms. And the *Guardian* had, by chance or design, acquired a global readership which felt the need for a news organisation which still had the resources to be out in the world and interested in it.

The opportunity was there. The revenues should, one day, be there – or so commercial colleagues believed. But, in the short term, we had a cash problem.

A paper like the *Guardian* had to have authority – especially in the informational chaos all around. We had to be trusted that we would, broadly, get things right; that we knew what we were talking about; and that we operated to high ethical and professional standards. We had to maintain range. Just 18 months previously we might not have thought that having an expert in banking would be the *Guardian*'s highest priority. We might have said, *The* Guardian *will never be known for its City coverage*. But how could we have got through the previous months without our indefatigable and shrewd banking correspondent, Jill Treanor?

To have influence, a newspaper must first find things out: i.e. it could not bail out of reporting. It could have – and should have – opinions – but they had to proceed from news. News before views.

So there had to be an irreducible core of what we did. We should still be able to write authoritatively from, or about, America, Western and Eastern Europe, Pakistan, Iran, Iraq, the Middle East, Russia, China, India, Afghanistan, South and sub-Saharan Africa, South America and the Far East.

To state the blindingly obvious: none of that came cheap. But, in an age in which fewer and fewer news organisations were going to care about international reporting, it seemed like a duty to maintain that focus. It could also be an opportunity. The *Economist*, in its main editorial on the threat facing newspapers, had written in 2006: 'As with many industries, it is those in the middle – neither highbrow, nor entertainingly populist – that are likeliest to fall by the wayside.'

When in doubt there was always a hotel within the M25 ring road around London to retreat to for discussions with commercial colleagues. The agenda for the latest one: if we were destined to be a much smaller organisation, what we would ditch and what we would fight for?

The previous 40 years had seen a huge expansion in what a newspaper did – including colour magazines and a concentration on lifestyle and the world beyond politics, culture and work. Much of it had been driven by the opportunities to attract advertising; but some of it had simply been an editorial wish to reflect worlds beyond the worthy, very masculine core of what a broadsheet newspaper had been for much of the nineteenth and twentieth centuries.

So – bolted on to news, politics, international affairs and finance – newspapers had started writing about fashion, clothes, food, drink, travel, sex, sexual politics, gender, children, families, emotions, leisure, love, cars, gardening, property, adventure, exercise, mental well-being, identity, time off and much more.

All those cost money to cover, as well. You could argue they weren't 'core' to what a newspaper was, but were now an expected part of a richer mix. Some brought in significant revenues, others less so. But the breadth of subjects, bundled together, certainly helped sell a printed newspaper.

But in digital? If we had to slash costs and didn't just want to salami slice everything we did?

A senior commercial colleague led the argument to drop all the 'softer' areas of coverage. We would be beaten by others in the digital space, anyway. Did we seriously think we could ever match the specialist sites that were springing up by the week to do fashion or food or travel? We had tiny digital resources compared with them.

The paper I had joined in 1979 had been pretty remorseless in all but ignoring what we ate, bought, aspired to or wore. There had been no features pages at all beyond one arts page, one comment page and one women's page. The Saturday paper was no different.

Was the new economic reality telling us to withdraw back to news and comment – and nothing but?

The commercial team was divided. What did it mean for them to ditch the areas that were most advertising-friendly?

The editorial team was pensive. A news-only digital *Guardian* might be very focused. But how many people would actually come to a website that was just news, news, news? Over the years the *Guardian* and *Observer* had found distinctive voices – light, serious, funny, irreverent, warm, personal – to cover the areas we might now think of as less essential.

Yes, others might do these subjects in more depth and comprehensiveness, but wasn't there a '*Guardian*esque' voice which would attract readers; which still counted? And which leavened what could otherwise be monotone – or even monotonous.

We broke for lunch, nothing decided.

Over lunch we talked about Philip Meyer's book, *The Vanishing Newspaper*, which suggested a business model for preserving and stabilising the social responsibility functions of the press in a way that could outlast technology-driven changes. This 'influence model' was based on the premise that a newspaper's main product was not news or information, but influence: societal influence, which was not for sale; rather than commercial influence, which was. Meyer's model explored how the former enhanced the value of the latter.

In the afternoon we talked about whom we were trying to influence. In the old world some 'quality' newspapers were primarily concerned with the decision makers – the people at the top of church, state, civil service, the armed services, cultural institutions, the universities, the police, the courts, the prisons, the embassies, the broadcasters, the banks, the trade unions. Famously, the economics editor of the *Times*, Peter Jay,[4] is said to have told a sub-editor who found it hard to follow his argument: 'I only wrote this piece for three people – the editor of the *Times*, the Governor of the Bank of England, and the Chancellor of the Exchequer.'

All journalists want to believe that what we do matters. In addition to the decision makers we think about the other opinion *formers*: other journalists; other editors in papers; radio and television stations making their editorial choices; publishers; think tanks; campaigners; bloggers; community activists.

Others pitched in: those two layers represented a very elite view of influence. What about non-elites: the young as well as the middle-aged and well-off? The non-white, non-UK readers now part of a wider eco-system of information who would increasingly have, and demand, a voice in the world? People who weren't at the pinnacles of power and who didn't simply aspire to be influenced by us, but to be part of influencing things. That was the world of social media. Sure, we could discount them – but that could just lead to a new 'horizontal' world (largely excluding newspapers) having ever greater influence while ours dwindled.

The *Guardian* and *Observer*, of all news organisations, ought to care what ordinary doctors, nurses, hospital orderlies, social workers, police-men and women, public servants, business professionals, teachers, artists, workers and managers thought. The work we were doing in build-ing communities was not about the one-way transmission of ideas or content. Nor was it the predominantly old newspaper model of passing down information from governors to governed, from elites and power to the mass of people without power or voice.

Influence in future would surely be a much more fluid concept. It would be about multiple-way connections. A digital news organisation could find a new importance with political systems which were strug-gling to find truly representative and responsive forms of government. This was a newly wired and networked world: we could play a crucial part by being a reliable, trustworthy element of it.

Any impact we had, or could imagine, now stretched far beyond the UK. Virtually every time a foreign correspondent returned to the office they would talk of how the *Guardian* – once respected but barely read 'abroad' – was now of growing influence on the streets as well as in corridors of power.

There was, undeniably, a global appetite for liberal, progressive anal-ysis of economics and politics, environment, science and social policy, underpinned by well-resourced reporting. If Meyer was right then our influence would be felt more broadly, and more persistently, the more other English-speaking news organisations decided they could not afford to stay engaged in the world.

The interesting thing about the discussion was that the editorial and commercial teams weren't necessarily manning the barricades you might have expected. It was one of those moments when not having shareholders made a difference to the conversation. Trust ownership was – plainly – not a magic wand. But it did encourage both sides of the enterprise to think about purpose and about values. Whether they would be enough only time would tell.

★

Away days mounted up. Board meetings and strategy sessions gobbled up time. It sometimes felt that day-to-day editing was pushed to the margins. One day, while deep in restructuring organisational flow charts, we would make an editorial mistake. In April 2008, we did: we accused Tesco, Britain's biggest supermarket chain, of not paying its fair share of tax.

If you're going to make a mistake of this sort, it's probably best not to make it against a company with gross global income of more than £50 billion a year and profits before tax of £5 billion. They were Goliath; we were David. And they were a very cross Goliath.

That was understandable. In common with most global organisations their financial structures were a complex maze of tax wizardry, havens, property unit trusts, intellectual property rights and creative accountancy. There was nothing improper or contrary to the law about all this. And, indeed, lawyers are kept very busy by the multinationals: one firm advising Tesco on a particular tax avoidance strategy employed no fewer than 90 lawyers on the project. The advanced tax planning undertaken today by most international companies is as intelligible to the average person as particle physics. The risk of getting something wrong – along with the lack of time, expertise or resources in most newsrooms – means there is very little coverage of tax. The so-called 'tax gap' – tax legally avoided by individuals and corporations – in Britain had been estimated at anywhere between $17 billion and $68 billion.

This was clearly a matter of high public interest – but fraught with complexity and danger. Even the managing editor of the *Financial Times*,

BREAKING NEWS

Dan Bogler, admitted at the height of the banking crisis: 'Unfortunately, financial journalists – and the *FT* has better-trained financial journalists than others – don't really understand this stuff, and they join a long list of people that starts with bank regulators, central bank regulators and money managers.'[5]

Tesco it turned out had, indeed, done their best to avoid one kind of tax – as the satirical magazine *Private Eye* was helpfully to disclose. But the company was innocent of the particular tax avoidance scheme we'd written about; and the sums avoided in a different avoidance scheme were considerably less. As I was later to tell parliament, we'd placed too much trust in the fact that one of the reporters was, most unusually, a trained accountant; and also in the opinion of another tax expert who had seemed to confirm our interpretation of the figures.

So, we were wrong. And once we realised it we – with sinking hearts – quickly apologised. It was a flawed piece of journalism, and we publicly said so – and stated frankly that we shouldn't have published it.

But Tesco wasn't going to settle for a quick apology. They were going through a phase of trying to silence their critics through litigation; in Thailand, they were pursing an action for criminal libel against a critic who faced jail and a multi-million-pound penalty for making some disobliging comments about the company.[6]

In the UK, they launched a blitzkrieg of litigation against the *Guardian* – and me, personally, claiming malicious falsehood. The company claimed that I had deliberately published something, knowing it to be untrue.[7] The truth was, as ever, much more mundane. My mind had been elsewhere in bumper-to-bumper discussions about integration, savings and internal reorganisation. I had read the piece in advance, but did not have the technical knowledge of high-level corporate tax structures to doubt the reassurances I'd been given.

Newspapers have always made mistakes, not invariably, or even mostly, from malign motives. The US Supreme Court Justice William Brennan Jr's landmark opinion for the majority in the *New York Times* v. Sullivan case in 1964 coined the phrase 'erroneous statements honestly made'. This remarkable judgment recognised the chilling effect – 'the pall of fear and timidity' – that the routine prospect of costly legal battles

174

inevitably causes on the press, and sought a way of offering protection to newspapers writing about matters of high public importance. But we had no such protection in the UK.

A full-scale defamation case – as we had seen with Hamilton and Aitken – develops an awesome momentum of its own. Letters rain in day after day, week after week – drafted by counsel, amended by junior partners, redrafted by senior partners, few of them earning less than £400 an hour. Their tone is alternately sneering, bullying, threatening and demanding. Within seven weeks of receiving the initial writ of libel, the *Guardian*'s costs alone of responding to the bombardment of demands from Tesco's lawyers, Carter-Ruck, and drafting a defence had mounted to more than £300,000.

Within two more weeks Carter-Ruck's costs had nearly doubled. The firm's lead partner claimed £46,000 for the 93 hours and six minutes he had toiled over the case (at £500 per hour). Another partner had clocked up £39,570 for 131 hours and 54 minutes. The accountants Ernst & Young eventually wanted £87,000 – it seemed to me for advising Tesco's lawyers on Tesco's own accounts. Berwin Leighton Paisner, the specialist tax lawyers who helped set up the offshore companies the *Guardian* had written about, billed Tesco for a further £87,000 – presumably for explaining to Tesco's lawyers the precise nature of the company's own tax structures. Three barristers specialising in defamation law charged for tens of thousands of pounds worth of perusing and advising.

These remarkable sums for explaining the tax structures were all the more ironic since Tesco contended that the *Guardian*'s error was an elementary, 'absurd' one. The total cost for both sides of fighting the action to the bitter end – which could have ended up largely being borne by either Tesco or the *Guardian* – could have been in the region of £4.5 million. All this for a case where any damages would have been relatively insignificant.

In the end, there was to be no great Aitken-style climax to this case: a judge intervened to put an end to the whole ridiculously drawn out and punitively expensive saga.[8] The months of fighting were concluded by altering a smallish number of words in the statement we'd made a few months previously and by paying £5,000 to a charity of Tesco's choice.

There was a serious mistake in the article, as we had quickly admitted. Tesco was entitled to make use of this country's legal remedies; its phalanx of lawyers, accountants and experts did nothing 'wrong' in the way they represented their client's interest. But there was also an outstanding public interest in journalists being able to investigate corporate tax avoidance without the kind of legal jeopardy we faced.[9]

Among the post-mortems posed after the dramatic implosion of the global financial system were searching questions about why the press failed to see it coming.

Lack of newsroom resources was agreed to be one answer. Fewer news organisations had the specialist knowledge to write about a complex subject like corporate tax avoidance or complex financial derivatives. Few had the money any longer to invest in drawn-out investigative stories. They didn't have the money to pay lawyers and accountants to vet material in advance to make it legally safe. And, if threatened with libel, they didn't have the money to defend their reporting.

There were many local newspapers which now, when faced with a legal threat, had no option but to cave in immediately. They literally had no budget to resist the prospect of a libel action.

The weakness of the press was slowly eroding its watchdog function, enabling the rise of fake news.

★

I had – as a result of the Tesco action – spent many, many hours looking into corporate tax avoidance and realised how widespread and commonplace the use of complex and artificial tax avoidance structures had become. So, instead of tip-toeing away from the whole subject, we resolved to launch a major series looking at more than 20 prominent British companies whose aggressive tax arrangements looked questionable.

We looked at, and tried to explain in simple terms, the so-called 'double Luxembourg', the 'Irish branches' and the 'Dutch sandwich'. Seldom, if ever, had this world previously been exposed to such prolonged and extensive scrutiny.

Newspapers are supposed to hold the powerful to account. But what if the powerful are not politicians – a relatively easy target – but advertisers? When newspapers had strong balance sheets that question should have been easy to answer. But in a world where advertising directors were finding it harder and harder to make their revenues, what were the dangers of 'compromise'?

Before our tax avoidance series launched I tipped off the head of advertising that there was a remarkable correlation between our biggest advertisers and the people on the list of 'offenders'. Even more notable was that the influential and giant advertising agency WPP had spent the past decade successfully running a series of elaborate, perfectly legal, avoidance schemes. They were responsible for much of the *Guardian*'s display advertising revenues. We would be writing about them, too.

The advertising director did not blink. That should be Newspapers 101 in any ethical media company. But, as the economics of news began to erode even further, the Chinese walls started coming down in some newsrooms. In time, a new kind of content – not quite advertising, exactly, but not quite editorial, as such – emerged. Someone thought of calling it 'native advertising'.

Anyone who looked unhappy at the prospect of this new hybrid animal was told they didn't get it. It was the future.

The deepening problem was an obvious one. Old-fashioned display or banner ads weren't working. In print that was less of a problem because, well, no one could ever measure whether or not print advertising worked. But in the new world of total measurability, advertisers demanded to know what was effective. A new metric became a CTR – a 'click-through rate'. And CTRs, never very high, had by 2008 declined to virtually zero. With the rise of mobile (tiny screens) and ad blockers (no ads) the problem was only going to become more acute.

A 'native ad', by contrast, didn't have to catch the eye and couldn't be blocked. It looked, smelled and quacked like editorial – but was, if you looked closely, 'sponsored', 'in feed', 'promoted' or 'recommended'. Unlike straightforward banner ads, native ads did get eyeballs. It was, in the lingo, a 'purchase driver'.

The purveyors of native advertising said it was 'better at building trust' than traditional display ads.

'Building trust' was what everyone wanted to do – business, media, institutions of all shapes and sizes. So this was win–win. But the genius of native advertising was that it 'built trust' by sowing confusion. And there was no reason to believe that the new 'trust' was going to be vested in the people actually publishing this new breed of content.

Or would it? Within no time at all there would be new news brands whose revenue models would largely be built on native advertising. Another way of looking at these companies is that they were essentially native advertising agencies with a shopfront of editorial. The window dressing of journalism gave a plausibility to something that would otherwise be dismissed as advertising, pure and simple.

But behind that simple notion was a vast, developing industry in mining as much data as possible about the reader. In the innocent old days you were anonymous. Just as, editorially, we had little knowledge who our individual readers were, so the commercial team – never mind the clients – only had a generic idea of broad categories of people to target. No one at all knew whether you had looked at a particular piece of advertising – quaintly labelled as such – in the *Guardian* or *New York Times*.

Round about 2008 that was all changing – fast. The deathwatch beetles were at work. I'm not sure how many of us fully understood the nature of the transformation in the early days. Antonio García Martínez's memoir, *Chaos Monkeys*, published in 2016, gives a fuller account of the rapid progress data-mining companies were making around this time. García Martínez was a PhD student in physics at Berkeley before moving to Goldman Sachs to model prices for credit derivatives en route to Silicon Valley to help monetise attention.

In media, money is merely expendable ammunition; data is power. With this new programmatic technology that allowed each and every ad impression and user to be individually scrutinized and targeted, that power was shifting inexorably from the publisher, the owner of the eyeballs, to the advertiser, the person buying them.

If my advertiser data about what you bought and browsed in the past was more important than publisher data like the fact that you were on Yahoo Autos right then, or that you were (supposedly) a thirty-five-year-old male in Ohio, then the power was mine as the advertiser to determine price and desirability of media, not the publisher's . . .

This is how online advertising works: money turns into pixels and electrons in the form of ads, which turn into a scintilla of attention in someone's mind, which after a few more clicks and electrons shuffling about, turns back into money. The only goal here is to make that second pile of money as large as possible relative to the first pile of money. That's it.[10]

That, even if we didn't all realise it at the time, was the world we were now playing in.

★

With the financial situation worsening, it was now obvious – to most – that we had to start to cannibalise the paper more aggressively, just as the West Coast crowd had told us we would in Oxford. We had to go web-first, posting things online as a matter of routine, even if the paper felt stale the following day for those who had already read the *Guardian* online.

We had begun with the City and the sports desks in 2006. It was apparent even to the digital sceptics that financial information was time-critical and that any news organisation which asked its readers to wait until the following morning's breakfast table was going to suffer. The same was true of football or baseball scores.

The foreign desk was now tip-toeing into web-first publishing, leaving the home desk – most aware of domestic rivalries – torn. Part of them wanted the professional satisfaction of being first with the news. Part of them felt the real deal was still the newspaper and that – by 'giving away' your best angles and quotes in the middle of the afternoon – you were simply gifting all your hard work to the enemy.

For a while we held the line on 'big properties' – exclusives which we felt would have a bigger impact if in print.

179

But at every turn the new rules of the digital game confounded us. In the old world a stonking print exclusive would start to leak out around 10 p.m. once other papers started seeing the first edition – unless, as sometimes happened, you kept the really big news out of the first edition to achieve real surprise the following morning.

But now we were learning that the internet behaved like a clattering of jackdaws: nothing remained exclusive for more than two minutes. An old-fashioned scoop – whether freely available or behind a paywall – would be rewritten or simply stolen, with or without attribution, in no time at all. We could invest days, weeks or even months on an investigation only to watch it spray out across the ether. The further it travelled in time or distance, the fewer people would be aware of where it had originated.

Sometimes the newspapers which most bitterly attacked the platform giants for destroying the economic basis of journalism were the worst offenders at pinching stuff from rivals, or the internet in general, without a word of credit.

Jackdaws had no shame.

16

Phone Hacking

It had been four years since Nick Davies had first broached the idea of writing about the media. The result had been every bit as problematic as I thought it would be – not least because he had been severely critical of the *Observer*'s reporting of Iraq, among other failures, as he saw them. This had not helped relationships between the two papers.

His book, *Flat Earth News*, had been published in February 2008. Part of it chronicled how so many newsrooms – obsessed with traffic and with ever-declining budgets – had started practising what he termed 'churnalism' – reporters with too little time pumping out material they had not sufficiently researched. Along with researchers from Cardiff University he'd surveyed more than 2,000 UK news stories from the four 'quality' dailies (the *Times*, *Telegraph*, *Guardian*, *Independent*) and the *Daily Mail*.

> They found two striking things. First, when they tried to trace the origins of their 'facts', they discovered that only 12 per cent of the stories were wholly composed of material researched by reporters. With 8 per cent of the stories, they just couldn't be sure. The remaining 80 per cent, they found, were wholly, mainly or partially constructed from second-hand material, provided by news agencies and by the public relations industry. Second, when they looked for evidence that these 'facts' had been thoroughly

checked, they found this was happening in only 12 per cent of the stories.

The implication of those two findings is truly alarming. Where once journalists were active gatherers of news, now they have generally become mere passive processors of unchecked, second-hand material, much of it contrived by PR to serve some political or commercial interest. Not journalists, but churnalists. An industry whose primary task is to filter out falsehood has become so vulnerable to manipulation that it is now involved in the mass production of falsehood, distortion and propaganda.

And the Cardiff researchers found one other key statistic that helps to explain why this has happened. For each of the 20 years from 1985, they dug out figures for the editorial staffing levels of all the Fleet Street publications and compared them with the amount of space they were filling. They discovered that the average Fleet Street journalist now is filling three times as much space as he or she was in 1985. In other words, as a crude average, they have only one-third of the time that they used to have to do their jobs. Generally, they don't find their own stories, or check their content, because they simply don't have the time.[1]

The book had had a mixed reception. 'A journalist turns on his own profession' was the headline in the *Sunday Telegraph*. John Lanchester in the *London Review of Books* found 'a genuinely important book, one which is likely to change, permanently, the way anyone who reads it looks at the British newspaper industry . . . his portrait of the British media could scarcely be any darker, or more convincing.'[2]

It was difficult to think of another comparable book – alternately pungently polemical and fiercely forensic – about newspapers. And it led to a sequel that would prove even more astonishing – and uncomfortable.

Nick came to see me in early March 2009 to tell me about new information which had come his way. For all his easy, urbane charm Nick was profoundly affected by the big set-piece investigations he became involved in. I could see he was living on his nerves. He lowered his voice. We would later shorthand this to the 'heart attack convo'.

Since *Flat Earth News* Nick had been looking at the criminal use of private investigators to ferret out personal information about the intended victims of tabloid stings. In January 2007 a *News of the World* (*NoW*) reporter, Clive Goodman, had been jailed for intercepting the voicemail of three people who worked at Buckingham Palace, along with the private eye who had helped him.

The editor, Andy Coulson, had resigned – he was now on his way to Downing Street as the media adviser to David Cameron – and the official story from News International was that Goodman had been a rotten apple: his phone hacking was a one-off.

Nick was here to tell me this story was not true. He'd been contacted by a source who had met him in a hotel room. This person told him that the idea that Goodman was the only person to hack phones was a joke. Loads of reporters were at it: it was how the *News of the World* had won so many awards. Hacking phones was the system, not an aberration.

I listened with interest and a faintly raised heartbeat. Nick's voice lowered more.

The police knew this at the time Goodman had been singled out as a rotten apple, but had done nothing about it. But now one of the other victims of hacking was suing and was trying to find out who had known what, and when they knew it.

How many victims were we talking about?

Nick had met a senior figure at Scotland Yard. The answer: thousands. So, not just one rotten apple then.

The person who was suing (he continued) was a man called Gordon Taylor, the chief executive of the Professional Footballers' Association – targeted partly because of gossip about his own private life, partly because he was the unwitting conduit for so much information about star players. Two of his close associates had also launched actions.

The *NoW*, rattled by this new legal action, had offered to pay Taylor an enormous sum – £400,000 plus £300,000 costs – to drop the action. Together with the payments to Taylor's colleagues, News International was offering to pay no less than £1 million to make the actions go away.

Nick had been told that the victims of hacking included the deputy prime minister, John Prescott, and the culture secretary responsible for overseeing UK media policy, Tessa Jowell. Dozens of *NoW* reporters and executives were implicated.

Most immediately, he had access to emails which showed that transcripts of 35 voice messages had been discussed between named reporters and editors. The rogue reporter defence was shot to pieces.

Nick's sources had told him that the deal had been approved by James Murdoch – son of Rupert and chair of News International. The silence money had been paid, and the court documents sealed. If Nick was right then Murdoch's most senior executive in the UK had agreed to a million-pound cover-up of criminal behaviour in his own company.

If Nick's proposal to write a general book about the media had been inflammatory, this was incendiary. The Murdoch operation, taken as a whole, was ruthless. If we merely wounded the company, it would close in for the kill. We already knew the police, for reasons best known to themselves, would not want to get involved. We would not have many friends in politics or the rest of the press. We would be on our own.

And yet it was clear what had to be done. A criminal conspiracy at the very top of one of the most powerful companies in the world? Could an editor really tell his reporter to drop the story and take on something less troubling?

I did look in the mirror that night and ask myself if I was up for it, which is something I thought only happened in airport thrillers. This was going to be lonely and, probably, horrible. It was going to be far worse for Nick than for me. I didn't look in the mirror for long. It had to be done. 'Piss or get off the pot' rattled around in my mind like an ear worm. It's not a bad saying for an editor. If you're not prepared to publish the tough stories, make way for someone who is.

The story ran mid-afternoon on Wednesday 8 July 2009. It detailed the conspiracy to cover up criminal behaviour. It implicated the Conservative leader's spokesman. It accused Murdoch's executives of misleading parliament. It pointed a finger of blame at the then press regulator, the Press Complaints Commission; and it asked why the police had turned a blind eye. It blew apart the rotten apple defence.

Fleet Street showed only mild interest in the story. Murdoch shrugged it off. The Metropolitan Police commissioner, Sir Paul Stephenson, asked an assistant commissioner, John Yates, to look into the matter. That, at least, was promising. Less promising was the reappearance of Yates later the same day to say he had investigated the matter and found nothing of undue concern.

The ground had been cut from under our feet – and now we were being summoned to give evidence to parliament's Culture Media & Sport committee the following Tuesday. By Friday night we were under attack from another wing of the Murdoch newspaper stable: a reporter from the *Sunday Times* was threatening to expose us for having used a firm set up by two former MI6 officers to help us investigate the giant American agrochemical company Monsanto. It was put to us that the firm had subcontracted some work to a private detective who had used questionable methods to target a Monsanto employee, i.e. the *Guardian* were stunning hypocrites.

We managed to see that particular smear off, not least because the supposed 'subcontractor' the *Sunday Times* was threatening to expose – a man named John Ford – had performed a great deal of blagging on behalf of . . . the *Sunday Times*, as he was later to admit. Nor was he the only one on the *Sunday Times*'s books. It had taken most of a train journey to Dundee locked in a toilet (for discretion on the phone, not ablutions) to push back against that. But it was a lesson in how the Murdoch organisation fought back. Later in the saga a senior executive on the tabloid *Sun* promised to use the pages of the broadsheet *Sunday Times* to show I was the 'biggest fucking hypocrite in the world'. It was as if the family titles were interchangeable in being used to target anyone with the temerity to take on the organisation.

By the Monday we felt quite alone. News International had released an official three-page statement rubbishing our work and exonerating themselves. The News PR operation had been working overtime in Westminster. All the allegations were, they said, false. Rebekah Brooks wrote to the chairman of the select committee saying we had deliberately misled the British public. The *Times* took a piece from another former Scotland Yard officer (now employed by Murdoch) pouring cold water on the *Guardian* story. It was reprinted in the sister paper, the *NoW*, under a full-page editorial attacking us.

The entire Murdoch UK newspaper organisation appeared to have been mobilised to call the truth fake; and to promote fake news as the truth.

The select committee hearing was promising to be torrid. Suddenly we were in the dock. I had been here before – 12 years previously, with many knives sharpened at the prospect of finishing me off over Jonathan Aitken.[3]

The one thing that gave us comfort was that one of Nick's sources – outraged by the perversion of the truth being peddled by the most powerful newspaper organisation in Britain – had agreed to him producing physical copies of the damning emails which showed the involvement of other *NoW* reporters and executives in the Taylor voicemail hacking.

Nick was by now as anxious and strung out as I'd ever seen him. Until he'd been given the green light by his source to produce the paperwork he hadn't been sleeping and had convinced himself this was the end for both of us. He later admitted he felt 'swamped with dread'. No individual journalist on his own could stand this kind of onslaught from police and press – and, now, parliament.

The ornate Victorian committee room was packed for the session, which was to be live-streamed. There were dozens of reporters there as well as a crowded public gallery and MPs and peers standing at the back to see the combat. I told Nick I would squeeze his knee under the table if I wanted him to shut up.

Nick began very much on the defensive, with the chair trying to cut him short. But the moment he started to distribute the paperwork, the atmosphere in the room began to change. MPs started to thumb their way through the documents. The mood turned. We were no longer there to be carved up. We hadn't delivered a knock-out blow, but we had survived. Parliamentary veterans said it was one of the most dramatic encounters they had ever witnessed in Westminster. The next day's *Times* carried little more than a hundred words on page 20.

Nick told me that the following day Rebekah Brooks, asked how the hacking saga would end, had replied: 'With Alan Rusbridger on his knees, begging for mercy.'

Almost exactly two years later Brooks resigned from News International. Two days after that, on 17 July 2011, she was arrested at Lewisham police station.

Those two years it had taken to fight off the Murdoch press's fury and prove that Nick had been right were lonely ones. You live in a democracy, you assume that there are numerous checks and balances to prevent powerful people from doing crooked things. For the first time in my adult life I doubted this was true in Britain.

We had presented strong evidence of a criminal conspiracy at one of the most powerful media companies in the world . . . and no one wanted to know. Not the police. Not parliament: the select committee to which we'd been summoned a few days after the story first ran was – initially at least – wielding a feather duster.

And not the press.

Dog doesn't eat dog, Alan, you know that. Fleet Street elders had told me so often.

The PCC – the press 'regulator', which we were all urged to defend as the fierce watchdog it wasn't – looked into the *Guardian* allegations. In November 2009, it not only effectively exonerated the *NoW* but reserved its criticism for the *Guardian*: 'its stories did not quite live up to the dramatic billing they were initially given.' I was caught off guard in Nairobi, but flew home and resigned from the PCC's code committee, which drew up the industry's ethical guidelines. It was the only form of protest open to me.[4]

'Phone Hacking Journos Cleared', trumpeted the *Sun*.

Meanwhile Nick's researches revealed a still darker story.

One day he came to tell me about a corrupt former private investigator, Jonathan Rees, who had been working for the *NoW* and who was now in jail, on remand for murder. He had been a business partner of another private investigator, Daniel Morgan, who had been killed by an axe to his head in March 1987.

Rees had served an earlier six-year jail sentence for planting cocaine on a woman to prevent her getting custody of her child in a bitter divorce case. Once out of prison he was rehired onto Coulson's *NoW* as one of four highly paid investigators using illegal methods that the editor apparently knew nothing about.

Now Rees was again in prison waiting to stand trial for the murder of Morgan. Under British court reporting rules, we couldn't write about that. But there was an election imminent – and every prospect that Coulson would, within weeks, walk through the front door of 10 Downing Street as press secretary to the prime minister. He would be one of the most powerful people in the country.

I wrote a leading article to accompany the story about 'Mr A' we ran on 25 February 2010. The anonymised story was an unsatisfactory way of alerting people to the ticking time-bomb should Cameron take Coulson into government, but our hands were tied.

However, there was nothing stopping us privately informing the most senior politicians about the situation. We made contact with Gordon Brown, the prime minister; with Cameron's chief of staff; and with Nick Clegg, the leader of the Liberal Democrats, to explain the full significance of an otherwise opaque story. None of it made any difference. By 11 May Cameron was prime minister, with Coulson at his right hand. Five weeks later News Corp announced that it was bidding to take full control of BSkyB⁵ – a move which, if it got political approval, would make them easily the most dominant news organisation in Britain. It was almost as if it had all been choreographed.

I saw fear in people's eyes when I talked about the story. No one wanted to make an enemy of Rupert Murdoch and his newspapers. That was understandable. For decades, he had relished his power to make and break people. He owned very nearly 40 per cent of the national press in Britain. The *Times* gave him entrée to the political circles he valued. At the other end of the operation, his hand-picked executives were employing criminals to dig up the dirt on the private lives of anyone they chose to target. Why make an enemy of such a man, or such a company?

The police did their best to put us off the scent. The Yard's head of communications, Dick Fedorcio, asked for a meeting with myself and John Yates, the assistant commissioner who had conducted the miraculously quick one-day investigation in 2009. They did their hardest to suggest that we were barking up the wrong tree while privately admitting 'it was a dirty business'. Another meeting was arranged with the commissioner himself, Sir Paul Stephenson. Again, the message was that we should ease up.

Then I got a call from someone at the heart of government suggesting to me – on a deeply private basis – that not only were we on the right track, but we were just scratching the surface. The source offered assistance via a middle man and warned me to watch out.

It was time to seek outside help. I rang Bill Keller, executive editor of the *New York Times*, and explained how we could not run the full Rees story; and also, how much of the British press was steadfastly ignoring the saga. Keller put three reporters on a plane that week. They stayed in London for the best part of six months.

We briefed them for four hours on their first evening and thereafter heard little about what they were up to, though Nick helped them in the background. They felt the need to check out every detail of our reporting for themselves – and then see how much further they could take it.

It was like the cavalry arriving. Ever since my stint in Washington in the late 1980s, I had had an enormous respect for the best of American reporting. To see these three reporters – who already had several Pulitzer prizes between them – move into action was a moment of pure relief. A sweet irony, to see watchdogs arrive to watch over the watchdogs.

The *NYT* published a 6,000-word account of the phone hacking saga at the beginning of September 2010.[6] It had taken an American newspaper to do what any British news outlet (or police or regulator or politician) had been free to do: to investigate an incredibly important and compelling story and find out whether the *Guardian* was right or wrong.

They confirmed all the essentials of Nick's reporting. They found their own sources within the *NoW*, including Sean Hoare, the paper's former show business correspondent, who told the reporters on the record that he had played hacked voicemail messages to Coulson both on the *Sun* and *News of the World*. 'Everyone knew [about phone hacking]' another source told the reporters. 'The office cat knew.'

The *NYT* story was the turning point. It was not just that they had produced many stunning new revelations. But they had meticulously confirmed virtually every word of Nick's reporting. From now on it would be hard to dismiss this as a *Guardian* obsession or an anti-Murdoch mission. A small cohort of lawyers was working away in the background, on behalf of a handful of rather courageous victims – Hugh Grant, Steve Coogan, Sienna Miller among them.[7] From now on the clock was ticking and various strands of newly rekindled inquiries acquired a momentum of their own. In short order:

- Early January 2011: The *NoW* suspended its news editor, Ian Edmondson, over claims of phone hacking, and Scotland Yard asked for new material to be handed over
- 14 January: The Crown Prosecution Service announced it would review all papers in the case
- 21 January: Coulson resigned from Number 10
- 26 January: Police launched Operation Weeting to look into phone hacking
- 9 February: Police announced they had found more potential victims
- 18 February: A judge ordered the private investigator Glenn Mulcaire to identify any other *NoW* journalists involved in hacking
- 5 April: *NoW* chief reporter, Neville Thurlbeck, and Edmondson were arrested
- 8 April: News International announced a compensation scheme and offered an unreserved apology to some of those suing the company
- 10 April: *NoW* published an apology for intercepting voicemails
- 14 April: Another senior *NoW* journalist, James Weatherup, was arrested
- 7 June: Sienna Miller settled for £100,000 in damages after several of her mobile phones were found to have been hacked into; News Group offered 'sincere apologies'

The denouement began with the revelation we published on 4 July[8] that the *NoW* had hacked into the phone of the abducted 13-year-old schoolgirl Milly Dowler, in the time between her disappearance and the discovery of her body some months later in 2002.[9]

There was widespread revulsion. Les Hinton, Murdoch's closest business confidant over decades, has since written that the story 'horrified' him.[10] The case was fresh in people's minds because the trial of Milly's murderer, a serial killer called Levi Bellfield, had just played out over two harrowing weeks at the Old Bailey. This was not about actors or sportsmen. Maybe the loss of a celebrity's privacy was distasteful. But a newspaper hacking the phone of a missing teenager triggered a surge of sheer disgust.

David Cameron condemned 'the dreadful act'. By the evening it looked as though the parents of two other murdered children – Jessica Chapman and Holly Wells – had also been targeted by Glenn Mulcaire. The following day's *Telegraph* reported evidence that 52 families bereaved by the July 2005 London bombings had also had their phones hacked by the *NoW*. With even the *Times* now condemning its sister paper, it turned out that families of soldiers of who died in Iraq and Afghanistan had been targeted. Advertisers started threatening to boycott the paper which was revealed to have behaved so disgustingly.

And then things starting happening so fast it was almost impossible to do justice to them. Within a very short space of time:

- Rupert Murdoch announced the closure of the *NoW*
- Brooks told a stunned newsroom they should be prepared for much more dirt to emerge
- Coulson was arrested on suspicion of conspiring to hack phones and bribe the police
- Clive Goodman, who had already been jailed for hacking, was re-arrested
- It emerged that millions of emails had been deleted from News International servers
- The prime minister, David Cameron, announced two public inquiries into press standards and ethics. He put his hands up for having 'done nothing' about persistent concerns about the dominance of Murdoch
- The government announced it was delaying the decision on the

BSkyB merger; £1.7 billion was wiped from the company's value
- Yates wrote a letter to me apologising for his mistakes
- Cameron opposed the BSkyB bid
- The BSkyB bid was dropped
- Brooks resigned
- Les Hinton, CEO of the *WSJ* and Murdoch ally for 50 years, resigned
- Sean Hoare, one of the *NYT*'s sources for phone hacking, was found dead – from, as it turned out, natural causes
- Brooks was arrested; Neil Wallis, former deputy editor of the *NoW*, was also arrested – it turned out he had been hired to give media advice to Scotland Yard and that the commissioner, Sir Paul Stephenson, had taken 20 nights' free accommodation at a health farm at which Wallis was the media consultant
- Stephenson resigned; Yates resigned
- Murdoch was called before a Commons select committee and announced: 'this is the most humble day of my life'
- Three separate police investigations into News Group journalism were launched
- The FBI started an inquiry into whether News Corp had broken the Foreign Corrupt Practices Act

These were the most intense few weeks of my life to date. The above narrative doesn't include repeated attempts by News International to fight back against us, nor the occasion when Nick – based on what he was hearing from internal NI sources – warned me we would both be put under surveillance by the Murdoch organisation (the warning was as vague as that). I had my house swept for bugs – only to discover the work had been subcontracted to people associated with Jonathan Rees (who soon fed the information back to the *Sunday Times*). I had it swept all over again – this time by former SAS personnel.

By the time the climax of the summer arrived with the Murdoch parliamentary hearing, Nick and I were hollow-eyed with adrenalin-suffused exhaustion. But that was nothing to the turmoil and chaos within a shell-shocked News Corp as the organisation struggled to cope with what had been revealed. It was now a fight for survival.

Hinton has described the impact on Murdoch himself – finding him late at night with an 'empty gaze . . . so ill and tired. He was so distraught I knew he wasn't thinking straight . . . he seemed almost on the edge of panic.' When Hinton heard the *News of the World* had been closed he was left speechless: 'it was a desperate move'.

The reaction from the rest of the press was interesting. The PCC – the so-called regulator which had criticised the *Guardian* while exonerating the *NoW* – had, in the middle of the chaos, abruptly withdrawn its report. I started receiving the odd phone call and email from other senior (and surprising) editorial figures around Fleet Street. *They hadn't realised. They should have known. First-class reporting. Got to hand it to you. Things had to change. The PCC was a busted flush: it was never a proper regulator, we all privately knew that. We needed to get our house in order. Murdoch had been running a rogue operation. Out of this could grow an opportunity.*

The industry had just launched a lobbying body to put its case more effectively: its promotional literature featured the *Guardian*'s phone-hacking stories. *We are fearless in taking on power – even on our own doorstep.*

There was a breakfast with two Fleet Street elders. *How can we rebuild something good out of this?* (Spoiler alert: that didn't last.)

In time, it was to transpire that the *NoW* was far from alone in using private detectives – and maybe not even the worst culprit. Many news-papers routinely used private agents to trace people through means both legal and illegal. In 2015 a court was told that the industrial scale of phone hacking at Mirror Group titles made the *NoW* 'look like a small cottage industry'.[11] The *Mirror* victims were awarded huge damages to reflect 'the length, degree and frequency of all this conduct', with the company admitting in court that its senior editors and executives had 'actively turned a blind eye' to phone hacking for years.[12]

The *Mirror*'s legal director, Paul Vickers, was central to the Fleet Street elders' later fightback against the government's regulatory proposals. He left the *Mirror* as the company set aside £60 million in provisions to pay damages and costs. He was immediately given a job as editorial legal director at the *Telegraph*, which later also hired Andy Coulson as a consultant.

The elders looked after the elders.

By 2015 the phone hacking scandal had cost News Corp up to a billion dollars in costs and damages.[13] Murdoch – desperate to protect his US operation – moved to restructure his company, splitting the newspapers from the entertainment division. The legal cases had now moved on to claim deliberate concealment and destroyed evidence at the *Sun* as well as the *NoW*. By then nearly 1,000 victims of intrusion had received damages, with more actions in the pipeline. Once Scotland Yard had run an honest inquiry they concluded that Mulcaire had had 6,000 victims, confirming what we had claimed way back in July 2009. The *Mirror* cases continue their way through the courts.

Coulson spent part of his 18-month sentence in prison. Four other *NoW* executives[14] – joined him in jail. Four others[15] were given a suspended sentence. Brooks, her husband and another executive were acquitted.

★

Nick Davies's account of these two years of his life was published as *Hack Attack*[16] in 2014. I recently re-read it in some wonder. If people in future years want to know what it was to be a brilliant investigative reporter – ingenious, unflinching, indefatigable, brave, resourceful – they should read Nick's book.

The elders of Fleet Street could never forgive him. The *Daily Mail*, which rarely carried long book reviews, devoted 3,000 words[17] to reprinting a *New Statesman* piece by its own in-house columnist Stephen Glover, who was repeatedly deployed in this way. He denounced Davies as 'The Man Who Did for the British Press'. Yes – literally. Not the man who saved the British press from a criminal and moral catastrophe – with all the dire consequences for democracy that were incipiently apparent for anyone with eyes to see – but the man who 'did for' the British press.

In Glover's account Davies was simply driven by a hatred for Rupert Murdoch and tabloid journalists. Why should anyone distrust Murdoch and the tabloid press more than the state? Glover seemed to find the question genuinely baffling. In any event, the press was now 'shriv-elling . . . crumbling, cowed and increasingly regulated' – and Davies was more than partly to blame.

The truth was more complex than perhaps Glover could imagine. Davies was certainly mistrustful of Murdoch. Who wouldn't be, having unearthed what he had and been met by such a wall of lies, dissembling, obstruction, threats and smears? But it was wide of the mark to say that Davies was motivated by a hatred of the tabloid press. In some respects, Davies's work showed his own Mirror Group training – in the directness of his writing, his love of human stories, his powerful sense of narrative.

More tellingly, his entire investigation – as I knew – had been aided and, at times, directed by people within the *NoW*. They hated the work they were given. They disliked the criminal methods and the bullying culture to produce ever-more sensational stories. James Murdoch, in closing the paper, paid tribute to the *NoW*'s 'proud history of fighting crime, exposing wrong-doing and regularly setting the news agenda for the nation'. In its 168-year history it had done all those things. But increasingly it had sold on intrusion and sex – the *News of the Screws*. It was the reporters who finally turned.

They weren't against tabloid journalism. They could – and did – defend a decent tradition of such reporting. They simply couldn't stomach its horribly corrupted form. That one or more commentators couldn't tell the difference spoke volumes about the paranoia of the *laager*.

*

It would be surprising if journalists were still using private investigators to do their dirty and criminal work for them. In that sense Davies's work had been an important cleansing agent. But *Hack Attack* is really about power – and how one media company had begun to frighten and corrupt so many corners of British life.

Any other company shaken to its bones by a dark period of corporate chaos and endemic crookedness would signal as publicly as it could that it had turned over a new leaf. The prime minister himself had said that the people at the top of News International 'must have no future role in the running of a media company in our country'.

But that is not how media elders work. If anything, they have to prove that the normal rules don't apply to them.

In 2015 – a little more than a year after she left the Old Bailey dock in some relief at being cleared of all charges – Rebekah Brooks was back, reappointed as CEO of Murdoch's UK newspapers. An MP who had been the victim of hacking by the company described it as 'two fingers up to the British public'. The next year James Murdoch, the subject of scathing criticism by Ofcom, the broadcasting regulator, was back running BSkyB.

As night followed day, in 2017 Rupert Murdoch – embattled in the US over revelations of similar chaos and ethical corruption within Fox TV – once again launched a bid to take full control of BSkyB.[18]

Murdoch's ability to survive what would have destroyed others reminded me of the speech in the Spielberg film, *Catch Me If You Can*. 'Two little mice fell in a bucket of cream. The first mouse quickly gave up and drowned. The second mouse wouldn't quit. He struggled so hard that eventually he churned that cream into butter and crawled out.'

Murdoch was that second mouse.

17

Let Us Pay?

George Clooney bought the rights.

Hollywood has always had a soft spot for the journalist-as-crumpled-hero narrative. Bogart in *Deadline*; Beatty in *Reds*; Al Pacino as Lowell Bergman; Redford and Hoffman as Woodward and Bernstein; Strathairn and Clooney himself as Murrow and Friendly. Robards as Bradlee, David Thewlis as Nick in the Spielberg film *The Fifth Estate*, about WikiLeaks. And now Clooney, son of a former TV anchorman, wanted to contribute another to the library of films celebrating the lonely reporter in search of truth. He commissioned two scriptwriters to produce a screenplay.

Nick's story – if it's ever made (a few studios declined the opportunity to upset Murdoch) – would be a worthy addition to the canon. So much for fiction. How, in real life, could one sustain the kind of reporting that he had done?

For well over 100 years journalists had not had to think very much about how their salaries came to be paid each month. Readers alone had, as previously observed, never handed over enough money to support a large newsroom with an investigative team. Advertising filled the void – not out of altruism, but because of the lack of alternatives. 'Best Buy', in the words of academic Clay Shirky, 'was not willing to support the Baghdad bureau because Best Buy cared about news from Baghdad. They just didn't have any other good choices.' And because they didn't have other choices, they over-paid for advertising.

Paul Starr's 2004 book, *The Creation of the Media*,[1] had traced the happy circumstance by which, for many decades, commercial entities produced critical public goods – or, more plainly, ad-supported newspapers produced investigative or accountability journalism.

Starr wrote a bleak piece in March 2009 predicting the media would face a crisis of legitimacy as, reeling from financial pressures, it retreated from its traditional role of reporting. 'When they were financially strong,' wrote Starr, 'newspapers were better able not only to invest in long-term investigative projects but also to stand up against pressure from politicians and industries to suppress unfavourable stories. As imperfect as they have been, newspapers have been the leading institutions sustaining the values of professional journalism. A financially compromised press is more likely to be ethically compromised.'[2]

David Simon, creator of *The Wire* and a former police reporter on the *Baltimore Sun*, made the same point around the same time: 'Oh, to be a state or local official in America over the next 10 to 15 years, before somebody figures out the business model,' he said. 'To gambol freely across the wastelands of an American city, as a local politician! It's got to be one of the great dreams in the history of American corruption.'[3]

Simon thought paywalls were the answer. Shirky – in September 2009 – thought the model for news was already so different from the nineteenth- and twentieth-century models that the eventual answer would lie elsewhere if we wanted to think of news as a public good which would be widely accessible to the public. The problem with paywalls for general news was that 'suddenly you have millions of people who are not as well served by the creation of public goods'. He elaborated in a lecture at Harvard:

> So, there's three methods for creating public goods. You go to the market, right? And things in the market are created when revenues can reliably exceed expenses. And then you expect some company to set itself up and provision.
>
> Secondly, you can have a public organization that has some source of income other than revenue, whether it is endowment, donations, taxes, whatever. It typically operates in a different legal regime.

Producing goods because they believe that that is the right use of that money and they are constituted to pursue those goals.

And then you can have social production where a group of people just get together and do something for themselves. Markets are how most cars are produced. Public goods are how much roads are produced. Social stuff is how most birthday parties are produced, how most picnics are produced, right? It has just not been a big feature of the landscape. But, now it is.

The problem we were facing, argued Shirky, was that newspapers had produced 85 per cent of the accountability journalism – and that whole system was suddenly at risk. You couldn't replace or recreate a newspaper in the twenty-first century. You needed to think about a new class of institutions or models to produce accountability journalism.

Shirky was often described – sometimes scornfully – as an internet optimist. But in Harvard in late 2009 he was anything but optimistic.

I think a bad thing is going to happen, right? And it's amazing to me how much, in a conversation conducted by adults, the possibility that maybe things are just going to get a lot worse for a while does not seem to be something people are taking seriously.

I think we are headed into a long trough of decline in accountability journalism, because the old models are breaking faster than the new models can be put into place.

To use the historical analogy from Eisenstein, from *The Printing Press as an Agent of Change*, there was a long hundred years between the Protestant Reformation and the Treaty of Westphalia. And that was a hundred years in which people almost literally did not know what to think. The old institutions were visibly not functioning any longer, but the nation-state as a new organizing principle was not yet in place. And those were, for many people, not a great hundred years. So, I have no idea how long this transition will take. But I don't think that some degree of failure and decay is avoidable. I think our goal should be to minimise the depth of that trough. But I don't think we can get away with a simple and rapid alternative to what we enjoyed in the 20th century — in part because the accidents that held that landscape together in the 20th century were so crazily contingent.

In sum, he thought, news organisations were necessary, but the sooner we started on 'vast and varied experimentation the better'.

★

But, in the middle of a global financial meltdown was it possible for already existing organisations to go in for 'vast and varied experimentation', or were we doomed to watch as others tried? It certainly felt as if we were experimenting – but maybe not on a scale or with enough resources to succeed.

The experiments included trying some hyper-local sites: interesting, but not our core business and too small a trial from which to learn. The science and environment pods were, on the other hand, producing fruit. On science, the editorial team had recruited a dozen academic bloggers and created a network whereby they could write for us, or simply cross-post from another site. We both won: we acquired additional interesting and authoritative voices: they were happy to be reaching far bigger audiences than previously. There was a similar story with environment. By co-operating with a variety of other green-tinged sites we had rapidly become the biggest environmental news site in the world. By March 2010 we had 2.6 million unique users a month just for that micro-site.

In our search for other voices we hired two prisoners – one serving (Erwin James), one former (Eric Allison) – to write about crime, punishment, miscarriages of justice and penal policy.

We ran a three-year experiment in using the new world of connectivity to look at development issues in far greater depth than any news organisation can ever have tried before. We picked one Ugandan village – Katine in the Soroti district – and wrote in great detail over three years about its education, health, governance and farming challenges. It was a village without power which had recently experienced a full hand of torments – famine, war, disease, poverty, drought. We partnered with NGOs and funded the project through reader donations and with help from Barclays Bank. One of the aims was to make the project a two-way one: i.e. we wanted to hear the voices of Katine residents rather than have them mediated through western journalists flying in from London. The experiment resulted in long-term funding for coverage of development issues from the Bill and Melinda Gates Foundation. Again, we were keen not to 'cover' development solely through the eyes of western reporters. We built up and trained a global network of locally based correspondents to tell us about labour, food, health, sex, drought, domestic violence, business, slavery and much more.

Some reporters had begun to use 'open' approaches to their work.[4] When a 47-year-old news vendor, Ian Tomlinson, died in the middle of the G-20 protests in London in 2009 Paul Lewis, a *Guardian* reporter who had joined as a trainee four years previously, had doubts about the official version of events – that Tomlinson had suffered a heart attack and that the police had come under a hail of missiles while rescuing him.

Lewis tweeted out an appeal for witnesses: any crowd in 2009 would include thousands of people with the means of recording events. A fund manager, back in New York, looked at the footage on his phone and found he had filmed the moment when a policeman struck Tomlinson from behind.[5] It felt like a distant echo of Peterloo.

Lewis again used Twitter the following year to investigate the death of an Angolan refugee, Jimmy Mubenga, on a British Airways flight on which he was being forcibly deported. The traditional instinct of reporters was not to let anyone else know in advance you're on a particular story. Lewis inverted that – and was rewarded by passengers on the plane who gave him eyewitness accounts of how Mubenga had been suffocated by security guards working for G4S.[6]

Lewis – along with his colleague Matthew Taylor – was again at the heart of the *Guardian*'s coverage of the riots that broke out in England in the summer of 2011. It was a week of chaos, flames, protests, looting and disorder in towns and cities across England. By the end of the week, five people had died and more than 1,500 had been arrested. It was a very difficult story for any conventional news desk to keep track of – fast moving, anarchic, scattered. However many reporters it fielded, any newsroom would still have been behind the story, or in the wrong place at the wrong time. Researchers (including ours) later identified an archive of 2.5 million associated tweets during the week.[7]

Night by night we would have 25 reporters out on the streets, feeding into a live-blog. Meanwhile, the data team started logging and collating all verified incidents and pinning them on a Flickr map. The *Guardian* became the most authoritative source of information by harnessing this live resource – and publishing it openly. On one day we had 6 million visitors to the site. The data team later collated more than 1,000 court cases of people accused of offences related to the riots. They then used that database to approach convicted rioters to hear their stories and to try and understand the root causes of the disturbances.

The reporting on Tomlinson, Mubenga and the riots all involved a combination of old-fashioned shoe leather and the power of social media. A reporter on their own could not possibly have the means or impact to match what Lewis and his colleagues were doing. Equally, social media on its own was quite often too unfocused, random or unreliable to match the highest standards of journalism. The combination of professional and amateur – as with the science blogs – seemed to be a powerful pointer to one future for reporting. We began to call it open journalism. It was an idea that was to catch on.

These techniques may seem less radical now, but they were virtually unheard of at the time. Some years later the *Washington Post*'s excellent reporter David Fahrenthold was to win the Pulitzer for his open-source reporting of Donald Trump in 2016. An NPR strategist, Andy Carvin, also broke new ground in 2011 with something clumsily labelled 'collaborative networked journalism', to become, for a while at least, the must-read source on the Arab uprisings. A veteran of social media, Carvin had begun retweeting testimonies, pictures and video from the protests in Tunisia – then Egypt and Libya. Although he had a network of blogger contacts in the region whom he used to check tweeted information, he also retweeted unverified material, inviting his followers to help establish its accuracy.

Eliot Higgins,[8] an unemployed British financial administrator, began blogging the Syrian civil war under the pseudonym Brown Moses from his front room in Leicester. By working entirely in the open – analysing social media and up to 450 YouTube channels a day – he became one of the world's leading experts on the weaponry being used in that conflict. Within a short period, he was attracting 250,000 page views a month and had been appointed visiting research associate at King's College London as well as joining the Atlantic Council's Digital Forensic Research Lab as senior non-resident fellow. He went on to help create a new website, Bellingcat, for people to investigate current events using open-source information.

We had used 'open' techniques in June 2009 at the height of the concern over the sums British MPs were claiming by way of expenses. When the entire database was released it consisted of 700,000 individual documents within 5,500 PDF files covering all 646 members of parliament. It would have taken weeks for a team of reporters to work their way through the material. So we asked the readers to help: we created a basic crowdsourcing app whereby readers could download any documents, comment on them and highlight anything that caught their eye. This act of sifting and commenting was of incalculable help to the reporters – and was enthusiastically embraced by numerous readers. Once again, pro-am worked to our advantage.

We did it again on tax – with complex corporate structures that would have taken days to understand. Sometimes we just threw a question out to the readers: we don't have the immediate knowledge to hand to interpret this offshore arrangement, but we know some of you will. Can you help us?

The resultant journalism was often better than we could do on our own. And readers felt involved in the *Guardian* and its reporting in a rather profound way. Was this a way of building a new basis of trust between a news organisation and its users/readers? Journalism was no longer something done, or sent, *to* you but a process that was open, transparent and confident enough to welcome the involvement of others. It was never going to be a technique for every story, but it was proving useful in many situations.

In time it became second nature for anyone with a mobile phone to share something they thought noteworthy – from casual witnesses to news stories to whistleblowers searching for a journalistic partner. Many Twitter sceptics melted away as it became apparent what a formidable reporting and publishing resource it was becoming – see, for example, the cascade of revelations over the shootings and killings by police in the US. The public instinct was to record, and anyone with a phone had better tools at their disposal than many professional journalists could have dreamed of only a few years earlier.

The eventual advent of live-streaming video from smartphones would have further consequences for live news: it would be raw, unfiltered, more immediate and more widely distributed than anything that preceded it. The revolution would be Periscoped. Or Facebooked. To begin with, reporters doubted whether the man or woman in the street would have the skills or experience to film and edit live footage. But then Snapchat and Instagram made that easy.

It was eventually impossible to imagine any newsroom standing entirely apart from this parallel world. Of course, the stream of material now flooding the ether was often random, opportunistic, inaccurate and messy. But that, surely, played to the advantage of an established news organisa- tion? Harness, contextualise, verify, explain: do all the things we did before. Only now we were part of a teeming ocean of information rather than the recipient of a trickle from the wires and with a few reporters on the ground. Our job had just become both much harder . . . and much easier.

As with Gutenberg, this was the beginning of an experiment whose future would be unknowable. How civic-minded would the public turn out to be? The optimists and pessimists watched from the wings, each convinced of the wisdom of their own arguments. The optimists held that, while there would inevitably be fewer journalists, there would be more journalism – that, collectively, people would be inspired by civic virtue to help separate fact from fiction – or, at least, help identify the closest kernel of the truth that could reasonably be deciphered. There was plenty of supporting evidence for this happening, with groups on Reddit or Twitter crowdsourcing their way to the truth.

The Clinton–Trump election of 2016 would give plenty of fodder to the pessimists. They concluded that most people were, on the whole, quite uninterested in being active participants in the news: they were happy simply to consume it, especially when it confirmed their prejudices. An alarming number were apparently willing to fuel and repropagate falsehoods. Reporters on the ground were stunned how many people had come to believe things that were simply untrue. These were educated and otherwise reasonable people who, ten years ago, would have read a city or state newspaper. They would have agreed the facts, even if they disagreed about their implications. Now even the most basic contours of news were contested.

Paul Lewis, by now based in the US, pronounced himself aghast at the conspiracies and fake news people relayed to him as fact – Sandy Hook was a hoax; Obama's parents were CIA agents; the Clintons secretly murdered one of Bill's accusers; Muslims controlled Europe; climate change was a fraud; three million Bernie Sanders votes were suppressed; there were Chinese sleeper cells spread across America. These fictions had gone mainstream.

When it came to the really important news, what would the wisdom of the crowd look like? Were the multitude of Facebook users more interested in dispassionate facts or in promoting versions of the world that support their prejudices? Were we collectively wired to want to sort fact from fiction? If so, why were so many people so receptive to fraudulent information? The success of these fake news stories was dependent on their being shared and re-shared; on people either assuming they were accurate, or turning a blind eye to the fact they were clearly fake ... because they coincided with some political belief or bias.

How this all works is, in 2018, barely understood at all. Many people, for instance, assert confidently that social media creates filter bubbles in which people happily live in echo chambers of their own making. But much academic research doubts whether this is actually true – in fact, claiming the opposite. One study after the Trump election suggested that social media users in fact use significantly more different news sources than non-users.[9]

Ten years after the mainstream launch of Facebook there was exhilaration over what had been unleashed on the world. And there was dismay. Some wanted to push forward at the frontiers, others to build up the barricades.

*

We were more on the side of pushing at the frontiers of experimentation. But it was also important to keep flexing the muscle of traditional investigative journalism. We had high-profile run-ins in 2009 with the global commodity traders Trafigura, over claims of toxic dumping. Barclays Bank were forced to wake a duty High Court judge up at 2.30 a.m. to issue a 'pyjama injunction' ordering us to remove a leaked document from our website.

Ian Cobain plugged away with a long series of revelations about torture and illegal rendition in the wake of the Iraq and Afghanistan wars – published in book form in 2012.[10] It would be half a dozen years later before one of his stories – that a Libyan dissident, Abdel Hakim Belhaj, had been tortured after being handed over by Britain to Muammar Gaddafi – was thoroughly vindicated. In May 2018 the prime minister, Theresa May, apologised for the 'appalling' case and the government paid £500,000 in compensation.[11] When Cobain's reporting of rendition and torture had originally appeared some people in the intelligence world did their best to persuade me Cobain was wildly off the scent. Felicity Lawrence investigated the murky world of food production – again leading to well-received books.[12] Maggie O'Kane was a powerful campaigner over female genital mutilation. Paul Lewis and Rob Evans unearthed an extraordinary saga of undercover policemen who had infiltrated protest groups, having prolonged relationships with women – and even fathering children – before vanishing from their lives.[13]

We investigated arms companies. We looked at the environmental havoc wreaked by oil companies in Africa and South America. David Conn quietly unearthed scandals in the business of sport, including years surfacing new turns in the case of the 1989 Hillsborough disaster.[14] Amelia Gentleman was not a traditional investigative journalist – but she developed a powerful strain of long-form reportage about social deprivation based on listening and the patient accumulation of facts.

We would expose the abuse and exploitation – including dozens of deaths – of migrant workers preparing the Qatar stadiums for the 2022 football world cup. Ben Goldacre also exposed a man called Matthias Rath, a German vitamin impresario who claimed that his pills were better for AIDS than conventional medication. Goldacre described Rath as a vile 'full-on fruitcake' who had helped cost the lives of tens of thousands of Africans needlessly deprived of effective treatments. He effectively accused Rath of manslaughter on a mass scale – and Rath duly sued us for libel. The successful defence of this single piece in a legal battle lasting 18 months cost an astonishing half a million pounds, not all of it recovered when Rath finally dropped the case.

We were – though of course the reporters would have disowned the word – building a brand. The more digging we did, the more people brought us more stories to investigate. Even those who didn't share the *Guardian*'s politics recognised the value of sustained and vigilant reporting.

The breaking – and defence – of all these stories was about editorial depth and resource ... and organisational resilience. As we came under a blizzard of orchestrated attacks over many of these stories we held our ground, just as we had with Hamilton and Aitken and Rath and the police federation. Good reporters needed tough, pragmatic lawyers behind them – and, over the years, we developed a resolute and wise team.[15]

The resilient news organisation was also there when its reporters got into trouble. At the end of 2009 our Middle East roving correspondent, Ghaith Abdul Ahad, was kidnapped in Kunar Province, North East Afghanistan. All work stopped for a week. Camp beds and inflatable mattresses were moved into the office. Security consultants arrived. We hit the phones to every former expert, diplomat and spook we knew.

We soon discovered where he was – held by armed bandits up an inaccessible valley in the mountainous region bordering Pakistan's Pakhtunkhwa province. That was the good news. The bad news was that he was likely to be sold on to the Taliban if we didn't manage to free him extremely quickly and that the gang had divided loyalties. It was not the easiest logistical problem to solve, but we got him out within six days.[16]

*

How, on present trends, would news organisations protect their correspondents in future? Or would they simply stop sending them? How could they maintain the will, let alone the ability, to carry on with challenging, expensive, time-consuming reporting?

The economic recession was continuing to bite horribly. Walter Isaacson, biographer of Steve Jobs, wrote the February 2009 cover story of *Time* magazine, announcing: 'the crisis in journalism has reached meltdown proportions. It is now possible to contemplate a time when some major cities will no longer have a newspaper and when magazines and network-news operations will employ no more than a handful of reporters.'

★

Up to this point virtually all mainstream general newspapers had, since the turn of the century, run free websites. Almost all those who had tried charging had given up.[17] One academic found that, in 1999, only two newspapers were still charging after an initial enthusiasm: the *Wall Street Journal* and the *Champaign News Gazette* in Illinois.[18] Another writer described the years 2001–7 as 'the frenzy of failed trials'.[19] There had, to date, been few successful experiments. Newsday.com, on Long Island, was the most recent experiment everyone was talking about: it had tried a paywall in October 2009 – and seen its 2.2 million unique visits a month shrink, by January 2010, to just ... 35.[20]

That was about to change. In June 2010 the *Times/Sunday Times* announced it would launch a 'hard paywall' – with users being charged £1 for a day's access and £2 for a week's subscription to both websites. The *Sun* and the *News of the World* would follow.

By this stage the *Mail* had overtaken the *Guardian* and was reaching 2.27 million UK browsers a day. The *Guardian* was on 1.87 million, the *Telegraph* on 1.55 million, the *Times* on 1.22 million and the *Independent* on 465,000. John Witherow, veteran editor of the *Sunday Times*, and I appeared on the BBC radio *Media Show* in May 2010 to debate the issue, hosted by Steve Hewlett,[21] in front of an audience.

Witherow explained the shared *Sunday Times* and *Times* sites would be separated (they had hitherto shared one URL) with an 'awful lot of multiple media, especially on the *Sunday Times* ... lots of graphics, whizzbang singing and dancing things in addition to what you get in the newspaper'.

He admitted that, in the middle of so much 'chaotic turbulence' going on it was 'a huge challenge, and something of a gamble'. The *Times/ Sunday Times* editorial budget approached £100 million a year.[22] The cost of a Washington correspondent alone − salary, travel, expenses − could approach half a million pounds. The Baghdad correspondent − including security − was nearer a million. Someone had to pay for it.

Hewlett asked how many readers they would lose by erecting a wall. Witherow frankly admitted they had no idea: 'We don't know . . . we assume the vast majority . . . easily 90 per cent.' It was still worth doing, he said. In some way advertisers would prefer a more select audience, 'because they know the sort of readers they'll be getting: the dedicated core of readers. It will more than balance out.' He hoped that people would sign up in their 'tens of thousands . . . we don't know yet . . . We'll just have to see.'

It was my turn. I said I welcomed the *Times*'s move: only by experimenting would we find out if paywalls worked. There might be many different economic models in the future.

If it worked would we follow, demanded Hewlett? 'Yes, you'd have to be crazy to be fundamentalist about this. None of us knows.'

I said I worried about the things you lost, journalistically, by going into a walled garden. We were interested in the gains of doing things openly and collaboratively. A fenced-off area of content meant turning your back on an incredible richness − being part of the way information now worked and was shared. I knew, for instance, that many *Times* journalists − though they welcomed the revenues − were conscious of writing for a much smaller audience and that would-be sources often preferred reaching a larger, and more, international audience; and for information to be freely findable over time.

Wasn't there a moral case for making people pay, Hewlett demanded? I quoted Jeff Jarvis's view of this meme: 'the entitlement argument . . . *this stuff costs us a lot to produce therefore you must pay us*'. It was an argument, as Jarvis pointed out, which didn't necessarily work elsewhere in business. In any event, Murdoch was on both sides of the moral case − with a free news website and TV news service (and a free newspaper) as well as a paid-for website.

I paid tribute to the *Times's* religious affairs correspondent, Ruth Gledhill, who, it seemed to me, had a very good understanding of how journalism in a digital age could be done. A physical newspaper was limited in its appetite for religious stories. Gledhill would write for it two or three times a day: the rest of the time she was a one-woman dynamo of blogging, linking, commenting, posting full texts of important documents or sermons, talking to her readers, and so on. She had made the *Times* essential reading for the community of readers she served. Putting Gledhill behind a paywall would kill that dead.[23]

It would be the end of the free exchange of the ability to use links – one of the central pillars, and glories, of the internet.

Was this an argument about protecting a newspaper or protecting journalism? asked Hewlett. We both agreed the days of the newspaper were numbered. I quoted Martin Sorrell, the biggest advertising guru in the world, who was predicting the digital side of his business would triple in short order. Not all of that would come to newspapers, but if, with a very large audience, we could similarly triple our revenues, we might be in with a good chance.

It was a good-natured debate, with neither of us sounding 100 per cent sure we were right. We were both vague on detail. Neither of us believed the printed newspaper was a long-term prospect. We both wanted journalism to thrive.

It was certainly a bold move by the *Times*. Of the three paid-for products Murdoch launched in 2010/11 – the *Times*, the *Sun* and the iPad newspaper, the *Daily* – two were to fail. The *Sun* dropped its paywall after falling drastically behind its free rivals, the *Mirror* and *Mail*. The iPad paper attracted 100,000 subs and was closed after 21 months, having burned through cash at $30 million a year. So, even within Murdoch's empire, the chances were stacked against success.

It was a clarifying discussion with Witherow because he was so honest (or vague) about the numbers of subscribers they anticipated picking up – 'tens of thousands' after losing 'easily' 90 per cent or more of the existing audience. To our ears those were frightening figures because we had such different readerships. Bluntly, the *Times* might be able to risk that loss of audience: it had affluent readers. We didn't.

For the *Times*, shedding the vast majority of their audience might just work because of the elite profile of the core *Times* reader. It was, in a way, a replay of a previous era of the *Times*, which had once used the marketing slogan 'Top People Read the Times'. In the mid-1960s it had gone for a bigger audience and, in the words of the economists Fred Hirsch and David Gordon, 'slid downmarket on an expensive spiral'.[24] Circulation soared – but they were not of the same social or wealth class as the existing readers and were therefore of little interest to the advertisers. After five years of large losses – £1.4 million a year (maybe £20 million in today's money) – the *Times* decided it made better business sense to go for a smaller readership. They actively sought to shed the readers of a lower economic bracket ... and could once more deliver better, classier, richer readers to advertisers. The paper was soon back in profit.

Those kinds of calculations would never, we thought, work for the *Guardian*, where we knew the average income of a reader even in 2016 was £24,000 – or £20,412 online. Our readers were educated, but they were not – financially or socially – elite. The median UK household disposable income in 2016 was £26,300.[25] If we had a small print readership and actively sought only a 'few tens of thousands' online – mostly in the UK – it was difficult to imagine a sustainable future for the *Guardian*.[26]

The author John Lanchester, writing in the *London Review of Books* in December 2010, was sympathetic to paying for news – but not behind a single wall for each newspaper. He, too, was glad Murdoch was trying something. 'If the *Times* paywall worked, we could all exhale and slap each other on the back and say "that was a close one" and forget that the business had once seemed doomed.' But he added: 'I should say that I don't know a single internet-minded person who thought that the paywall experiment had any chance of succeeding.'

His analysis of the *Times* experiment after six months – disentangling much opaque data about different kinds of subscriptions – was that the numbers 'were not just bad, they're terrible ... I would imagine that the loss in revenue from online advertising, a direct result of the precipitate crash in web traffic, would more than wipe out the revenue from the paywall. In fact, I'd be amazed if that weren't the case. Nobody is going to follow Murdoch down this route.'

Lanchester predicted that print editions would soon be junked and that the 'irresistible logic' pointed to a Spotify or iTunes-style payment mechanism. That implied that many newspapers would make their content commonly available for the payment of a monthly subscription. For a flat monthly fee you could browse across many titles within a 'walled garden'.[27] Blendle, a Dutch online news platform, had tried the so-called iTunes model: it aggregated articles from a variety of newspapers and sold them on a pay-per-article basis.

Lanchester concluded, 'Walls are not the way forward, but walls are not the same thing as payment, and without some form of payment, the press will not be here in five years' time. I hope one of the big organisations is working on this idea or something like it, because for print newspapers, the clock isn't just ticking, it's ticking louder and faster.'[28]

I personally wasn't against a Spotify model, but the *Guardian* – the tiniest corporate player, if large digitally – was not in a position to make it happen. The GMG Board and executives overwhelmingly did not think a paywall would work for the *Guardian* at this stage. Among its reasons:

- There were too many free sources of news competing with us. In the UK alone the BBC (revenues £4.6 billion), ITV, Sky (£5.9 billion), Reuters, the *Telegraph*, the *Mail*, the *Independent*, the *Mirror*, the *Huffington Post* – never mind the myriad specialist websites now serving sport, culture, science, fashion, music, film, etc. In the UK there was free radio and many free newspapers as well.[29]
- The available research (e.g. a Boston Consulting Group study in 2009) showed the UK low in the rankings of countries prepared to pay for news. BCG concluded: 'Paid online news would have a negligible impact on industry revenues (though) its impact on operating profit would be more significant. The willingness to pay would disappear if a disruptive free model emerges.'[30]
- We started from a much lower base in terms of bundling digital and print subscriptions. The *Times* and *Sunday Times* together sold 1.6 million copies compared with 656,000 for the *Guardian* and *Observer*.
- Only a third of our digital audience was UK-based. Two thirds lived abroad. Foreign readers couldn't be tempted to buy a digital

subscription off the back of a printed newspaper and we had no chance of building a larger audience abroad if we demanded they pay. Possibly in the future, but not now.

- The *Huffington Post* was, we heard, eyeing up international expansion. It would be free. Others were bound to follow.[31]
- The advertising team still believed that if we could build a large enough readership – particularly in the US – they could, in time, monetise it.

The NYT – which took a different route (a metred paywall) at the beginning of 2011 – started from a completely different position: a very large (and comparatively affluent) audience in the US which it was already monetising very effectively. Of all general (i.e. non-financial) newspapers this experiment has met with the most success. Initially sceptical, I came to think that – in time, once we had built a *much* larger readership – this might eventually be a model for the *Guardian*. But, at this stage, it didn't look right for us.

There were one or two commercial dissenters, but this was the overwhelming majority view. Most Board members wanted to concentrate on continuing to build reach – while getting better data on new readers. The editorial floor was broadly against paywalls, as well. Some would settle for whatever worked. Some clung on to a fundamental belief that journalism cost money to produce and therefore had a value. But most liked writing for a huge, and growing, global audience and didn't relish the idea of retreating to a relatively tiny UK-only pool. It was true of reporters, who did not warm to the idea of putting an off-putting (£) on their Twitter links. It was particularly true of foreign correspondents, who found they had a greater influence and impact in the regions they were covering than ever. There were fewer internationally accessed news organisations ... and the *Guardian* was now firmly cemented as one of them.

The digital natives were, unsurprisingly, the most vocal in believing that it would be a disaster to hide the *Guardian*'s journalism behind a wall. They just didn't believe the world was going to work like that in future or that younger readers would ever pay. Sure, you could – in the short-to-medium term – bundle print and digital together and effectively sell online access to middle-aged readers as a 'reward' for print. But when the time came to switch off the presses would you really be left with a sustainable business model?

The truth was, no one knew.[32]

*

Around this time Emily Bell came into my room with one of her Great Pronouncements. This one was not necessarily mad, but it was heartfelt. The digital world was going to divide between open and closed. We were at a fork in the road. The tech world could see it in the differing approaches of Google versus Apple: for them it was an article of faith that open would always beat closed. The Columbia Law School professor Tim Wu was to write about this argument later, questioning whether (in the wake of a golden period by Apple) it was still true. His conclusion: 'closed can beat open, but you have to be genius. Under normal conditions, in an unpredictable industry, and given regular levels of human error, open still beats closed.'

Wu conceded that the idea that 'open beats closed' was a relatively new one. For most of the twentieth century the opposite was usually believed to be true. But in a networked world the collective endeavours of many would win. AOL's walled garden proved no match for the open Web. 'An open product can also take advantage of collective, voluntary contributions of the masses, a point emphasized by [Harvard law professor] Yochai Benkler. Consequently, an individual Wikipedia entry might be lousy and contain errors, but the entire corpus will remain impressive.'[33]

This was what Emily wanted to talk about. She had come down from a meeting with a couple of engineers and the head of advertising. It was a decision every company was going to have to take.

There was no question in their minds: the *Guardian* had to be open side.

Open was not exactly the same as free. Some newspaper models would in time have a close and collaborative relationship with readers – and link freely to the world wide web – while trying a subscription or membership model.

Instinctively I agreed. I didn't like the idea of newspapers as closed worlds. Much of what we'd tried to do to date had been about knocking down the walls between the journalist and the reader – beginning with the readers' editor. It was there in the collaborative reporting we had been pioneering. It was there in the API open platforms we had used; there in Comment is Free; there in our science and environmental platforms; there in our wish to take our journalism to where the readers were, rather than insist the readers come to our platform to read it.

But it was a difficult idea to explain simply – and it was difficult to convince people that this was not necessarily the same as the debate about free versus paid. It was certainly true that charging for content behind a very hard paywall precluded some aspects of openness. But we were coming to believe we had to work out how journalism was best done in the twenty-first century before retreating to the apparent safety of nineteenth-century payment models (which might not, in any event, work for everyone now).

How about with hindsight? Some years later – in 2016 – I asked Emily, by now director of the Tow Center for Digital Journalism at Columbia University's Graduate School of Journalism and on the Scott Trust, about how she now thought of this distinction between open and free. This was how she put it, with the distance of some years, and from her perch as a much-consulted thinker about anything digital:

> You know, the natural endpoint of paying for news is the individual version of the Bloomberg Terminal, which means that the richest people have access to the best information. It's another way in which you can see division between the haves and the have-nots widening.
>
> I get that journalists have to be paid; and, if necessary, paid through subscription; and if the subscription keeps them out of an increasingly compromised advertising market; and if the subscription is easy and it's going well; then I have absolutely no objection to it whatsoever.
>
> But I still think that journalism, as a field, expends this enormous amount of intellectual energy and resource on building walls and keeping people away from really high-quality news and information,

which is incredibly important to the operating of a democratic society. And I don't understand why it is so controversial to say that's not a good state of affairs. The *Guardian*, to me, always had to be … an organization that used its endowment, foundation and status, to really push what that meant. So I think I was probably more ideologically committed to free.

I wasn't so ideologically devoted to free, but I was to open. I was intensely interested in the *Guardian* exploring all the implications of the latter. And, of course, I shared Emily's concerns about the best information being restricted to those who could pay for it, while the rest fed on scraps. But then I wasn't the business brain in the company. This was going to have to be a close and never-ending conversation between the editorial vision, the engineering opportunities, the public value and the commercial realities.[34]

Shortly after catching up with Emily in 2016, I was at a London dinner hosted at the Savoy Hotel by the *New York Times*. There was much talk of Donald Trump and of the *NYT*'s success in sustaining a metred paywall since 2011. At the end of the meal the executive editor, Dean Baquet, thanked the guests for their discussion about politics and business models for news. He was happy with the *NYT*'s position, but he asked whether anyone else around the table shared his concern about the new reality in which 98 per cent of Americans were now excluded from the *NYT*'s journalism and might well have to make do with substandard information?

The table, until then quite voluble, fell quiet. The question hung there as we bid our farewells. It was the rarely-articulated 'gated community' question. In a world of almost limitless information, the best would be available only to the more affluent. The rest of America would make do with an ocean of free stuff; some true, some fake.

The next day I emailed Dean to thank him and to commend him on his question. 'Thanks my friend,' he replied. 'And yes I fear a world of only rich elite media. I may be comfortable sitting at dinner in the Savoy but I'm also a guy who grew up in a poor neighbourhood in the American South. And I'm not so confident the people like a young Dean will be able to afford the reports we all edit. That would not help the divide that plagues the world.'

The *New York Times* had performed brilliantly during the election campaign: it had done everything you could ask of a serious newspaper. But 13 days after the dinner Donald Trump was elected 45th President of the United States.

The proportion of bad news to good news in the US was, by then, frightening. A study of Twitter in November 2016 by Oxford academic Robert Gorwa found that professional news content and 'junk news' were being shared in a one-to-one ratio.[35]

For every piece of 'real' news, people were consuming stuff that was fake, propaganda or conspiracy theories.

One to one.

Worse still, studies showed that very nearly two thirds of 'average people' did not know how to tell good journalism from rumour or falsehoods.[36]

The ability to tell fact from fiction had reached a tipping point.

*

Why did it matter?

Why did it matter that journalism – serious journalism, not celebrity or lifestyle clickbait – continued to be created, and consumed, by as many people as possible?

In the 1920s there had been a famous and prolonged public discussion between the philosopher John Dewey and the journalist/social critic Walter Lippmann. In crude terms Dewey believed that the press played a crucial role in creating an educated public and that a better-informed public would, in turn, make better decisions about elected representatives. That process would, in turn, create a better democracy. Lippmann was not so sure. It was a nice idea in theory, but he was more sceptical about the nature of the press, the function of journalism and the capacity of the public to participate in democratic discussion. The modern world was too complex for the public to play the role that liberal democracy demanded.

The argument[37] was played out over some years in books and articles and was revived decades later by media academics and theorists, not least Noam Chomsky, who was much struck by Lippmann's description of the manipulation of consciousness as 'the manufacture of consent'.[38]

Lippmann thought participatory democracy was a romantic ideal based on an unrealistic idea of the ability of the masses to engage in public affairs in meaningful ways. Dewey similarly believed in a factual basis for public debate – but that democracy should not be left to insiders or elites. 'It is not necessary that the many should have the knowledge and skill to carry on the needed investigations; what is required is that they have the ability to judge the bearing of the knowledge supplied by others upon common concerns.'

Dewey worried that the public was in danger of abandoning the public square for the sake of entertainment and would be more vulnerable to propaganda. In any case, how were the elites and intelligentsia to discover the best policies, if they were to be isolated from the masses? 'In the absence of an articulate voice on behalf of the masses, the best do not and cannot remain the best, the wise cease to be wise.'

Lippmann certainly had little sympathy with the distortions of the press brought about by the ownership model and commercial imperatives of the American press. 'A great newspaper,' he wrote, 'is a public service institution.'[39]

The debate had many modern resonances. The club or the mob? Was the social-media sphere the babbling of the ignorant, or was it more representative of true public feeling – emotion as well as intellect – than any political system ever previously devised? Do comment threads matter? Would Donald Trump have been elected if there had been a more effective, representative and professional media? Alternatively, would the elites have had a better idea of the forces that nurtured Trump if there had been a healthier local press to alert them?

What did it mean when an Oxford-educated British Cabinet minister[40] could proclaim in the middle of the Brexit referendum that 'people have had enough of experts'?

Old debates, new echoes.[41]

18

Open and Shut

Best of times, worst of times. This period might have been an extremely unsettling one in many ways – but there was also a feeling that journalism was there to be re-made and re-imagined. That was – intellectually and practically – beyond absorbing.

What was open journalism, if such a thing existed? We constantly looked outside, at how the rest of the connected world was now behaving. What would a future look like – assuming we were planning for the long term rather than simply muddling through with a hybrid print–online newsroom?

After a series of sandwich lunches to talk about it – including technologists as well as journalists – we hesitantly articulated ten principles of how post-print open journalism might look:

1) It encourages participation. It invites and/or allows a response
The age of the printing press was essentially a one-way, top-down form of communication. This age was different. 'Allow' felt weak. I preferred 'invites'.
2) It is not an inert, 'us' or 'them', form of publishing
A continuation of the same thought. A PDF document was an example of an 'inert' thing, as was a newspaper page or some iPad editions. There was not much a reader or user could contribute to a printed page.

3) It encourages others to initiate debate, publish material or make suggestions. We can follow, as well as lead. We can involve others in the pre-publication processes

We would not simply get into a pattern of publishing . . . and inviting a response. That was not truly interactive. If we truly believed our readers knew more than we did in many respects then they should sometimes lead us – both before we set out on stories, and after.

4) It helps form communities of joint interest around subjects, issues or individuals

A newspaper was a single bundle of carefully chosen, but – in some respects – random, material. Within the readers of a newspaper there were numerous communities of interest, knowledge, passion or geography. We would like to connect these communities and be at their centre.

5) It is open to the web and is part of it. It links to, and collaborates with, other material (including services) on the web

This was Emily's 'be of the web, not just on it'. We wouldn't just plonk our material on the internet as though it was just another distribution channel. We'd use links and knit everything we did into the most powerful system of communication ever seen.

6) It aggregates and/or curates the work of others

'Out there' would be material that complemented, challenged, clarified, broadened or expanded on what we did. As well as linking out to it we might want to use some of it ourselves as, for instance, we were doing in science and environment. We could be both a platform and a publisher.

7) It recognises that journalists are not the only voices of authority, expertise and interest

A big one for some, but not for others. In a way a statement of the obvious – but still challenging to some people's exclusive notion of 'professional journalism'.

8) It aspires to achieve, and reflect, diversity as well as promoting shared values

We all knew there was a problem of diversity within newsrooms. These guidelines to open journalism would surface and amplify other voices.

9) It recognises that publishing can be the beginning of the journalistic process rather than the end

A story did not end with publication. Often that was when a story began its life. We should listen to the response to a story and work out how to incorporate it.

10) It is transparent and open to challenge – including correction, clarification and addition

We should, wherever possible, be more open about the sources of our information and our methods. We should welcome challenges to our journalism. When things were wrong or needed clarifying, we would correct or clarify.

Not all our journalism had to look like this: some reporters just wanted to get on with shoe-leather reporting. But there was enough in these principles to suggest the ways in which digital-only journalism might develop.

Two outsiders came to represent striking illustrations of new ways of working. Neither – which may have been significant – had been trained as a journalist. Neither worked in a conventional newsroom. They were inventing new forms of engagement for themselves.

Glenn Greenwald, then in his early 40s, had trained as a litigation attorney in New York before starting an investigative blog which frequently touched on surveillance. It caught the eye of Salon, the West Coast website, which hired him in 2005. By the time Janine Gibson, our US editor, approached him to move to the *Guardian* he was living in Rio with 13 rescue dogs. His newsroom was his kitchen. By then his personal 'community' of readers was approaching a million.

Nothing about Greenwald was conventional in journalistic terms. For one thing, he had strong opinions and was not afraid to use them. This did not accord with classic J-School ideas of journalism as a search for dispassionate, objective truths. Later, I tried to persuade the *New York Times* to give him a byline on a news story. They simply wouldn't. He was not their idea of a proper reporter.

Equally singular was the fact that no one had ever told Greenwald about how a proper reporter works. *You come in in the morning, make some calls, write your story, press 'send' and then go for a drink.*

Greenwald, in his innocence, thought the most interesting point of the day was when he pressed 'send'. That was when the story began its real life. People would start responding to it, attacking it, praising it, sharing it, adding to it, pointing out errors, suggesting new leads. In his untutored innocence, he thought: *How wonderful and fascinating!*

So Greenwald would make himself a cup of tea and watch those chains and sparks of reaction. If he'd made a mistake he wanted to know about it as soon as possible so that he could correct it. If there were things that were missing, he added them. He got new ideas for next week's column. Readers could check things that weren't clear. He could add detail or sources or links if people doubted him.

During the hours immediately after publication his story would improve.

This was the inverse of how most reporters used to work. Greenwald was not afraid of stirring it if, on Twitter or other platforms, people jeered or threw rotten tomatoes. He gave as good as he got.

He insisted we suspend the normal rules of moderation for his column: there would be no moderation. He didn't believe in what he thought of as 'censorship'. He would rather talk to sceptics or trolls than have them filtered out. When I last looked he had nearly a million followers on Twitter and had tweeted 72,000 times.[1] He was quite happy – excited, even – to believe that some of his readers knew more than he did. He would learn from them.

One certainly did. His name was Edward Snowden.[2] And Glenn Greenwald, not 'a proper reporter', helped the *Guardian* win the Pulitzer prize.

The second rule breaker was a Dutch journalist who had trained as an anthropologist. At the age of 26, Joris Luyendijk found himself switching careers and becoming a newspaper correspondent in Cairo. After a few years doing what foreign correspondents do – from Lebanon and East Jerusalem after Egypt – he wrote a book, *People Like Us*,[3] which was as much about the failure of journalists adequately to explain the Middle East as it was about the region he had set out to cover.

His book sold extremely well. He was disenchanted about conventional journalism. One interviewer reported: 'Luyendijk quit conventional journalism because he was always being railroaded into telling a linear story, packaged for one-off consumption. In the new net world, he believes, it will be possible to tell many stories, work on their development with other people in the agora via crowdsourcing, be open about saying "I don't know", be provisional in drawing conclusions, and endlessly return to the same subject. The agora exists in perpetuity; the debate never ends.'[4]

Luyendijk returned to his paper,[5] which allowed him to spend 2009 writing a weekly column about the electric car: he convinced his editor that if the Indians and Chinese started using petrol cars, the planet's future would not look good.

Most journalists would begin by doing sufficient research to convince most readers that they knew their stuff. Joris did the opposite: he frankly admitted this was an issue he knew very little about. But with the help of the readers (some of whom were bound to know much more than he about batteries, materials, storage, pricing, charging, urban design, etc.) he would soon find out.

Like Greenwald, this was an inversion of normal rules. The readers – conventional wisdom would have it – would scoff at Luyendijk. *Your job is to find out stuff and then pass it on.* That wasn't, in fact, the reaction of most readers. I suspect many of them thought the opposite: *At last a journalist who's not bullshitting us.*

I met Luyendijk in June 2010 in unusual circumstances: we were both guests of the Queen of the Netherlands. The entire royal family sat through our presentations on the future of journalism. I struggled to imagine the British royal family doing the same.

Was there anything else Luyendijk knew little about, but considered important? He thought for a moment, and answered: banking. We were still in the grip of the financial crisis triggered by the baroque excesses of financial wizards. It was up there with the most defining stories of our time, yet he was not convinced journalism had done a brilliant job, either before or after the crash.

We hired him. He began a weekly column the following year in the same way – a confession of personal ignorance on the subject he was about to address. His initial pitch to his projected subjects was blunt: everyone hates you, anyway – why not let me understand and explain in a way conventional journalism might struggle to? Mix an immensely complex subject with the internet, narrative journalism and anthropological fieldwork . . . and something interesting might emerge at the other end.

It did. His columns over the next two years humanised the world of finance more than anything else I'd read. At the end of it I understood the processes, motivations, codes, frailties, hubris, chutzpah, isolation, hierarchies, addictions, relationships and risks of the City of London far better from him than from anything I had derived from the financial pages. The subsequent book[6] shot to the top of the non-fiction bestseller charts.

Here were two (untrained) reporters coming at the work of journalism in entirely new ways. They both climbed off the platform and established a new kind of horizontal relationship with the reader. They used a different kind of voice. Some readers felt able and willing to contribute. Even those who didn't could see a writer being transparent about their workings,[7] and – where they existed – prejudices. My inclination was that their readers trusted them more – which is why they ended up with such large and devoted followings.

Not all journalism was going to look like Greenwald and Luyendijk's. But their experimentation did suggest that twenty-first-century technologies would enable profoundly different ways of doing journalism if you were willing to throw away some very entrenched assumptions of what journalism was.

*

Barely ten years previously our way of understanding what readers wanted from their paper was not much more sophisticated than it had been in 1821. You recruited a panel of readers (loyalists, 'occasionals', young, old) and put them in a room with a copy of the paper and a felt tip marker or scoresheet. After a couple of hours you looked at the results.

Here's one from January 2000. We learn that the best-read story of the day was 'Mowlam Said Yes to Drugs',[8] on the front page. Also that 61 per cent of readers read the whole story, and 39 per cent some of it. Another story on page 4 – about the worst ever fall in the quality of the UK's air – fared less well: 24 per cent read all of it; 21 per cent read less than half, but at least some. And 51 per cent read none of it, or virtually none of it.

What was a news editor to do with these roughly hewn figures? If you have an extrovert woman in public life confessing to taking drugs as a student ('and, unlike President Clinton, I did inhale') and you stick it on page one, it's perhaps not surprising many people read it. Half our readers, on this evidence, aren't much bothered by the quality of the air we all inhale, by contrast. Should we therefore do less on environmental stories? Or, conversely, put environmental stories on the front page because, objectively, they're more important?

Editorials usually scored extremely poorly – less than 10 per cent of readers were apparently interested in what 'the paper' thought about the great issues of the day. But they were (we thought) essential to defining the paper's values and in asserting our influence on the corridors of power. Sometimes a sentence or two might be read out on the radio in the morning, signalling 'the *Guardian* view'. We would, in defiance of our readers' apparent indifference, carry on publishing editorials.

This 2000 survey looked at six different 'products' across the week – including the main section of the paper, the weekend magazine, the jobs and money section, and the G2 features section. The last page found: 'the vast majority of all six products go unread by most readers – the perception of choice rather than actual reading behaviour is an important motivation to purchase'.

That seemed to mean that we give our newspaper readers a bundle, or package. Most of them wouldn't bother to read most of it. But they liked the thought it was there.

Ten years later this scattergun approach – throwing the newspaper over the wall at the readers – seemed merely comical. To a new breed of engineers it was worse than comical: it was almost offensive. At a hack day they decided to build their own in-house analytics platform so that journalists could see in real-time which stories were being read – and how, for instance, a change to a headline might affect search traffic. They called it Ophan.[9] Chris Moran, the *Guardian*'s digital audience editor, said that Ophan was 'all about informing decisions around content'. This hadn't happened overnight, of course. We had gradually been able to get a better fix on who was reading what. To begin with, this seemed to pose a dilemma: who should see the figures? Would it not be demoralising to a leader writer or a particular reporter who discovered that almost no one was reading their work? If you gave the tools to desk editors would you not also have to give them clear guidance about how to interpret the data? If your mission was more traffic at any cost then it was relatively simple: stop commissioning stories about worthy issues. That road essentially led to Mail Online or Buzzfeed – at least until the latter realised it didn't want to be that sort of website.

If it wasn't all about clicks then . . . what?

A whole generation of West Coast engineers were working on finding an algorithmic answer to that question. For a start, who's choosing? If the reader's in charge, you could ask them to create a personalised dashboard of stories. They could decide whether they read about pot-smoking politicians or air pollution. Or you could machine-monitor their reading habits over a period of time and give them more of what it seemed they liked. That looked like the Facebook way of doing business.

But let's suppose there's still a role for human judgement. The 27th story about phone hacking or arms bribes that you know almost no one will read? The review of the violin recital at the Wigmore Hall in London or the academic study of food production? The worthy report on climate change that is every bit as bleak as the previous worthy report on climate change? You could more or less guarantee very few people will read any of those. But was each, in their own way, a form of public service? Did the *Guardian*'s attention to each matter – and, in its way, help define the *Guardian*?

For quite a while, we didn't let that data widely loose into the newsroom. But Ophan was different. Now everybody could see everything. What did we want to know or measure? Unique users was one metric.

They were like newspaper readers – you wanted lots of them, partly in order to boast to advertisers how many people they could reach. Unique users were not quite the same as unique browsers, mind you. We had to 'de-dupe' the single user who accessed the *Guardian* from her home laptop, her office desktop, her mobile phone and her iPad. Four devices, maybe only one user.

Page views was another metric. A click could be matched to a user coming directly to the site or from Facebook, even if it was the same person. They were at least easy to understand, even if considered a little old-fashioned by some. Others wanted to dig deeper and track, minute-by-minute, the number of page views coming directly from, say, the front page as opposed to those arriving from Google, Twitter or Facebook.

But even that was a two-edged sword. A front-page editor with the traffic monitor at her elbow might see that, after an hour or so, a particular story was dipping in clicks. Time to replace it with something else? Quietly slide it off the front page?

That started to happen. Sometimes it was the right decision. Sometimes it would drive me mad. We'd have invested weeks on some investigation or long read. This was the kind of story that defined our journalism. So not enough people were reading it? That didn't mean we shuffled it out of view after an hour or so.

Moran would patiently try to educate us in how to balance the wisdom of the machine with the experience of the hack. An investigation into families being evicted from their homes was a strong, important, power-ful illustration of a much bigger issue in Britain – affordable housing. Ophan shows it doing well within minutes of publication, but within four hours it's tailing off. It's not doing well with Google referrals because no one else is writing about these evictions. Getting it into Google news was probably not going to happen, but it might fare better on Twitter and Facebook.

The news editor monitoring how the story was faring could break down the audience by geography and by device – desktop browser, tablet, app or phone. Other organisations (Buzzfeed, for example) placed more emphasis on the social shareability of stories. We'd rather know how many people were actually reading the article, rather than simply generating tweets.

If not clicks, if not sharing: maybe we should measure attention time – how long people stay within an article page before leaving? We could monitor exactly how many words they'd read, or whether they were merely skimming. We could now tell whether a reader bounced in and out of the *Guardian*; or whether they stayed to read something else.

These methods of measurement became commonplace in digital-only start-ups such as Chartbeat or Upworthy, but were relatively rare in newsrooms until recently. Pretty soon attention to metrics would no longer be optional. Advertisers increasingly wanted to know more and more about who was reading what – and for how long. If you couldn't sell on reach then maybe sell on 'engagement'.

Ophan was, in short, a formidable tool – but one which, understand-ably, made many people nervous. Journalism had never been a science. We older hacks believed in judgement and instinct: the great tabloid editors, we said, had an almost supernatural feeling for what people wanted to read. At the other end was 'eat your peas' journalism. *We think this is good for you. You don't think you need to know about the growth of ultra-conservative Wahhabism in Saudi Arabia. But we're here to tell you should be interested. One day you will thank us.*

If you believed in gut editing then Ophan was anathema. Moran admitted that his first attempts to introduce journalists to data 'was greeted as warmly as if I was bringing in a bucket of nuclear waste'.[10] He continually tried to reassure people he wanted a data-informed news-room, not a data-led one.

Some embraced it. When Janine Gibson created the first proper *Guardian* newsroom in New York she placed the data guy right next to the front-page editor. Why wouldn't you?

*

The readers, when you talked to them, sometimes confused you. Even if education classified advertising was draining out of print, we still wanted to keep teachers reading the *Guardian* – not least because we wanted to retain the (albeit much reduced) recruitment advertising. We would create a better education website. More reporting, more attention to the concerns of teachers.

What did the readers think? There was a bit of a shrug about 'more reporting'. The answer was unexpected – to journalists. If we really wanted to be useful, why not create a website where any teacher could share learning resources with each other?

Are you sure? Because, like, we're journalists. We do news.

They were sure. We built it: they came. Pretty soon thousands of teachers were sharing their lesson plans on Tudor history, particle physics, ox bow lakes and transitive verbs.

This wasn't quite journalism. It was, if you like, a sort of public service. But it had a commercial rationale – we continued to make money from education if only we could keep a community of teachers hooked in to the *Guardian*. Wendy Berliner, our former education correspondent, had returned to the paper after a spell as editor of the *Times Education Supplement*. Once she'd realised what the teachers wanted, she created it. She helped build a community of 350,000 registered educational professionals.[11] The professional networks, with 750,000 registered users, brought in nearly £11 million in revenues in 2015. Not riches compared with print revenues. But the alternative – losing these communities of interest – seemed worse.

*

We developed a one-minute version of how to explain open journalism. I took the example of the theatre critic. We had been lucky enough to employ Michael Billington since 1971. He was our 'expert' at the first night of a new play at the National Theatre. The *Guardian* would always want its critic at the show.

What about the 900 other members of the audience? Would some of them have interesting perceptions about the play? Of course. Would it be interesting to allow them the opportunity to give their own feedback? If the *Guardian* didn't, someone would. They could tweet about it, go to Facebook or any of the free specialist theatre and culture sites springing up – the arts versions of TripAdvisor.

We'd like to hear from the others in the audience. If we did, we'd have a richer panorama of views about the play rather than simply the voice of one critic on one night. Maybe we could ask Billington to spend an hour exchanging views with the best of the fellow theatre-goers.

We *could* decide not to do this. We knew enough about social media to know the audience would find ways of sharing their views; and also that prospective play-goers (and advertisers) might well end up on another culture or theatre site offering the sort of peer-to-peer recommendation that was exploding all over the internet. So we'd end up pitting Billington against the new competition.[12]

Bring it on, some said. Billington is Billington: he's enough of a name and is a brilliant enough writer to take on the internet. In fact, we should be charging for him, he's so good.

To argue against that seemed to be to question the worth of a professional critic. My instinct was to want both – the professional *and* the amateur: a) because it was journalistically richer; b) because not to, risked opening the door to social media and other free alternatives.

Out of an audience of 900 maybe only 30 would want to contribute something. Their involvement might be no more than giving a star rating or writing a short review. It could be a question for Billington – maybe as a 'freemium' benefit. I had seen Billington in a room with *Guardian* readers and how some revered him. Was this one more example of ways to break down the walls between writers and readers?

Many colleagues bought the theory. Making it happen, for an organisation with so many other priorities, was quite another thing.

Our film critic, Peter Bradshaw, reflected on how his own role had changed in the two decades he had been working at the *Guardian*. 'It used to be that people read the review and then saw the film. Now it's the other way round: they see the film and then, on the way out of the cinema, get out their smartphones and read your review. And then they start vehemently letting you know what they think. You get reviewed! It's been a sobering experience for all critics to realise that the one-party state of media and publishing – which lasted from the invention of the printing press in the middle ages to about 2004 – is over.'[13]

'Open' became something of a mantra within the office – doubtless to the irritation of some, and to the excitement of others. It was too general a word to be an ideal piece of motivational shorthand, but it was a big enough umbrella to include a number of ideas about what we could be experimenting with. If it was simply an editorial aspiration it could never fly: the commercial side of the organisation needed to be convinced that this mantra would work for them, too. So we looked outside the newspaper for others who had come to the same conclusion. They were not hard to find. For many in business, public service and academia, open was – in the jargon of the day – the new twenty-first-century operating system of much corporate and intellectual life.

The Canadian consultant Don Tapscott's 2006 bestseller, *Wikinomics*,[14] had told the story of how encyclopaedias, operating systems, mutual funds, mining, law enforcement, the auto industry, pharmaceuticals and more were being transformed by tapping into teams numbering in their thousands or even millions. He called it collaborative innovation. His post-crash 2011 sequel, *MacroWikinomics*, went further. When we met to discuss his ideas, he said:

> I mean the industry that brought us Elvis and The Beatles is now suing children as a key part of its business model. The old model of the corporation typified by General Motors? Well, it went bankrupt. We have industrial age governments that can't seem to deliver services to people that they need and that are appropriate. We have old models of science, of the university, and of education. Universities are losing their monopoly in higher education. We have the very best model of learning that 18th-century technology can provide.
>
> Then there are our models of democracy where you vote and I rule. All of these come out of the industrial age: mass production, mass distribution, mass media, mass marketing, mass education, mass democracy – all of them are models whereby content, whether it's information or products or whatever, is delivered one-way to passive recipients. But for each of these institutions that are failing,

there are now sparkling new initiatives that show a whole new civilisation. We don't know exactly what it will look like but the contours are starting to come clear.

His book titles were a play on the achievement of Wikipedia – a million people creating an encyclopaedia ten times the size of Britannica and in 190 languages, for negligible cost. Linux – denounced by Microsoft for being socialist – had done it on operating systems: 'No one owns it – but it has some big customers . . . like China.' The industries and systems which had been slow to adopt open models – newspapers, the music industry, government, healthcare, financial services – had stalled or were in various stages of atrophy or failure.

Tapscott avoided the term crowdsourcing, but he used the example of Proctor & Gamble looking for a molecule that would take red wine out of shirts. They employed 9,000 chemists but there were a million chemists outside the company – an 'idea agora' – whose knowledge they could harness. The answer might come from London or Taipei.

'In every industry we're starting to understand that talent is not just inside our boundaries.' According to Tapscott half of all P&G innovation was, by 2011, coming from outside the company. There was internal resistance – Not Invented Here (NIH) resentment – which P&G had tried to reverse with financial incentives for Proudly Found Elsewhere (PFE).

Tapscott thought media was a classic example of why closed systems – one-to-many, using old technologies to publish a narrow range of views, often based on the whims of a proprietor – could not compete with the highly distributed, many-to-many or one-to-one with 'awesome neutrality'.

I was interested in how widely Tapscott's ideas were shared and trawled for like minds.

*

Eric Schmidt, the then CEO of Google – thought of as being on the open end of the tech spectrum – certainly believed in the notion. 'I worry about the seduction, the dangerous allure of closed systems,' he told me on a visit to the *Guardian*. 'After all, they're ordered, they're always correct, they're always structured, they're very efficient. But that's not how the world really works. Open systems are messy and complicated and hard to work with but, ultimately, the transparency, all the new voices, and so forth, produce a much larger pie to have a good chunk of in your business, your personal life or in everything you're trying to do. It's better for democracy, it's better for corporations and it's better for you as an individual.'

I found further examples all round.

- Glaxo Smith Kline (GSK) had been a traditional pharma company, owning everything it did. When Andrew Witty took over as chief executive, he began to think of GSK as one of the largest research organisations in the world with 99 per cent of the research capacity existing outside the company. He gave me an example of publishing all 13,000 chemical structures (out of the two million they had discovered) that showed some degree of activity against malaria, 'for any scientist to now pick up and start to work from'. In addition, they were intending to open-source data from all the failed trials (99 per cent of all research) so that other scientists could learn from them.

- Albert Ferrer, former right-back at Barcelona Football Club, talked to us about how that team had effectively mutualised itself. The club was owned by its members – they all got a vote on who should lead the organisation. It made sense because the fans had a real sense of belonging. Ferrer explained how it had also grown out of the region's history in the twentieth century. 'With Franco we had a dictator, and we couldn't somehow express ourselves. People didn't accept this Catalan thing. Probably the only way that we could express ourselves was through Barcelona – and then we used the club to give our opinion in terms of everything, political and sporting.'

- John Sulston, the Cambridge biologist who had won the Nobel prize for his work sequencing genomes in the open, was another voice I sought out. As soon as he discovered information he released it immediately, and without patenting it – believing all the data should be open and public. 'It's all pre-competitive, nobody gets any advantage,' he explained. 'So as an absolutely essential part of getting that kind of collaboration to work, you remove the base of the competition. People do this in industry all the time. This word "pre-competitive" is very good. It means that they may share the funding so at least they're not expecting to compete over acquiring this particular bit of knowledge.'

And then there was the movement to open publishing in science – and the complications around copyright and economic rewards, which, in some ways, overlapped with the news business. Open publishing was certainly happening in universities and academic publishing, with the irresistible movement to an open-access system and the Public Library of Science (PLoS).

Under the old system, the authors of a scientific paper didn't pay. If accepted by peer reviewers, the cost would be met by libraries or individual subscribers. The information was free to publish, but expensive to consult. With more and more scientists emerging in developing countries this became a barrier to their work and careers. One answer was to make information available to people in low-income countries. Others decided to publish in an open-access way – with the author paying. The downside was that this introduced barriers on the supply side. Some journals responded by waiving fees from anyone from poorer societies. Another model was to charge for hard copies of papers or academic books, but to make the material free online.

'It's really quite important we deal with this because we're wasting the potential, otherwise, of the internet and the whole electronic communication,' said Sulston. 'Just like the situation with the genome databases, we gain hugely if we can click without barriers from one journal, one publication, to another. Ideally what one wants, as you have with PLoS, is that you have your document you're reading and it's full of hyperlinks that allow one to click and go to another one, no barrier, if the other one is also open access.' For Sulston, these considerations of open access in science and open access of data in an equitable way had huge implications for society. 'It's something that we're really neglecting in the conduct of our societies and in the conduct of the world.'

So 'open' – as a system or philosophy – did seem to have powerful advocates across business, technology, science and academia. That didn't mean easy solutions had magically arrived, but there was an awareness of the benefits – if not of new ways of organising things.

The commercial side of the *Guardian* increasingly bought into the idea – indeed, started using it enthusiastically in our marketing and conversations with advertising clients. They understood it, because so many of them were waking up to similar digitally induced challenges. But with the news business there was, of course, the perpetual tension between journalism as a form of public service and a historic economic model built on advertising and profit.

*

The philosopher Ronald Dworkin used the analogy of the lighthouse to me when we were talking about all this stuff over a drink one night. The lighthouse sends its light out to all ships, regardless of whether or not they pay for its service. They can all take advantage of the information sent out by the flashing beacons in a non-exclusive and non-competitive way: i.e. those who do not pay cannot be excluded from consuming the signals . . . and their consumption of the warning lights does not reduce the consumption of others. Ronnie explained to me, as a non-political philosopher, that the lighthouse had been used by many economists, from John Stuart Mill onwards, as an example of a public good.

In media we have had the BBC as a kind of lighthouse – paid for by near-universal subscription by anyone in the UK who owned a television set and (pretty much) universally available. It is a wondrous news organisation, employing roughly 7,000 journalists around the world, with the highest editorial and ethical standards. It sends its beacon out into the world, including to hundreds of millions who don't pay for it. It is a public service.

At the *Guardian* we – of course – shared the irritation of colleagues on other papers that it was so widely available and of such high quality that it was extremely difficult to compete with. There was regular moaning from fellow newspapers that the BBC stood between them and making a fortune from paywalls – an argument which ignored the reality that newspapers around the world were in trouble – BBC or no BBC. The difficulties of the American press could hardly be blamed on competition from public-service broadcasters.

The indignation that the BBC should behave like an open public service reached its peak in a scathing attack on it by James Murdoch in the 2009 MacTaggart lecture in Edinburgh. 'Dumping free, state-sponsored news on the market makes it incredibly difficult for journalism to flourish on the internet,' he complained. 'Yet it is essential for the future of independent journalism that a fair price can be charged for news to people who value it.'

He added – without apparent irony as the scion of a family which dominated the national newspaper market in the UK: 'We seem to have decided to let independence and plurality wither . . . as Orwell foretold, to let the state enjoy a near-monopoly of information is to guarantee manipulation and distortion.'

He famously ended: 'The only reliable, durable, and perpetual guarantor of independence is profit.'

Attacking the BBC's editorial and ethical standards was a cheeky move for a Murdoch to make, mired as he was in a moral and corporate disaster of his own – a person who, within two years, would be denounced by the prime minister as someone who should have 'no future role' in the running of a media company.[15]

So the open model of news certainly had multiple detractors. But even when I was irritated by the commercial strength (and occasional over-reach) of the BBC, I couldn't rid myself of a feeling of gratitude that it was there. Amazingly, a lighthouse model of public service news had survived for the best part of 90 years and was – despite the odd self-inflicted crises and ceaseless attacks on it – still easily the most trusted news route in the country, if not the world.

An Ofcom[16] review of all news sources in 2011 asked people to name the one news source they trusted most. A substantial 59 per cent nominated the BBC – by a country mile the winner. The Murdoch papers did not compare well – with just 1 per cent volunteering the *Sun* or the

Times. The primary reasons for naming the BBC were that people found it impartial, unbiased, accurate, trustworthy . . . and independent.

When asked to compare the BBC with other news sources the answer was the same: the BBC was the clear winner on trust – with 87 per cent compared with 48 per cent for the *Times* and *Guardian*, 44 per cent and 33 per cent for the (very profitable) *Telegraph* and *Mail*, and 15 per cent for the *Sun*. The public seemed not to agree that profit was the only guarantee of independence . . . or anything else they most wanted from journalism.

A lot of academics watching the industry from the outside placed the open *v.* closed debates in a longer historical context. Quite a few who knew their press history were doubtful if the media industry could ever adapt to openness because its history had been predicated on being closed.

Jay Rosen, a thoughtful sociology professor at NYU in New York who later became involved in a new journalism start-up,[17] put it like this when I dropped in on him in 2011 – for 200 years there had been two different ways of profiting from news, the newsletter model or news for the public:

> The oldest way [of news information] was a private good for rich people. The first people to be paid as correspondents were in the pay of rich merchants in the 15th and 16th centuries, who needed to know about conditions and trade in cities other than the ones they lived in. The value of the information was not just that it kept the merchant informed about what was happening over the horizon – but that *nobody else had that information*. It was an exclusive good for a producer class. That's the newsletter model for profit in news. Part of the value is that the information you paid for *doesn't circulate widely*: that gives you the advantage.
>
> The other way of profiting from news is to cut the price to make it free, or virtually free, to get as broad an audience as you can to be able to sell that attention to advertisers or sponsors – but also to build up power or influence by speaking broadly to civil society so that people can't ignore what you publish. The power

and influence that come from that broader marketplace become essential to the business.

Those two models – the newsletter model and news for the public – were very different models. So the choice for news organisation is whether to go back and become a private good for a producer class or address the public.

Clay Shirky also believed that open models helped cultivate a civic sense of participation: a closed-off media organisation became a newsletter rather than a newspaper. 'Openness says: "we're here alongside you and if you know a piece of information you tell us; and obviously when we know something we'll tell you." Openness is the way we learn the most, the fastest. It's the way you can tell not only the story but give the underlying resources.'

To Jeff Jarvis, professor of digital entrepreneurship at CUNY, openness took away the power of the old elite – in education, government and media. 'It's threatening to them. It's a symbol of the revolution of this age. I think we're moving to the era of publicness, and it's just begun. We cognate the world differently. There's no beginning and middle and end. These tools of publicness are the tools that enable people to find each other, gather together and act – and haven't we seen that in Egypt and Tunisia? It's going to be a crucial factor in the infrastructure of the society we will build next.'

We were, in other words, in the middle of a pea-souper fog – with many voices strongly calling for us to feel our way back to where we started. 'Open' felt to me an inherently plausible explanation for the way the world was going, but it was a difficult concept to nail down – not least because, with an intensifying gravitational pull towards paywalls, some people would insist on substituting the word 'free'. If you believed that journalism would in future gain much power and relevance from being open to new networks and systems of information sharing, then you were sometimes branded the Taliban of Free.

If free didn't work financially (and the commercial team at the *Guardian* appear to this day to believe it will) then we could always switch to a paid-for model. We would at least have a much larger audience by having achieved reach. But being 'open' felt fundamental in understanding how information and individuals behaved in the digital age: horizontal more than vertical.

The *Guardian*'s then marketing director, David Pemsel,[18] wanted to find a way of explaining 'open' to a wider audience of potential advertisers and readers. Together with the advertising agency BBH, we devised a short 'docudrama' imagining how the modern news media would cover the story of the Three Little Pigs boiling the Big Bad Wolf.[19] The fairy-tale pigs (in costumes from the Royal Ballet) were thrust into a brutal contemporary 24/7 news cycle of stories, tweets, YouTube videos and social media. The implicit point was that the *Guardian* existed in a world of multiple sources, with myriad bursts of noise. We could harness the best, repudiate the worst. We could filter the static, be responsive to the powers of the crowd.

The film went down well with most readers – and with most advertisers. The digital disruption threatening to capsize our industry was washing over so many sectors and walks of life and some of our readers perhaps 'got it' more naturally than beleaguered colleagues. As Jarvis said: 'You can't stop publicness or openness. It's an inexorable movement in society – every sector of it, not just media and journalism but business, government, education and how we interact with each other.'

★

2011 began with our heads still above water – just. Boardroom discussions continued to focus on two alternatives: invest or cut? We could a) try to take advantage of the global digital opportunity that seemed to be in our grasp; or b) batten down the hatches to get through the short-term cash squeeze and the recession and come back in a year or two once the fog had cleared.

Neither route was great. The first course risked financial overstretch if revenues didn't materialise. The second course could mean we simply missed the digital bus. If we retrenched now and took ourselves out of the game we might never get back in it.

The number crunchers looked at the likely digital growth. By 2015/6, if we held our nerve, we should be generating nearly £18 million revenues in America, and maybe £65 million in all (up from £29 million in 2010/11). If we did nothing we'd preside over a 10 per cent decline in overall revenues and would have to go in for some tough cost-cutting just to stay still. The Boards went for option a). But we had to force more cost savings through and be more decisive about priorities. Already our editorial budget was back where it had been in 2006, despite working much longer days, in multiple media, seven days a week. It was projected not to grow (barring pay rises) for four years.

We made two big decisions.

First, we would be a digital-first organisation. Not web-first; digital-first. Second, we would make print a slower, more reflective read which would not aspire to cover the entire waterfront in news.

The two were, obviously, connected. We had already been 'web-first' for some time – i.e. we would normally publish material online without having numerous debates about whether to save it for print. 'Digital-first' was a larger statement of intent. We would now clearly prioritise digital within the organisation . . . while also producing a newspaper. That would – once again – require us to change processes, priorities, budgets . . . and journalism.

All news desks would now focus on how best to cover news as if there was no newspaper – and with mobile devices now very much in mind. A small team would be tasked with producing a paper that complemented the faster, live coverage on desktop and mobile. It would be slower-paced, much of it pre-planned and with a greater emphasis on analysis and context. It would be more like *Newsnight*, the late-night BBC current affairs programme, and less like the evening news.

A newspaper is highly labour intensive. On most days we felt as if we started well digitally and then, around mid-afternoon, the entire operation would lurch as all hands rushed to the other side of the building to get the newspaper done. A sizeable production shift of copy-editors and lay-out staff appeared early afternoon and then worked heads-down on print until late evening. More pre-planning of 'slower' print content meant a more even workflow all day. How radical were we prepared to be? Some news organisations had even outsourced their copy-editing process; parts of the *Irish Independent* were now edited in the South of France; soft *Telegraph* features were turned out for £45 a page (London cost up to £200) in Australia; the *Miami Herald* was partly produced in India[20].

But all this was getting very difficult to manage. We were doing more with standstill budgets. Mobile and multimedia were begging for attention and resource, but we didn't have either. We were planning 10 per cent cuts in newspaper pagination and had learned that paid-for iPad editions – hailed by Rupert Murdoch as the saviour of the industry – were expensive and labour intensive to produce and with only modest revenues.

And then there was America. Since 9/11 we had grown to be number four in news sites in the US – behind the *NYT, Washington Post* and *Wall Street Journal* – but now bigger than the BBC or the *Economist.* These new readers were wealthier than their UK *Guardian* counterparts – an average income of $81,000. Three quarters of them were American, a quarter British ex-pats.

We had still spent nothing on marketing in the US, and we didn't know enough about these new users. But commercial colleagues were convinced they could make money from this large, and growing, audience. All but a handful of 1,400 newspapers in the US were now essentially local. Huge staffing cutbacks – 30 per cent was the average, though some bigger papers such as the *Washington Post* had gone much further – meant less foreign coverage.

The opportunity was there, and we now had one of our best editors, Janine Gibson, a former media editor in her late 30s, in place. There was no cheap way of doing it: we would need an office, writers, editors, social media, multimedia and so on. There would be no point in doing run-of-the-mill American coverage: we could never compete. But if, in addition to our internationalist credentials, we could specialise in a few key aspects of the US news agenda, we could start to make waves.

*

Returning foreign correspondents were often the most evangelistic about the *Guardian*'s new visibility and influence. Jack Shenker had been at the heart of the protests in Tahrir Square in Cairo that had been one of the rallying points of the protest movements sweeping through the

Middle East[21]. Shenker – young, stubble-chinned and described by the *Spectator* as 'a throwback to an older, more romantic age when foreign correspondents were angry, partisan and half-crazed with frustration at the stupidity of the powerful' came into my office to tell me how the daily live-blogs had been so influential on the ground: 'Our coverage had a monumental impact. The *Guardian*, along with Al Jazeera, were the two news outlets that everyone on the streets were following – not just in Cairo, but in surrounding cities.'

We had, for a while, translated the live-blog into Arabic. 'That was a revelation,' said Shenker.

> At a time of fast-moving events people were desperate for updated information that they trusted because there was a lot of misinformation being spread. The *Guardian* became the one place on the web that people could go to which had a regional grasp of everything that was going on minute by minute.
>
> It manifested itself in the *Guardian* being emblazoned on banners and placards across Tahrir Square. On the day Mubarak resigned – just hours before he fled – a preacher in his midday sermon was citing the *Guardian*. In the journalism we were doing on the ground we tried to stay as honest and unbiased as possible. With so many aspects of the revolution arising out of collaborative digital networks, the fact that the live-blog was so well-adapted to that format and the way it incorporated other voices really resonated with people and struck a chord. We were breaking stories that even the local media weren't getting. The first accusations of the army torturing people inside the Egyptian museum was a revelation, as well as things we revealed about negotiations behind the scenes . . . people were very grateful for what we did.

In Shenker's reporting from Tahrir Square I saw further echoes of the reporting – from St Peter's Square, Manchester – that had led to the *Guardian*'s founding. Both involved peaceful political uprisings in which it was vital to have independent witnesses on hand to either record or discourage violent retribution from the state. In the attempted revolutions that followed it was more and more vital that all citizens – not just elites – had access to timely information that they could trust.

This was part of what was meant by open: the ability for our reporting to be read by everybody. Very few people in Tahrir Square or Cairo would have been reading the *New York Times* or London *Times*: they were now, to some extent, gated communities.

Some argued that it was ever thus: that high-quality information had always come at a price. But the difference now was the ubiquity of low-quality information. There was an ocean of fake news, propaganda, rumour; careless, and deliberately wrong, information swilling all around. So-called mainstream media was actually being marginalised. What had once been fringe media was now becoming the true mainstream.

Just as with the English riots, we were placing ourselves at the heart of vital stories – combining our own reporting and analysis with the other voices we recognised to be reliable and worth reading. We were able to do it by having several knowledgeable, experienced Arabic-speaking members of staff in London and the region, as well as enough reporters like Shenker on the ground.

The *Guardian*'s influence was reflected in growth. In November 2010, we had been reporting traffic of 37 million – up 22 per cent on the year before. By October 2011 we had grown that to 60 million – up another 57 per cent.

In London, the Leveson Inquiry – established on the back of our reporting – was in full swing investigating an ethical catastrophe for newspapers.

In a separate universe a young Australian called Julian Assange was hell-bent on revolution. He despised journalists. But he had hundreds of thousands of top-secret documents in his backpack and was beginning to feel desperate . . .

19

The Gatekeepers

In January 2010, Hillary Clinton, then US Secretary of State, made a rather good speech at the Newseum in Washington D.C. about the potential of what she termed 'a new nervous system for the planet'. She described a vision of semi-underground digital publishing – 'the samizdat of our day' – that was beginning to champion transparency and challenge the autocratic, corrupt old order of the world. But she also warned that repressive governments would 'target the independent thinkers who use the tools'. She had regimes like Iran in mind.

Her words about the brave publishing future could well have applied to the rather strange, unworldly Australian hacker quietly working out samizdat methods of publishing the world's secrets in ways that were beyond any technological or legal attack. Little can Clinton have imagined, as she made this much-praised speech, that within a year she would be back making another statement about digital whistleblowers – this time roundly attacking people who used electronic media to champion transparency. It was, she told a hastily arranged State Department press conference in November 2010, 'not just an attack on America's foreign policy interests. It is an attack on the international community.'

In the intervening ten months, unnoticed by most of the world at the time, Julian Assange had developed into a most interesting and unusual pioneer in using digital technologies to challenge corrupt and authoritarian states.

Assange had made the journey from anonymous hacker to one of the most discussed people in the world – at once reviled, celebrated and lionised, sought-after, imprisoned, self-exiled and shunned. He had been catapulted from the obscurity of his life in Nairobi, dribbling out leaks that nobody much noticed, to publishing a flood of classified documents that went to the heart of America's military and foreign policy operations. From being a marginal figure invited to join panels at geek conferences he was suddenly America's public enemy number one. A new-media messiah to some, a cyber-terrorist to others. As if this wasn't dramatic enough, in the middle of it all two women in Sweden accused him of rape. Oh, and Steven Spielberg's people were on the phone to the *Guardian* wanting to buy up the rights to the story.[1] You couldn't make any of it up.

The media and public were torn between those who saw Assange as a new kind of cyber-messiah and those who regarded him as a James Bond villain. Each extremity projected onto him superhuman powers of good or evil. The saga became even more confused in December 2010 when, as part of his bail conditions, Assange had to live at Ellingham Hall, a Georgian manor set in hundreds of acres of Suffolk countryside. It was as if a Stieg Larsson novel had been passed to the writer of *Downton Abbey*, Julian Fellowes.

But – despite the tensions and the shouting matches and the disappearances and the threats and the silences – we produced some rather important reporting. As Sarah Ellison's *Vanity Fair* piece on the subject concluded: 'Whatever the differences, the results have been extraordinary. Given the range, depth, and accuracy of the leaks, the collaboration has produced by any standard one of the greatest journalistic scoops of the last 30 years.'[2]

*

The series of stories which grabbed the attention of media, politicians and public around the world began on 25 July 2010. At this stage there were three media organisations involved in addition to WikiLeaks itself – the *Guardian*, *Der Spiegel* and the *New York Times* (another collaboration with Bill Keller). We had once again gone to the *NYT* because a) the quantity and scope of the documents (390,000 reports from Iraq alone) was greater than the *Guardian*, on its own, could do justice to in the time available; and b) because the US First Amendment protection for free speech might come in handy. Journalists in the US have a much stronger constitutional protection than their counterparts in the UK.

On the first day we published 14 pages and the relevant Pentagon cables, which we, along with the other two media partners, redacted. Assange published a very great number of 'threat reports'. It was the beginning of a fundamental difference of opinion about the responsibility involved in handling such sensitive material. The three editors felt we were treading on delicate security and ethical eggshells. The logistics – three (and, later, five) publications with different deadlines across three time zones – were complex enough. They became even more complex when we learned that Assange had given some of the documents to other news organisations.

Relations further soured over the continued involvement of the *NYT*, which Assange despised and which had run an unflattering profile of him. It was the most complicated editorial project any of us had been involved in. Different news organisations had divergent views on the sensitivity of particular regions or cables (the *NYT* was reluctant to publish material about Yemeni collusion with the US military, for example, whereas the *Guardian* and later *El País* felt this was an important story).

Publication came in waves. On 25 July we released our respective versions of the Afghan war logs. The *Guardian*'s coverage ran over 14 pages – too much for a general reader to absorb, but it was never certain that we would be free to publish a second day's coverage. We focused on civilian deaths and a special operations group, Task Force 373, which targeted the Taliban. Assange meanwhile simultaneously published all but 15,000 'threat reports'.

The Iraqi war logs, based on nearly 400,000 reports, were scheduled to run two weeks later on 8 August, though by now relations between some of the media partners and Assange were already cooling. By then we also had access to 250,000 diplomatic cables.

No news organisation had, at that stage, ever had to handle such quantities of raw data, and it tested the ingenuity of our systems engineers[3] to build a search engine capable of making sense of it. Once it was up and running David Leigh, the most experienced and tenacious of reporters, was able to get to work – a process he likened to lowering a hook into a pond and seeing if any fish came up. 'Within a week or two, it was clear to me that there were about two dozen stories, each of which would normally be the splash story on the front page of the paper.'[4]

An already complicated relationship with Assange became infinitely trickier when he was accused of rape by two Swedish women in the third week of August. Nick Davies made his own enquiries and strongly warned against any assumption that Assange had been set up. He was a partner in the series of revelations, but the *Guardian* had no obligation to defend him against charges of sexual misconduct, especially as he seemed to be distributing misinformation about what had happened. Quite the reverse.[5]

In October we published the Iraqi war logs, including revelations of torture of prisoners by Iraqi forces; on the use of private contractors in war; and on Iran's involvement. The format in which we released selected cables enabled the public to search within them.

Nothing about the arrangement was simple. But – after a late-night stand-off in which Assange marched into the office with lawyers at his side blisteringly to denounce us all – we were, sort of, back on track.

By 28 November the publishing consortium – expanded at Assange's invitation to include *Le Monde* and *El País* – had more than 160 articles ready for publication and more in the pipeline. They ranged from revelations about US diplomats spying on UN officials; to Saudi Arabia urging the US to bomb Iranian nuclear plants; to relations between China and North Korea. Each cable the five publishing partners intended to use was subject to redactions. At the height of the operation we had more than 25 editors and reporters involved at the *Guardian*.

The secrecy around such publication is double-edged – necessary to protect the security and exclusivity of the material, but in danger of creating a bubble of self-reinforcement. At once stage I asked our columnist (and former *Times* and *Evening Standard* editor) Simon Jenkins to read through the stories we'd prepared just for a reality check. He'd not been involved in any aspect of the editing, and I wanted his frank assessment of the stories and any risk they might pose. His verdict: we had no choice but to publish.

We learned much from each other. I was nervous when the *NYT* told us they would be going to the White House for comment a week before publication. In the UK, few newspapers would consider doing that for fear of injunction. In the US, where a newspaper cannot realistically be injuncted,[6] a more grown-up dialogue between state and media is possible. This was a lesson which was lost on the British authorities – up to, and including, the subsequent Snowden reporting.

We published. The sky did not fall in. The opponents of publication made repeated assertions of the harm caused by the release. Some years later, I was sitting with a senior intelligence figure as he predicted grave consequences of the Snowden revelations. We'd have blood on our hands, he told us.

'But you argued that over WikiLeaks,' I protested. He waved his hand dismissively. WikiLeaks was insignificant.

'But that's not what you said at the time!'

*

The Iraq documents and diplomatic cables were, to date, easily the biggest leak of classified material in history. The relationship with Assange did not survive – quite the opposite. He became the bitterest of critics, protesting (in the third person) on Twitter that he had suffered 'five years being detained [as 'editor'] without charge after you invited him to the UK to be your source'[7] – a very Assangeist mingling of causes and effects. Assange was either an editor or a source: he couldn't be both. In fact, Chelsea Manning was our (and Assange's) source. Nor had Assange been detained: he had sent himself into exile, for something that had nothing to do with his, or our, editorial activities.

Everything about working with Assange was difficult. The writer Andrew O'Hagan, who was supposed to ghost Assange's autobiography but ended up writing a short, brilliant account of his months failing to do so, recorded 'how deeply adversarial WikiLeaks was in its relationship with its friends. Julian treated his supporters as subjects, and learned nothing when they walked away. He hardly mentioned the right-wing press that called him a criminal and a traitor: he expended all his ire on the journalists who had tried to work with him and who had basic sympathy for his political position. In a bank safe, I have dozens of hours of taped interviews with Assange in which he rails maniacally against the *Guardian* and the *New York Times* . . . Before my eyes, and with no regard for me or my tape recorder, he snapped the olive branch proffered by those he hated.'[8]

As flawed and impossible as he could be, Assange was – in his early days at least – visionary about the possibilities of the internet, disclosure and free speech. If he were ever charged for the specific activities in which we were jointly engaged, I would – of course – give evidence on his behalf. I believed then, and I believe now, in the value of our carefully edited and redacted publication.

But Assange was a new breed of player in the digital age. The old rules were not his rules. He belonged nowhere and had no identifiable political creed. He was a shape-shifter, a libertarian anarchist, a stateless provocateur – and, in future, even the most powerful states were going to have to work out how to deal with the ultimate asymmetry of one person declaring war on the system.

This, like it or not, was the new eco-system of publishing.

Our collaboration with other media organisations was also a new thing – and led to other partnerships that took advantage of being able to leverage technology, scale and constitutional protections. One news-paper acting alone might be picked off and intimidated or silenced: that became much harder if they were part of an international consortium of publications.

Yes, of course, Assange could have published some (or, as he eventually did, all) of the material himself. He had a very small team of assistants – mostly (not all) very young developers. But, as we were to discover, they struggled with the magnitude of the task, at least as we defined it.

He saw it differently. Much of the editing on which we prided ourselves was, to his eyes, unnecessary if not positively repressive. The niceties of libel law didn't concern him. He was happiest dumping raw documents into the public domain and letting nature take its course. It wasn't for him to make assessments of the significance of a particular cable about India, Uzbekistan, Brazil or Myanmar. The internet could do that for itself. Let people around the world pick through the entrails of US foreign policy deliberations. He took crowdsourcing to its ultimate conclusion.

As more conventional publishers we faced considerable challenges in dealing with this new breed of actor who defied any categorisation or control. We were different animals.

Journalism – to us – involved careful choices about responsibly publishing the material we considered to be of public interest. Assange's challenge – not an unreasonable one – was *Who gave you the right to sit in judgement or determine the 'public interest'?*

I once remarked to a senior intelligence figure that the British and American governments, instead of condemning our role, should go down on their knees in thanks that we were there as a careful filter. Without newspapers, they would be dealing with a much scarier and intractable problem. Some of the wiser heads tacitly understood that. But how contemptuous Assange would be of such a thought. How he would despise even my contact with such a person, or the fact that I leave him anonymous in this narrative.

Assange appeared to have contempt for all journalists and for journalism itself. As he went it alone and became ever more isolated – metaphorically and literally – he veered off in directions which made even his staunchest supporters uncomfortable.

But he did pose some difficult questions for practitioners of journalism. I sympathised to some extent with a looser idea of allowing the wider world – in a controlled way! – access to raw data rather than acting as a sometimes-impermeable filter. We were besieged by requests from colleagues around the world begging for sight of documents relating to particular regions or governments. We declined nearly all of them: that led to Pandora's box. But who were we to appoint ourselves as gatekeepers?

And then there developed new and troubling issues about the motivation of sources. I have generally believed that – overwhelmingly – an editor has to disregard motivation. All kinds of people leak material to newspapers from all kinds of motives, many of them not shiningly honourable. Put the motives aside and look at the documents: what story do *they* tell? If they disclose matters of considerable public importance, that is (nearly) all that matters. We might want to let the reader know about the apparent purposes or biases of our sources, but they shouldn't necessarily colour the decision to publish.

But – years later – Assange, solitary and reclusive, intervened in the 2016 US presidential election in ways that troubled many. In the month before voters went to the polls WikiLeaks assiduously published a steady barrage of hacked emails – more than 100,000 in all – from the campaign (the Democratic National Committee leaks) and Hillary Clinton's team (the Podesta emails). Clinton had been seven points ahead of Donald Trump at the beginning of October. In December 2016, she singled out both the WikiLeaks documents and FBI director James Comey's announcement that he had re-opened enquiries into her communications as significant contributions to her defeat.

That may or may not have been true. But what if the emails were 'intelligence porn', to use Comey's description of them to a Senate hearing? The claim is that WikiLeaks was essentially laundering information that might have been hacked by Russian intelligence with the purpose of destabilising the election of a foreign power.[9]

Assange's defence about what he described (using the language of newspapers) as an 'epic scoop' was straight down the line: the classic right to know. In a statement released on the WikiLeaks website in November 2016 he elaborated: 'It is an open model of journalism that gatekeepers are uncomfortable with, but which is perfectly harmonious with the First Amendment ... It would be unconscionable for WikiLeaks to withhold such an archive from the public during an election.' He contrasted his behaviour with the notorious failure of the *NYT* to publish evidence of illegal mass surveillance of the US population for a year until after the 2004 election.

'The First Amendment does not privilege old media, with its corporate advertisers and dependencies on incumbent power factions, over WikiLeaks' model of scientific journalism or an individual's decision to inform their friends on social media. The First Amendment unapologetically nurtures the democratization of knowledge. With the internet, it has reached its full potential.'

Having argued for our own model of 'open journalism', there was something about Assange's behaviour in late 2016 that did, indeed, make me feel uncomfortable. Was that because – as he would doubtless put it – I was a 'gatekeeper', unable to let go? Was it old-fashioned to think there was something qualitatively different about acting as a conduit, or cut-out, for information obtained by foreign espionage (if that's what he was subsequently doing)? Was the releasing of vast quantities of unmediated raw data 'journalism', as he described it? Did it matter? Were we reaching a stage when the distinction between 'journalism' and other forms of publishing information was so blurred as to be meaningless?

'If it's true information, we don't care where it comes from,' was Assange's riposte to what he saw as liberal hand-wringing. 'Let people fight with the truth, and when the bodies are cleared there will be bullets of truth everywhere.'

To Raffi Khatchadourian of the *New Yorker*, there was a difference between someone like Chelsea Manning or Edward Snowden and the exploitation of hacking by foreign powers: 'State-sponsored information warfare is nothing like what activist hackers and whistleblowers do,' he wrote in an August 2017 article. 'The latter take personal risks – with their freedom, and their reputation – to release information that matters to them. For a state, there is no personal risk, no courage, and the content may not even be terribly important. The release of a huge archive filled with arcana and gossip carries its own symbolic weight, especially during a moment of political volatility: an institution that seems permeable does not seem strong – and an institution with secrets looks duplicitous, no matter how benign the secrets may be. This is something that Russian intelligence appeared to understand: the leak is the message.'[10]

The executive editor of the *NYT*, Dean Baquet – a 'gatekeeper' who, with Jill Abramson, his predecessor, had collaborated with the *Guardian* on the WikiLeaks and Snowden releases – was asked about his views of 'gatekeeper' versus 'open' in a BBC interview:

> Early WikiLeaks now feels like some halcyon [exercise]. [The Iraq and diplomatic cables] were such a powerful and important mission-driven data dump. It was about how governments operate. It inspired

parts of the Arab Spring. It was clearly journalistically newsworthy. It seemed that the source was idealistic. But we're now in an era when governments are weaponising hacking. But I still think, even though it makes me queasy, that if someone gives us information that's really important and vital for people to know, we've gotta figure out a way to publish it – even if the source is part of the story.[11]

So, yes, he would have published some (not all) of the DNC and Podesta material – but with two provisos: a) he would only have published the material he considered significant and important; b) he would do his best to be transparent about the sources and their motives. He would not consider the private lives of public figures to be of public importance.

Once, to do journalism, all you needed was a knowledge of shorthand and to read a couple of books on law and local government. Now the best journalists had to be moral philosophers and students of ethics.

The speed of change was both dizzying and relentless. We could sense that we were caught up in a new world of possibilities and disruption. We were, to some extent, helping to drive it. But the accelerating and violent forces buffeting journalism meant there was never enough time to pause and reflect.

*

There's clearly a gulf here between two views of how information behaves, or should behave, in the horizontal twenty-first century – the difference, if you like, between irrigation and spraying. The gatekeepers – the irrigators – were throwbacks from the vertical world: we would sift, evaluate and contextualise for you and let you see only what was, in our view, important. The sprayers believed in splattering the information indiscriminately into the world and letting citizens decide. That was the new democracy of information.

I felt torn. I was a gatekeeper who believed in open journalism. I had spent my working life with journalists whose judgement and ability I admired and depended on. But I could also understand a growing scepticism about self-appointed arbiters of news in an age when much information fought to be free.[12] Journalism wasn't a profession with recognised, universal standards. It was not like brain surgery or mechanical engineering. A Fox News presenter's idea of journalism might overlap only marginally with that of a desk editor on the *New York Times*. The *Daily Mail* – combative, proudly biased, often intrusive – practised a form of journalism very different from the cool, impartial, restrained BBC or National Public Radio. What did the processes of the *Sun* and *FT* have in common?

Journalism was more a craft than a profession. But it was not even like woodworkers, electricians or plumbers – in which there were agreed methods of working, along with ongoing training and certification. At the moment of its greatest trial – because the money to support it was disappearing and the competition from other sources multiplying – its lack of definition was troubling.

Now, in 2018, I am not, primarily, a journalist – just a reader, a consumer of news, a voter. And still I am confused. I quite often find myself disliking and distrusting some of the traditional gatekeepers and their methods, even if I know the classic defence of free expression requires one to defend the sometimes loathsome. I am deeply suspicious of Assange – in his way, also a gatekeeper – but am in sympathy with the idea of allowing the mass of people access to the same information the gatekeepers used to monopolise.

I revere the work of many journalists. I desperately want the institutional estate of a free press to thrive. I find many aspects of the new landscape of alternative media liberating and enriching. Other parts of the informational chaos I find repellent and disturbing.

Whose side am I on? Do I have to take sides? What is the best synthesis of these multiple lenses on life?

*

These are questions which niggle away with virtually every passing week, if not day. In January 2017 Buzzfeed published explosive – but unverified – allegations about the Russian government's alleged cultivation, support and assistance of Donald Trump as he mounted a bid to become president.[13] They were based on a dossier of intelligence about Trump, including his financial dealings and graphic claims of sexual acts said to have been documented by the Russians. Buzzfeed journalists had done their best to investigate the contents of the dossier but had not been able to verify many of the claims – nor to disprove them.

There were many reasons not to publish this document – and, indeed, it transpired that several news organisations were in possession of it and had not, to date, let their readers in on the fact of its existence, far less its contents.

We fall back on the classical nostrums of our craft. Journalism is about separating truths from untruths – and aspiring to publish only truths. Why would we publish material if we had an imperfect idea if it was true or not? In a 'post-truth' world of fake news, isn't it all the more vital that journalism sticks to what it does? If we publish only the truth, that will distinguish our brand from the rest of the seething digital ocean with its turbulent, roaring tides of stuff – true stuff, untrue stuff, malicious stuff, vapid stuff, explosive stuff. We are the sifters, the irrigators. The rest is spray.

And I believe all that. All the same, in January 2017, I – as a mere reader – felt grateful that Buzzfeed had published the dossier of material about Trump without knowing fully what was true or not. I felt irritated that the document – potentially so important – had been kept from public gaze … particularly when less explosive raw material about Hillary Clinton had been so freely sprayed around before the November presidential election.

Buzzfeed may not – in their haste to be first – have published the 35-page document well, i.e. with sufficient context, redactions and caveats. But the dossier appeared to have originated from a reputable source, a respected former MI6 officer, Christopher Steele; and a synopsis of its findings had been in circulation, including to Presidents Obama and Trump. It was reported that those who had read it included the former Senate Democratic leader, Harry Reid; the Arizona Republican John McCain; and the FBI Director, James Comey – and that the FBI already had copies of many of the memos.

It was further reported that journalists at the *NYT*, the *Washington Post*, Yahoo News, the *New Yorker*, CNN and *Mother Jones* had been briefed about, or possessed, the dossier. *Mother Jones* wrote a story on 31 October 2016 – just a week before election day – in which the author, David Corn, said 'Mother Jones has reviewed that report and other memos this former spy wrote.' It quoted very selectively and briefly from the document.[14]

Here was a new asymmetry of information. The sprayers ensured that voters were treated to tens of thousands of raw Clinton emails: the irrigators decided the voters should not be trusted with much more explosive – and raw – information about Donald Trump ... until it was too late to make any difference.

Many in the old world vented their fury at Buzzfeed for playing by the new rules, rather than the old ones: their behaviour, they said, stank. Corn, who had allowed his readers only a peek in late October, was dismayed at the publication: 'Even Donald Trump deserves journalistic fairness.' Brad Heath, an investigative journalist for *USA Today*, protested: '"not how journalism works ..." decide for yourself if it's legit'.

The editor of Buzzfeed, Ben Smith, was having none of it. To his mind, this was precisely how journalism should work in 2017. Why should American citizens be denied sight of a document that was circulating at the highest levels in the US government? 'Our presumption is to be transparent in our journalism and to share what we have with our readers.' Very similar words – in a different context – have been used by the *NYT*'s Baquet, in saying how uncomfortable he feels when he knows things his readers don't.

One story – a hugely important one – and no consensus about how to publish it, or even whether it should be published. It was emblematic of the shifting arguments over what 'journalism' was, or was becoming.

★

The British gatekeepers found themselves on trial – or, at least, subjected to the unforgiving glare of a judicial inquiry – with the Leveson Inquiry into the culture, practice and ethics of the British press, the government's response to Nick Davies's reporting, which opened on 14 November 2011.

The two-part inquiry had been set up in July 2011 by the prime minister, David Cameron, in the wake of the phone-hacking revelations. By then the police had contacted nearly 200 potential victims of phone hacking and had a further 3,870 names to contact.

Cameron told the House of Commons that a senior judge, Lord Justice Leveson, would scrutinise the culture, practices and ethics of the press along with the failure of the current system of regulation. A second inquiry would later look at the extent of unlawful conduct at the *News of the World* and other newspapers along with implications between newspapers and the police.[15]

Until this point the British press financed its own self-regulatory body, the Press Complaints Commission, which could order corrections and, on rare occasions, criticise newspapers which broke its own code of conduct. The British press had defended this organisation as tough and rigorous – right up to July 2011, when the elders had admitted it was pretty toothless after all and should be replaced by something tougher and more rigorous.

Just over a year later the judge published his mammoth 2,000-page report into what he'd learned. There followed another two years of wrangling before a new regulator was established to oversee the workings of journalists and try to correct the wrongs of the past, or at least prevent them happening again. Unfortunately, the solution cooked up between politicians and the press was so convoluted it was virtually impossible to describe, let alone implement.

Brian Leveson was an amiable, no-nonsense judge in his mid-60s who had spent a career in largely criminal practice at the Bar. Nothing in his previous life had prepared him for his lengthy close encounter with Fleet Street. Nor did Fleet Street take kindly to having an outsider poking his nose, however well-meaning, into their affairs. The inquiry was a long and tense affair, often bristling with mutual incomprehension and bruised mistrust.

Leveson appointed six assessors to help him with expert areas of evidence, including three distinguished journalists – Sir David Bell, formerly of the *FT*; Elinor Goodman, ex-Channel 4; and George Jones, former political editor of the *Telegraph*. There was immediately a row as to why there wasn't an assessor with tabloid experience.

Separately, the editors of the 'broadsheet' titles – the *Guardian*, *FT*, *Times*, *Telegraph* and *Independent* – formed a little breakfast club. Together, all five titles represented just 18 per cent of the complaints against all national newspapers. We weren't perfect. But in a typical year, according to studies, well over 50 per cent of all complaints were against just two newspapers – the *Daily Mail* and the *Sun*.[16]

American colleagues were baffled by the entire inquiry, finding it impossible to imagine any form of regulation on the press – by anyone. Some British journalists were in the same camp: there was plenty of criminal and civil law to punish errant reporters or editors. Why did you need regulation as well? And wasn't it hopelessly old-fashioned, in the age of global digital media, to be singling out British print-dominated companies for special treatment?

The old-fashioned point had some substance. As to the assertion that criminal law was enough – the riposte was that it hadn't worked over phone hacking. The police had ignored evidence and held only the most cursory of inquiries. There would always be the suspicion that a hugely dominant media organisation felt some degree of impunity from police and politicians, not to mention the scrutiny of the rest of the press. That was why a level of regulation was widely considered necessary. The question was: who could be trusted to do the regulating? How could you create a body that was truly independent both of the press itself, but also the government?

The answer Leveson came up with was complicated by the fear that – as in the past – particular media companies might simply boycott the regulator, as Richard Desmond, the former pornographer who owned the *Express*, had done by refusing to pay his dues to the previous regulator, the PCC. Such a boycott would wreck the credibility of any new system. So Leveson played with the idea of carrots and sticks to marshal everyone into the fold.

His chosen carrots and sticks were linked to the British libel laws – giving more protection on costs to people who were properly regulated while making it potentially punitively expensive for anyone outside the regulatory system.

So far, so good. On a brisk December morning in 2012 no fewer than 19 Fleet Street editors gathered for bacon rolls and granola at the Delaunay hotel near the Strand to consider the 47 main Leveson proposals – and unanimously agreed to 40 of them without very much haggling.[17] The meeting was ably chaired by James Harding, the then editor of the *Times*, who brought along Phil Webster, his respected political editor, to keep the minutes.

The collected editors agreed with most of Leveson's suggestions for a new, independent regulator, along with its financing, powers and processes. The group agreed to provide an arbitration service to keep the costs of more serious complaints down. In future there would be a whistleblower hotline for journalists concerned about ethical lapses within their newsrooms. Equally, reporters who refused to act unethically would have contractual protection against disciplinary action.

Leveson himself was said to believe he had come up with the mildest possible remedies – and most of Fleet Street agreed at the time. If anything, there was a sense of relief that we had got off relatively lightly.

After this broad accord matters became more complicated. For some days the minutes weren't circulated on the grounds, said Harding, that one of the editors present had had second thoughts. This was a novel view of what minutes were for. There was, apparently, some displeasure that the *Guardian* had carried a brief report of the meeting: champions of openness evidently did not like their own deliberations exposed to daylight.

From that moment on the lights went out. The elders took back control. The press side of the argument was decided in smaller, less open groups. Harding, who had been fair and open in his chairing, was – coincidentally – sacked from the *Times*. The fightback – long, arduous, bitter and, for the most part, decided behind closed doors – began.

The really complicated sticking point was how to implement the carrots and sticks. Leveson believed you needed some 'legal underpinning' to make it work – i.e. you had to pass a short bill that would give the force of law to any measures on costs or penalties in libel actions. The media negotiators volubly argued that this was, in effect, statutory control of the press. They weren't having it – and they were fully prepared to use their own megaphone to get their way. Far from being a mild response, Leveson was now denounced as the end of 300 years of press freedom – or so editorials and columns argued loudly and repeatedly.

The government (and this is where it got ridiculously convoluted) responded with a too-clever-by-half idea of side-stepping the law by the front door. Instead it suggested awarding the proposed press regulator a 'back door' royal charter – a peculiarly opaque medieval instrument more usually reserved for Oxbridge colleges or professional bodies. In truth, a royal charter is, itself, statute, but one that is decided at the pleasure of the government of the day[18] rather than parliament as a whole. If you were against statute you should be against a royal charter. But some editors wobbled.

There followed attempts at political deal-making every bit as closed-off as Fleet Street's own deliberations. The proposed carrots and sticks were clumsily botched. The victims of phone hacking, part of an umbrella group that included academics and media professionals, dug in for the full Leveson as opposed to the Leveson Lite package they believed to be under negotiation. The whole process could barely have been messier.

In the end, the closed circle of elders who were running things decided to go ahead with their own (non-Leveson compliant) regulator and defy parliament to take them on. One of their number invited me to tea at the Savoy hotel and produced some sheets of paper from his inside pocket. *This was how it was going to be.*

He was contemptuous of our little broadsheet breakfast club, about which he seemed remarkably well-informed. Its members would either do what they were told or were irrelevant. He ticked them off one at a time. I felt a twinge of pity for my granola colleagues, apparently (in his words) overridden by their corporate superiors or regarded as super-fluous. The unmistakeable message to me was: *You're on your own.*

I said I'd go away and think about it. My teatime companion's mood darkened. His blunt advice was not to think about it for too long: *If you don't do what we want then I wouldn't want to be in your shoes.*

The *Guardian* didn't, in the end, join the Independent Press Standards Organisation (IPSO), the new regulator, when it started: nor did the *FT* or the *Independent.* The National Union of Journalists similarly refused to endorse it, calling it a 'pointless so-called regulator'. Having been responsible for the investigation which led to Leveson we felt we had to respect the strong opposition to the new body from the victims of phone hacking. And, in any case, we were no more convinced of the true independence of the new 'regulator' than the first person chosen to lead it, a retired judge, Sir Alan Moses, who was (initially, at least) privately and publicly sceptical of its governance. The previous regulator had not behaved well towards the *Guardian* over phone hacking. Was this new body going to be much better?[19]

Leveson and its aftermath did not inspire huge confidence about Fleet Street and its openness. It closed ranks, responding with paranoid aggression to outsiders trying to help it think through the main issues. I came to know many of the victims, academics, politicians, think-tankers, lawyers and broadcast journalists who were – for mostly genuine and disinterested reasons – trying to help find a solution to the difficult questions posed by Leveson. Some of them had a record in journalism as fine as any of the current crops of editors or proprietors. But to a small cabal in Fleet Street – editors, business leaders and one or two lobbyists who had never done a day's journalism in their lives – they were all anti-press freedom fanatics who must be rebuffed, denounced and crushed.

This siege mentality led to one of the maddest single editions of any newspaper to have been published in modern times. In mid-November 2012 – just before the publication of the Leveson report – our media commentator, Roy Greenslade, was told to stand by for a shock story in the *Daily Mail* and was invited personally to preview it in the newsroom before publication. Such an unusual call suggested impending dynamite, but Roy explained he was currently in Brighton. The *Mail* couriered the proofs to his house – a round journey of 130 miles. We held our breath.

Roy rang me a couple of hours later when the dummy pages arrived. He was baffled. The *Mail* had decided to devote 12 pages – twelve! – to a massive 'special investigation' into Sir David Bell, one of Leveson's assessors. Roy had flicked through the eye-popping headlines fulminating about this supposedly sinister figure with a minor role in the inquiry. He couldn't find a story. An angry but rambling editorial concluded that Bell was 'an elitist liberal' and that if people like him were about to determine 'the public interest and what newspapers should be allowed to print' it would be curtains for 300 years of press freedom in Britain.

I knew David Bell slightly. If I wanted to run an investigation into a shadowy spider at the heart of the British establishment, Bell wouldn't be in even my top quarter of a million potential targets. He was, in the best sense of the word, a do-gooder living an unexceptional post-retirement life of public service on the boards of assorted charities, schools and trusts. A former managing editor at the *FT*, he had risen to being CEO and then chair of the *FT*. He had been knighted for service to business, the arts and charity. Now in his late sixties, he cut an affable, slightly old-fashioned figure as he busied himself with education, churches, ballet companies or the homeless.

Bell's crime in the eyes of the *Mail* was that he had also sat on the board of a body called the Media Standards Trust (MST), which – the clue was in the name – was sometimes critical of media standards; and that, together with his fellow board member Julia Middleton, he served on another body – an organisation called Common Purpose – which ran harmless-looking leadership programmes. Most neutral commentators couldn't see much to write home about. Peter Wilby, writing in the *New Statesman*, called it a 'masterpiece of "link" journalism. Show that X sits on the same committee as W who is married to Y whose cousin Z once spent a night at the house of the mass murderer V and, hey presto, X is "linked" to V and therefore to mass murder.'

As a declaration of war on Leveson (as it was widely read to be) it was, to put it kindly, unhinged. All 12 pages. I cannot think of a single other recent occasion when a mainstream Fleet Street paper so abandoned all sense of reasonable news values or proportion in order to butcher the reputation of a mild and decent person.

But the tone was set. It was now all-out war on Leveson. In the period after the report's publication there were thousands of articles about the inquiry and its aftermath, with Fleet Street's coverage overwhelmingly negative. One study – by the hated MST – found the *Mail* carried 33 negative articles for every positive one; at the *Sun* the ratio was 29:1.[20] The inner circle of media elders involved in setting up IPSO – with 90 per cent of weekly national newspaper circulation – decried Leveson as an existential threat to press freedom. The general approval at the Delaunay breakfast, minuted by the man from the *Times*, was conveniently forgotten.

The *Times* ran five negative articles about press regulation to every positive one.[21] The names of Milton, Wilkes and Defoe were invoked.

I didn't much like the royal charter fudge either. The carrots and sticks, all lawyers agreed, had been badly drafted and need revisiting or abandoning. Hacked Off, the pressure group associated with the victims, could also at times be strident and inflexible.

But there *was* a case to answer. The unchecked criminality within newsrooms was a moral catastrophe for British journalism and its role in our democracy. It was our Enron, our Volkswagen, our Deepwater, our subprime crisis. It was depressing to watch colleagues retreat into the bunker and use their own bully-pages to close down debate by savaging anyone who offered even constructive help in rebuilding trust in the press. I loathed the threats and abuse directed at anyone who dared to disagree.

But the elders eventually got their way.

As the phone-hacking legal cases spread into the *Sun*, the Murdoch organisation – now once again led by Rebekah Brooks, editor of the *Sun* between 2003 and 2009 – made a last minute confidential legal settlement. The January 2018 deal meant that there would be no public hearing of allegations of wrongdoing by James Murdoch and Brooks.[22]

It also meant that, six weeks later, the government led by Theresa May could announce it was reneging on David Cameron's promise to hold a second part of the Leveson Inquiry, intended to look into criminality in the press. Lord Justice Leveson himself published a long letter vigorously disagreeing with the turn of events.

The decision to drop the inquiry suited everyone in the sealed government–press bubble. The weakest prime minister in living memory, her administration paralysed by splits over Brexit, May desperately needed allies in the press. And the press desperately wanted the second part of Leveson not to happen. Everyone was happy.

A week later the *Sunday Times*'s main private detective, John Ford, broke cover to express bitter remorse over his work in delving into the lives of hundreds of targets: 'I was untrained, untutored and I was nothing more than a common thief, even though I tried to dignify my activities as artistry under the catch-all title of blagger.' He was particularly ashamed about his fishing expeditions to dig into the private affairs of some politicians. 'It was grossly invasive, shameful, immoral, wrong and it was not news.'[23]

Ford had been at the heart of the News International attempt to smear the *Guardian* after our first story about the Gordon Taylor settlement. In May 2018 he came to see me in Oxford, accompanied by the former *News of the World* investigative reporter Graham Johnson. Ford, a former actor turned blagger, opened his heart about the shame he felt over his years of targeting people on behalf of *Sunday Times* executives and reporters. His contrition felt genuine.

The new evidence of what you might kindly call 'ethical flexibility' at the *Sun*, Mirror Group titles and *Sunday Times* – and, in a different way, the *Telegraph* – could have been at the heart of Leveson 2. Which no longer existed.

*

The dripping contempt for 'the liberal elite' or their supposed notion of 'public interest' was the bitter stuff of deeper culture wars. But Leveson and its aftermath clarified how much confusion – or, more accurately, straight disagreement – now existed about the nature and purpose of what we did.

It was becoming more and more evident that there was no neat agreement on what journalism in the public interest looked like. The *Daily Mail* employed many outstanding reporters – we occasionally employed a few of them – but the relentless, bruising, sometimes brutalising editorial ethos of that paper in recent times had little in common with the BBC or the *FT*, any more than the newsroom at Fox TV had much in common with that of the *New York Times* or *Washington Post*.

Even among the so-called legacy media organisations there was a yawning divergence in attitudes to what journalism should, or could, be. Scarcely a week passed without a withering attack from the *Mail* on the BBC's editorial ethos or standards. Periodically the *Mail* editor would castigate the *Guardian*, Channel 4 or the *FT* – either personally, anonymously or through willing surrogates. There was never a flicker of irony or humility in the eyes of the most-complained of newspaper (1,214 PCC complaints in 2013) bellowing contempt at the most trusted/ethical news organisations in the country (e.g. the *FT*, seven complaints).[24]

The elders' fury at Leveson was dressed up in invocations of Cobbett, Swift or John Delane. But there seemed little that Leveson himself was proposing – as opposed to botched subsequent wrangling – that would inhibit robust commentary or investigations into matters of genuine public significance. Article 10 of the Human Rights Act – as it was being interpreted in the (English as well as European) courts – was gradually proving a reasonable protector of public interest journalism.[25]

What, then, did they fear? The real fury – also apparent in denunciations of European jurisdiction concerning privacy – was reserved for judges who stood in the way of the lucrative pursuit of sex scandals.

In 2011 there had been a spate of so-called super-injunctions – court cases intended to gag the press, which themselves were covered by an injunction. Not only could a newspaper not write about something, they couldn't even tell their readers what it was they weren't allowed to write about. In 2009 the *Guardian* had been subject to such an order, obtained by the international trading company Trafigura, who were accused of arranging for the dumping of toxic oil waste in West Africa in 2006, making thousands of people ill.[26] Trafigura went to court to stop us publishing something from an internal report which included a scientific study containing damning evidence of the potentially toxic nature of the waste. The judge went further than banning us from using the document: he prohibited us from revealing that Trafigura had even been to court. The case was labelled RJW and SJW so no one could ever know the identities of the parties in the case.

The company was so intent on stopping publication of the document it even attempted to prevent the reporting of parliamentary proceedings in which the matter had been raised. Twitter made a mockery of the attempt to gag parliament as well as the press, and the company backed down. After a five-week battle the *Guardian* was able to publish details from the suppressed report.

That seemed an open-and-shut case of the misuse of injunctions, never mind super-injunctions. But what about cases where nothing more important was at stake than, for instance, whom a footballer went to bed with?

Let's just take two from 2009. The first concerned a footballer we can only call MJN.

MJN was married. He was said to have had an affair with a lingerie model. The model wished to tell, or rather sell, her story about the 'relationship' to the *Sun*. Indeed, she *had* told her story – 'MY FLING WITH PREM STAR' but the paper had not been allowed to name the 'love rat' because there was a GAG ON AFFAIR.

Under British law, a court was obliged to do three things:

1) Give due consideration to freedom of expression (Article 10 of the Human Rights Act, based on the European Convention on Human Rights)

2) Balance that right with another right under Article 8 – an individual's right to privacy

3) Consider the relevant journalistic codes of practice which might, for instance, justify intrusion into private life on the grounds of public interest.[27]

The *Sun* had not argued there was any public interest in the story. In fact, it hadn't even turned up in court. MJN said he assumed this had been a private relationship: he'd never courted any publicity in relation to any aspect of his private life. He was worried that publication would cause him and his wife 'enormous distress and embarrassment'.

The court agreed.[28] It injuncted the *Sun*. The case was heard in public, but the judgment was anonymised so that the claimant's name would be protected.

As you read this, some years later, are you outraged? Do you think it is your human right to know who MJN was and what he was up to? Do you care?

Anyone with any legal knowledge would know that – given the *Sun*'s failure to argue any public interest in the story – this was the only possible result.

Or here was another footballer who had strayed from the marital straight and narrow. The court called him TSE, and his one-time lover ELP. The *Sun* wanted to spread the relationship all over its front page and had offered ELP a lot of money to spill the beans. Neither of the love-birds wanted to do that.

The *Sun* argued – in print, but not in court – that they must expose the footballer because he was a hypocrite. In court, they did not attempt to argue any public interest in front of the judge, or even to resist the injunction. But in public they were furious: 'NEW ACE GAGS SUN ON ROMPS REVELATION'.

Mr Justice Tugendhat allowed the injunction.[29] In the absence of any pretence at public interest he couldn't do otherwise. At the end of his judgment he made a sharp comment on the way these cases – and there had been several of them – were reported by the press.

He noted that editorials often claimed that the courts were being used to protect rich footballers and other sportsmen. But, he said, many people seeking privacy injunctions were women and children; he listed nine such cases. Some were claimants who were gay or lesbian. Some of these cases weren't even about sex.

His words fell on deaf ears. There was outrage in several newspapers, claiming to hear the march of the jackboot in Britain. There was a line we, collectively, were expected to take: this was a sinister new intrusion on freedom of the press. We must all write editorials denouncing the creeping privacy law.

Some papers used the ban to attack Europe, the European Convention, the European Court, the Human Rights Act, human rights themselves – such was their fury at a process that had, on the face of it, tried to balance human pain and public benefit in a sober and humane way.

One judge who heard many of the cases was denounced repeatedly and personally. He was not only wrong, he was *amoral*.

The *Sun* periodically returned to the bones of the case – presenting a 'damning dossier' of 'the rich and famous whose filthy laundry was buried under big-bucks privacy injunctions ... about their sleazy antics'.[30] The orders, it said, often flew in the face of freedom of speech and the public interest – even if it was a public interest they never actually argued at the time in court.

Other journalists found it difficult to get worked up. Most of us (say, on the *Times*, *Sunday Times*, BBC, *FT*, *Economist*, etc.) had at times been bombarded with actions for ... you name it: libel, contempt, data protection, official secrecy, attempts to make us reveal our sources or even sequestrate our assets – all of those. But at the *Guardian* we had never been threatened with an action over privacy.[31]

The tabloids have a business model – one which, partly, involves intrusion into the privacy of people in the public eye. In comparison with some other business models, it's not a bad one. The public's appetite for scandal subsidises the coverage of politics. Take away the sleaze and the sex, and kiss goodbye to reportage of Westminster: that's how they argue it.

But you wondered at all the puffed-up outrage. Was the *Sun* editorial team itself free of 'filthy laundry' or 'sleazy antics' any more than any other newsroom? Journalists – and even some proprietors – were not known for leading saintly lives, any more than footballers. During the phone-hacking trial it emerged that, for six years, the (married) editors of the *Sun* and *News of the World* had been having an on-off affair together while regularly exposing the sexual antics and hypocrisy of others. I expect they (quite rightly, in my view) regarded these relationships as private. But shaming of others was a business model.

Did it matter? The *Sun* and *Mail* can surely have their economic imperative and their ethics; and the *Guardian* and *FT* can have theirs. We can rub along in peaceful coexistence. That's how it used to work, in a kinder age before newspapers began using the techniques of the secret police to spy on their targets.

But now journalism was facing an existential economic threat in the form of a tumultuous recalibration of our place in the world. And, on both sides of an increasingly scratchy debate, there was a hesitancy about whether there was any longer a common idea of journalism and what really mattered.

20

Members?

It was time, we all agreed in 2012, to get closer to the readers. It was time to meet them.

In print, we were nearing reliance on a loyal rump who were remarkably tolerant of repeated price increases. We wanted to reward their loyalty, to explain as openly as possible the seismic changes that had happened – and would happen more. And we wanted to explore different kinds of relationships and communities in this new world.

Over the road from the old offices in Farringdon Road, we had built a little café and lecture space and had begun to stage events, debates and public conversations involving *Guardian* and *Observer* journalists. For years we had sponsored the Glastonbury, and the Hay and Edinburgh book festivals, where thousands of readers would congregate, meet and exchange ideas. We experimented in giving a physical and human form to something that had previously been bound by newsprint and text.

Live events were gaining in salience, whether in music or at book festivals. Why not try a weekend festival in Kings Place in London and invite the readers in? Too often, journalists' only connection with their audience was through below-the-line comments. That was not always pleasurable. What if we met them face to face?

The building – only part of which we occupied – had numerous surrounding spaces, halls, galleries, bars and cafés. Imagine if we took the constituent bits of a newspaper and matched them with a space and with readers. Crossword fanatics could meet their fellow addicts and setters in one room. Theatre lovers could discuss drama with our critic, Michael Billington. Politics junkies could sit in on an editorial conference. We could have big main-stage debates for the more general readers. And we could use the occasion to tell people about the revolution in their own newspaper.

In the absence of a conventional owner, older *Guardian* readers tend to be very proprietorial about 'their' paper. Over the years I'd see them carbon-dating themselves by editor. 'I started with Wadsworth,' an elderly loyalist might say; or 'I began reading under Hetherington.'[1]

Thousands of readers turned up for the Open Weekend in March 2012.[2] Fiona Shaw read love poetry; the artist Jeremy Deller talked about his latest work; the star of African music Fatoumata Diawara performed songs; the economist Jeffrey Sachs discussed the Euro crisis with our economics editor. Younger editorial staff were charmed to find how nice *Guardian* readers were in person: their previous exposure had sometimes been coloured by the less charming corners of the comment threads.

On the Sunday morning, I did a session on newspapers, the digital economy, open journalism and the future of digital with Clay Shirky. Shirky ended up describing various different ways of getting readers to part with money. It was a pivotal conversation in shaping the immediate relationship between the *Guardian* and its readers. Out of it grew the membership scheme which – by 2017 – was being acclaimed as a crucial element in the future funding of the paper. Shirky told the audience over their first coffees of the day:

> The *Chicago Sun-Times* talks about this in terms of selling a product. You are buying content. The *New York Times* calls their model 'the digital subscriber model'. You are subscribing to a service. The *LA Times* calls theirs a 'membership model'. You are joining a club, or a community.
>
> These are really three different metaphors. News as product, news as service, news as community. Or I should say, a relationship between the reader and the newspaper organisation as customer relationships, subscriber relationships, membership relationships.

So, literally for the first time since 1830, in the US we are re-negotiating how we think about the relationship between the reader and the newspaper publication . . . What's fascinating is that it's not a fight about the business model any more, which is where all the heat has been for much of the last ten years. That part seems largely done. The fight now is how the newspapers are going to tell the readers about that relationship, and what the readers are gonna do in response. I think the metaphor we settle on, or maybe we'll settle on a range of metaphors, is really going to affect the culture of the news business, because form follows funding. At some point the self-conception of the people in the newsroom is gonna respond to the reader–newspaper relationship.

Which model did he favour?

There's advantages and disadvantages to each. If you say to somebody, 'I'm selling you a product . . .' the advantage is its complete continuity with the business of printing since Johannes Gutenberg. 'I made a thing, and you give me money, and I give you the thing.' So the advantage of that is cultural continuity, for the people inside the newspaper.

The disadvantage is, it's not actually true. So if I'm told I'm paying you for content, and I give you money, and then I look around and I see that 90 per cent of the people who show up are not giving any money, and they're getting exactly the same content, I'm feeling not very good about that. So . . . I think this creates a really submerged risk: the readers will start to think that this is not a very good customer relationship.

The subscriber model goes further. It says, essentially, 'This is a service.' We are in the client services business. You are essentially a client of ours. You have certain rights and responsibilities when you give us this money. But journalism as a service then moves you from stocks, to flows. You start thinking less about content that I put out every 24 hours, and you start thinking about the kinds of services you can enable. So, that is a more web-like way of thinking about it.

Membership goes all the way to maximising the loyalty premium, as in 'God forbid the *LA Times* go out of business.' Membership maximises the 'God forbid' premium. What we don't know yet is, is the service-oriented, subscriber model better? Or are some papers really going to end up like National Public Radio? Where the thing that keeps them going is a less than 10 per cent group of the readers who – even though they don't have to – every year put forward money because they're saying, 'God forbid there not be WNYC' or 'God forbid there not be a *Guardian*.'

We tried the different propositions on the Sunday morning audience of *Guardian* readers. No one was very keen on the Gutenberg model. There were some, but not many, takers for the subscriber model. We tried the third proposition – the 'God forbid' model. Readers liked the thought of being members of the *Guardian*. They also liked the idea of the *Guardian* being open to others, even if they hadn't paid.

It was Dworkin's lighthouse model.

Shirky told them they were voting for the 'public goods' model – ensuring that the reliable news source they personally valued remained an accessible force in the world at large.

The resonance is a little bit different in the US, because we don't have many public goods any more. We've been doing away with them over the decades. But I will say this: the special case of information is that, since the marginal cost of giving someone access to a story is zero (not the fixed costs, the fixed costs are not zero, but the marginal cost is zero), it's possible for a small group of people to be committed to actually providing a resource that makes society better, even for people who don't pay.

You still have to make the pounds and pence add up at the end of the day. But in terms of the newspaper's historic function as a value to the common weal, that is certainly the model that is best in terms of openness and turning consumer product into a civic platform.[3]

In the weeks and months following the weekend we began to explore the consequences of pursuing that audience's clear preference for a membership model. Madeleine Bunting started the work along with commercial colleagues. At first the Board was sceptical of the external consultants she brought in, who reported they had never seen a 'brand' in which the 'customers' had such loyalty. Over time the penny dropped and they realised that *Guardian* loyalists were very loyal indeed.

The problem was that 'membership' could look like three different ideas:

1) A plastic bucket: *please give us your money*. The commercial department initially shied away from this. 'How,' they asked, 'could you pitch to luxury advertisers if you behaved like a charity?'

2) A loyalty scheme: *we will reward you with two-for-one offers and events*. But everyone did that nowadays, from supermarkets to colleges. And an events business, in particular, ran the danger of being London-centric.

3) Mutualisation: *you can own a share of the* Guardian. More like the Barcelona Football Club model. This met with off-the-scale enthusiasm from readers – but less so from the GMG Board and the Scott Trust, who worried about control or influence.

Nevertheless, there was an idea in there somewhere that appealed both editorially and commercially if we could only refine it. Eventually, the Board enthusiastically embraced the idea of membership, with projections of up to £15 million a year profit within a few years. By June 2017 the paper announced that around 185,000 readers had become members and were paying for print and digital subscriptions, while there had been more than 190,000 one-off contributions.[4] At the end of 2017 the *Guardian*'s new editor, Kath Viner, predicted[5] that this reader-revenue model would enable the *Guardian* to break even by 2019. In all, there were 800,000 contributors – including members, subscribers and donors.[6]

Others have tried versions of the same idea. The Dutch journalism platform De Correspondent secured an initial $1.7 million in crowdfunding from 20,000 members – subsequently adding another 20,000 at around $65 a year (they reckoned that was the equivalent of 750,000 subscribers in a country the size of the US).[7] Their model was an open one: 'The greatest untapped source of knowledge in journalism is the readers themselves,' co-founder Ernst-Jan Pfauth wrote in December 2015. 'Our platform allows journalists to function as true discussion leaders, inviting readers to share their expertise and then respond with their own findings. This collective research leads to richer, more well-founded stories.'[8]

The website – which announced in early 2017 it was going to launch an American edition – declines to take any advertising. Members were promised they would be the first to receive articles, personalised newsletters, the opportunity to chat with correspondents and access to member events. The site boasts that its 31 beat reporters (with titles such as 'progress', 'technology and surveillance' and 'sports and analytics' correspondents) don't chase the latest headlines, but cover structural developments – with the aid of their members (which they call 'a knowledge community').

Correspondents are encouraged to pick the brains of members about what to cover and how to cover it. They sometimes share their first drafts with readers, encouraging them to comment and suggest edits before a text is published. 'There are business advantages because we turn those readers into more loyal readers,' says Pfauth. 'When they participate that leads to a stronger bond between the journalist and the reader.'[9]

For Jay Rosen, the NYU professor advising De Correspondent on its move into the US market, it is all about 'optimizing for trust'. For him the key elements are transparency about data, sources, and 'what motivates the reporters' journalism'. He added a list of other qualities: 'getting better at listening *to* the internet, even as you publish *on* the internet . . . adding my knowledge to yours to make for a better product . . . when responding to criticism, and sorting the valid criticism from the invalid, is considered a vital newsroom skill'.[10]

Without any revenue from advertising, De Correspondent may yet struggle to make the sums add up. But its dedication to making its members integral to its journalism was impressive – and maybe easier to achieve in a start-up[11] than by coaxing an established media organisation to change the habits of 185 years.

By 2011 we had grown to be the second most-read English language newspaper in the world, tucked in behind the *NYT* – not bad for a tiny little British newspaper. The *NYT* had more than 30 million online readers – yet was still making 80 per cent of its revenue from the sales and advertising of just 900,000 newspapers. There was, in all commercial leaderships, a nervousness about the pursuit of traffic alone and whether digital advertising would, in time, really begin to deliver larger chunks of revenue.

There was especial anxiety around engagement metrics. A 2010 Pew analysis found that the average visitor spent only 3 minutes 4 seconds per session on the typical news site. That compared with 2005 figures showing that about half US newspaper readers spent more than 30 minutes reading their daily paper. Most audiences were built of up many fly-bys, with a small nucleus of loyal fans. In between there were people categorised as regulars and occasionals. The *Guardian* commercial team, led by David Pemsel, focused on a strategy of moving readers 'from unknown to known'. Suddenly data was all: we needed to know all we could know about our users and devise ways of engaging them more deeply. Advertising was, to put it crudely, more effective if you could target a 45-year-old female primary school teacher living in Cornwall differently from a 32-year-old male investment adviser living in London's docklands.

But it would take time. As a 2011 Tow Center report on the state of play noted: 'Rapid audience growth is often accompanied by thin engagement.' Search engines drove traffic – but the visitors were often snackers. Users who arrived through social read more articles and stayed around longer. 'The argument about whether it's more important to build large audiences or engaged audiences has not been settled,' wrote the authors.[12] Newspapers' accounts were notoriously opaque so it was difficult to get a complete grip on how others were faring. We asked a media commentator, Peter Kirwan, to take his best stab at looking at ten *Guardian*-like newspapers in eight different countries. The pattern across all titles was strikingly similar: revenues which had already been in decline fell off a cliff with the financial crisis and were still declining around 10 per cent a year in 2012. The *Washington Post* had suffered a 56 per cent advertising revenue decline in six years – from $596 million to $265 million in 2011. It was the same story at *El País* in Spain and *Le Monde* in France. Everyone was trying to make up for the decline by charging much more for the printed paper and by sacking staff. At Fairfax Media in Australia 1,900 jobs had gone in three years: *Le Monde*, the *Washington Post* and *NYT* had suffered 30 per cent headcount cuts in six years.

It was very difficult for outsiders to understand the position of the *Times/Sunday Times*. In 2009 the papers were reported to be losing £87 million. By the following year the losses were down to £45 million. In 2011 the company apparently performed a further transformative miracle – slashing a £45 million loss to £9.5 million. A closer look at the accounts found that the company now only employed 542 staff – the full-time journalist employees. All the directors, accounting, depreciation, printing, advertising and distribution had been outsourced elsewhere in the Murdoch empire. Our own finance department was mystified. They calculated that, on a like-for-like basis, the *Times* and *Sunday Times* losses were nearer £60 million – a bit more than the *Guardian*'s £57 million or the *Washington Post*'s $53 million loss in 2012. But it was almost impossible for an outsider to tell.[13]

The downsizing of editorial staff was a difficult issue for everyone. The *Guardian* had been shedding jobs – but with virtually 100 per cent union membership among journalists, and a workforce that threatened strike action if any member was compulsorily sacked, progress was slower than on rival titles where firings were swift and 'clinical' or 'brutal', depending on the victim. Even the most senior *Guardian* editorial executives were union members and it was by no means clear to me that all of them would support compulsory redundancies.

Cutting cost out of editorial budgets – and we cut a lot – was inevitable. But it came at a journalistic price. In the past decade, the productivity of colleagues had rocketed as they worked longer hours producing more material faster for multiple platforms and across different media. Asking a smaller team to carry on producing the same output was punishing, and we began to have concerns about the mental welfare of an increasingly stressed workforce.[14]

Should we, in retrospect, have cut more editorial costs faster? Probably. In repeated editorial presentations I emphasised that we would almost certainly have to shrink at some point. The Board had a choice of whether to downsize now – while producing two newspapers as well as expanding digital operations – or at some point in the future, perhaps when print finally came towards the end of its economic life.

We weren't remotely out of the woods, even with an anticipated endowment of around £1 billion. But the real envy in Fleet Street commercial departments was directed at the *Telegraph*, which was still turning in profits in excess of around £55 million before tax. Editorially, it may have been unstable, chopping and changing editors and switching directions of travel. In November 2009 its then editor, the ambitious 40-year-old Will Lewis,[15] decamped from the shiny new hub-and-spokes newsroom in Victoria to set up a digital outpost near Euston station in North London. He was given a large budget and a team of 50 in order to 'capitalise on cutting edge ideas' and 'drive new revenue streams'.[16] Six months later Lewis was gone; a year later the Euston Project was no more.

Nevertheless, the paper kept throwing off cash. A 2012 paper from Enders urged us to be more like the *Telegraph*. Our 'bundle' of content no longer made any sense, they argued. Our revenues in 2011 were 85 per cent of what they'd been in 2005. The *Telegraph*'s were 103 per cent. The *Telegraph* had also cut their costs by 24 per cent – we'd only cut by 10 per cent. Why?

It was a reasonable question. How could we explain the £94 million gap between our performance and theirs? We turned to our director of strategy, Steve Folwell, an able mathematician whose school of hard knocks was McKinsey before joining the *Guardian*. He explained in three simple steps what the *Guardian* would have to do to match the *Telegraph*:

> **Step 1:** If we start with the *Guardian*'s pricing, advertising revenue per copy and variable costs, and assume that we had the *Telegraph*'s readership and subscriber numbers, we would achieve approximately £65 million additional profit

Step 2: If we had the same audience AND the same pagination as the *Telegraph* (which is about 12 per cent less than ours), annual profits would increase by a further £12 million, i.e. GNM would have annual profits of £43 million

Step 3: If we then additionally assumed that the *Telegraph*'s 22 per cent fewer editorial ccms (column centimetres) translated to a correspondingly smaller editorial budget (a very crude assumption), then profits would increase by a further £15 million, i.e. GNM would have annual profits of £58 million

So, Steve concluded, '£92 million of the £94 million difference between our results can likely be explained by the *Telegraph*'s larger readership (by far the most important factor), their lower pagination, and their, potentially, smaller editorial budget. The rest is rounding.'

That gave some clarity. But the real story was more complicated. And far more interesting . . .

21

The Trophy Newspaper

In mid-afternoon of 17 February 2015 the veteran chief political commentator of the *Daily Telegraph*, Peter Oborne, launched what Fleet Street journalists sometimes term a 'marmalade dropper'.[1] The 3,000-word blog was both a public letter of resignation and a furious excoriation of the ethical standards of a newspaper once considered as decently British as warm beer or rained-off cricket.

Oborne's piece on the Open Democracy website was headlined: 'Why I have resigned from the *Telegraph*' and, in the words of a long-running UK television advert, it did what it said on the tin.

Oborne turned fiercely on the paper for which he'd written a column for the past five years. He laid out a sorry story of declining editorial standards, including knowingly printing untrue stories and a demeaning chase after web traffic. He claimed the distinction between advertising and editorial departments had been eroded and that articles were routinely suppressed, removed or commissioned for commercial reasons. He concluded that he had a duty to make his concerns public because the *Telegraph*'s coverage of certain issues amounted to a 'form of fraud' on its readers. The paper responded by describing Oborne's piece as 'an astonishing and unfounded attack, full of inaccuracy and innuendo'.

Some of the allegations in the article would have been familiar to readers of *Private Eye*, with its regular chronicle of editorial arrivals, sackings, feuds and commercial interference at the 160-year-old title.

But this was the first time an insider had broken cover. And not any old insider.

Oborne, 58, was a generally admired author and commentator with a dozen books and numerous television documentaries to his name. With his crumpled tweed jackets, deliberate courtesy and unruly mop of dark brown hair he cut a rather old-fashioned figure in what remained of Fleet Street. He was most commonly termed 'maverick' – a label, he'd doubtless counter, that tells you more about the dull managerialism of politics and journalism today than it does about him. And he might, after a drink or two, say it rather forcefully.

In a previous incarnation at the *Express* he famously ended up in the River Thames after a long and liquid lunch. In the manner of a Wodehouse character he promptly dripped his way to the nearby Savoy Taylors Guild and purchased a new suit before returning to work. More recently, he had developed a keen investigative and libertarian streak, reporting sometimes contrarian documentaries on Zimbabwe's President Mugabe, the war in Afghanistan, corruption in cricket, the Iranian 'nuclear myth' and what he saw as the crimes and evasions of Tony Blair.

The peg for the Open Democracy piece was the failure of the *Telegraph* to pay more than cursory attention to a series of allegations about the global bank HSBC, and tax avoidance – a mounting scandal which had begun in the *Guardian* and had been given saturation coverage by the rest of the UK nationals and broadcasters, as well as other papers around the world. An investigation by an international consortium of journalists involving more than 50 global media outlets found that the bank had helped its wealthy clients evade hundreds of millions of pounds' worth of tax.

The bank's bosses eventually issued a full apology, accepting that the episode had caused 'horrible reputational damage'. But *Telegraph* readers read little of the story after it first broke on 10 February 2015. The paper's coverage largely concentrated instead on the supposed hypocrisy of HSBC's critics.

For Oborne, this was the moment to break cover. 'At that point, I thought, "Oh sod it, I really can't, in all conscience, ignore this, and just go quietly,"' was how he put it to me some months later.

'I found there was a pattern. What had happened was that the commercial side of the paper had become very powerful and was able to determine news content. One person said to me that the head of advertising was the effective editor of the paper.'

Was Oborne right? The question nagged away in my mind for a few days as the rest of Fleet Street had some fun repeating the allegations and while the *Telegraph* furiously responded. And then the story faded from view, leaving only *Private Eye* to continue chronicling the comings and goings at the paper it used affectionately to call the *Torygraph*.

If this had been a car manufacturer, oil corporation or a bank, Fleet Street's finest would undoubtedly have pursued the story rather more vigorously. As it was, they moved on, with no one digging.

Was this simply a world-weary acceptance that journalism is a rough-and-tumble profession of villains as well as angels? Was it a secret admiration that the *Telegraph*, almost alone out of Fleet Street, had consistently turned in really solid profits? Was it a feeling that you don't wash your trade's dirty laundry in public? A sense that most of us live in glass houses and shouldn't start lobbing stones?

The question still nagged away. Surely it mattered if one of the leading serious newspapers in a western democracy goes a bit rogue? Our public narrative is that we – professional journalists – stand apart from the world of information chaos because we deal in the truth. We can be trusted. If the truth had been corrupted at one of the best newspapers, surely this merited more than a footnote?

Was Oborne right? I made a few phone calls to people who used to work at the *Telegraph*, to see what they'd made of it. Entirely right, virtually all of them said. In fact, this was just the tip of an iceberg. 'Speak to X,' they'd advise me, 'he really experienced the sharp end of it.' I'd speak to X, who would come up with further examples of things he confessed he was now slightly ashamed of. 'But you should speak to Y . . .'

The former staffers were – within limits – very open about what they said had happened when they had worked at the *Telegraph*. Some appeared to feel guilt they had not stood their ground more firmly. Most spoke with sadness about a paper of which they still felt genuinely fond. Some displayed the relief of the confessional.

The limits were that virtually all of them demanded anonymity before agreeing to speak. Some of them sheepishly explained they had signed non-disclosure agreements as part of their financial settlements and could not be seen to talk. With others, you felt a sense of fear that bad things might happen if they were to go public with any criticism.

One very experienced former executive would not speak to me on his own phone; or communicate via email; or meet me in any public space. 'They're quite effective and ruthless,' he said when we eventually met at my home. 'If I were to go public, you know, they would unleash the dogs. I mean, Oborne, bless his heart, had the courage to do what he did.'

I discovered that this fear of the Barclay family was not confined to journalists.

The story that Peter Oborne told matters because the *Telegraph* still has immense influence in British public life. For many years its reputation was as a house journal for the Conservative party, but with straight, detailed reporting. 'It was a comprehensive factual newspaper with a clear division between Comment and News coverage,' says Roy Greenslade, Professor of Journalism at London's City University. 'It really did cover the news terribly well.'

Oborne thought that the paper represented 'the quiet decency and pragmatism of British conservatism' read by 'decent people with a stake in the country'. The paper still has some outstanding reporting and famously embarrassed the entire British political class for weeks in 2009 by drip-feeding details of their outlandish expense claims into the public domain.

But the saga of the *Telegraph* also serves as a cautionary tale about the commercial, editorial and political pressures on all newspapers as they struggle to adjust to the new economics of digital news. In the past three decades, as the new economics of news have bitten with a vengeance, five of the main national UK newspaper groups have changed hands. Their new owners have included two crooks (Maxwell and Black); a former soft pornographer (Desmond); an ex-KGB agent (Lebedev); as well as the Barclays, the pair habitually referred to by *Private Eye* as the 'weirdo twins'. Rupert Murdoch, who had problems of his own, was one of the few constants.

In an age when billionaires (from Bezos at the *Washington Post* to Zell at the *LA Times* to Kushner at the *New York Observer,* not to mention a host of oligarchs in Russia, Turkey and beyond) are queuing up to buy distressed media assets, the private ownership of legacy newspapers merits scrutiny.

'It's a great cautionary tale,' says one former senior-ranking *Telegraph* executive. 'As more and more papers become trophy wives for rich industrialists or tech tycoons, the temptation's going to be to use it for influence.'

★

If one journalist epitomised the old *Daily Telegraph*, it was Bill Deedes. The veteran journalist, former editor and columnist, said by some to be the model for William Boot in Evelyn Waugh's novel about journalism, *Scoop*, began writing for the paper in 1937 and saw more than half a dozen editors and three proprietors come and go before dying in 2007. He was still writing for the paper well into his nineties.

Deedes had himself edited the paper in gentler times, when it was owned by the Hartwell family: he would later join his proprietor on the Conservative benches of the House of the Lords as Lord Deedes of Aldington. Deedes, whose son Jeremy was also for a time CEO of the company, oversaw the editorial pages of the paper from 1974 to 1986. His owner occupied a suite a few floors above him in the art deco building at 135 Fleet Street. Hartwell's 5th-floor rooms were decorated along the lines of a gentleman's club, with a white-gloved butler and a rooftop lawn.

Lord Hartwell did not interfere in the political line of the paper. The board of directors comprised one marquess, a baronet, four peers, a banker and a former American ambassador.

His family had owned the title since the late 1920s and grew it from selling 84,000 copies to well over a million – the combined circulations at one point of the *Times*, the *Guardian* and the *Independent*. Hartwell may have had a butler, but he drove himself to work in a brown Mini: he was no Citizen Kane.

Similarly, Deedes, as editor, was no Ben Bradlee. 'He was one of the most unassuming men I had ever met,' wrote the former *Independent on Sunday* editor Stephen Glover, of his time as an editorial writer in the early '80s . . . 'He saw his task as creating a little pool of tranquillity for himself and his personal staff.' Charles Moore, who followed Deedes into the editorial chair some years later, remembers someone who was 'actually very good at news and not very good at comment. He used to always see the front page and think about it, and so on, but he wasn't giving the orders.'

But in the mid-'80s the Hartwell money ran out. In swooped the Canadian multimillionaire Conrad Black, who also sat for a while as a Conservative peer before himself running into financial difficulties, not to mention prison. The imposing building – with its neo-Graeco-Egyptian facade – had by then been sold to Goldman Sachs, which may serve as some sort of metaphor for the triumph of finance over journalism. There are many more bankers than reporters in today's Fleet Street.

For a decade, the *Daily Telegraph* was edited by the former war correspondent Max Hastings, who wrote an internal memo describing the paper, then selling 1.2 million copies a day, in 1985:

'The *Daily Telegraph* is a middlebrow paper,' he wrote. 'A cynic might suggest that the *Telegraph* is for people who think they want a serious paper but really don't . . . The *DT* is also "nice". Our readers regard the press in general with distaste and even if they read the *Mail* or *News of the World*, they feel secretly rather ashamed of doing so. We are trying to ensure they never feel ashamed of themselves . . . this is an honourable newspaper.'[2]

But as Conrad Black – in turn – stumbled, ownership of the *Telegraph* passed in 2004 to the Barclay brothers, a pair of reclusive identical twins who split their lives between the tax haven of Monaco and an island in the middle of the English channel on which, having imported a reported 1,000 workers, they built their own mock-gothic castle. The twins had dabbled in newspapers previously, buying the ill-fated *European* newspaper from Robert Maxwell in 1992 and the *Scotsman* in 1995. David and Frederick Barclay paid £665 million for the *Telegraph* and the *Spectator* – a sum described by former *FT* editor Andrew Gowers as 'eye-popping'.

Few people had ever met the secretive new owners of the *Telegraph*: virtually the only publicly available pictures of them dated from the time they received their double-knighthoods from the Queen in 2000. Nor could anyone really understand why they had been so tenacious in pursuing ownership of Britain's leading Conservative broadsheet. Even in 2004 there were many easier ways of making money than buying a newspaper. The twins seemed relatively uninterested in political influence and not at all in what Conrad Black termed 'the passport to other people's drawing rooms'.

Nor did the twins – let alone Aidan Barclay, David's son, who managed the business on their behalf – have much of a sense for journalism or newspaper life. Their dislike of any form of interest in their lives or businesses led them into several legal battles with other journalists. And – with virtually no experience in journalism – they struggled to find editors they trusted to steer their newspapers into the future. Before the twins bought the *Telegraph* there had been just six editors in 81 years. In their first 11 years after buying the *Telegraph*, the paper had had at least six more: an average span of just under two years. At the *Scotsman*, which the brothers purchased in 1995, the life expectancy of an editor (eight in ten years) was just over a year.

★

But who were the Barclay brothers? Facts about the twins are thin on the ground. When Bloombergs set out to profile the new owners of the *Telegraph*, Aidan Barclay wrote back: 'We do not consider our financial, business or charitable affairs to be of public interest as we are not answerable to shareholders, or indeed members of the public. We would prefer if you did not write about us at all.'[3]

David and Frederick Barclay – born 1934 – had grown up in West London, the sons of a travelling salesman. By the time they made their move on the *Telegraph* at the age of 70, they owned more than 50 companies around the world, including the Ritz hotel in London. In 2004 their empire was generating more than $7.5 billion in annual revenue and the businesses employed 40,000 people.

The money initially came from buying and selling property, later expanding into shipping, mail order, hotels, car dealerships, retail and energy companies. One former banker who has monitored their careers sums them up as 'classic asset strippers . . . their modus operandi is to either find a company that is unloved by its parent and are able to acquire it on the cheap or they spot something that's been mispriced in the underlying valuations of the business and they extract that pretty mercilessly within a relatively short period of time'.

The reclusive family's reticence with the press did not always dissuade reporters from trying. The brothers have twice sued British journalists in France. A BBC *Panorama* reporter, John Sweeney, was pursued for breach of privacy and then convicted of criminal libel in France for remarks he had made on BBC Radio Guernsey. In 2005 the *Times* was sued in France – once again for criminal libel. The brothers were upset that the *Times* had accused them of being 'twins who swoop on owners in distress'. They won this battle, securing an apology over the 'asset stripper' tag.

Charles Foster Kane, the central character in *Citizen Kane*, famously imported 100,000 trees and 20,000 tons of marble to build a castle in the desert – modelled on the Californian palace William Randolph Hearst built for himself. In 1993 the Barclay twins purchased the island of Brecqhou, an inhospitable windswept 158-acre island of granite and bracken neighbouring the island of Sark (population 600) in the English Channel off the coast of Normandy, and set about building their own mock-gothic turreted and moated fortress. Designed by the classical architect Quinlan Terry, it is reported to have cost anything between £40 million and £60 million. That included the cost of planting olive groves, an 80-foot-long banqueting room, a swimming pool, a library with a hand-painted ceiling inspired by the Sistine Chapel, and 22 cannons, to be fired on special occasions.

By 2017 the Barclay brothers' assets included Littlewoods, a former direct-mail company which they merged with GUS retail group; the Ritz hotel; and Yodel, a loss-making home delivery company. All their main companies had common directors – including Aidan, his brother

Howard and an accountant, Rigel Mowatt. Mowatt, for instance, had 30 directorships at 29 active companies in addition to 45 reassigned directorships and 29 appointments at 29 dissolved companies. There were now no marquesses or peers on the *Telegraph* board – just two members of the Barclay family along with four close lieutenants.

The structuring of the ownership and debt in the Barclays' companies is extraordinarily complex. One former banker – who (in common with virtually everyone involved in this story) spoke on condition of anonymity – said it had taken him 'five man months' of investigation before he felt he had begun to understand the structures and finances of the Barclays' empire. During the course of his enquiries he worked with another expert in forensic accountancy, who commented: 'You know these guys have spent a lot of time and a lot of effort making sure that this is not easy.'

The difficulty arises from the movements in ownership and value as companies within Barclay ownership are variously 'gifted' to parent or grandparent companies and moved onshore or offshore. Pension assets leave the UK to move offshore. Brand new shelf companies are created, either on- or offshore. Valuations are variously written-down or inflated with the same directors on both sides of deals.

The ownership of the (Brexit-supporting) *Telegraph* is, while also entirely legal, similarly complex. Its immediate parent company is Press Acquisitions Ltd, incorporated in the UK, which the directors regard as being ultimately controlled by the twins' family settlements. Press Acquisitions' immediate parent company is May Corporation Ltd, incorporated in Jersey, a tax haven.

But nothing is quite that simple. In February 2015, the *Guardian* reported that it had emerged that the group was ultimately owned, via a series of companies, by another company based in Bermuda, a leading tax haven. All 150 million shares in May Corporation are held by another Jersey-based company called Press Holdings Limited. All 267 million shares in Press Holdings are held by a company called B.UK Limited, based in Hamilton, Bermuda.

★

The Barclay brothers' style of business was illustrated by the way they launched all-out war on a hotelier whose property they wished to purchase – against his will and in ways which appeared to intersect with the newspaper business.

Paddy McKillen had a taste of the ruthless business style of the Barclays when he received a phone call one morning in January 2011 to tell him that the brothers had bought out his two partners at Claridge's hotel and 'that effectively I'd be gone at the weekend'.

McKillen, a Belfast-born property developer and hotelier in his late 50s, discovered that the Barclay brothers had been quietly plotting to buy out the two partners – both of them in some financial difficulty – with whom he owned the luxury London hotel, along with the Connaught and the Berkeley.

'I was shocked, stunned,' recalled McKillen, sitting in blue jeans and a white shirt in the lobby bar at Claridge's. 'It was like your worst nightmare, and it was a complete surprise attack. This is what the brothers are good at. They're good at lining up all their advisers and running and hitting.'

'They are very effective stealth buyers,' Charles Sherwood, a partner at London-based Permira Advisers Ltd, told Bloomberg for a 2004 profile of the brothers. 'They come out of nowhere and move quickly.'

McKillen decided to fight – 'I never built my business for 35 years to have it washed down the toilet.' And thus began a titanic battle in the courts, both in Ireland and London.

The Irishman managed to find someone else to refinance his debt, backing from a senior Qatari royal Sheikh Hamad Bin Jassim, known as HBJ.

News of that backing, which broke in March 2014, was attacked in an unusual place in the autumn of 2014 – the tiny *Sark Newspaper*, which started smearing the former Qatari prime minister, highlighting his support for McKillen and claiming links between Qatar and the financing of terrorist activities around the world. The *Sark Newspaper* is edited by the Barclay brothers' manager on the little island next to Brecqhou, on which the twins built their castle. Legislators on Sark have complained that they are subject to abusive and intimidating attacks in the paper.

More prominently, the *Telegraph* titles, led by the Sunday paper, published more than 30 articles between 20 September and 16 November 2014 making allegations about Qatari funding of terror groups, among them the Islamic State. The articles included eight front-page stories and four editorials.

Intensive coverage of Qatar, in itself, could be seen as quite coincidental in the *Telegraph*, if not the *Sark Newspaper*. But that was not how it was seen by many internally. One senior editor on the daily said he had no doubt about where the pressure for the stories came from. A reporter who had banking stories suppressed said, 'We were given a complete free rein on Qatar, for example. We were told to splash out – "Money is no object on Qatar."

'Of course, I'm very game for having a go at Qatar because I think they're an appalling regime in lots of ways, but now you've told me I've got to get Qatar, right? It was just ridiculous. And they were so kind of shameless in the way that happened.'

According to McKillen the younger Barclay brothers – Aidan and Howard – eventually sued for peace at a Christmas 2014 meeting at the Connaught. McKillen kept his hotels.

McKillen says he tasted something else in the battle for Claridge's – the power of aggressive businessmen who also happen to own an influential newspaper.

'The Barclays didn't think that we would stand up, because they have strength, they have immense, immense influence in the *Telegraph*,' he said. 'Politicians didn't want to touch this issue. No politician wanted to get involved . . . they were too afraid of the *Telegraph*. The paper annihilated every politician in this country with the expenses scandal.

'Other journalists told us straight that their owners have an agreement, maybe unwritten agreement, that they don't write about other owners. So there was negative and one-sided press through the four years . . . we definitely were second-class citizens during that time.'

★

On the *Telegraph* newsfloor the journalistic staff – under pressure to meet financial targets – grew to learn that some stories were more welcome than others.

The *Financial Times* did some digging into the extent to which the *Telegraph*'s owners might not wish to antagonise HSBC, reporting in April 2015 that the Barclays were restructuring a £1.25 billion debt securitisation programme involving HSBC during the period when the paper was said to have discouraged negative stories about the bank.

A spokesperson for the Barclay brothers told the *FT*: 'For anyone that understands financial markets or media to think that the editorial decisions of a newspaper can possibly influence the credit committee of a large multinational bank...is misguided and just plain wrong.'

Nevertheless, several sources within the *Telegraph* do claim that journalists were told to tread very carefully while covering banks, and HSBC in particular. One former senior executive with direct knowledge of events remembers HSBC pulling advertising from the paper after an exposé about its involvement in money laundering.

'We went on a sustained charm offensive to get the advertising back but [HSBC CEO] Stuart Gulliver played hard-to-get. You couldn't write anything negative about them after that.'

The executive remembers a subsequent headline about HSBC losing a lot of value in one day as shares tumbled. 'There was a big inquest,' he recalled. 'How could that have happened? You felt yourself upbraided. There'd be lights flashing in your mind about this company or that company. '

Virtually every former *Telegraph* executive I spoke to talked about the sensitivity of covering banks. There would be instructions to 'go easy' on some. One executive told me: 'There have been times that I have been told to do things that I refused to do that have involved a bank.'

A 2012 *Telegraph* investigation claimed that HSBC was at the centre of a major HMRC investigation after it opened offshore accounts in Jersey for serious criminals living in the UK. The bank tried for a late-night injunction to prevent publication, but the newspaper won. 'We were kind of very pleased with ourselves,' remembers one journalist involved in the story. 'But then, the next day, it all kind of started disappearing.' A reporter familiar with the situation said the instructions came not from the *Telegraph*'s own lawyers but from lawyers acting for the Barclay brothers. 'Basically, you know, they had to delete everything ... The reporters had to delete all the emails, every email that they had with HSBC, you know, that, literally, had HSBC in it, they had to search and delete all of that.'

Oborne looked into these and other stories while researching his piece: 'I forensically investigated every case, I forensically investigated the relationship between HSBC and the *Daily Telegraph*. It became clear to me that this was, in journalistic terms, a corrupt relationship, i.e. HSBC was able to determine the content of what was written about it. You know, it stopped negative material appearing about it in the *Telegraph*.'

But was Oborne right in his overall reporting and verdict?

Here were some of the responses to that question from some of the most senior editorial executives who worked on the paper at the same time:

– 'Completely right, if anything, you know, just the tip of the iceberg. He only scratched the surface . . . I don't think he quite appreciated how right he was and how much, you know, there were so many other stories and examples of things, things that were wrong.'

– 'He hit the nail on the head.'

– 'When I read Peter's piece, it absolutely struck me as something that, you know, someone should have said a long time ago but, for whatever reason, no one ever had the guts to say it, and I certainly didn't have the luxury, as it were, of Peter's position, because, when I left, I had to sign the usual compromise agreement etc. So I was gagged. But what he said basically was, undoubtedly, true, in terms of what had been going on at the *Telegraph* over a long period, and it's one of those slow processes that build steam.'

One former reporter said:

> I, and various other people who had been at my level, just thought, 'It is the tip of the iceberg.' This was a glimpse of what we'd always known and always, you know, moaned about in the pub but never had quite been put to paper.
>
> I remember, it must have been 2010, around the time of the election campaign, HSBC bought a complete wraparound ad of the

entire paper, which is obviously a very unusual thing for a proper broadsheet to do. I remember [former editor Tony] Gallagher screaming, effing and blinding, at the ads chief in front of the entire newsroom about how, you know, this was unacceptable and he was just completely overpowered and, I suppose, the way that that spilled into the newsroom and we all knew it was going on for years.

★

The Barclay brothers had been dabbling in newspapers for some time before buying the *Telegraph*. They had bought the *European*, a newspaper founded by Robert Maxwell, in 1992 and then closed it in 1998 having lost a reported £70 million. In 1995, they purchased the *Scotsman* for £85 million, selling its historic central Edinburgh site to developers who turned the newspaper office into a luxury hotel.

In 2004 the brothers hired as their CEO Murdoch MacLennan, a quietly spoken Scot who was managing director at Associated Newspapers, owners of the *Daily Mail*. Within a year the editor of the *Daily Telegraph*, Martin Newland, resigned.

Editors came and went. Within the first four years of MacLennan's time there were four different editors of the *Daily Telegraph* and an equal number of editors at the sister paper, the *Sunday Telegraph*.

I asked one of the former editors what MacLennan was like to work for. He paused before quoting Churchill on the Germans: 'He's either at your throat or at your feet.'

Even his detractors concede that MacLennan delivered consistent profits at a time when many other Fleet Street newspapers were struggling to keep their titles in the black. But the trend was downwards. In 2013 the paper made £57 million profit after exceptionals: in 2014 the profit had dropped to £46 million, with profit margins hovering around 18 per cent. By 2016 the operating profit was down to £32.2 million. In January 2018 the paper was selling 385,000 copies a day and had been overtaken by the *Times* (440,000). Of these, just 149,000 were sold at full price. In July 2018 the paper announced that pre-tax profits had halved from £27.1 million to £13.7 million.[4]

Profits had been maintained through a combination of ruthless commercial drive and cost-cutting. One former senior executive remembers:

> It was a kind of ritual every year: MacLennan would send a letter to staff saying, you know, 'Doing incredibly well, investing a lot, it's all going brilliantly well but the conditions are very difficult and I fear we may have some difficult decisions ahead.' And then he'd say, 'Can you take out 10 per cent?' And that was every year.
>
> So we were taking that kind of money out every year and we'd basically line a whole bunch of people up and shoot them. The days when we did it were so dreadful. We used to have to book a number of rooms upstairs and each of us would divvy up the rooms and we'd have people queuing out the rooms, you know queuing up outside to come in and be shot, and it was just terrible.
>
> One of the things that they would not tolerate is anything that put advertising revenue at risk and I think the advertisers cottoned on to the fact that the *Telegraph* was an easy touch. You could threaten the *Telegraph*, or complain to the *Telegraph*, and you would immediately get, you know, bad stories spiked, better advertising deals offered.

Another executive who worked closely with MacLennan said: 'He comes across as this gentle, avuncular, soft-spoken, nice human being. He's got this incredible, the most supremely developed reptilian brain of anyone I've ever met. He's just got that extreme survivor instinct.'

MacLennan is an important part of the *Telegraph* story because of Oborne's assertion that even the head of advertising – never mind the CEO – could override the editor. But that, of course, was not the official story told by the *Telegraph*.

MacLennan's witness statement to the Leveson Inquiry was unequivocal: 'The editor decides what is published . . . I can confirm that I am not involved in determining which stories, including "exclusive" ones, go into the paper or are published on the website.'

On the witness stand MacLennan confirmed that Aidan Barclay similarly 'leaves the editorial side entirely in the hands of his editors'.

He added: 'Our readers demand honesty and integrity as a given. That's what we seek to protect at all costs . . . I live daily with a concern about the brand reputation of our titles.'

This was not quite how Dominic Lawson remembered things when he was editor of the *Sunday Telegraph*, later telling a House of Lords committee that Aidan Barclay had asked him not to run a story about the then home secretary, David Blunkett, on the grounds that, 'He is a very important man and that he might be around for some time.' The story ran. Lawson was sacked shortly afterwards.

Lawson told the House of Lords three years later: 'One of the problems, if you have a situation where there was a very high turnover of editors . . . is that that makes the editors frightened. They feel that their tenure is a weak one and that makes them more likely to defer to that kind of pressure.'

The Leveson Inquiry also saw a handwritten letter from MacLennan to David Cameron dated a few months before the 2010 general election: 'As I said when we sat down for dinner, we desperately want there to be a Conservative government and you to be our next prime minister. We'll do all we can to bring that about and to give you great support in the gruelling months ahead, and as we are no fair-weather friend, we'll be there with you too when you're in Downing Street.'

In the run-up to the 2015 general election the *Telegraph* once again proved itself a reliable friend – sending hundreds of thousands of emails on the day of polling to readers, urging them to vote Tory – an act which earned them a £30,000 fine by the UK's data regulator, the Information Commissioner's Office. The ICO ruled that the email was a 'marketing communication' not an editorial one.

*

The third member of the management team, each of them supposedly more powerful than the editor, was the then head of advertising, Dave King.[5]

King, say those who worked with him, operated from a desk on the floor with his sales team and also an upstairs conference room reserved for him. He's a tennis player and is described as fit, always dressed in one of two uniforms – a suit and tie on days when he was meeting with clients, and on other days jeans and a blue blazer. He is, according to one senior journalist, 'old school'.

'He's a bully, really,' says someone who has worked closely with him. 'He is ferociously competitive, very determined, myopic, only really knows how to manage people in one way, which is to have them have some fear. And, yeah, he rants and he raves and he, he's a very odd character. Clients really love him.'

Senior editorial executives describe how the King–MacLennan team worked. One recalls: 'MacLennan would ring up the editor and say "spike that story" and the City editor would – and it was on pain of death, as it were . . . Sometimes after it was published you had stories that were put up and that were immediately taken down, or taken down a day later . . . There are countless examples . . . we published story X and, the next thing you know, the person concerned complains to Aidan, who complains to MacLennan, who complains to the editor or the section head. It was made clear we were being ordered to take the story down or edit the story, or change it. And this was the kind of thing that happened all the time and people were abused and shouted at.'

Other former executives gave numerous examples of cases where editorial control had been eroded, if not overridden. There would be pressure for flattering profiles of CEOs of companies which might advertise. One described how 'lumps of advertorial' written, at the commercial team's insistence, by well-known staff correspondents, were put into the paper.

'Journalists clearly felt uncomfortable doing it but basically knew that if they didn't do it, they were going to make their own lives very difficult.' A senior editorial figure said of the things he was asked to do: 'It was contrary to everything I knew about journalism for the past 25 years, it went against all my natural instincts.'

Were these pieces labelled advertising? 'Oh, well, you know, they tried to make them look like advertising to keep us happy but, really, when they were printed, it was very difficult to distinguish.'

One journalist described how a culture developed where 'it just gets ingrained in people's behaviour and, actually, you know, the pressure doesn't have to be that overt. It's just there, as it were, and people just assume x, y, z is going to be too difficult to print so they don't, they kind of just don't bother.'

One day there might be pressure to stop writing negative stories about supermarkets: 'There's a lot of money coming from Tesco. Be nice to them . . .' An executive claimed that the advertising department started sending someone along to editorial conferences 'so they'd know what was coming up'.

Another former senior executive maintains: 'Dave would sometimes erupt onto the editorial floor and say, you know, "Your story is costing us. We lost five hundred grand [£500,000] from [company X] because of you. Don't run those fucking stories." You know? Or "Why didn't you puff my watch supplement better? You know, as a result we've lost business."'

The executive tells the story of a *Telegraph* promotion of the *Despicable Me* film. To the dismay of the commercial department the culture desk only gave the film two stars out of a possible five. No one in editorial knew what kind of coverage had been promised to the client, or what financial consequences would flow from the mediocre review of a film the paper was supposed to be promoting. 'So the next thing that happened was [*Telegraph* client director] Melanie Danks marched onto the floor and started shouting at the head of Culture, saying "You fucking take orders from us now."

'And then there was a whole negotiation involving various high-ups . . . about, you know, could we bring it up to four stars? And then, in the end, there was some big complicated compromise of bringing it up to three stars. Anyway, there were moments that were darkly comical which, when we look back now, we just think this was unreal. And that happened quite a lot.'

In December 2015, the UK's advertising watchdog criticised the *Daily Telegraph* for running an article that praised Michelin tyres without making it clear to readers that the piece was a paid advertisement. The Advertising Standards Authority found that an advertorial on the *Telegraph*'s website for Michelin tyres was 'misleading' and must not appear again in its original form.

'Who did we learn not to offend?' muses a former executive. 'HSBC and Stuart Gulliver, for a while [Barclays chief executive] Bob Diamond and Barclays Bank. Who else? Lloyds . . .' His voice trailed off as he recalled multiple acts of self-censorship.

> There was also this weird world where MacLennan would inter-
> vene on stuff, not having had a complaint from anybody, but he
> would act pre-emptively. Ryanair, I know, pulled advertising
> in protest at a story. Online did a sort of 'Ten Things We Hate
> About Ryanair'. Ryanair promptly cancelled £250,000 worth of
> advertising and, as a result, the advertising people went screaming
> to MacLennan, who came screaming down, and said: "Pull that
> story." So the Ten Things We Hate About Ryanair was pulled
> off the site, and Ryanair never reinstated the money. So, in other
> words, we kowtowed and got nothing for the kowtow. That was
> the great dark irony.

Numerous former journalists at the paper asserted that the compa-ny's CEO – MacLennan – was, contrary to what he told the Leveson Inquiry, actively engaged in making demands of editorial.

'They were just "Leveson Schmeveson". They just did not care. There was absolutely no sense of impropriety. It was just all, you know, "This is our train set and this is how we run things."'

★

Oborne says he feels sadness over what has happened. 'It still contains quite a lot of the elements which it always has. I mean, the readers remain, a lot of them do remain loyal to it, and for very good reasons, you know,' he told me.

> It still has some very good, terrific, news coverage. But I think it is
> taking liberties with its readers now.
> I do think it represents the destruction of a particular kind
> of conservatism. There is a quiet conservatism about England, or
> about Britain, and it's being gradually replaced by a neo-conserv-
> atism. Neo-conservatism is completely different to conservatism,

it's hostile to all things which conservatism is for, like institutions, morality, rule of law, history, tradition. And it's becoming a neo-conservative paper, and so you're destroying the traditional English, or British, conservatism with this other platform, or a large part of it.

One former editor told me:

If they treated their newspapers like they treated the Ritz, all would be well: they lavish care and attention on the hotel. No one questions whether there is a doorman or waiter too many, or tries to pare back on essential staffing. They have put the *Telegraph* in the [courier firm] Yodel mindset of their business, whereas it should be in the Ritz bit – as a prestige bit. It has high cultural importance to Britain. No one goes to the Ritz and says, 'there aren't enough waiters', or 'the food is stale'. It's a recipe for success.

There's not, it seems, much to be done about a newspaper that is alleged to have abandoned the ethical framework that has governed the best journalism over centuries. The new UK press regulator, IPSO, founded in 2014 to 'uphold the highest professional standards of journalism', took no interest in the Oborne allegations about his old paper. It was, a senior figure told me, difficult to get at the truth and, anyway, what aspect of the industry's Code of Practice had been breached? Within five months of being established the new regulator was shrugging its shoulders at the thought of investigating 'standards'. IPSO is funded by a body called the Regulatory Funding Council, which has four seats for representatives of the national press. One of them was Murdoch MacLennan.[6]

I asked one executive why senior editorial staff did not stand up more? He answered that the instances of commercial pressure 'happened all the time and people were abused and shouted at . . . Tony [Gallagher] absorbed constant pressure . . . constant editorial interference from upstairs.'

Bill Deedes, the former editor, similarly shrank from public confrontation with the new breed of Barclay executives in charge of the paper as he neared the end of his life. In a 2006 phone call to his biographer, Stephen Robinson, Deedes said that his beloved paper was now being run by a 'stinking mob'.

The remark was picked up by Peregrine Worsthorne, a former editor of the *Sunday Telegraph*, in a 2008 review of the biography published in the Barclays-owned *Spectator*.

In the text he submitted to the magazine, he wrote of Deedes's decision to speak out against the Barclays: 'Deploring their recent bout of sackings, Deedes calls them "a stinking mob".'

But the published version had been altered to make it appear that Deedes was attacking not the Barclay brothers, but the staff of the paper: 'Dear Bill lets his last colleagues feel the rough edge of his tongue, calling them "a stinking mob".'

Worsthorne said he was told before publication that the text had to be altered in order to avoid upsetting the twins. He was offered the choice of dropping all references to the Barclay brothers, or the review not running.

'It totally stands on its head what Bill was really like,' Worsthorne told the *Guardian* as he filed a complaint to the press regulator. 'It is the main Conservative right-wing influential journal and it's hard to believe that it has become so subservient to a proprietor who lives abroad and has no interest in these things.'

Three months later the magazine apologised – though in early 2018 the review remained, uncorrected, online.

From beyond the grave Bill Deedes had, you might argue, sort of made his point.

★

Getting at the inside story of editorial 'compromises' at the *Telegraph* took a few days' work: a couple of lunches and a dozen or more phone calls. The story of how a great newspaper was compromised was there to be written – if anyone thought it important enough. Apart from *Private Eye*, the rest of the press, after an initial flicker of interest, mostly turned a blind eye.

Did it no longer matter to other journalists if the best of journalism was so easily corrupted? Was it simply an unwritten code of *omertà* that stopped other publications from doing what they would have done with relish if it had been any other kind of business or proud institution? Or was journalism feeling so beleaguered that it was our duty to circle the wagons?

Journalists love the narrative of the watchdog: *We hold power to account.* But we didn't much like holding our own power up to the light. And we resented it bitterly if others tried.

James Murdoch's famous epigram – 'The only reliable, durable, and perpetual guarantor of independence is profit' – didn't work with the *Telegraph*. It was quite easily the most profitable British quality paper. But the drive for profit came at a terrible cost to its independence.

No one could take any pleasure in the story of how the integrity of the *Telegraph* had – for a considerable period – been badly compromised. The eagerness of *Telegraph* executives subsequently to share their unhappy experiences with me was testament to their professional decency. Equally, their fear of losing their financial settlements through speaking on the record did not speak to a spirit of corporate transparency. None of the four main named executives in this chapter – Aidan Barclay, Murdoch MacLennan, Melanie Danks or Dave King – wished to comment on the claims made by their former editorial colleagues.

22

Do You Love Your Country?

On 3 December 2013, I was led into a parliamentary committee room in Westminster to justify journalism. It was not a trial, but it felt like one. Waiting in the very next room were two of the most senior police officers in the country, who were investigating whether I should be prosecuted. Some Conservative members of the committee were determined to force admissions out of me and would, I felt sure, quite like to see me in jail. The hearing was being broadcast live. One slipped word of self-incrimination could have profound consequences.

It is rare for editors to be called to parliament to justify something they have published. Almost exactly 250 years earlier, in 1763, John Wilkes[1] had been one: hauled in front of MPs to be accused of sedition and treason after publishing issue number 45 of his scabrous newspaper, the *North Briton*, which had been blisteringly rude about King George III.

The Home Affairs committee was notionally looking into counter-terrorism. But today they wanted to know about Edward Snowden, the former National Security Agency (NSA) operative who had given the *Guardian* and others a very large number of top-secret NSA and GCHQ[2] documents showing the extent of the surveillance by states. Such a leak had never happened before. The NSA was so hermetically closed it was known as No Such Agency.

The UK's Intelligence and Security committee had met a month earlier in a dramatic hearing in which Britain's three senior spy chiefs ventured into the public glare for the first time to denounce the Snowden disclosures. The head of MI6, the urbane former diplomat Sir John Sawers, had told MPs that Britain's adversaries were 'rubbing their hands with glee. Al-Qaeda is lapping it up.' He had smoothly delivered the next day's headlines.

The British press, in contrast to the overwhelming majority of journalists in virtually every other country, had not bent over backwards to support the *Guardian* in publishing the Snowden revelations. Some had been openly hostile. A former broadsheet editor had written that newspapers had no right to determine the public interest when it came to security. An *Economist* writer had suggested he would have marched Snowden to the police if he had brought him the story. Once again, the British press could not agree what the public interest looked like.

The MPs arranged in front of me in a horseshoe did not, on the whole, look friendly. I was on my own.

The committee chair, the maverick Labour MP Keith Vaz, opened the questions. He came from a Goan family and had settled in England at the age of six after a period in Aden. We had not been going for long when he lobbed what felt like a fizzing grenade in my direction. 'You and I were both born outside this country,' he said. 'But I love this country. Do you love this country?'

For a split second I was speechless. There was so much bound up in that question: my Zambian roots;[3] the tension (if any) between journalism and patriotism; or between journalism and the national interest; or between journalism and national security. I recovered to say my patriotism was rooted in the idea of a Britain that allowed a free press that could report on such matters. There were countries where the security services told editors what they could or couldn't write. They weren't democracies. I was proud to live in a country that didn't behave like that. Or words to that effect.[4]

An MP called Michael Ellis, formerly a star of the Northampton Bar, tried repeatedly to get me to admit criminal behaviour. He had done his homework: he was pretty sure that, by transporting an encrypted disk of secrets, we had infringed section 8(16) of the FedEx conditions of carriage. That was easily enough batted away. Another MP, Mark

Reckless, soon to defect to UKIP, was more focused on proving I was guilty of crimes in breach of section 58A of the Terrorism Act – punishable by up to ten years in prison.

One of the Labour MPs colourfully compared my interrogation to Stalin's feared state prosecutor Andrey Vyshinsky. Some of the questioning was actually more Inspector Clouseau. But the intention of some of the MPs was clear: they wanted to see me behind bars.[5] As I left the room the two police officers entered to confirm that they were, indeed, on my trail.[6]

★

The outlines of the story are, by now, familiar from two major films (including an Oliver Stone biopic) as well as books, articles and numerous academic studies. Edward Snowden, a 29-year-old former contractor for the NSA, had made contact with Glenn Greenwald, a *Guardian* columnist, and asked to meet him in Hong Kong, where he was in hiding, along with the material he wished to share. This was the most significant leak of intelligence secrets in history.

The events inside a Hong Kong hotel room one week in early June 2013 were, indeed, the stuff of drama. Less dramatic, but equally intense, were the soul searching and problem wrangling back in London. It was, by a mile, the most complex story we had ever handled – logistically, ethically, legally, editorially, technologically. It made WikiLeaks look easy.

From the very first there were multiple decisions. Greenwald, as already discussed, lived in Rio with his partner, David Miranda, and 13 rescue dogs. I had never met him. Snowden had also contacted Laura Poitras,[7] a gifted filmmaker with, it seemed, a marked antipathy to mainstream media. I had never met her either. Finally, Snowden was also in touch with Barton Gellman, a senior writer for the *Washington Post*. He was – to all intents and purposes – a rival.

My first knowledge of the Greenwald contact came from Janine Gibson, our US editor. She was speaking on an open phone line and was circumspect. We switched to a form of encrypted communications, over which I learned we had to decide whether to send Greenwald to Hong Kong to meet a man who wanted to spill a lot of secrets.

Do you go? The *Washington Post*, under the editorship of one of the best, Marty Baron, decided no: it was too legally fraught. Janine and I decided yes. But, given we'd only been working briefly with Greenwald, we thought we should also send a reporter from London, the wise and experienced Ewen MacAskill. Thus three journalists – MacAskill, Greenwald and Poitras, all rumbling with mutual suspicion – ended up in room 1014 of the Mira Hotel in Hong Kong with a young man they learned was called Edward Snowden. He had been there a few days in a room cluttered with unwashed clothes and half-eaten hotel food.

Both Poitras and Greenwald had near-contempt for much of the establishment media – especially the 'fear-driven, obsequious' *Washington Post* and *New York Times*.[8] They had no reason to believe the *Guardian* would be any different, even though Greenwald was writing for the paper. This story needed audacity. They saw MacAskill as a 'company man' sent to babysit them. They'd had no time to learn that MacAskill was – beneath his austere, sometimes monosyllabic lapsed-Presbyterian facade – a tough, radical and unrelenting reporter who could be relied on in every circumstance. Nor did they know that, in Janine, they had a calm, tenacious editor of great flair and judgement.

The clock was ticking. Snowden believed it was only a matter of time before the NSA swooped on him. Greenwald was sceptical the *Guardian* would ever run the story. Poitras, filming every moment for a tense documentary that would later win an Oscar, was with Greenwald. They still hadn't had time fully to digest the documents Snowden was carrying. Janine and I – on opposite sides of the Atlantic – were scrambling to get legal advice and to work out how on earth we could communicate securely. We were working across three time zones. None of us got much sleep.

The lawyers were blunt in their advice that we should tread with great care, if only because the Obama administration had betrayed a keen appetite for pursuing whistleblowers and their journalistic collaborators. In order to demonstrate proper diligence, we had to engage with the US authorities. Nearly 20 years of dealing with assorted governments, lawyers, writs, injunctions, spooks and police had been good training for this moment.

By Thursday Snowden, Poitras and Greenwald smelled either coward-ice or betrayal on the part of the *Guardian*, though they had begun to respect MacAskill. They threatened to take the story elsewhere – and started making contact with other media outlets. They could even publish it themselves. In 2013 whistleblowers and their collaborators didn't need newspapers. They could simply recruit a team of volunteers to edit and release as many documents as they wanted to. Greenwald consulted friends about this idea: they told him he was mad. A single operative against the most powerful nation on earth was not an even fight, they told him. He needed the resources, protection and experi-ence of an established media house.

Greenwald and Poitras were unconvinced. They couldn't conceive of a reason the *Guardian* appeared to be dragging its feet – other than that we were 'fear-driven'. They gave us a deadline: if we hadn't published by the end of the day, they were off. It was hopeless trying to co-ordi-nate all this from London, so I jumped on a plane to New York. I told Janine that, while I was airborne, the decision on publication was hers.

On one side the NSA, the White House, FBI, MI6, the British government and GCHQ. On the other a reporter ready to publish the story himself – with the *Washington Post* simultaneously preparing its own Snowden documents for publication. While I was in the air, some-where over Newfoundland, Janine gave the go ahead. At 7 p.m. EST the *Guardian* published the first Snowden revelation – the disclosure that the NSA was using top-secret court orders indiscriminately to collect the telephone records of millions of US customers, regardless of whether they were suspected of any wrongdoing.

The reaction was instantaneous and explosive. The story led most bulletins in the US that evening – and, as we published more revela-tions, for days to come. Former Vice President Al Gore linked to the Verizon phone records story on Twitter to question: 'Is it just me, or is blanket surveillance obscenely outrageous?'[9] The first week culminated in Snowden outing himself through the *Guardian*.

By now I was overseeing the story from the *Guardian*'s shabby chic offices at 536 Broadway, New York. The story disclosing Snowden's identity went live at teatime on Sunday 9 June. It was 10 p.m. in

London – a mad time, in print terms, to break such a major story. But in New York the printed newspaper in London was of no relevance. For years people had argued you needed print to have impact. But here we were publishing the story with the biggest global impact in the *Guardian*'s 190-year history and we gave no thought to print. It was a vivid moment of realisation of the *Guardian*'s potential to seize space at the centre of the international stage.

The loft-like newsroom in Soho was fairly empty that Sunday afternoon as we pressed the button to reveal the mild-mannered, almost scholarly 29-year-old who had been behind the string of revelations about the extent to which the US intelligence agencies had apparently co-opted civilian and commercial digital networks to create an infrastructure of surveillance that George Orwell could only have imagined.

Sunday afternoons are a quiet time for the US TV networks. For a full hour, the monitors in the newsroom stayed with pre-filmed discussion programmes and documentaries. And then the dam broke. For days thereafter every TV monitor on every channel was Snowden. And more Snowden. And then more Snowden.

As the *Washington Post* joined in the revelations, we kept to a routine to stay focused on responsible publication. Both criminal and civil lawyers were by our side much of the day. We were in continuous contact with the intelligence agencies and the White House. With every story, we took to assembling the team of reporters and editors in the backroom of the office and reading the draft copy aloud. It is a very good discipline. The eye can sometimes skate over danger or error. Reading something slowly in a group can expose any flaws much more effectively.

Al Gore's tweet had been a taste of the arguments to come. For every attack on our decision to publish these revelations there would come support from all points on the political spectrum – including from former presidents, cabinet ministers, legislators and lawyers. To many in the intelligence community Snowden was a traitor who damaged national security. To many in business, civil liberties, journalism, academia, technology and politics he was a hero. Some people suggested he be executed. Others were already suggesting he should receive the Nobel peace prize. There was no one agreed public interest.

Someone had to make the decision: the editor.

As with WikiLeaks, I kept testing my judgement with others. I was convinced that – providing we judged each story on its merits and took great care to maintain a conversation with the agencies – we should continue to publish. As with phone hacking, I looked in the mirror. This was a story that could land me in jail. Was it worth it?

I liked what I saw of Snowden and, as importantly, trusted Ewen's judgement: he thought he was sincerely motivated. But, in the end, it was the documents, not the source, that counted. What story did they tell? Was a significant public good served by publication? How did that public good measure up against the possible harm?

The case against publication was obvious enough: that the intelligence techniques of a western democracy are the deepest secrets of the state and that, by revealing them, you could alert its enemies and compromise its powers of defence. That was a formidable hurdle to surmount in my mind. I hope I never forgot it.

What were the countervailing public interests in favour of publication? As the stories multiplied I drew up a list of ten:

• Consent. Should citizens be allowed to know about the new technologies that had been deployed since the beginning of this century to collect, store and analyse every byte of their digital lives? Should there be a wider discussion of how, in a digital age, the distinctions between 'home' and 'foreign' intelligence appear to be increasingly blurred? What does meaningful 'consent' mean and how can it be reconciled with the agencies' desire for secrecy?

• Parliamentary/congressional approval. Should legislators have had a say before these new mass databases and collection techniques were implemented? Some congressmen, MPs and peers had voiced their dismay that they were kept ignorant of existing capabilities while being asked for more. What should informed democratic legislative consent look like?

• Legality. Most of the laws under which this activity happens were passed in an age of crocodile clips and copper wires. Was it right that analogue laws should be stretched to cover digital spying? Had everyone in the various intelligence agencies told the truth and behaved legally within their own frameworks? Several members of congress doubted this. The Director of National Intelligence, James Clapper, admitted he gave the 'least untruthful' answer to a question by a member of the Senate Intelligence committee. Declassified documents released from the FISA courts show repeated violations by the NSA. The recent Gibson report on rendition implied that our own agencies had been less than frank with Westminster's Intelligence and Security committee. A former Master of the Rolls, Lord Neuberger, found in 2010 that MI5 (the same MI5 whose word must never be questioned by journalists!) had deliberately misled parliament and had a 'culture of suppression' that undermined government assurances about its conduct.

• The private sector. Much intelligence nowadays piggy-backs on the capabilities of private tech and telecom companies. How many of these companies went beyond what they were legally required to do? Do their customers and shareholders have a right to know how their information is shared behind users'/subscribers' backs and on what legal (or voluntary) basis? How would that work?

• The integrity of the web itself. The UK government was keen to point out the £27 billion-a-year cost of cybercrime, yet there was evidence that the basic security of the digital platforms used by all of us had been weakened for the benefit of the NSA. Cryptologists, business leaders and privacy experts had been appalled to learn about what the NSA and GCHQ had been up to. President Obama's own review panel of security experts echoed his concern: 'the US Government should . . . not in any way subvert, undermine, weaken, or make vulnerable generally available commercial software.' Did Sir Tim Berners-Lee's views on the web count as much as the spies'?

• The risk to the digital economy. US and UK digital entrepreneurs were gravely concerned at a potential backlash against western tech companies which, it was estimated, could cost them tens of billions of dollars over the next few years. Just before Christmas 2013 the leaders of all the major West Coast tech companies expressed their alarm to President Obama. Did they have a right to be heard – and informed?

• Relationships with friendly governments and institutions. The normally NSA-friendly head of Senate oversight, Senator Dianne

Feinstein, ordered a complete review after the US tacitly admitted that the agency had been bugging Angela Merkel's phone. The US also promised to stop spying on other allies. The Australians were caught trying to bug the phones of the Indonesian president and his wife.[10] When was it right for the west to spy on its friends – and did we mind when they spy on us? What were the new rules of the game – or was it best left to whoever has the best technology?

• Privacy. The collection of billions of digital and telephonic events a day represented the most staggering potential invasion of privacy in history. Security advocates painted this in a benign light, saying that it was merely 'metadata', which they compared to old-fashioned records such as phone billing. Privacy experts vigorously disputed this and said that metadata gives a near-complete picture of an individual's life. What were the implications for medical, financial, journalistic, legal and sexual records and general individual privacy? Who represented these arguments in any oversight mechanisms?

• Everyone agreed that intelligence involved intrusion – and that it was vital that the work of the agencies was effectively and independently overseen. But were the oversight mechanisms up to the job? (We were later to see a public display of many legislators' unfamiliarity with technology in April 2018 when Facebook founder Mark Zuckerberg grappled with the incoherent questioning of several Senators who appeared to have rudimentary knowledge of what social media was, or how it was funded.)

• Proportionality. Was there convincing evidence that bulk data collection and storage was necessary and proportionate? Security chiefs insisted yes. At least three US Intelligence oversight Senators said they hadn't seen such evidence. Ditto a federal judge. President Obama's own review panel expressed outright scepticism.

The Snowden documents, in other words, raised multiple issues which a great many people would consider to be of real public concern. That there had been so little open and informed debate about these matters was down to the fact that the world had never been allowed this much information about the quite startling development in the capacity of the intelligence services in the age of digital. As a society, we repeatedly examined the extraordinary implications of the Panopticon[11] age in which we were now living . . . except this.

In the middle of the revelations I ended up debating with Stewart Baker, a former general counsel of the NSA, in New York. He was candid about the real meaning of the word 'metadata'. 'Metadata absolutely tells you everything about somebody's life,' he said. 'If you have enough metadata, you don't really need content . . . [It's] sort of embarrassing how predictable we are as human beings.'

Baker also showed some grounding in the first amendment: 'Look, once the stuff is in the hands of journalists, the journalists are absolutely protected. But if I met Snowden tomorrow he'd be in jail for the rest of his life.'

It was a small irony that a former lawyer for the NSA had more respect for the independent role of journalism than some journalists.

Back in the UK, things weren't quite that simple.

*

After a while the centre of editing gravity was split between New York and London. Snowden, more by luck than design, had ended up in Moscow. MacAskill was back in London with a thumb drive of documents. Greenwald had flown home to Rio, Poitras to Berlin. In Kings Place we set up a third-floor bunker free of any computer that had ever been connected to the internet or with any other electronic equipment. We devised a two-signature password system and put 24-hour security outside the door.

But Britain doesn't have a first amendment. Nor had we ever had a Supreme Court case such as that involving Daniel Ellsberg, who in 1971 had leaked classified documents about the Vietnam War – the so-called Pentagon Papers – to the *NYT*.[12] It was, in many ways, a similar situation to Snowden. Should the state be allowed to injunct a newspaper to stop it endangering national security?

President Nixon knew what he thought about Ellsberg: the *NYT* was acting treasonably. His Deputy National Security Advisor, General Al Haig, described the publication as 'a devastating . . . security breach of the greatest magnitude of anything I've ever seen'.

The first judge to hear the case, Judge Murray Gurfein – a federal judge appointed by Nixon – did not agree: 'The security of the Nation is not at the ramparts alone. Security also lies in the value of our free institutions. A cantankerous press, an obstinate press, a ubiquitous press must be suffered by those in authority in order to preserve the even greater values of freedom of expression and the right of the people to know.'

The case rapidly progressed to the Supreme Court, which debated what was meant by 'damage to the national security'. The judges supported Mr Justice Stewart's standard, which was 'direct, immediate, and irreparable damage to our nation or its people'. Mr Justice Bickel had proposed a test that would permit an injunction only 'when publication could be held to lead directly and almost unavoidably to a disastrous event for the country'.

The *New York Times* won 6–3. Mr Justice Black said that 'in revealing the workings of government that led to the Vietnam War, the newspapers did precisely that which the Founders hoped and trusted they would do.' The press had a duty, he said, 'to prevent any part of the government from deceiving the people and sending them off to distant lands to die of foreign fever and foreign shot and shell. I believe that every moment's continuance of the injunctions against these newspapers amounts to a flagrant, indefensible, and continuing violation of the First Amendment.'

I read that judgment on the plane back from New York having just met James Goodale, the *NYT* lawyer at the heart of the case, who had written a new book about it: the judgment sent shivers down my spine.

Here was a judge – not a journalist – delivering an unflinching endorsement of the essential role of a free press:

> The word 'security' is a broad, vague generality whose contours should not be invoked to abrogate the fundamental law embodied in the First Amendment. The guarding of military and diplomatic secrets at the expense of informed representative government provides no real security for our Republic. The Framers of the First Amendment, fully aware of both the need to defend a new nation and the abuses of the English and Colonial governments,

sought to give this new society strength and security by providing that freedom of speech, press, religion, and assembly should not be abridged . . .

The greater the importance of safeguarding the community from incitements to the overthrow of our institutions by force and violence, the more imperative is the need to preserve inviolate the constitutional rights of free speech, free press and free assembly in order to maintain the opportunity for free political discussion, to the end that government may be responsive to the will of the people and that changes, if desired, may be obtained by peaceful means. Therein lies the security of the Republic, the very foundation of constitutional government.

The words were so clear, so tough and so eloquent. The effect of the judgment was to give American journalists confidence that it was virtually inconceivable that their government would ever again seek in advance to prevent a newspaper from publishing something. I took measures to ensure that a copy of the Snowden files was in the US, beyond the hands of the British government, which was likely to be less squeamish about marching into a newspaper office.

At first, we shared some material with the foundation-supported ProPublica. Its editor, Steve Engelberg, dispatched a digitally savvy young reporter, Jeff Larson, to work alongside our own James Ball. They looked like teenage versions of Woodward and Bernstein. In time, we realised that we would need more resources – and more institutional muscle – if we were to withstand the anticipated governmental pushback. Once again I reached for the *NYT*. Their executive and managing editors, Jill Abramson and Dean Baquet, immediately flew over to London.

The two papers were, in some senses, rivals. We both realised that co-operation could be advantageous, even essential. But I was still the one who would go to jail, so I typed out our conditions for collaboration on a side of A4. The main stipulation was that the *NYT* (and also ProPublica) wouldn't use the archive as a bran tub to go fishing for stories unrelated to Snowden's primary focus. I knew there were documents about Afghanistan, Iraq, even Kenya, in the archive. We weren't going to look at that. This was about surveillance and civil liberties, not the wartime use of intelligence. The *NYT* agreed. Sometimes I think they (and ProPublica) wished they hadn't, but they stuck by the agreement.

The expected call from the British government finally came. The Cabinet secretary – the most powerful unelected figure in the machinery of state and the prime minister's closest official aide – would like to visit me. He turned up in my office first thing on Friday 21 June. The government was grateful for our responsible behaviour so far, he said, in tones of polite reasonableness. But enough was enough.

British menace comes in many disguises. On the surface, there was nothing intimidating about Jeremy Heywood, Quaker and Oxford-educated with a playful little Tintin quiff of hair. But there was an edge of steel in his voice as he implied he was the nice guy and he wouldn't like me to meet his rough friends. 'A lot of people in government believe you should be closed down, and that the Chinese are behind this.'

He pointed to the block of social housing across the canal from my office. 'I wonder where our guys are,' he (possibly) joked. 'Do you know how many Chinese agents are on your staff?'

If we had some, it would be nice to know.

I told him it would be particularly pointless trying to stop us from publishing. The archive was in New York, Berlin and Rio. Did the government really want a world in which Glenn Greenwald – who would certainly resign from the *Guardian* – was free to carry on regardless? 'The PM worries a lot more about the *Guardian* than an American blogger,' he replied suavely.

Two weeks later the tone had changed. Heywood reappeared, accompanied by the official Downing Street spokesman Craig Oliver, a former BBC journalist. This time there was no small talk, just an ultimatum: *We can do this nicely or we can go to law.* The pair would not be specific about what kind of law: whether the police would march through the front door or the government would go down the civil route to injunct us and order us to return all the Snowden material.

I said we were still working on the documents and that it wasn't for politicians to determine when a newspaper story had run its course. If they were worried about the Chinese in the flats opposite, why not send in some information security advisers to see if there were any flaws in the way we were holding the material?

Of course, I could see their anxiety. The trouble was that the British authorities were stuck in a mindset about official secrecy that was the polar opposite of the Americans' ('we hate you having it, but we recognise and respect your right to report'). In New York a call to the NSA or White House would, within minutes, be put through to someone familiar with the document a reporter wanted to refer to. There would then be a grown-up conversation in which the agency would explain any concerns about particular elements. If there were especial sensitivities, they would explain why. Reporters found these guidance sessions useful, and we would sometimes change our judgements on the basis of them.

The UK government, by contrast, operated a long-standing NCND policy – 'never confirm nor deny'. Two agencies preferred only to deal with one of two nominated and trusted journalists within any news organisation. GCHQ were – at least initially – on the far edge of a spectrum of refusal to engage at all.

More frustrating still, there was a 'voluntary' semi-official understanding that news organisations would operate with the Defence Advisory (DA) Notice system. This meant that if you were thinking of publishing sensitive security or intelligence matters, you were strongly advised to ring an official – usually a retired rear admiral or air vice-marshal – and describe what it was you were considering. The retired military man would seek an opinion from chaps on the other side of the fence before coming back to you with 'guidance'.

With one exception (our first story referencing GCHQ, out of fear we would be injuncted), we did indeed always liaise with the air vice-marshal. In time, we even invited him into our morning conference. In fairness to him, he played the whole saga with a straight bat: in fact, he was so fair that Whitehall subsequently demanded a full inquiry into a system which they obviously felt was inadequate. But it was no substitute for the page-by-page discussions we could routinely have in the US.

When the story was finished I put this difference in operational styles to one of the most senior figures in British intelligence. 'We'll never move from NCND,' he said briskly.

'But if your overriding concern is to prevent damage, why not engage with reporters?' I asked. He was unbudging. NCND was the past – and the future.

Three days after the second Heywood meeting, Craig Oliver rang me sounding flustered and cross. 'You've had your fun. Now it's time to hand the files back.' After six weeks of rather un-urgent dealings, the government suddenly wanted the material returned or destroyed. Immediately.

The one hopeless option would have been to engage in a legal battle. An injunction would have prevented the *Guardian* from reporting anything more on the story. Greenwald would obviously resign and continue with the revelations – and he definitely didn't believe in engaging with the agencies before publishing.[13] Any legal action could take two or three years and cost millions. We (and the government) would watch impotently as the *NYT*, *Washington Post*, ProPublica, *Der Spiegel* and Laura Poitras had a field day with the material we no longer had.

We were certainly not handing anything over to the government. We owed it to our source not to do that. So – given that we had another copy in the US – destruction of the London copy was the least worst option.

A couple of days later two GCHQ technicians arrived to supervise the destruction of the machines we had been working on. Like Heywood, they looked at the buildings opposite the *Guardian* and speculated whether the Russians might be focusing laser beams on the plastic cups of water on my desk, thereby rendering their vibrations into microphones. On Saturday 20 July three *Guardian* executives armed with angle grinders and drills took it in turns to dismember an array of circuit boards, drives and chips under the watchful instructions of the mysterious men from GCHQ.

We were left with the dossier intact – in New York – and a variety of mangled circuit boards in London. Quite what the point of the exercise was remains a mystery. The UK authorities showed little interest in the material we held at 536 Broadway – either in destroying it or advising on keeping it securely. Similarly, they offered no guidance to the *NYT, Washington Post* or Greenwald on information security. It felt like a piece of theatre designed to satisfy hawks in Whitehall. The former deputy prime minister Nick Clegg gave a glimpse of the mood towards Snowden inside government in his autobiography:'The whole security establishment, backed by Number 10, the Home Office and all Conservative ministers, focused exclusively on the man and not the ball, working themselves up into a lather of indignation at his personal conduct, rather than grappling with the wider issues that his revelations clearly raised.'

He added: 'I, however, believed from the outset that the Snowden revelations had simply exposed something that I had long felt to be the case: that the laws and rules governing the deployment of surveillance techniques, and the manner in which surveillance powers were held to account, were being outpaced by huge technological change . . . [it was] a debate that urgently needed addressing.'[14]

Some weeks later the mayor of Leipzig visited to award the *Guardian* an honour in recognition of free speech. He said he found the destroyed hard disks a chilling icon – reminiscent of burned books. I found the image of destroyed computers disturbing, but also a symbol of optimism, precisely because we were able to carry on publishing. The internet was the thing the authorities feared, the thing they wanted to master. It was the space in which we might all find darkness as well as light. But the very reasons the state wanted to tame, penetrate and control the digital universe were the same reasons which made it an instrument of liberty. What was unpublishable in Britain was publishable elsewhere. Infuriating to the British state, no doubt. But, we would all agree, wonderful if the information in question was trying to escape the control of China, or Turkey or Russia or Syria.

*

In trying to explain to hostile legislators why the subject might be more complex than they imagined, I'd ask if they knew about Tor. Most didn't – even ones who were notionally supposed to be overseeing intelligence. Tor, I'd explained, stood for The Onion Router and was free software designed to help anonymous communication.

Tor had been substantially funded by the US government, both as a way of cloaking the online identity of government agents and informants and as a tool for dissidents to escape surveillance, torture or death under authoritarian regimes. So – a good thing. And it could be argued there was a real public benefit in letting dissidents know whether it was still safe to use.

But, of course, Tor was also used by paedophiles, money launderers, terrorists and drug barons. For that reason, it was – in the eyes of others – a bad thing. Intelligence and law enforcement agencies wanted to break its encryption and certainly didn't want the bad guys to know whether or not it was safe to use.

So, it was both a good thing and a bad thing. There was a public interest in knowing it's safe and a public interest in *not* knowing whether it's safe.

For an editor in possession of documents like Snowden's or WikiLeaks', where is the ethical framework that might help his decision on whether or not to publish? The 'public interest' is supposedly a clean, simple concept – but what if there were multiple public interests, one contradicting another?

Some attacked us when we did publish something[15] on this – including an NSA presentation titled 'Tor Stinks' which concluded: 'We will never be able to de-anonymize all Tor users all the time.' But it was also clear that the NSA did operate and collected traffic from some nodes in the Tor network. And – such was the open-source nature of Tor – there was, we were reliably told, nothing in the *Guardian* reporting that had not already been surfaced online for those who specialised in such things.

Revelations about attempts to create 'back doors' into hardware or software incensed the developer and security communities. 'The NSA not only develops and purchases vulnerabilities, but deliberately creates them through secret vendor agreements. These actions go against everything we know about improving security on the internet,' wrote the respected encryption expert Bruce Schneier.[16] 'This is why so many products push out security updates so often. And this is why mass-market cryptography has continually improved. Without public disclosure, you'd be much less secure against cybercriminals, hacktivists, and state-sponsored cyber attackers.'[17]

But how many in newsrooms, congress, courts or parliaments really understood the terms of the debate? After every terror outrage a politician would demand an 'end to encryption' before an official presumably had a quiet word to explain why that was either impossible, or not such a good idea. In nearly every terror attack it emerged that the perpetrators were known to the authorities. The problem was not so much identifying them as the capacity to monitor them sufficiently once they had come on the radar of police or intelligence services.

They had the needles: the problem was the haystack. And now they wanted an even bigger haystack.

But that was not the debate that ensued in Britain – partly because a large segment of the British press had, like Clegg's description of government, decided to play the man not the ball. In their gut, they didn't like the look of Snowden just as, instinctively, they quite admired the inhabitants of Vauxhall Cross, Thames House and Cheltenham.[18] In the British psyche spies are all about James Bond and Bletchley Park. The Germans – and even the Americans – had good recent-enough reasons to be more circumspect.

There was muted support when, on 18 August, Glenn Greenwald's partner, David Miranda, was detained for nine hours at Heathrow airport under Schedule 7 of the UK Terrorism Act 2000. He had (unknown to us) been acting as a go-between for Laura Poitras and Greenwald. Section 7 is intended for the purpose of determining whether the detained person is engaged in instigating acts of terrorism.

The former lord chancellor Lord Falconer, who had helped introduce the Act, did react sharply, pointing out that 'publication in the *Guardian* is not instigating terrorism . . . Schedule 7 does not contain a power to detain and question journalists simply because the state thinks they should not be able to publish material because of the damage publication might do, or because they do not approve of where the information came from.'[19]

A few weeks later a former editor of the *Independent*, Chris Blackhurst,[20] wrote a hostile piece headlined 'Edward Snowden's Secrets May Be Dangerous. I Would Not Have Published Them.' The sub-heading read: 'If MI5 warns that this is not in the public interest who am I to disbelieve them?' He admitted he had been 'served' several DA notices in his time and on every occasion had decided not to publish.[21]

He was not alone. Several newspaper editorials adopted a similar line. The respected former editor and historian Max Hastings thought Snowden was a traitor and we were 'deluded fools'. He wrote in the *Daily Mail*: 'I cannot for the life of me imagine what harm can result from MI5 accessing the phone calls, bank accounts, emails of you, me or any other law-abiding citizen.'[22]

Both pieces left me blinking. Hastings, whom I greatly admired, might dislike Snowden – but, as a historian of the twentieth century, could he seriously not imagine what harm could result from a state awarding itself the power of total surveillance over its citizens?

Blackhurst and the other editorial writers who adopted a similar line were even more baffling. I could understand colleagues disagreeing with our decision to publish, or with the way we published. But I was confounded by an insistence that an intelligence agency should be the arbiter of the public interest.

It didn't require much knowledge of history to know how the government or administration of the day will regularly insist it is not in the public interest to publish something. The greatest journalists didn't meekly acquiesce. Did we have to refight the battles of the eighteenth century in which Wilkes and his heirs risked their lives to establish that journalists should be allowed to form an independent judgement of the public interest? That's what the Fourth Estate meant – an institution that stood apart from, and independent of, all other centres of power.

A press which demanded unfettered freedom to write about the sex lives of footballers *in the public interest* wanted a government agency to determine the national interest when it came to the ultimate power to see into all of our lives.

The Pentagon Papers was the classic example of a newspaper vigorously disputing the state's assertion that publication was not in the public interest. In the Steven Spielberg retelling of the story, Tom Hanks and Meryl Streep (as Ben Bradlee and Katharine Graham, *Post* editor and owner) are heroic figures for defying the Nixon government. Would Blackhurst, one wondered, have quietly shredded the documents if General Haig had had a quiet word and told him it wasn't a good idea to publish them?

Recent history was crowded with further examples of editors (or in some cases, politicians) not rolling over when governments told them they defined the public interest:

- In the 1930s Winston Churchill received numerous disclosures of secret information about Britain's readiness for war: his sources included senior Foreign Office officials and RAF officers, all of whom were in breach of the Official Secrets Act (OSA). While he was not prosecuted, Sir Maurice Hankey, Secretary to the Committee of Imperial Defence, chastised Churchill in October 1937 for obtaining and gathering information from serving officers within the War Office. '[The leakers] jeopardise their official careers by their action, for a slip might prove disastrous to them . . . I feel in my bones that these unofficial communications are all wrong, that the thing is infectious and subversive to discipline and that the damage done to the Services far outweighs any advantage that may accrue.'

- In 1957 the *Daily Sketch* was threatened with prosecution if it published a photograph of a new vertical take-off aircraft. The paper did not publish. A fortnight later Duncan Sandys, Minister of Aviation, released pictures of it to every newspaper. The threat of prosecution was, in effect, a form of press embargo.

- In 1970 the government of the day oversaw the prosecution of Jonathan Aitken, a young journalist and Conservative parliamentary candidate, together with a source, Colonel Douglas Cairns, and Brian Roberts, the editor of the *Sunday Telegraph*. (This was the same Aitken who would later sue the *Guardian* for libel.) The paper had published an article revealing a 'secret' Biafra War plan. 'There were allegations that the trial was a political one, brought by a government infuriated by revelations that it had been less than truthful,' according to David Hooper, a leading media solicitor, in his 1987 book *Official Secrets*. The journalists were acquitted on the direction of the judge, Mr Justice Caulfield, who said: 'It would be absurd for a government official to have the power to dictate to an editor what he should or should not publish . . . It may be that prosecutions under the OSA can serve as a convenient and reasonable substitute for a political trial.'[23]

- The government tried in 1967 to prevent the *Sunday Times*, under its then editor Harold Evans, from publishing a true account of the case of former MI6 operative Kim Philby, and his life as a double agent. The foreign secretary at the time, George Brown, having failed to prevent publication, publicly accused Evans of being a traitor and of 'giving the Russians a head start . . . for God's sake stop'.

- The Attorney General of the day in 1975 threatened to prosecute Evans and the *Sunday Times* for publishing extracts from the diaries of Richard Crossman, the former Labour minister. The Treasury solicitor said it was 'not in the public interest'. The courts disagreed.

- In 2004 the *NYT* sat on a story revealing that the George W. Bush administration was spying on its own citizens with warrantless wiretaps after being told by the NSA director, Michael V. Hayden, that it was not in the national interest to publish.[24] Only after the story was about to emerge in book form did the *NYT* publish it. The story won the 2006 Pulitzer prize. In 2013 Hayden told the *NYT* he could not demonstrate any harm to national security from the publication – then or now.

Journalists may often make wrong decisions – but the assumption has to be that newspapers are free to make those wrong decisions and, if necessary, be held responsible afterwards. It was so strange to see writers and editors in 2013 willing to concede this principle when judges had, in general, been so much more robust in their defence of the press. I preferred the robust language of the *NYT* when, even after the

Pentagon Papers verdict, the Nixon administration decided to prosecute the reporter, Neil Sheehan, under the Espionage Act.

> The indictment of Neil Sheehan for doing his job as a reporter strikes not just at one man and one newspaper but at the whole institution of the press of the United States. In deciding to seek Mr. Sheehan's indictment, the administration in effect has challenged the right of free newspapers to search out and publish essential information without harassment and intimidation. Neil Sheehan is not a criminal. He is a newspaper reporter . . . who acted in the finest tradition of American journalism. The *Times* published the Pentagon Papers after a thorough review by the paper's responsible executives . . . because we felt it was our duty in the public interest to do so.
>
> During its effort in court to prevent publication of the Pentagon Papers, the Government asserted that dire consequences might result from disclosure of this material. The *Times* had carefully considered this possibility and had concluded there was no such likelihood . . . What did happen was that this large and significant body of information bearing on a vital national question was made available for the first time to the American people and to historians and analysts now and in the future. The administration's ultimately unsuccessful effort to prevent publication of the Pentagon Papers was without precedent in this country. Now the administration has gone a big step further by seeking to punish a reporter personally for his part in a major story . . . The course that the administration has set for itself is dangerous. A free press is at the very heart of a free society.[25]

Once the Snowden coverage had died down politicians moved swiftly to ask the Law Commission – the UK body charged with updating legislation – to consider reforming the laws around official secrecy. The Law Commission's draft proposals[26] decided that the government of the day should be the arbiter. Editors using their own judgement risked longer jail sentences and would not be able to argue a public interest defence. The same thing happened in Australia, where journalists now face ten years in jail if they report on certain intelligence operations.

★

Edward Snowden could easily have published his concerns and/or revelations himself. He chose not to. He deliberately went to journalists he thought would understand the significance of what he was disclosing and asked them to make their own judgements. It was, to some extent, an act of faith in journalism. Whether whistleblowers will behave in such a way in future is unknown. There would, of course, be no incentive in taking such disclosures to newspapers if they declined to print them.

The verdict on the story came in many shapes and sizes. It ricocheted around the world, amplified by some excellent reporting in the *NYT*, *Washington Post* and *Der Spiegel* in particular. Politicians, tech giants, lawyers, judges, civil libertarians and academics all reacted. Commissions of inquiry were set up all over the world and court actions launched, while the West Coast digital giants, horrified at the potential damage to their businesses, scrambled to improve their encryption. The US Director of National Intelligence, James Clapper, claimed that Snowden had accelerated the development of commercial encryption by seven years.[27] Snowden tweeted in response: 'Of all the things I've been accused of, this is the one of which I'm most proud.'[28]

Among multiple responses to the revelations:

- In December 2013, a federal judge in Washington ruled that the bulk collection of Americans' telephone records by the NSA exposed by Snowden was probably unconstitutional and 'almost Orwellian'.
- In the same month one of two review groups set up by President Obama in response to the *Guardian*'s reporting issued a report that unequivocally rejected the notion that privacy and civil liberties must be sacrificed in order to achieve a balance with national security. *Liberty and Security in a Changing World* included 46 recommendations

for reforming Intelligence Community programmes and practices, several of which would go a long way toward protecting Americans' rights. The report was sceptical about the practical and ethical value of collecting general, as opposed to specific, data. It wanted privacy rights for non-US citizens. It believed the government should fully support strong encryption and secure communications, not subvert them. There should be more transparency about sweeping surveillance programmes and court opinions. It recommended better oversight, a reform of NSA governance and the practices of secret courts.[29]

- In January 2014 President Obama implemented new guidance imposing some restraints on the collection of non-Americans' data.[30] (This was followed in February 2016 by Obama signing the Judicial Redress Act giving citizens of some countries recourse to challenge the mishandling of their personal information in US courts.[31])

- The UK Investigatory Powers Tribunal (IPT) ruled that a GCHQ–NSA data-sharing agreement had violated human rights for seven years.[32]

- In May 2015 a federal appeals court in New York found that Section 215 of the Patriot Act, which was used systematically to collect Americans' phone records in bulk, was illegal.[33] The following month the Freedom Act was passed, ending the US government's bulk collection of domestic phone calls. This was the first time Congress had restrained US surveillance powers since the 1970s.[34]

- In June 2015, in a legal action brought by Amnesty International, Liberty and others against the UK government, it was found that GCHQ's covert surveillance of two international human rights groups was illegal.[35]

- In October 2015 the EU's highest court, the Court of Justice, declared that an international commercial data-sharing agreement allowing US companies free-flowing access to large amounts of European citizens' data was no longer valid. Europe no longer considered the United States a 'safe harbour' for data because the NSA surveillance exposed by Snowden 'enables interference, by United States public authorities, with the fundamental rights of persons'.[36]

- In May 2016 the US Attorney General, Eric Holder, said that

Snowden had performed a public service in triggering a debate: 'We can certainly argue about the way in which Snowden did what he did, but I think that he actually performed a public service by raising the debate that we engaged in and by the changes that we made.' He said Snowden had caused harm, but added: 'I think in deciding what an appropriate sentence should be, I think a judge could take into account the usefulness of having had that national debate.'[37]

- In October 2016 Microsoft chief legal officer Brad Smith credited Snowden with alerting the industry to the importance of privacy rights. 'I think our whole industry needed to react to what we learned in the wake of the Snowden disclosures,' he said. 'We learned things of which we were not aware. And we came away from that with a renewed determination to protect privacy.'[38]

- In November 2016, 15 former staffers to the Senate Church committee[39] urged lenience for Snowden, citing the benefits of his actions, the care that he took and the leniency extended to others (such as General Petraeus) who disclosed classified information.[40]

- In December 2016 the EU's highest court ruled that 'General and indiscriminate retention' of emails and electronic communications by governments was illegal,[41] in a judgment that could trigger challenges against the UK's new Investigatory Powers Act – the so-called snooper's charter. The action was in response to a legal challenge initially brought by the Brexit secretary David Davis, when he was a backbench MP, and Tom Watson, Labour's deputy leader, over the legality of GCHQ's bulk interception of call records and online messages.[42]

- In September 2017 the UK's top security court, the Investigatory Powers Tribunal (IPT), ruled that the European Court of Justice (ECJ) should decide whether the UK's bulk collection of communications data, tracking personal use of the web, email, texts and calls, was legal.

Journalism had done what journalism was supposed to do: placed matters of high importance into the public domain so that debate and challenge could follow.

While there was scattered support for what we were doing from some quarters – notably, from the libertarian right and liberal democrats – the political pressure to have the *Guardian* prosecuted was growing. One MP, Julian Smith – later to become government chief whip – was dogged in trying to get me into jail. In late October 2013, he called a special Westminster debate accusing the *Guardian* of 'a terrorist offence'.

The *Guardian*'s system of governance provided great protection since neither Board nor Trust was constitutionally allowed to interfere with the journalistic decisions of the editor. So, when a small group of MPs demanded a meeting with Liz Forgan, chair of the Scott Trust, to insist she put a stop to the coverage, she was able to respond that – short of sacking me – she was literally powerless to intervene.

The *Mail* appeared to side with the MPs. Its coverage fell just short of actually calling for the *Guardian* to be prosecuted – but there was not an ounce of support for the paper, even in the teeth of a police investigation and a growing political firestorm. One article, almost certainly approved by the editor, accused the paper of 'glorying in betraying Britain . . . Treachery is too strong a word, but it is impossible to find any decent motive for what the Guardian has done.'[43] Snowden, two weeks later, was denounced by the paper as 'a hypocrite and moral coward'.[44] We were Chelsea Manning's 'leftie puppet masters', according to another head-line a fortnight later.[45] In the space of a few months the paper returned repeatedly – almost obsessively – to denunciations of our coverage and questions about our patriotism. The paper explicitly mentioned our 'single-handed responsibility' for the Leveson Inquiry and wondered why we shed no tears for tabloid journalists arrested for alleged crimi-nality after being 'shopped' by their own news organisation.

Anyone familiar with the *Mail*'s journalism could read the tea leaves here. The *Guardian* had been cut adrift.

It got worse.

In early October 2013, the *Mail* was the target of widespread criticism for the terms in which it attacked the late father of the Labour leader, Ed Miliband. The paper claimed that Ralph Miliband, a Belgian-born Marxist academic who had come to the UK in 1940 to escape the Nazis, was a 'man who hated Britain'.

When Miliband – who had played his own part in the post-Leveson discussions – defended his father, the *Mail* doubled down in an editorial headlined: 'An Evil Legacy and Why We Won't Apologise'. It added: 'The father's disdain for freedom of expression can be seen in his son's determination to place the British press under statutory control . . . If he crushes the freedom of the press, no doubt his father will be proud of him from beyond the grave, where he lies 12 yards from the remains of Karl Marx. But he will have driven a hammer and sickle through the heart of the nation so many of us genuinely love.'

I didn't agree with all of the younger Miliband's post-Leveson proposals, but this was frothing stuff about both Milibands, father and son. It was hardly surprising that Paul Dacre was roundly criticised in many quarters, including by a number of writers at the *Guardian*.

For such a bruiser (not always a bad quality in an editor), Dacre could be remarkably thin-skinned. A week later he turned the dial up to ten and hit back most vituperatively about Snowden – combining the attack with bile against Leveson and resentment about the criticism over Miliband. It was as if months of fury and frustration over Leveson, regulation, phone hacking, super-injunctions and the rest had all exploded in a splattering rage.

The paper splashed on a 'blistering' private briefing from the head of MI5 claiming we had 'handed a gift to terrorists'. Our own correspondent, Nick Hopkins, had been at the same briefing and described how he had sat at the edge of the group of reporters eagerly lapping up the hostile remarks. Everyone in the room knew the game.

The following day's *Mail* had no fewer than three commentaries attacking the *Guardian*. 'Why All This Country's Enemies Will Be Grateful for the Schoolboy Vanity of the *Guardian*', shouted one headline over a piece by Douglas Murray, director of the right-wing Henry Jackson think tank, which said our behaviour was 'worse than criminal'.[46] Another commentary inside, by an ever-pliant in-house columnist, accused the *Guardian* of entering shameful 'realms where no newspaper should venture'.[47]

But it was the editorial – headlined 'The Paper that Helps Britain's Enemies' – that was most deadly. It argued (once again) that it was not for journalists to make judgements about publishing material about intelligence gathering. And then, rubbing in as much salt as it could muster, the leader compared the *Guardian* unfavourably with the detested Ralph Miliband: 'True, he hated so much about this country . . . and, yes, his ideas chimed more with Stalin's than with Churchill during the Cold War. But he fought for Britain in the war. And never once, as far as we are aware, did he give practical help to our enemies. Nor was he ever accused by the head of our security services of putting British lives at risk. Isn't that a great deal more than can be said for the *Guardian*?'

At any other time (and there were many) one would shrug. Paul Dacre was famous for his editorial feuds and splenetic outbursts.[48] There was an element of theatre about one Fleet Street dog mauling another – a Kabuki-style dance. But Dacre knew the police and government were circling around the *Guardian*. He was, still, widely regarded as the King of Fleet Street. This was the monarch's wink.

It was a clarifying moment: Thursday 10 October 2013. For years I had been schooled by the Fleet Street elders that we should all circle the wagons when one of us was attacked. And now I was watching the wagons receding into the distance over the horizon, with one of them giving a single-finger salute.

After morning conference, I sat down and tapped out an email to several of the editors around the world I most admired. I attached the *Daily Mail* editorial and said that if they wanted to respond I'd happily find space for them in our edition of 11 October.

The response was immediate and overwhelming. By the late afternoon more than 35 editors, former editors and academics from four continents had penned robust, forthright and tough defences of the Snowden stories and the need for independent newspapers to hold governments – and their intelligence services – to account.

It was a humbling show of solidarity. Most of the editors, including those from India, Israel and the US, were well-accustomed to making difficult choices about intelligence material. The editors from countries such as Germany, Poland, Austria and Italy were writing from within-living-memory experience of the catastrophic abuse of state power. Not one of them argued that journalists should surrender such decisions to the state.

Here were some of the contributions:

'Journalists have only one responsibility: to keep their readers informed and educated about whatever their government is doing on their behalf – and first and foremost on security and intelligence organisations, which by their nature infringe on civil liberties.'

– Aluf Benn, editor-in-chief, *Haaretz*

'One does not have to admire Julian Assange or Edward Snowden to recognise that their revelations, filtered by scrupulous journalists, have served the fundamental democratic interest of knowing what our governments are up to and how they may be abridging our rights.'

– Jacob Weisberg, chairman, the Slate Group

'The Snowden affair, one day, will be understood as a historic milestone at which democratic societies began to realize that the political cost of new technologies still needed to be negotiated. Hans-Magnus Enzensberger, one of Germany's last great intellectuals and certainly not a leftist, sees it as a transition to a post-democratic society. And had the Snowden files not opened our eyes to this transition already, the way how the current debate about these documents unfolds, certainly did.'

– Frank Schirrmacher, co-publisher,
Frankfurter Allgemeine Zeitung

'There is a superficial appeal in the argument that intelligence "professionals" know better than editors what information must be suppressed, even if it has already escaped their control . . . Arrogant though it sounds, the fact is that experienced editors and correspondents who deal daily in the subject matter of "national security" know better than most judges and prosecutors whether a given piece of information could seriously threaten lives or damage national defence. Moreover, if in doubt, we have . . . demanded persuasive argument that distinguishes between a genuine threat and mere bureaucratic embarrassment or inconvenience.'

– Max Frankel, former executive editor, the *New York Times* (who edited the Pentagon Papers in 1971/2)

'The accusations of "irresponsibility" [claimed about] the *Guardian* sound familiar to my ears. *La Repubblica* repeatedly received this kind of allegations too, after the numerous investigative reporting that we published to reveal Silvio Berlusconi's network of corruption, abuse of power and manipulations during the many years in which he was at the head of the Italian government . . . But the role of a free press in a democratic country is to be the guardians – not the spokesmen – of power. Media is part of the check and balances system of a healthy democracy and they would betray their duty if they only reported what the power considers legitimate to reveal to the public opinion.'

– Ezio Mauro, editor-in-chief, *La Repubblica*

'Intelligence agencies in the United States and elsewhere have acquired enormous capacity to monitor the communications of their countries' citizens, residents, and those who live elsewhere. While the purpose is counter-terrorism and other foreign intelligence, surveillance of such massive scale has sharply eroded the privacy that many citizens feel they are entitled to enjoy in a democracy that respects individual liberties. Citizens in a democracy are given the right to decide for themselves how to strike the proper balance between privacy and national security. They cannot do so, however, unless they know what their government is doing. A highly intrusive surveillance apparatus has been built without public knowledge and public debate.'

– Martin Baron, executive editor, the *Washington Post*

'The *Guardian* did what newspapers were invented to do: to make well-reasoned editorial judgements . . . In my 28 years as a journalist, I cannot think of a single topic that would have been more justified being debated publicly in a democratic society than Edward Snowden's, Glenn Greenwald's and the *Guardian*'s revelations of these last few months.'

– Armin Wolf, deputy editor-in-chief, ORF-TV, Austria

'From the Pentagon Papers on, there is a whole history of authority crying wolf. I don't know if this is another. What I do know is that the current attacks on the *Guardian* echo those levelled at the *Sunday Times* in a number of investigations. We took national security as seriously as anyone but over 14 years the barriers erected against legitimate inquiry on grounds of national security . . . proved spurious or self-serving . . . Hell, let's not ask questions at all. Let's not scrutinise those with the power and ability to carry out widespread surveillance on their own citizens. Let's keep the public in the dark, rather than serving their right to know. And when the state acts unlawfully, let us look the other way. Then we will truly have the society our enemies wish upon us.'

– Sir Harold Evans, former editor of the *Sunday Times*

I read these contributions with a surge of relief. There was relief because such a barrage of international support would make any prosecution of the *Guardian* much harder: it must have dawned on the authorities that if the *Guardian* editor was going to be arraigned in the Old Bailey there would be a queue of global editors-in-chief halfway down the Strand in support. But the greater relief was to read such unflinching articulations of what journalism stood for – some of them from towering figures in our profession.

The contrast could not have been greater. In the UK, the great litmus test of a free press – with all the ritual invocations of Milton and Defoe – seemed to be whether you were allowed to write a shagging story. But I doubt that any of these editors from other counties would ever dream of writing such a thing. That was not what the press was for. On the other hand, Snowden was a story of outstanding importance and, yes, it really, really mattered that a newspaper could, and would, publish it.

At a time of great crisis for the press – when its ultimate justification was the public interest served by journalism – it was hardly a good sign that newspapers still couldn't agree what the public interest looked like.

★

So here was this odd thing. While a sizeable slice of Fleet Street sucked their thumbs or turned their backs, the defence of – or, at the very least, serious engagement with – the Snowden disclosures was coming from the courts, from politicians and from civil society. At the height of the revelations the American ambassador to the UK invited me to his residence for tea to discuss the issues. He said he thought we had behaved responsibly. The secretary of the DA Notice committee, in front of a room full of *Guardian* journalists, confirmed that he had seen nothing in our coverage that had endangered any lives. His deputy said he felt that much of the material fell into the category of embarrassing rather than damaging.

Others rallied in support of the journalism. A member of the Cabinet, the business secretary Vince Cable, issued an immediate riposte to the *Mail*: 'I think the *Guardian* has done a very considerable public service. What they [the *Guardian*] did was, as journalists, entirely correct and right . . . There's the *Guardian* acting as a newspaper, bringing things to public attention, things that shouldn't have happened that did happen, and they have brought that out. That's their role, and they have done that very well and courageously.'[49]

Nigel Inkster, former deputy chief of MI6, initially played down the potential damage. 'I sense that those most interested in the activities of the NSA and GCHQ have not been told much they didn't already know or could have inferred,' he said.[50] In an opinion piece for the *New York Times*, security specialist Bruce Schneier wrote: 'The argument that exposing these documents helps the terrorists doesn't even pass the laugh test; there's nothing here that changes anything any potential terrorist would do or not do.'[51] Some intelligence insiders were vocally critical; others were dismissive of claims of damage. Jean-Paul Laborde, EU counter-terrorism co-ordinator, Council of the European Union, explicitly stated there was 'no evidence' that terrorists had been assisted by the Snowden revelations.[52]

Over subsequent months it became apparent how widespread were the concerns about the powers and oversight of the so-called five eyes alliance of intelligence agencies.[53] In the UK, some of the most vocal support came from right-wing libertarians such as David Davis MP. The Republican congressman who wrote the Patriot Act declared himself appalled it should have been used in ways he never intended. Jim Sensenbrenner[54] wrote that the Act was never intended to hand the US government the kind of powers Snowden revealed it had awarded itself.

Silicon Valley chief executives, including Apple's Tim Cook, visited the *Guardian* to discuss the issue. There was also a memorable *Guardian* private dinner in Davos attended by Eric Schmidt from Google; inventor of the world wide web, Tim Berners-Lee; the boss of Vodafone, Vittori Colao; former Swedish prime minister Carl Bildt; the founder of LinkedIn, Reid Hoffman; and Fadi Chehadé, CEO of the body charged with co-ordinating the internet. If you were a serious technologist or entrepreneur, you got what Snowden was talking about. It was real. It was vital. It was important. Not one of them questioned the public interest in publication: quite the opposite.

But the threat of prosecution never quite went away. More than four years after the first revelations the British police confirmed that the investigation into *Guardian* journalists was still active,[55] bringing in officers to do specific functions such as 'analysis, forensic and detailed searches'. They declined to say how much the inquiry had cost.[56]

I engaged in public debates, including at the heart of Whitehall: it was right, I thought, that an editor should go out and defend such a controversial story. To his credit, the director general of MI5, Andrew Parker, asked me in to his headquarters once the story was all over to talk to around 80 intelligence operatives. The reception was respectful, rather than warm, but it felt constructive that we should each hear the other's views.

As the immediate threat appeared to recede, the international press organisation WAN-IFRA sent a delegation to look into the threat to press freedom in the UK. Their report concluded: 'In short, the *Guardian* newspaper has been a frontline defence against what has been the most unprecedented recent attack on press freedom in an established democracy. The international press has flocked to the publication's side to denounce the pressure and support its journalism, firmly regarded to be in the highest (global) public interest. WAN-IFRA's mission to the United Kingdom was an extension of this solidarity and a reaffirmation of the need to protect the values of investigative journalism.'

The international delegation accused the UK government of intimidation and questioned the relative passivity of so much of the British press. 'Why rival publishers have been so silent over their support for the *Guardian* remains a definitive low point, especially given the current impasse in the regulation debate and the apparent need for solidarity within the media fraternity. There was a perception among some who spoke with the WAN-IFRA delegation that this lack of support could be in response to the *Guardian*'s revelations of the phone-hacking scandal that exposed News International journalists to arrest and prosecution. Others suggested support for the *Guardian* over Snowden has been limited for sound, principled reasons about national security and the public interest.'[57]

Who knows? That I hadn't – so far – ended up in jail felt quite substantially due to a worldwide community of serious journalists rallying to the *Guardian*'s side to assert this was, indeed, what journalism was supposed to be.[58] The story achieved further endorsement in the sheer number of global prizes showered on our heads. We were celebrated in the Swedish parliament; with the prestigious Ortega y Gasset award in Madrid; in Leipzig; with the European Press prize, the George Polk award, the British Press awards, an Emmy and many more. And, to crown it all, in April 2014 Janine Gibson and I went up to the dais at Columbia University, New York, to receive the 2014 Pulitzer prize for Public Service on behalf of the *Guardian* team.[59]

For public service. That felt good.

I have dwelled on Snowden at some length partly because it was an important and difficult story: it demonstrates, more than almost any other episode in my time as an editor, why the institutional strength and independence of the press is so imperative.

And then there was the public interest.

With rising oceans of competing information all around, journalists were casting around for the last hill to fight on. *You need proper journalism because . . .*

But how did that sentence end? Because . . . *we are independent of all other forms of power*? Because . . . *what we do is in the public interest*? If we couldn't agree on what the public interest looked like, how could we expect others to rally to that bedraggled cause? If we so easily shrugged off our hard-won right to make editorial judgements independent of the state, then could we really claim to be a proud and separate fourth estate?

There were many other problems in differentiating what we did from the best of what others did. But Snowden illuminated some of the difficulties in defining our trade and why it mattered.

23

Whirlwinds of Change

Another huge story, another Hollywood movie. The Oliver Stone directed biopic *Snowden* appeared in the autumn of 2016.[1] The *Guardian*'s journalism was making global waves – and was being rewarded with seriously increased readership. In October 2014, the *Guardian* overtook the *NYT* to become the leading serious English-language newspaper website in the world.[2] From being a minnow – the ninth-biggest paper in Britain – that was quite a shift in scale.[3]

Ahead of us in the ComScore newspaper website league table stood three Chinese websites and Mail Online.[4] We were ahead of the BBC, the *Washington Post* and *Wall Street Journal*. That felt good for all sorts of reasons. Two stood out: first, we were well on the way to delivering what the commercial team had asked: a large enough audience, particularly in the US, to be of interest to advertisers.

We now – nearly – had enough reach. Would the revenues follow?

But, more significantly, we had got there while still doing the stuff that journalism was – at least in our reckoning – supposed to do.

Going for numbers was routinely denounced as a betrayal of editorial values, usually summed up in one word: clickbait. Everyone using social media knows clickbait: the grabby tweet or headline to lure you to an article that doesn't deliver. And everyone knew websites that thought they could attract huge numbers by doing little or no serious journalism, but packaging the content well.

We may have been guilty of the occasional clickbait lapse, but a more common criticism of the *Guardian* was the opposite: we were worthy. And there was some truth in that. But how amazing to be (almost) the most popular serious English-language website in the world while being a bit too worthy. No one – surely – would read you if you banged on about climate change, security, civil liberties, education, international development, human rights, economic inequality, social mobility, the environment, feminism, housing, race, science, faith, prisons, tax avoidance, slavery, politics, fiscal policy, Europe and all that stuff? But they did.

We broke virtually no celebrity news or gossip. We tended to ignore peoples' private lives. All this appeared – for our readers – to be a positive, not a negative.

There was clearly a huge, and global, appetite for significant news presented seriously. There was a need for it.

But was there a sustainable market for it?

Having a properly staffed New York office meant that we could hand over the editing of the website after London went home. New York could then hand over to Los Angeles. We were close to becoming a fully resourced 24/7 news operation.

That eventually happened in a curious way.

In the autumn of 2012 I had a weekend phone call from a senior Australian politician. He planted the idea that we should think of starting an Australian edition of the website. The Murdoch domination of the Australian press scene was overwhelming, but it had historically been counterbalanced to some extent by the Fairfax titles, especially the *Sydney Morning Herald* and the *Age*. But the Fairfax group was at that moment in some danger of being taken over by Australia's richest person, an iron ore magnate named Gina Rinehart.[5] In 2017 *Forbes* valued her personal wealth at $16 billion: she could have financed Fairfax from her small change. The group's journalists feared she would turn the papers into cheerleaders for the mining industry. Suddenly, the Australian media scene looked very unbalanced indeed.

It was a nice idea, but unaffordable ... unless a philanthropist, concerned about media plurality, could be found to support the idea. Within weeks just such a figure emerged – Graeme Wood, a digital entrepreneur in his sixties who was passionate about the environment.[6] He was willing to underwrite the first few years. If we turned Guardian Australia into a going concern, we'd pay him back. If not, he was happy to write the investment off.

It was an interesting new model of financing journalism. Wood obviously had to understand he would have no say at all in the editorial stance of the operation. It appeared he did. Kath Viner skilfully launched Guardian Australia in May 2013, having hired a clutch of star performers from News Corp and Fairfax, along with one or two young digital natives. By late 2017 the operation had a monthly audience of 2.6 million and had overtaken the *Age*, (Australian) *Daily Telegraph* and *Herald Sun*.[7] It was expected to break even by 2018.

In addition to covering Australia and the region, we now had a team working in the same approximate time zone as much of Southeast Asia. By the time the London operation opened up they had a head start on other news organisations which had to gear up from scratch.

Wood's donation was a pointer to other forms of philanthropic support for journalism. We had, over the years, taken money from Barclays Bank (development stories); the Joseph Rowntree Foundation (analysing the English riots); as well as Soros (coverage of North Korea, Sudan, Tehran) and Bill and Melinda Gates (a global development hub). We looked at modern day slavery with help from a $700,000 two-year grant from Humanity United – which threw up two extraordinary investigations into migrant worker abuse in Qatar's preparations for the World Cup, and established a direct link between slaves on boats in Thailand and the prawns being sold in western supermarkets. A three-year campaign to try and stem female genital mutilation was backed by UN Secretary General Ban Ki-Moon and attracted funding from the UN's population fund, UNFPA, among others.

We were also granted $3 million from the Rockefeller Foundation for a microsite, Guardian Cities, which created a hub for reporting urban life and the future of cities around the world. In the first three months of establishing the project there were more than 3 million unique visitors.

Did such funding cause us ethical dilemmas? The dangers were obvious, and we did our best to be transparent about them, with clear rules so that people understood what it was they were reading. The most high-profile stories were followed up around the world: none were subjected to criticism for the accuracy or quality of our reporting.

Newspapers have long claimed their journalism was not influenced by the advertising they take. Nor was it clear that taking money from an NGO on transparent terms was less 'ethical' than native advertising, or being funded by a billionaire who might well have a hidden agenda and unspoken influence on the papers he was funding. Jeff Bezos appears, so far, to have been a model owner of the *Washington Post*. The same can be said of Pierre Omidyar, funder of the *Intercept* website.[8] The same fastidious hands-off approach could hardly be said of generations of press barons from Hearst, Northcliffe and Beaverbrook through to Murdoch, Desmond, Maxwell, Berlusconi, Tiny Rowlands and the Barclay brothers.[9]

★

There was no such thing as a steady state any more. The moment you felt you'd cracked the web along came Web 2.0. Once you'd grappled with desktop, there was mobile. No sooner did you feel at home with search than you were told it was all about social. The minute you'd learned the basics of audio podcasting the commercial team (not to mention Facebook) were mouthing the latest mantra: pivot to video. You'd get up to speed on platforms, only to be told it was all about personalisation. You might think you understood data, only to learn it was now all about structured data. You'd crack your platform strategy only for Mark Zuckerberg to change his mind.

Joanna Geary,[10] whom we'd hired in 2011 to look after social media, posted on Facebook in late 2017:

> About 10 years ago I thought I might need to learn Ruby on Rails
> [to build web apps] to understand what's going on in journalism.
> Then, about 5 years after that, I thought I might need an MBA.
> Now, the qualifications I need are probably in:
>
> Computer Science
> Data Science

Natural Language Processing
Graph Analysis
Advanced Critical Thinking
Anthropology
Behavioural Sciences
Product Management
Business Administration
Social Psychology
Coaching & People Development
Change Management

I think I need to lie down ...

We had recruited two stars of the digital news universe – Wolfgang
Blau from *Die Zeit* in Germany and Aron Pilhofer from the *New York
Times*[11] – and relaunched the website in a design that worked much
better over desktop, tablet and mobile. They, in turn, had recruited a team
of stellar developers and product managers, including some refugees from
the BBC. Time spent with them in the bar at the end of the day was
rarely wasted. The best of them had an idealism about the possibilities
of journalism that made some editorial colleagues look jaded. At other
times the talk over the drinks revealed technology moving at a such a
speed that I sometimes felt only just capable of keeping up.

I was coming up to 20 years in the job. Soon it would be time to hand
over to someone whose understanding of the emerging digital landscape
would be more instinctive.

My thoughts began to turn to life after the *Guardian*. An organisation
without a proprietor needed to tread delicately in matters of succes-
sion-order to ensure a continuing thread of values and purpose. This was
especially true of the Scott Trust, which had virtually no parallel in news.
By unhappy accident it looked as though the CEO and editor-in-chief
could both be stepping down around the same time as the chair, Liz
Forgan: three out of four of the key posts needing to be filled at the same
time. That would leave just GMG chair Neil Berkett – who had no previous experience of the journalism business and who lived part of the year

in his native New Zealand, as well as in South Africa and Australia – as the sole remaining figure of continuity at the head of the organisation.

Liz Forgan and I decided to take time to think about how to balance change with continuum. Meanwhile the speed of transformation at the *Guardian* and elsewhere remained relentless.

The *New York Times* had just commissioned a big internal innovation survey from its future publisher, A.G. Sulzberger,[12] on its own structures and processes (more product managers, product editors, data analysts, etc.; more attention to mobile); we kept reviewing ours. What seemed right at one moment looked wrong six months later. And vice versa.

Blau and Janine Gibson wrote an internal response to the *NYT*'s innovation report that asked some uncomfortable questions. Imagine, they wrote, that a young descendent of C.P. Scott were to conduct a similar review of the *Guardian*:

- Would a young C.P. Scott notice that we mostly benchmark ourselves against other newspaper sites, despite the fact that neither readers nor advertisers still think in such categories?

- Would this young owner take issue with the fact that the *Guardian* strives to be global yet is almost exclusively staffed by UK nationals?

- Would she or he think that digital news organisations need team structures and reporting lines that allow for much faster and much more frequent decision making and prioritising than mature newspaper newsrooms require?

- Would she or he be supportive of redefining journalism well beyond the pioneering work that has already been done in defining the *Guardian*'s principles of 'open journalism'?

- Would she or he be able to support the understanding that coders, developers and product managers represent professions that are as integral to journalism as writers, editors or reporters?

- Would she or he encourage the *Guardian* to dream big and to take on the significant risks of truly trying to become the world's leading, most courageous and most influential news organisation that is financially self-sustainable?

It became clear that there were two long overdue and major pieces of internal re-arrangement.

The first was an (or another) attempt to resolve the tension between producing a printed newspaper (one main deadline a day, all text and static pictures) and a stream of 24/7 journalism for mobile. On one level we managed it well, but it was an immensely difficult thing for any desk editor to juggle the conflicting demands of analogue and digital news. And it was not clear that we could truly transform the newsroom culture as long as we still seemed ambivalent about priorities.

The answer – this was mid-2014 – was for the main editing desks to be remade as digital-only. A separate team – at a little distance from the main commissioning desks – would produce a newspaper at the end of the day. They could repurpose any material for print but – save for the main two or three stories of the day destined for the front page – would not have a hand in commissioning it.

This was – of course – an immensely unpopular move among older, inkier hands, who saw it as the final betrayal of print. They took to calling it the *Yo! Sushi Guardian*: their role (as they saw it) reduced to taking menu items off a conveyor belt. I sympathised, but the circulation was now 180,000 and falling at around 8 per cent a year. No editor could look at the future of print and feel sanguine. The *FT* was now down to selling 55,000 copies Monday to Friday – less than 30,000 at full price. The *Telegraph*, which had sold more than a million copies a day 12 years earlier, was now selling half that.

Every so often a commentator would pen a 'print is here to last' column. But the true figures – available to circulation managers inside the magic circle – showed an inexorable decline. By March 2018, whatever the headline figures claimed, the number of print copies being sold at full price in the UK made for alarming reading. The *Telegraph* now sold just 149,000 copies at full price; the *FT* 29,600; the *Guardian* 96,000. The *Times* – still much cheaper than its rivals – sold 194,000 at full price, but distributed another 90,000 in 'bulks'.

The second change was related – and was one that had been niggling away in my mind ever since Emily had, late in the day, thrown a spanner in the great reorganisational discussions of five years earlier. With mobile, the world was remorselessly speeding up, with people accessing their phones up to 150 times a day. The commercial and product teams insisted that if we weren't constantly up to date, with minimal load and refresh speeds, we would soon – in their terms at least – risk becoming irrelevant.

We had reorganised to make sure we had a capacity for breaking news and fast-reacting stories. What about creating a slow team?

We established an editorial board – bringing the editorial writers together with columnists and editors under the leadership of Jonathan Freedland.[13] We decided to run three long reads – essays of up to 4,000 words – per week in the paper and online, and hired a former *New Yorker* editor, Jonathan Shainin, to commission them.

The idea was that this group could have time to think, read, discuss – and come up with articles (and podcasts and films) that were more reflective and analytical. No desk editor – supervising the minute-by-minute hose-pipe of news – could be expected to see the bigger picture and context. The new editorial board soon found its own rhythm, inviting specialists and foreign correspondents into the circle as required. Some colleagues who were not inclined to embrace the *Yo! Sushi Guardian* were slightly reassured. This was more like the slow-food movement: it also helped separate news and comment, a nod in the direction of the more distinct editing functions on American papers.

We were less successful in working out how to scale-up to serve the global audience that was now coming to the *Guardian* multiple times a day. We had, more than most, maintained a reasonable team of full- and part-time correspondents around the world. But our coverage of Africa and South America was patchy (just two full-time correspondents for one continent and one for the latter).

In the old world, a paper or news agency would have dispatched another correspondent or hired a stringer. We played with the idea of covering the world by themes, or beats. Open journalism implied drawing more heavily on the work of local journalists rather than simply sending from London or New York. With two thirds of our readership non-British we discussed making the 'main' edition of the *Guardian* an international one – with the option of choosing a British, US or Australian edition from a drop-down menu.

Two senior German and French colleagues – Blau and Natalie Nougayrède (a former editor of *Le Monde*) – were perpetually frustrated that the *Guardian* didn't seize the opportunity to embed itself more aggressively as the leading English-speaking newspaper in Europe. They were doubtless right, but we simply didn't have the bandwidth to expand.[14] And we didn't have the money. The commercial team drew up a budget of £8.5 million they would like to invest on video (video advertising was said to be growing at 96 per cent year on year),[15] not to mention another £7 million on America.[16] That, they believed, was where the money would be.

By now the GMG Board benefitted from the advice of experienced business and banking non-execs and had recently recruited two New York-based directors with extensive knowledge of advertising and new media.[17] If we could reach a top five in the quality news rankings starting from scratch, the commercial team thought they could make $40 million a year in revenues within three years. At the start of 2016 traffic was growing 55 per cent year on year and the team was predicting revenues of $17 million – up $6.5 million on the same period.

The speed of transition was a hard thing for the Board to judge. The GMG Chair, Neil Berkett, whose career had included running Virgin Media in the UK, was torn. He thought that, in all probability, we would end up having a significantly lower cost base. I agreed. But should we grow first, in order to shrink later – a continuation of 'reach before revenue'? Alternatively, if we knew that print would die one day, why not just do it now? We could take a big hit – with considerable redundancies – and transform ourselves into a digital-only operation sooner rather than later.

Cautious Board discussions rejected that option. Berkett – feeling more relaxed about the cashflow now we had realised most of the endowment – demanded a 'Bee-hag'. Seeing my blank expression, he explained that a BHAG was a 'big, hairy audacious goal'.[18] He was prepared to write a large cheque if we came up with an exciting enough vision.

We were not short of ideas, but everything about future revenues felt too unknown. There were more away days. McKinsey had been brought back into the building.

No one was raising any urgent red flags. But there was, for a while, a slight feeling of rabbits and headlights.[19]

But, while the consultants consulted, the deathwatch beetle was still at work.

In Menlo Park, California, 5,000 miles away, the engineers and developers had been intensely querying the world of data – in particular interrogating the advertising software companies. By 2012/13, according to Antonio García Martínez in his book, *Chaos Monkeys*: 'Facebook, Google, and others have achieved the holy grail of all marketers: a high-fidelity, persistent, and immutable pseudonym for every consumer online. Even better, they've joined that to your real-world persona, the one that shows up bleary-eyed at two a.m. at a Target in El Cerrito looking for tampons or a six-pack of Natural Light.'

The bridge between the 'real-world you to the browser version of you' was a super-rocketed, steroid-pumped, algorithmically-boosted version of Pemsel's 'anonymous to known' mission. I had sat in countless meetings with commercial colleagues in which they talked about persuading readers to part with an email address, or a home postcode, or even a telephone number. But that amount of personal information – particularly in an age of mobile – couldn't begin to compete with the real-time window into users' lives which the new tech companies could now accumulate – and which, according to Martínez, they 'sold and resold a bazillion times a day to whoever is willing to pay for it'.

In early 2015 Facebook were riding to success

> ...atop a tsunami-esque wave nobody had predicted, or at least hadn't predicted to arrive right then and so quickly. In this case, that wave was mobile usage, which in the span of a few months in 2013 suddenly constituted the majority of Facebook usage. This was a turn of events that completely upended Facebook's monetization strategy, making everything that came before mostly irrelevant, or at least secondary.
>
> Facebook regeared the entire Ads team to focus on mobile, squeezing every advertiser, big and small, to spend as much as possible on Facebook mobile ads. It was one of those instantaneous pivots that were breath-taking in their speed and focus.

While Martínez watched 'top-quality publishers often us[ing] advertising as a crutch to help monetize the digital presence whose business model they hadn't figured out', Facebook revenues rocketed from $7 billion in 2013 to $27 billion three years later. Google, meanwhile, was also making mindblowing amounts of money from advertising – $67 billion in revenues in 2015, growing to $79.4 million the following year.

It was, perhaps, only a matter of time before the privacy implications of this digital gold rush based on the mining of our lives would become fully apparent. They did – with an ear-splitting crash – in the aftermath of the Cambridge Analytica exposé in the *Observer* in early 2018. But, for now, the money was – for the West Coast giants – simply washing in.

The annual Reuters Institute for the Study of Journalism 'Digital News Report' for 2016 did not make cheerful reading about the crisis gripping newspapers the world over: 'Across our 26 countries, we see a common picture of job losses, cost-cutting, and missed targets as falling print revenues combine with the brutal economics of digital in a perfect storm.'[20]

Much of this was due to revenues being sucked out of minnows, who were left gasping for air as the West Coast giants began to hoover up the advertising dollars in earnest. Google and Facebook were expected to together control 63 per cent of all digital-ad spending in the US in 2017 according to eMarketer.[21] By December 2017 Rupert Murdoch estimated that 85 to 90 per cent of incremental digital-advertising expenditure was going to the West Coast duopoly. (The big platform players disputed these figures.[22]) In January 2018 Murdoch suggested the mega-platforms should start paying news publishers for content.

The problem hit the new digital players as hard as the old ones. Mashable, once valued at $250 million, was looking for an emergency buyer by the end of 2017. The founder of *Vice*, Shane Smith, called the 'patrimony' of Facebook 'the biggest problem of the world': 'Unless you are on those platforms, you're dead, but if you are on those platforms then you're not making money, so therein lies the rub and that's going to be the biggest challenge in media going forward.'[23]

Over at Buzzfeed – which had ridden the Facebook tiger as enthusiastically as anyone – the founders watched in dismay as they missed their 2017 targets by as much as 20 per cent, about the same margin as the *Wall*

Street Journal. The company responded by ditching staff as ruthlessly as the legacy players had for a decade or more.

Just before Christmas 2017 the website's founder, Jonah Peretti, joined the chorus accusing the West Coast duopoly of leeching on the journalism created by news providers, new or old: 'The media is in crisis,' Peretti wrote. 'Google and Facebook are taking the vast majority of ad revenue, and paying content creators far too little for the value they deliver to users. This puts high-quality creators at a financial disadvantage, and favors publishers of cheap media: fake news, propaganda and conspiracy theories, quickly re-written stories with sensationalistic spin, shady off-shore content farms, algorithmically generated content, and pirated videos.'

The laws of supply, demand and scarcity were impacting on the commercial side of the business as bitterly as they had hit the editorial side. The world now had a huge surplus of ad space. Prices began to plummet – hastened by the growth of programmatic advertising, in which machines, rather than human beings, traded advertising, some of it through real-time actions.

All this impacted on the new team at the *Guardian*. I had stepped down at the end of May 2015 with the commercial board pronouncing themselves pleased with the shape the company was in.[24] Digital advertising had been growing healthily: £68 million in 2014 followed by £82 million in 2015 and projected to rise to £100 million in 2015/16. After all the ambitious striving after 'reach', the revenues seemed finally to be arriving. Patience was, finally, being rewarded – surely? On top of this were digital subscriptions and membership/events – predicted to be making £27 million by 2019/20 – along with some foundation funding.

But, in common with most other players – even the successful and most digitally native ones – few people had anticipated the extent of the advertising market turmoil in 2015/16. By January 2016 the trading conditions were suddenly looking distinctly fragile, with print revenues falling more sharply than anticipated and digital advertising slowing down dramatically. The paper was heading for a £53 million loss – and the *Guardian* was far from being the only news organisation feeling a sudden pinch. The new team did not propose a radically different business model. There would still be no paywall. A more ambitious form of membership was to be the chosen route, as was continued investment in America, which Viner saw as 'critical to our future'.[25] But it was clear that severe belt-tightening was going to be needed – and was doubtless overdue.[26]

I had much sympathy with the new editor, having – like most *Guardian* editors – lived through more than one serious financial crisis myself. On the one hand Viner and Pemsel had the safety net of more money in the bank (more than £1 bn still in 2018) than any *Guardian* editor in history could have dreamed of. On the other hand, they were being bitterly buffeted by a global disruption of news that must have felt beyond control. It was to be a tough introduction to the life of editing.[27]

But by mid-2018 conditions had eased again. Revenues were back up to £216 million. Clay Shirky's little acorn idea of a membership scheme had grown to a three-tiered programme drawing in nearly a million contributions from readers (570,000 regular paying supporters and 375,000 one-off donations). America and Australia – now 'on a secure financial footing' – were very much at the heart of the international ambition. The *Guardian* was reaching 150 million browsers each month and a billion page views per month. There was no talk of paywalls: even so, reader revenues had overtaken advertising. And digital revenues – at £109 million – had, for the first time, overtaken the £107.5 million of print revenues. The paper was confidently talking of hitting break-even in 2018/19.[28]

The long-planned and crafted, patient route to digital sustainability was finally imaginable.

★

But back just before Christmas 2014 I had been sitting by a log fire, glass of wine in my hand, wondering about regrets. I had just announced I would be stepping down as editor – to take effect after the imminent general election in May. What would I miss? What could we have done better?

Maybe it was the unseasonably mild weather outside, but my thoughts turned to climate change. Even the best-intentioned news organisations struggled with the subject. It wasn't hard to compile a list of reasons why:

- With some, it came down to ownership – a sceptical or uninterested proprietor. Or leadership: 'My editor doesn't believe in it.'

- Highly regulated or 'impartial' organisations (the BBC, for instance) struggled to reflect the weight of scientific agreement while also airing the existence of critical views.[29]
- Journalism is better at rear-view mirrors than looking into crystal balls. It's good at recording what happened yesterday; less comfortable at predicting what might happen in 20 or 30 years' time.
- News thrives on the novel, the changing and the unique. But climate change is always there, and the story varies little from month to month.
- There *are* dramatic stories which are – quite probably – related to climate change. But the best scientists are cautious and meticulous about evidence. Most will be reluctant to attribute specific extraordinary weather-related events (hurricanes, floods, droughts, fires, etc.) to global warming.
- Science reporting needs care and expertise. The economic crisis in the press has seen the shedding of knowledgeable specialists and the shrinking of environmental teams.
- Many newsrooms are now driven by metrics: what drives traffic? What leads to more subscribers? If not enough people read climate change stories, why run them?

The pattern of coverage in the UK and US was depressing. Academics who studied climate-change reporting found a dismayingly high amount of misleading information, where there was any coverage at all. It was a story that – even in the best papers – rarely found its way onto the front page, or leading a TV news bulletin.

If the science was even approximately right, this was a bewildering neglect. Within the lifetime of our children there were quite likely to be huge impacts on the habitability of the planet, with untold consequences for health, security, resources, migration, food, economics and disease. Can anyone name a bigger story?

Neglect was one thing. Far more disturbing, as a journalist, was to see some in our profession fielding as their main commentators on the subject writers who appear to be totally unqualified to be taken seriously. To take one example: James Delingpole is a prolific commentator used by the *Sun* and the *Spectator* (not to mention Breitbart) to opine on climate change. Delingpole has a degree in English literature and admits 'it is not my job' to read peer-reviewed papers, but to be 'an interpreter of interpretations'. He has, for instance, dismissed evidence that the Great Barrier Reef is in any kind of danger as fake news.[30]

In one article for Breitbart he summarised his beliefs: 1) Man-made global warming is evidently and demonstrably not a problem; 2) The people who pretend otherwise are crooks, liars, idiots or shills; 3) Fossil fuels ... are the ideal solution to our energy needs; 4) Renewables are a waste of everyone's time – and always will be.

He ended: 'There is copious evidence to support all these statements and it's really about time those of us on the winning side of the argument stopped pussyfooting around and apologising for being 100 per cent right. That should include everyone in the Trump administration. This is a revolution; we've got truth and justice on our side; we owe the enemy nothing – and we really shouldn't count our job done till we've crushed them, seen them driven before us and heard the lamentations of their women.'[31]

How can we put this kindly? Delingpole writes entertainingly enough in a sub-Boris Johnson sort of way but when it comes to climate change he's about as authoritative as a carpet slipper. And yet he was regularly given space by mainstream newspapers and magazines to spout dangerous nonsense – let's call it fake news – about something people who do know what they're talking about consider to be a devastating threat to our species. At the same time Delingpole and his fellow travellers criticise the BBC's coverage as 'warmist propaganda'.

An average reader is left not knowing what or who to believe. The classic defence of the press in the twenty-first century – we are a beacon of trust in a sea of dross – crumbles into a dust of mistrust: *They're all as bad as each other.*

America has its own Delingpoles working for Fox and other outlets. Meanwhile, the overall volume of climate change coverage on ABC, NBC, CBS and Fox News has decreased steadily – airing a combined 50 minutes the whole of 2016 – a 60 per cent drop on the previous year.[32] A Canadian academic, Jennifer Good, analysed two weeks of hurricane coverage on eight US TV networks – 1,500 stories in all. 'Trump' was discussed in 907 of them. Only 79 (5 per cent) even mentioned climate change.[33]

★

What could we do in the following five months – my final stretch as an editor? It was not that we had under-covered the subject or given undue space to ignorant voices. But were we moving the needle? I had just spent a couple of days with Bill McKibben,[34] a former *New Yorker* staff writer who now headed up an environmental pressure group, 350. org, who persuaded me that we were making the mistake of leaving the environmental team to cover the subject. 'The science is now settled,' he argued over a lunch in Stockholm. 'You should be getting all your specialists to cover it – politics, defence, economics, food – you name it.'

In January 2015 we called together a broad cross-section of specialists, together with some developers and a young digital trainee who had come from a background of political activism. If reporting on its own wasn't any longer imprinting this issue in the front of readers' minds, perhaps we should couple reporting with some overt campaigning.

We had generally shied away from that kind of activism. There were a handful of subjects – female genital mutilation, free speech – where we felt no obligation to be even-handed. But on most subjects we felt the greatest service to the reader was to let them understand both sides of an argument. I'm not saying we always adequately succeeded in this, but that was the aim.

Climate change felt like a subject where the evidence was stacked enough on one side of the argument to do something more akin to campaigning. But what sort of campaign?

George Monbiot, a veteran environmental columnist, argued that the only thing that would really change the course of history was getting agreement for a particular form of wording in the upcoming Paris climate talks. He may have been right, but it was difficult to turn a dense 120-word policy paragraph into a campaign.

We liked McKibben's very simple framing of the problem in three numbers:[35]

1) 2 degrees C: the target for the maximum 'safe' rise in temperature – a figure which had been endorsed by 167 countries
2) 565 gigatons: the largest amount of carbon dioxide humans could put into the atmosphere by mid-century and still hope to stay within two degrees
3) 2,785 gigatons: the amount of carbon already contained in the proven reserves of fossil fuel companies and stores, i.e. the fossil fuels we're currently planning to burn.

The maths was elementary: the human race could not use anything like the existing reserves of fossil fuels and still hope to preserve life as we knew it. That implied that there were vast stranded assets which could not, in time, possibly be valued as they currently were.

The beauty of the figures were that few people contested them. During the course of our subsequent campaign I did a podcast interview with Ben van Beurden, CEO of Shell. Even he did not quarrel with McKibben's framing of the maths.

But how to turn that into a campaign? We settled on something around divestment from fossil fuels. We thought a direct appeal to financial institutions would produce limited results. But what if we asked enlightened investors or funds to consider divesting? There were two funds in particular we decided to focus on: the Wellcome Trust and the Bill and Melinda Gates Foundation. Both were forces for good in medicine and health. Both conceded that climate change was the greatest possible threat to health. And both had, to date, declined to divest.

We would call it #keepitintheground.

Wellcome and Gates were a bit puzzled when we told them what we were up to. They were used to being the good guys. I had an amiable cup of coffee with Jeremy Farrar, the Wellcome Trust director, and a long, thoughtful email from Bill Gates. Both disagreed with our campaign. So, to be fair, did some colleagues. We decided at an early stage that we would podcast all our discussions – including disagreements about the aims we were pursuing.[36] We were a newspaper, not a political party or a bank. If you couldn't be transparent about differences within a newsroom, you weren't living your open values.

Living those values meant I also had to make the case to the GMG Board that they should also consider divesting from fossil fuels. There was no requirement for the Board to be bound by the *Guardian* editorial policy: indeed, editorial independence more or less implied the opposite. But the Board listened carefully to the arguments and, by late March, had decided to sell all its investments in coal, oil and gas companies. Berkett called the move – at £800m the largest fund to have divested – 'a hard-nosed business decision' justified on ethical and financial grounds.

The attraction of the campaign was that it enabled readers to be more than passive and fatalistic recipients of disturbing information over which they had no control – one reason, research had shown, why people didn't like reading about climate change. We told them how to divest their own pensions; how to lobby their schools, workplaces, unions or faith groups. We invited them to write to the boards of Wellcome and Gates – and they did. Their letters, some of which we published, were all the more powerful for being written from the heart.

We then asked readers to feature in a film – reading lines directly spoken to Bill Gates. Two days running, we wrapped powerful images and texts round the printed paper so that it was impossible to ignore the statement we were making. We coupled the campaigning with reporting from China, India, Canada, the Pacific islands and South America. We again took over the front page of the paper to list all the most polluting companies associated with oil. On the desktop, we interrupted reading with a large slick of oil apparently sliding down the screen.

We gave our content away to any other publisher who wanted to use it – vastly extending the 3.5 million people who had read the material on our own website. We commissioned poems. Famous actors, including Jeremy Irons, Gabriel Byrne, Maxine Peake and Michael Sheen, volunteered to record them for free. We held events, we sold t-shirts.

We were making a two-pronged argument. One was ethical (think tobacco, arms, apartheid); the other financial (stranded assets). Slightly to our surprise, the Prince of Wales endorsed the 'clear, compelling' campaign. Even more unexpectedly, the second prong seemed to land more effectively than the first. The governor of the Bank of England, Mark Carney, went on BBC News using Bill McKibben's three numbers to wave a large red flag at financial institutions, warning them of the long-term value of investments in carbon-related stocks.

The hashtag #keepitintheground somehow stayed – used, for instance, by the French president in December 2017 in a tweet announcing that his was the first country to ban any new oil-exploration licences with immediate effect. An *FT* comment piece about the behaviour of investment institutions by John Plender remarked: 'something momentous is going on'.[37]

What had been a trickle of divestment became a stream. Universities, pension funds and sovereign wealth funds began to get their money out of the most polluting fossil fuels, with pledges to ditch $2.6 trillion from coal. Cambridge University blacklisted coal and tar sands companies. Within a year the *FT* was reporting a poll that showed two thirds of adults agreeing that fossil fuel investments were risky. In March 2016, the Bill and Melinda Gates Foundation sold its entire holding in BP. One year after Paris nearly 700 institutions had committed to some form of divestment, to the tune of $5 trillion. In December 2017, New York state announced it was starting to divest the state retirement fund from fossil fuels.

We were, of course, not the only campaigners in this space. And the extent of divestment was still, in the overall scheme of things, a trickle. But, for a few months, we had succeeded in grabbing attention and focusing it on the most important story in the world. And we had, it seems, made something of a difference. I still believed that such overt campaigning should have a limited role in news media. But, if you were going to make an exception, the long-term survival of the species was as good as any issue.

My Christmas regret was at least partly answered. It was time to tiptoe away . . .

Epilogue

This is a story half told. There is no ending, happy or otherwise. It would be nice for this book to have been a retrospective from the shelter of the other bank, safely reached. But, for the great majority of news organisations, the other bank is still tantalisingly distant. For many, it's practically invisible.

By 2017 the legacy media had developed an understandable obsession with the GAFAT companies – Google, Apple, Facebook, Amazon and Twitter – which, in their view, were working to different rules on a hopelessly tilted playing field.

The old-media view was simple: the Gafaters stole their content; built an audience around it; sold that audience to advertisers; gave almost nothing in return; took virtually no responsibility for the content they hosted; got a free pass on the regulations that burdened traditional media; and – to cap it all – paid virtually no tax.

It was all, in other words, deeply unfair. But, however unjust, many companies felt they had no choice but to play by the new rules. A Reuters Institute report in late 2017 discovered fatalism within newsrooms and management. Social media was, they nearly all agreed, a vital bridge to the next generation of audiences. As the platforms grew, so legacy media – which could never dream of rivalling the Gafaters for scale – would weaken.

'The strategies of legacy organisations must now be inflected through the prism of platforms,' said the report.[1]

In Axel Springer's view: 'They have a scale, they have the direct customer relations, they have the data, they have all the insights, and they can connect the dots, and they are doing this a lot better than we will ever be able to . . . I see a huge, huge, huge threat coming up through Google and Facebook . . . it's frightening.'

Legacy media's strategic sovereignty is reduced. The power of the platforms means lower ad revenues, less control over the context in which content is consumed, less contact with readers, and poorer data. The dilemma facing publishers is that to be in the game, you need to be on the platforms. Yet being on the platforms means less money, less control, and less scale.

But being 'on' Facebook grew ever more complex. Studies showed that only about half of the users of Facebook could remember the original source of a story.[2] And Mark Zuckerberg, like all new media players, changed his mind a fair amount. In early 2018 he announced that news would appear further down in everyone's newsfeed. The respected digital analyst Frederic Filloux announced: 'Consider us notified. Facebook is done with journalism . . . it has been a pain in the neck from day one . . . publishers should stop whining and move on.'[3]

But the idea of Facebook abandoning journalism wasn't great news for the legacy news organisations, who – however much they loathed the West Coast monsters – knew that platforms provided the best way of reaching a massive, and younger, audience. The old players – with varying success – used their editorial megaphones and their lobbying muscle to try to get some equity into an arrangement which, to them, resembled anarchy. Their number one aim was to get Facebook to admit it was a publisher, not just a pipe down which content flowed. That meant they would have to face the same responsibilities – and costs and regulation – as others. To the *Daily Mail*, Facebook was a 'deeply tarnished, filth-peddling, tax-dodging, pusillanimous, terror-abetting behemoth which targets the vulnerable with bile and hatred'.[4]

Not all the traditional players would use such language. But, as unease grew over the extent to which Facebook's laissez-faire processes were being manipulated to dark ends, there was something of a broader backlash against companies which were seen as greedy, out of control, arrogant and destructive of social and democratic fabrics.

Facebook's Mark Zuckerberg countered with a 5,000-word manifesto to his 1.86 billion users which couldn't have been more different in tone.[5] In some ways, it struck me as sharing some of the idealism and high-mindedness of Scott's 1921 essay about what a newspaper was for.[6] However disingenuously, Zuckerberg claimed not to have regarded Facebook as just a business. Scott believed in journalism as a mission rather than a route to profit. With the advent of new technology, he wrote in 1921: 'more and more we shall take our pulpit seriously and preach to all the world'.[7] But – like Zuckerberg nearly 100 years later – he also thought about the influence on the 'life of a whole community'. Zuckerberg's manifesto spoke of wanting to 'develop the social infrastructure to give people the power to build a global community that works for all of us'.

Or so he said.

A visit to Facebook's stunning Frank Gehry headquarters[8] – suppos-edly the largest open floor plan in the world – suggested a culture of thinking, collaboration and working a million miles away from the traditional newsrooms of some of its accusers. A nominated interlocutor would listen politely to old media's complaints before patiently explain-ing how Facebook was like no other company that had ever existed. Traditional regulatory responses or pigeon-holing wouldn't work. They were doing something totally different.

There was something in that. Many observers – however much they disliked the company – agreed it would be hard to regulate something so vast and so global in a satisfactory way. Some academics began to develop normative standards (e.g. dealing with hate speech, falsehood, free speech, privacy and so on) to which Facebook could sign up, and which could then be monitored – assuming the company was prepared to be more transparent. A big assumption.

And then, in the spring of 2018, the legacy media finally drew blood. A long and lonely investigation by one *Observer* reporter, Carole Cadwalladr,[9] had picked away at the part played by a shadowy political consulting firm, Cambridge Analytica (CA), in using vast troves of personal data harvested by Facebook to target voters in American and UK plebiscites.

Two things changed the impact of Cadwalladr's campaign. In association with the *NYT* and C4 in London, the *Observer* produced a whistleblower who was prepared to speak on the record. And C4 sent in undercover reporters to elicit damning admissions from the company's top brass about its unlovely modus operandi.

Both CA and Facebook initially responded with legal threats before the dam burst, at one stage wiping $80 billion (14 per cent) off the latter's market value.[10] At one level, many Facebook and Google users knew that their ability to use free email, search and messaging services came at a price – the surrender of quite significant amounts of their personal data. But the arithmetic of the harvesting – as many as 87 million profiles of friends and friends of friends – suddenly made Facebook look creepy.[11] In the words of one Google artificial intelligence expert, not only could the platform be used as a totalitarian Panopticon, it was also a 'psychological control vector'.[12]

Edward Snowden had shone a light on the state's power to delve deeply into an infinite number of lives. Some had been outraged, others had shrugged. Now, some of the shruggers sat up straight and howled foul. As Zuckerberg struggled to frame an adequate response, a mob demanding regulation, if not actual dismemberment, soon made itself heard.

There were also some calmer voices, even from the mainstream press. Don Graham, the 72-year-old former *Washington Post* publisher, who had also served on the board of Facebook until 2015, urged against regulation. His mother, Kay,[13] had battled President Nixon over Watergate. Where were these apolitical regulators going to materialise from? It was a question of free speech.[14]

The Cambridge Analytica crisis was real enough. But it coincided with two popular movements in which social media had acted as a global bushfire. The hashtags #MeToo and #TimesUp had been used by millions of women to amplify the full implications of the outing (by the *NYT* in October 2017) of Harvey Weinstein's abuse of women.

And – almost simultaneous with the Cambridge Analytica affair – millions of Americans came together under the banner of #NeverAgain to demand gun control in the wake of the massacre of 17 people at a Florida high school.

These horizontal waves of connection, co-ordination and action were signals of the benign power of social media to demand change and to transform culture. But they came against a backdrop in which the arrogance and opaqueness of some of the GAFAT companies which enabled those connections were laid bare.

Those who yearned for simple truths about so-called 'new media' were frustrated by the fact that a single narrative – good or bad – didn't work. Some turned to public broadcasting models such as the BBC as an example of a business model that – in contrast to the free market – did actually sustain quality journalism.

Others argued the opposite. Once again, there were demands that the West Coast giants should do more to support old-fashioned journalism. Once, meeting a Facebook interlocutor – this time in a less futuristic space in central London – he turned the question around. 'This journalism you think we should be supporting, what does it look like?'

It was a genuine enquiry, and the glances among his colleagues suggested it was one they had been grappling with themselves. *If you think we should be sharing our revenues in the cause of some kind of public benefit, how do you define that benefit?*

For all its mildness and politeness, it was the deadliest and most profound question.

What is journalism? Who gets to do it? Do you all agree on a core set of standards and ethics and methods? Do you all agree on a common concept of public interest? Do you want us to support the Mail Online*'s sidebar of shame? James Delingpole's climate-change coverage? Or just local news or investigative news? Help us understand.*

There were senior figures within both Facebook and Google who were very troubled by aspects of the information chaos they had partly enabled, and who valued some – but not all – of the things that the old information order produced. They felt most traditional news executives didn't understand algorithms. Some of them would privately admit they didn't understand journalism.

★

Where to start? How to get honesty into the narrative we tell about journalism – the modern equivalent of David Broder's 'partial, hasty, incomplete, inevitably somewhat flawed and inaccurate rendering . . .'

Let's start here: there *is* no one thing called 'journalism'; no single entity called 'news'; no single recognisable identity for a 'journalist'.

Try drawing a map of things we call 'news'. There is straight news and adversarial news; subjective news and objective news. There is news as public service and news as entertainment. There is exclusive news and commodity news. There are investigations; there are campaigns and there is advocacy. There is breaking news and there is slow, considered news. There is analysis, or news with context; explanatory news. There is news as activism. There is opinion dressed up as news; there's eyewitness news; first-person news; or scoops of interpretation. There may even be sponsored news or advertising dressed up to look like news.

Within one news organisation virtually all those forms of journalism may exist under one roof. We took it for granted that the reader understood what was going on and that they could differentiate one kind of journalism from another. But now – at the time of journalism's greatest crisis – the defence of 'journalism' seems infinitely more complicated.

In an age of information chaos and crisis, journalists feel they have to win the argument that there is a category of information – let's call it 'proper' news – which is better than, and distinct from, all the other stuff out there.

Winning that argument seems crucial to the future of journalism. If you want to make people pay for proper news, you have to make the case that proper news has a value – and not purely financial – that the other stuff lacks. Or you may want your proper news to be a more attractive environment for advertising than the wild west of the world wide web. Or you may simply want people to trust your proper news because it was produced by proper journalists . . . and the other stuff wasn't.

Because I was a journalist for 40 years, my instinct is – of course – to stand shoulder to shoulder with 'proper news'. I hope I have sketched enough here to demonstrate the necessity of strong media institutions that can pay for, and defend, the work of reporting the world around them. I hope I have suggested why societies which do not have a flow of agreed factual information are not good societies. If this book were not already too long, I would include an appendix of journalists – on numerous papers, big and small – who do heroic work on a daily basis.

If only the information systems could be tidily divided between the trusty old media and the flaky new ones. But let me highlight two opposite syndromes – I'm going to call them 'useless proper news' and 'proper other stuff' – to show the difficulty.

Useless 'Proper' News

The 2016 UK referendum asked voters for a simple 'yes' or 'no' to settle whether Britain should remain a member of the European Union. Whichever side of the debate you were on, it was commonly accepted that this was the most significant decision the UK had taken in generations.

Though the question on the ballot paper appeared to be a simple one, the decision was, in fact, mindnumblingly complex – with untold consequences for trade, agriculture, security, jobs, the economy, education, migration, human rights, the courts, regulation, food standards and much more.

Faced with such a stark choice, what might a country want from its journalists? The answer is, surely, obvious. *We, the voters, would want to understand the facts on both sides of the argument, presented as neutrally as possible, so that we could make up our minds on the basis of the fullest possible understanding of the risks and opportunities.* That was the Dewey role of the journalist.

We might add this: *We get that this is a complex issue, so we would greatly value the skill of reporters in presenting complicated material in an accessible way. Conversely, please don't insult us by assuming we can't deal with complexity. Even more strongly, we ask that you don't pretend that this is, in fact, a simple choice when it obviously isn't.*

Having done that essential and basic job of proper journalism, if you would like to tell us your *view as a newspaper, then fine. Better still, we would appreciate a spread of views.*

That is not, in fact, how much 'proper' journalism behaved. Indeed, quite a few influential newspapers started from the opposite position:

*This is a simple question on which we, as a newspaper, have a very strong opin-
ion. Our opinion will be very evident in most of what we do and we will not
trouble you with alternative views. We will do some reporting of the campaign,
but most of it will be around the personalities rather than the issues.*

Over the four-month campaign, the Leavers hugely outgunned the
Remainers in the press. A Reuters Institute study found that, factoring-in
reach, 48 per cent of all referendum focused articles were pro-Leave,
with just 22 per cent pro-Remain.[15] Three quarters of all articles in the
Express were pro-Leave, followed in partisanship by the *Mail*, *Sun* and
Telegraph.[16]

The billionaire owner of the *Express*, Richard Desmond, was a
prominent supporter of the main pro-Brexit party, UKIP, giving it £1
million in 2015 on top of the £300,000 he had given the previous year.[17]
Over at the *Sun*, the management spent nearly £100,000 publishing a
pull-out poster backing Brexit, forcing its parent company, Murdoch's
News Group Newspapers, to register as an official Leave campaign
group with the Electoral Commission, which was regulating spending on the campaigns.[18] The cost of the poster made NGN one of the
largest spenders among 48 groups whose finances were revealed. Apart
from that, the *Sun* spent more time campaigning for future British pass-
ports to be 'patriotic' blue than in explaining how their readers' jobs or
services might be negatively impacted by a vote to leave.

But the four-week campaign was, for some editors, just the icing on
a cake they had been baking for a decade or more of anti-European
coverage. Few readers of the Euro-hostile press would, over time, have
been exposed to arguments that membership of the EU brought any
benefits at all. In addition, the two main mid-market tabloids repeatedly
splashed on negative stories about migrants – 72 splashes in the *Express*
and 56 in the *Mail* in the run-up to the referendum. One academic study
found they used the same language to describe the movement of water,
insects, or epidemics. Migrants were 'swarming, swamping, storming,
invading, stampeding, flocking, over-running, and besieging the UK'.[19]

Editors were quite frank about what they were up to. The then
Express editor, Hugh Whittow, proudly admitted that the referendum was the culmination of a five-year 'crusade', including a 'unique

24-page supplement' carefully setting out the case for a UK with-drawal published five years before it actually happened. To him, this was what journalism was: 'Those who voted on June 23 to be free and independent were surely delivering a similar vote of confidence in the newspaper industry.'[20]

So the issue of European membership was, for many years, filtered through an unrelentingly hostile lens – a bit ironic given that the same papers regularly protested that the internet creates 'filter bubbles' in which users are only exposed to views with which they agree.

If the coverage had nonetheless been accurate that would be some mitigation. But the same Brexit-boosting newspapers were – according to the European Commission itself[21] – the leaders in perpetrating myths about how the EU would destroy British sovereignty: bananas will have to be straight; cows will have to wear nappies; milk jugs will be banned; Bombay mix will be renamed; women will have to hand back old sex toys, and so on.

One of the reporters who delighted in this style of reporting was Boris Johnson, the *Telegraph*'s man in Brussels in the early 1990s. One of his former colleagues, Jean Quatremer, wrote of his technique: 'Johnson managed to invent an entire newspaper genre: the Euromyth, a story that had a tiny element of truth at the outset but which was magnified so far beyond reality that by the time it reached the reader it was false.'[22] Johnson became one of the leading architects of Brexit and, later, British foreign secretary.

The campaigning organisation InFacts secured ten corrections to inaccurate pre-Referendum stories after complaining to the press regu-lator IPSO – including the *Sun*'s explosive, but unsupported, claim that the Queen backed Brexit. But, according to InFacts director, Hugo Dixon, it took an average of 89 days for the newspapers to set the record straight.

Just days before the vote, the *Mail* splashed on a story reporting 'yet another load of migrants arrives in UK declaring WE'RE FROM EUROPE – LET US IN!' This, as the paper acknowledged the follow-ing day, was untrue: the migrants were from Iraq and Kuwait, not Europe. A small correction appeared on page two.

The hectoring and misrepresentation did not end with the vote. The *Mail* – and to some extent the *Telegraph* – used their front pages to accuse and, effectively, bully those who disagreed with their views on Europe. Three examples stand out:

1) Judges. Three High Court judges ruled that the government would need parliamentary consent before it could start triggering procedures to leave the EU. The *Mail* responded by running mugshots of the judges over the headline 'Enemies of the People',[23] a phrase with an ugly ancestry that could be traced back to the early days of the Soviet Union. A strapline said there was fury over 'out of touch' judges who had 'defied' 17.4 million Brexit voters and who might thereby trigger a constitutional crisis. But this was all legally illiterate nonsense. The judges – as the Supreme Court was to confirm – were simply interpreting the law. In western democracies, we treasure the independence of the judiciary. Only in the editor of the *Daily Mail*'s mind were they 'enemies of the people'.

2) MPs. Theresa May's decision in April 2017 to call a general election was reported by the *Mail* with the blaring headline 'Crush the Saboteurs'[24] – supposedly what the prime minister had 'vowed' to do to those whom the *Mail*'s strapline referred to as 'Remoaners' (people who continued to disagree with the *Mail* over Brexit). In seeking the return of British parliamentary sovereignty, the *Mail* regarded dissenting MPs' voices not as legitimate debate but as sabotage.[25] (In the event, far from crushing those who disagreed with her, May lost her overall majority in the election.)

3) MPs. The democratic endorsement of a general election vote was still not sufficient for the *Telegraph* and *Mail*, who continued to gun for MPs with principled disagreements over Brexit. The *Telegraph*, once the most understated of broadsheets, produced a front page dominated by 15 photographs of MPs intending to vote against another stage of the parliamentary Brexit proceedings under the headline 'The Brexit Mutineers'.[26] When, a few weeks later, the government was defeated the *Mail* echoed the *Telegraph* treatment with photos of the rebel MPs under the sneering headline 'Proud of Yourselves?'[27]

An MP – Jo Cox – had been murdered in the run-up to the referendum campaign by a far-right extremist who shouted 'Keep Britain independent' and 'Britain first' as he shot and stabbed her. On those grounds alone, a newspaper editor might think twice before running headlines that were certainly experienced as intimidating, some of which were followed by death threats.

But the bigger point, for present purposes, is an editorial one. The 1920s classic Dewey justification for journalism – that it creates better-informed citizens who can thereby make more considered choices about their society – simply didn't work with Brexit.[28] A group of influential editors decided their job was to advocate, not inform. They deliberately created filter bubbles of partial information that would, they hoped, deliver the result they (or their proprietors) wanted. If that included also handing over money to political parties or printing propaganda, so much the better.

Was that 'proper' journalism?

'Proper' Other Stuff

In the binary argument over journalism in a digital world it became an article of faith to some that the internet was largely dross. You needed professionals to bring you reliable information because only they could be trusted [insert brain surgeon comparison]. Twitter – with its restrictive character limit – was widely held up as a place of simplicities, hatred and ignorance. All that was true, but only partly. If, as a journalist, that's all you chose to believe then you were blind to how Twitter was also a place of expertise, intelligent debate and genuine dialogue.

'My readers know more than I do,' Dan Gillmor had written in his 2004 book, *We the Media*,[29] nearly two years before Twitter was born. It was a statement of the obvious: that out there in the 'audience' were the people we were writing about. They did it: we wrote about it. We might write better than they did, but the chances were that they were more knowledgeable.

In time, these knowledgeable voices began to appear on Twitter. For the first time in history they had their own means of mass communication. At first, they were constricted by the format. But then came the invention of a new format: the thread – a sequence of tweets making an argument or advancing a proposition. Suddenly the straitjacket of 140 or 280 characters melted away.

In the right hands the thread is a fascinating new form. Over many tweets a writer can develop quite a sophisticated argument. Each tweet can be accompanied by a screenshot or link to supporting evidence. Each tweet can be individually commented on or shared.

Take, as an example, a 47-tweet thread by an American political analyst, @EmporersNewC [sic] on 10 July 2017.[30] In 20 minutes he posted a cogent narrative about Britain's position within the EU over a generation or more. It showed how the UK had negotiated improvements in foreign policy, fisheries and agriculture. He mined old Conservative and Labour manifestos for examples of both parties trumpeting their successes in bolstering processes and collaboration. The thread ridiculed inconsistencies, U-turns and contradictions in arguments. The singer Billy Bragg likened it to 'an old folk tale that draws you in, then catches you out'.

This was an entirely new form of . . . let's call it 'journalism'. No newspaper could have attempted this exercise in print: the tweets plus supporting screenshots would simply have taken up too much space. Few traditional journalists would sit down and answer responses, supplying more evidence where appropriate, as these tweeters did. In terms of depth, research and analysis it quite easily surpassed much of what passed for proper journalism.

Multiple groups took to these new media. I happened to follow a lot of lawyers, but there are medics, police, soldiers, bankers, farmers, academics, teachers and nurses there if you look for them. Without too much trouble you can find dozens and dozens of interesting lawyers – quick-witted, pithy, argumentative, wide-ranging, open to debate . . . and expert. It's sometimes painful to see them picking apart the legal coverage in 'proper' newspapers. Example: in October 2017 the *Sun* attacked a 'clueless' judge for his handling of a case involving a terrorist, Lee Adebolajo.[31] Over a thread of 18 tweets @BarristerSecret patiently explained the judge's thinking, concluding he was far from clueless.[32]

Or take a screaming *Daily Mail* headline in December 2017: 'Another Human Rights Fiasco! Iraqi "caught red-handed with bomb" wins

£33,000 – because our soldiers kept him in custody for too long.'[33] Almost everything about that was wrong: £30,000 of the £33,000 was in fact for beating and inhuman treatment: and the Iraqi had been cleared of being involved in bomb-making. One barrister, Adam Wagner, patiently sat down just before midnight – because he knew what effects such stories have on citizens' perceptions of human rights – to compose a calm 17-tweet thread urging people to read the judgment (supplying a link) or, at least, a summary of it.

Wagner expressed sympathy for soldiers having to operate in dangerous conditions. He had acted for many of them himself. But he concluded: 'So as painful and difficult as this process is, it's important. I desperately want us to have an Army we are proud of, which sets an example to others and is a proper ambassador for British values. So these cases are important.'[34]

Wagner's thread was infinitely more rounded, comprehensive legally coherent – and accurate – than some players in the 'proper' media. The *Mail* later corrected several aspects of its report.

★

This is the twenty-first-century reality: that old and new media are part of a continuum of information in which traditional definitions of news overlap and blur.

The truth is that it is difficult to map the new eco-system of information in a neat way with – at different ends of a spectrum – 'proper' mainstream media and 'other stuff'. Much of the information being produced by non-professionals is just as reliable, informative and useful as that produced by journalists. Vice versa, some information produced 'professionally' is weak, unreliable, unethical . . . and even untruthful. You could call it 'fake'.

The style of quite a lot of the journalism produced in recent years by the *Sun* or the *Daily Mail* has, it seems to me, less and less in common with that produced by the BBC, the *New York Times* or the *Financial Times*. Not, 'nothing' in common, but 'less'.

The *Mail* – not always, but often – can be aggressive, intrusive, hectoring and partisan. Its website is driven by an obsession with the very celebrity culture its print counterpart affects to despise. It has polit-ical objectives which it pursues relentlessly. The BBC and *NYT* are, in some ways, the opposite. Their tone is cool and impartial. Their news operations are discouraged from having political ends. They are gener-ally motivated by what's important rather than what sells. They do not go in for bullying.

So the nagging question keeps returning: at the very time when jour-nalism itself is crying out to be defended – what is it? Who gets to do it?

We are back to the polite question from the Facebook executive: 'What is this thing that you would like us to support, or subsidise?' How do we answer? Who gets to answer?

We know what journalism used to be in the age when only one small group of people in society could do it. Journalists were skilled at it. People willingly parted with money for it. And the business worked, not least because news companies were also very good at marrying advertising with consumers.

But now advertisers could often reach consumers much more effec-tively through other channels. People were much more reluctant to part with money for news. And, however you measured it, there was wide-spread scepticism, confusion and mistrust about mainstream journalism now that plausible alternatives existed.

The crisis today goes further. On the eve of Donald Trump taking office, the respected NYU media academic Jay Rosen published a bleak blog post titled 'Winter is Coming' in which he argued that 'so many things are happening to disarm and disable serious journalism . . . at the darkest time in American history since WWI'.

He began with an ever-more severe economic crisis for news combined with the lowest levels of trust in news media in living memory, citing the First World War as a time of particular censorship and suppression of dissent. He added in a 'broken and outdated' model for political journalism (based on 'access' or 'inside' reporting which misses broader connections with the public). Then came a lack of diver-sity in newsrooms; weak leadership and 'thin institutional structures' in the American press. The mistrust of the media was mirrored by low levels of trust in most institutions and their leaders – the very people journalists were writing about. Then came an organised movement on the political right to discredit mainstream journalism and the increasingly dim prospect that there was even a fact-based debate to which journalists could usefully contribute. Media companies increasingly subordinated news and political debate to entertainment values; while finally, Facebook was slowly taking charge of the day-to-day relationship with users of the news system.[35]

So that was the perfect storm that had been brewing for years and which now glowered over the struggling realm of journalism. There were still bright beacons of hope: the grotesque distortions, evasions and menace of the Trump presidency were more than matched by some magnificent reporting by, among others, the *New York Times*, *Washington Post* and the *New Yorker*. But most journalism was struggling to reconcile the commercial, technological and editorial imperatives of the new age.

A more dispiriting – and probably typical – example of new ways of doing things was brought home to me by a young local news reporter I met in 2017 after giving a talk in London. She told me she worked for a title, owned by a large British news conglomerate, which was, to all intents and purposes, a front. The physical office in the community she was reporting had long since closed: she worked from another newsroom 30 miles away. Reporters had to produce a set quota of stories a day to meet daily online website targets, so rarely left their desks. Her newspaper copy was sub-edited by people she had never met, a hundred miles away. She still had idealistic notions of journalism and was keen to learn. But, at 24, and after only a few years of working as a journalist, she was already one of the most senior reporters in the office. The others had long since jumped ship. So, a few months later, did she.

A look at her erstwhile website was as crushing to the spirits as the *NYT* was uplifting. One was produced within a hollowed-out organisation that had – with this bit of the operation in any event – lost any sense of service to a community; the other was still resolutely holding power to account, a reminder not only of what great, serious journalism could do – but also that there was an evident hunger for it.[36]

Sometimes it helps to spend time in countries where journalism is, literally, a matter of life and death. In the past two years, I led missions to Kenya and Ukraine on behalf of the New York-based Committee to Protect Journalists. Neither country was newsless, but in both countries news was direly threatened. In Kenya, the government was slowly choking off the economic lifeline that state advertising had once provided. In Ukraine, as in Kenya, there was a sense of impunity: that you could threaten, defame, gag or even kill a journalist without any consequences.

But what brave and resourceful journalists I met in both places! To them, journalism wasn't a game. There was no world-weary cynicism. There was, in some, a determination to keep a flickering light of scrutiny alive even if it came at the cost of their lives. They were driven by a strong sense of the link between journalism and public duty.

'Public' is, to some in the twenty-first century, a difficult word. We value public services, public spaces and public goods – but we sometimes struggle to know how to discuss them, create them, run them, fund them, regulate them, support them or measure them. We speak of public benefits and 'the public interest' without ever satisfactorily defining them. In the UK, we treasure a public health service – but not to the point of financing it sufficiently. We trust a public service broadcaster above all private news providers – but regularly revile it.

Newspapers once created a form of public square – assisted by other public entities such as public libraries and public post offices. The US Post Office Act of 1792 circulated newspapers free, or at a very modest rate. Post offices and their attached public reading rooms made newspapers, along with government documents, widely available. Newspapers were considered public resources 'as free to all comers as to the person to whom they rightfully belong'.[37] To Alexis de Tocqueville's eyes, 'the post office was the only entity with the organisational capability to circulate the information of public significance that was essential to sustain America's bold experiment with democracy'.[38]

The ultimate defence of journalism is that it remains a public good. But how do we measure, or value, such a public good at a time when, in the words of the political philosopher Michael Sandel, 'markets – and market values – have come to govern our lives as never before . . . Markets leave their mark. Sometimes, market values crowd out non-market values worth caring about.'[39]

Such talk in relation to news, a decade ago, would have been dismissed as the bleating of liberals – the despised 'subsidariat'[40] who weren't commercial enough to produce decent journalism that the public wanted to read. But now the boot was on the other foot. Faced with the overwhelming scale, popularity[41] and sheer turbo-charged commercial power of the West Coast digital giants there was now an outcry against the havoc that free markets had inflicted on the traditional press.

A decade ago, the idea of a public subsidy – to cover courts, councils or public authorities, for instance – was rubbished by newspaper elders: it smacked of the sort of French-style handouts that had (in their view) neutered much of the European press. By early 2017 there was barely a murmur of disagreement as the UK government diverted £8 million a year from the BBC's £3.7 billion-a-year licence fee to pay for 150 'local democracy reporters' funded by the corporation, but employed by 'qualifying news organisations'.[42]

But what was the public interest that needed to be served? A decade ago some newspapers screamed themselves blue in the face over the right to expose philandering footballers. But who, today, would look into the eyes of Facebook executives and say with a straight face that these things were of overwhelming public benefit that demanded support?

And, if they did, would Facebook listen?

In fact, Facebook was listening, in its own way. At the beginning of 2017 it launched a project to collaborate with journalists to tackle issues such as training, technology, fake news and news literacy 'to equip people with the knowledge they need to be informed readers'. A parallel $150 million, Google-funded digital news initiative subsidises numerous projects in 29 countries around such things as metrics, personalisation, online discussions and involving readers.

Metrics were the new big thing – and one on which the editorial and commercial side of news organisations could agree. The new new world was about collecting as much data as possible on each reader so as to be able to serve them better (editorial) and monetise them (commercial). Groups of editors and CEOs gathering in Oxford for regular Reuters Institute forums in 2017 wanted to share notes about processes, teams and tasks; about sponsored content; about pricing points for paid content; and about the best software for drilling down into the performance of individual stories. One editor had banned stories on subjects that, according to his desktop graphs, did not drive subscriptions.

All this was important and, in their shoes, I would probably have been pre-occupied by similar things. But it was much to harder to see, measure, or understand the rapid development of a new kind of public realm – an unfamiliar horizontal world formed of billions of daily interactions between people.

Some queried the importance, or even the existence, of this new realm. Some disliked it and set little value on it. Some acknowledged it; but opted to ignore it because it was not what 'we' did. As with hurricanes and climate change, it was difficult to make causal links between extreme events (Arab Spring, Trump, Brexit, the 2017 British general election result, etc.) and new forms of societal arrangements resulting from changed information systems and hierarchies. But many journalists found themselves consistently wrong-footed by public behaviour that they failed to anticipate. The UK satirical magazine *Private Eye* had much fun devoting pages to the inaccurate predictions of eminent columnists and editorialists; and to their subsequent head-scratching retractions, apologies and explanations.

But the wider point was that journalism – whatever it was: a craft, a toolkit, a method, a discipline – was failing in its job sufficiently to understand how newly rearranged societies were now working. New networks were having a literally incalculable effect on how connected citizens thought, behaved, informed themselves and voted. The historian Niall Ferguson explored how these new forces were operating in his 2017 book *The Square and the Tower*: the tower represented hierarchical control, while the square represented social networks – 'the structures that human beings naturally form'. As Tim Harford summarised Ferguson's sweep through 500 years: 'Networks flourished in the years 1450 to 1790; hierarchies reasserted themselves until around 1970, and networks have been making a comeback ever since.[43]

Ferguson was not alone in thinking these new arrangements were far from benign: 'The reality is that the global network has become a transmission mechanism for all kinds of manias and panics, just as the combination of printing and literacy temporarily increased the prevalence of millenarian sects and witch crazes . . . The contamination of the public sphere with fake news today is less surprising when one remembers that the printing press disseminated books about magic as well as books about science.'[44]

★

Like these new systems or not, it was impossible not to be curious about how human beings, given the tools to communicate with each other as never before, were using them. It might take computer and social scientists many years to understand more fully how these new networks were operating. But journalism doesn't have many years to wait for answers. Some might still want to stand apart and take refuge in the tower. But, meanwhile, what was happening in the square?

Some used the word 'publicness' to describe new ways of interacting that, at their best, built trust; thrived on open collaboration; and enabled people with experience and authority to be heard. How did these new techniques of publicness compare with the habits of the tower?

The question was worth asking because, in theory, the complete answer to fake news should be . . . journalism. People have always published and spread falsehoods. Journalism was widely considered one of the most effective ways of distinguishing the true from the untrue in a timely way. The irreducible purpose of a newspaper is to do just that.

What had never existed before was a system for the instant dissemination of lies in such infinite volumes. For a while journalism looked as if would be capsized by the sheer scale of what was happening. The bigger problem was that journalism itself was so ill-prepared for the moment of crisis. If only people trusted journalists more, society would have a system in place for dealing with fake news.

If only . . . we were back to issues of trust and the paradox that popularity, economic viability, editorial quality and trust did not inevitably go hand in hand. There was something about the present age that made people suspicious of the claims that journalism made for itself – along with many other institutions of the tower. And some of the new conventions of information were, in their publicness, an improvement on some historic practices.

Take two: the correction and the link.

For all the concern about fake news and the casualness with which inaccurate and distorted information spread, there was also a widespread instinct to correct things that were wrong, or untrue, or unclear. The timescale for correction shrank. Often within seconds – certainly within minutes – of falsehoods being spoken or published, someone in the eco-system would challenge or correct them.

Of course, to some players that made no difference. But the best practice among people who wanted decent information to circulate was quickly to acknowledge error. A wrong tweet would, for instance, be quickly conceded; and then deleted or corrected, sometimes with an apology. In my experience of the Twittersphere when that happens, people move on.

Journalists should have no conceivable interest in publishing wrong information. It's the opposite of what journalism should be doing. Uncorrected errors corrode trust. But, even in 2018, it is often not a simple matter to secure a correction from some traditional news organisations.

Many newspapers or websites will now carry a small paragraph indicating where complaints should be addressed. Many will be dealt with, visibily or invisibly. Relatively few errors are publicly acknowledged. In extremis there will be a correction or clarification. In the UK, if the matter is referred to the regulator, IPSO, the average delay in dealing with a complaint is 35 days.[45]

There are journalists who will monitor social media and respond quickly if they have got something wrong. But, in general, the mentality of print was that corrections were laborious and unwelcome and should be conceded only where the alternative (a legal action, an IPSO case, a public spat) was worse. And the mentality of print is a difficult mentality to slough off.

Early in the book I quoted the definition of journalism coined by the *Washington Post*'s David Broder: 'a partial, hasty, incomplete, inevitably somewhat flawed and inaccurate rendering . . .'

Honest journalists know that is what our business is. So do most readers. So maybe the biggest step we could take towards winning trust in the square is to do what Broder suggested 31 years ago – 'label the product accurately'.

It is a safe assumption that one of the reasons that social media is so spectacularly popular is that people can often find an authenticity there that they feel is lacking in so many areas of corporate, political, commercial, governmental and journalistic communication.

Most people do not these days (if they ever did) expect journalism to tell them the whole 'truth';[46] nor should we promise it. We can certainly be truthful. We can tell truths. We can – and should – stick to things we know to be true.

But 'the truth' is usually more complicated than space or time allows. It depends on who is willing to speak; on what documentation is publicly available; on who is lying to us or spinning us. The deadline is our enemy. Resources are ever more scarce. It's human to make mistakes. Historians, with the luxury of time and documentation, know how elusive the truth is. Why should journalists, usually in much more testing circumstances and against the clock, be expected to deliver it so easily? An honesty about the limits of journalism – as well as its powers and benefits – would win, not erode, trust.

So that would involve baking open and transparent systems of correction and clarification into the journalistic process. It might involve finding a journalistic voice that was sometimes less declamatory, less certain; more tentative, more collaborative, more involving, more enlisting.

Is it imaginable that more journalists would curate their articles after publication in the expectation that the pieces could thus quickly be improved once in the public domain? Or do we consider that an article is an artefact which, once issued, stands? To embed a greater willingness to make correction an intrinsic tool of journalism would certainly require massive organisational and attitudinal change. My instinct is that kind of change is probably unavoidable, even if it's not actively sought.

And then there's the link . . .

The best users on social media link. Linking to your source is, of course, something that academics and scholars have done since medieval times – whether in marginalia, glossed psalters or, in more recent times, footnotes.[47] Academics cite their sources in order to assist other academics; to be transparent about their scholarship; to make their work checkable and, thus, trustable.

It's quite striking, in contrast, how few journalists routinely link. Even fewer link usefully – e.g. to the relevant report, poll, document or court judgment. I know the feeling. You're writing at speed. A copy editor is standing over your shoulder. Have I really got the time and inclination to go back and insert a bunch of URLs?

But the link is your pathway to trust. It says: *Don't take my word for it: here's how I know what I know.* The reader can, if they want, check your sources to see how reliable they are and how faithfully you've represented them.

An entire book could, of course, be written on journalistic sourcing. All reporters know that people will often speak more honestly if allowed to speak anonymously. The use of non-attributed quotes can contribute a truer understanding of a subject than if a journalist confined him/herself to quoting bland, on-the-record quotes. There are some areas of reporting – national security, for instance – where it is very difficult to persuade anyone to speak on the record. On the other hand, journalism which isn't believed has failed.

In the past – at the risk of labouring the point – readers had few alternatives. It was difficult, if not impossible, to seek out original documentation or alternative narratives. So readers were more or less obliged to take our word for things; and if we were wrong, who was to know? In an age of publicness things could barely be more different. Yet how many news organisations carry on as though nothing has changed?

*

This book opened in an age – within the careers of a great many journalists still working – when the reader was largely a distant, unknown and passive figure. Now, 20 years into the digital revolution, many news organisations still feel as if we can't quite make our minds up about what relationship we want with the people who read or watch us.

We want their money, of course. We're keen on harvesting their data.[48] We'd like them to send us stories if they stumble across them. There was a time when we valued their opinions – but, in many cases, that experiment is being jettisoned. A clutch of news organisations have begun to announce they no longer want to hear their readers' views. *Vice* bailed out in December 2016 ('We don't have the time or desire to continue monitoring that crap moving forward'). National Public Radio (NPR) had closed down comments five months earlier ('not providing a useful experience for the vast majority of our users'). Others followed suit, some arguing that social media in general was the new arena for people to have their say.

In any period of great disruption it's probably desirable to hold two contradictory thoughts in your mind: that the revolution will be less profound than it feels; and, conversely, that it will be much more radical.

If the former's true it's possible that, after a period of experimentation in our relationship with the reader, things will revert to a more traditional state of affairs. Most readers, it may turn out, don't want to be involved in the news: they just want to read or watch it. Some of them will be happy to pay for that. We will treat them like consumers.

If the latter's true – that the revolution has barely started – then news organisations may, by contrast, have a whole lot more innovating still to do. We will almost certainly want to draw readers in; to engage them; to win their trust; to ask for help; to be ever more open; to change some significant things about the way we do journalism.

★

I think back to the *Guardian* readers who assembled in our morning conference room during our Open Weekend in March 2012. One of the reasons for staging the weekend was a feeling that we should be more forthcoming about the likely upheavals ahead. The older readers, in particular, felt a sense of ownership of the paper. Editors came and went; readers were the lifetime loyalists.

Several of the group sitting on the yellow sofas that day were medics, or primary school teachers, or criminal lawyers or local council employees. They were acute in their comments about the paper and the website as well as being courteous and knowledgeable about current events. Their commitment to the *Guardian* – and to the principle of its journalism being widely read around the world – was such that several of them would have volunteered to be involved in it.

We never went that far.

We toyed with the idea of turning the *Guardian* into a mutual organisation, owned by its readers and run for the public benefit. We never did that either. We were too intensely occupied by phone hacking, Snowden and the rest to give the ideas the concentration they needed. And, in any event, the commercial team were pretty sure their own strategy would come good. As of early 2018 it seems to be.

In 2008 a *Guardian* colleague, Alison Benjamin, wrote a book called *A World Without Bees*[49] – a warning that we should pay more attention to the health and well-being of bees because, were we to lose them, our planet would be done for. I feel the same about reporters. Reporters are the bees of the world's information systems. Without reporters like Nick Davies, or like the late Anthony Shadid of the *NYT* or Marie Colvin of the *Sunday Times*, both of whom died stubbornly trying to keep the public informed about important truths – we're in serious trouble.

All the anguish over economic models for newspapers, how do we – crudely – get 'them' to pay for news, even to think it's important, have taken up startling amounts of energy that might equally well have been spent on the more fundamental questions that have been asked of journalism. But newspapers, in their raggedy way, have always been reliant on whatever economic system was driving the commerce of the day. The question now is how will it be sustained in the age of the hyper-global corporation: the untaxed, rootless entities that know more about us than our own mothers. Will they destroy, or support, a critical, independent, professional cadre of people and news outlets that – at their best – perform an ever-more necessary public service?

As 2018 progresses – and as I am writing these lines – nobody knows for a certainty what's going to work with the news business, financially at least. Donald Trump may have been terrible for America, the world at large and the future of the species, but he has, in some ways, been good for news. He has – with his prolific lies, and his bullying menace towards decent reporters and newspapers – reminded people why journalism matters. A good many journalists have risen magnificently to the challenge.

Will the Trump Bump last? Will the public rediscover their appetite for good, old-fashioned reporting and investigations? Will Facebook and Google sweep all away? Might there, in the end, be no conventional economic model for news? Will the re-making of journalism be far more radical than most people can currently begin to imagine?

William Goldman famously said of the movie business: 'Not one person in the entire motion picture field knows for a certainty what's going to work. Every time out it's a guess and, if you're lucky, an educated one.

'Nobody knows anything.'

We do know that readers and listeners and viewers across the world depend on – even love – the news outlets that promise, and deliver, honest, enquiring, brave journalism.

And we know that – as well as the dross and the fakery and the hate and the lies – there are wonders in the new world of information: people connecting with each other through networks of humanity, complexity, experience, expertise and decency.

These two worlds – old and new – continue to collide in a fog of mutual suspicion and misunderstanding. But collisions can also release energy. The combination of the best of these worlds could yet be formidable.

These are signs – sputtering, but hopeful. If the world wakes up in time then we may be all right. Trust me, we do not want a world without news.

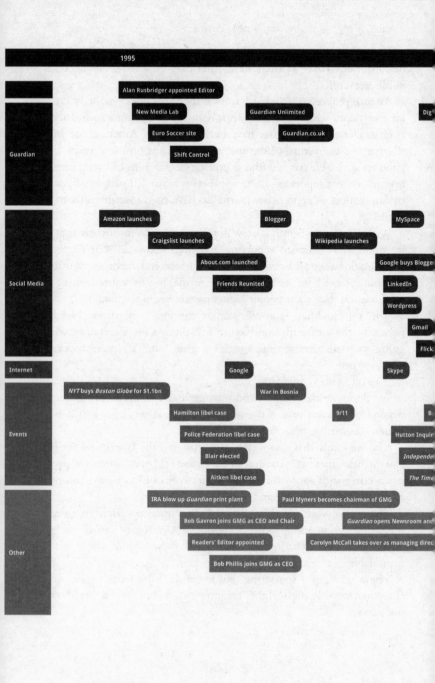

1995

Guardian
- Alan Rusbridger appointed Editor
- New Media Lab
- Euro Soccer site
- Shift Control
- Guardian Unlimited
- Guardian.co.uk
- Dig

Social Media
- Amazon launches
- Craigslist launches
- About.com launched
- Friends Reunited
- Blogger
- Wikipedia launches
- MySpace
- Google buys Blogge
- LinkedIn
- Wordpress
- Gmail
- Flick

Internet
- Google
- Skype

Events
- NYT buys Boston Globe for $1.1bn
- Hamilton libel case
- Police Federation libel case
- Blair elected
- Aitken libel case
- War in Bosnia
- 9/11
- B.
- Hutton Inquir
- Independe
- The Time

Other
- IRA blow up Guardian print plant
- Bob Gavron joins GMG as CEO and Chair
- Readers' Editor appointed
- Bob Phillis joins GMG as CEO
- Paul Myners becomes chairman of GMG
- Guardian opens Newsroom and
- Carolyn McCall takes over as managing direc

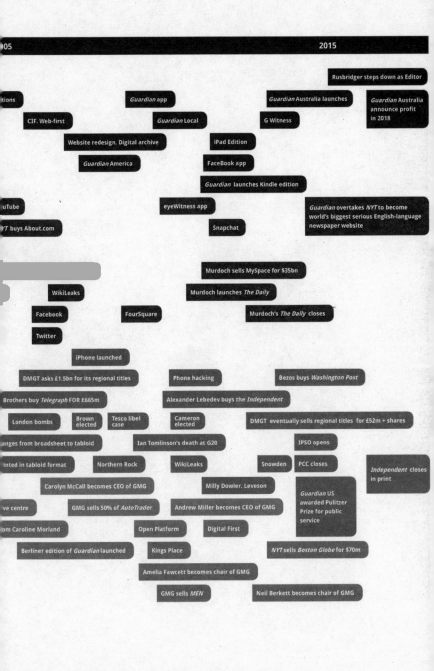

2005   2015

Rusbridger steps down as Editor

...tions   *Guardian* app   *Guardian* Australia launches   *Guardian* Australia announce profit in 2018

CIF. Web-first   *Guardian* Local   G Witness

Website redesign. Digital archive   iPad Edition

Guardian America   FaceBook app

Guardian launches Kindle edition

...uTube   eyeWitness app   *Guardian* overtakes *NYT* to become world's biggest serious English-language newspaper website

...YT buys About.com   Snapchat

Murdoch sells MySpace for $35bn

WikiLeaks   Murdoch launches *The Daily*

Facebook   FourSquare   Murdoch's *The Daily* closes

Twitter

iPhone launched

DMGT asks £1.5bn for its regional titles   Phone hacking   Bezos buys *Washington Post*

...Brothers buy *Telegraph* FOR £665m   Alexander Lebedev buys the *Independent*

London bombs   Brown elected   Tesco libel case   Cameron elected   DMGT eventually sells regional titles for £52m + shares

...anges from broadsheet to tabloid   Ian Tomlinson's death at G20   IPSO opens

...inted in tabloid format   Northern Rock   WikiLeaks   Snowden   PCC closes   *Independent* closes in print

Carolyn McCall becomes CEO of GMG   Milly Dowler. Leveson   *Guardian* US awarded Pulitzer Prize for public service

...ve centre   GMG sells 50% of *AutoTrader*   Andrew Miller becomes CEO of GMG

...om Caroline Morland   Open Platform   Digital First

Berliner edition of *Guardian* launched   Kings Place   *NYT* sells *Boston Globe* for $70m

Amelia Fawcett becomes chair of GMG

GMG sells *MEN*   Neil Berkett becomes chair of GMG

Bibliography

Addison, A. *Mail Men: The Unauthorised Story of the Daily Mail: The Paper That Divided and Conquered Britain.* London: Atlantic Books, 2017.

Aitken, J. *Pride and Perjury.* New York: Harper Collins, 2003.

Anderson, C. *The Long Tail.* New York: Hyperion Books, 2006.

Arendt, H. *The Origins of Totalitarianism.* Berlin: Schocken Books, 1951.

Benjamin, A. and Benjamin, B. *A World Without Bees.* London: Guardian Books, 2008.

Broder, D. *Behind the Front Page.* New York: Simon & Schuster, 1987.

Brown, C. 'State of the American Newspaper. FEAR.COM'. *American Journalism Review,* Vol. 20 No. 10 (June 1999), pp. 50–71. Available at: http://ajrarchive.org/Article.asp?id=3230

Campbell, W.J. *1995: The Year the Future Began.* California: University of California Press, 2015.

Carey, J.W. 'The Press and Public Discourse'. *Kettering Review* (Winter 1992) , pp. 18–19.

Chippendale, P. and Horrie, C. *Stick It Up Your Punter: The Rise and Fall of the Sun.* London: William Heinemann, 1990.

Clegg, N. *Politics: Between the Extremes.* London: Bodley Head, 2016.

Davies, N. *Flat Earth News: An Award-winning Reporter Exposes Falsehood, Distortion and Propaganda in the Global Media.* London: Chatto & Windus, 2008.

Davies, N. *Hack Attack.* London: Chatto & Windus, 2014.

Dean, M. *Democracy Under Attack: How the Media Distort Policy and Politics*. Bristol: Policy Press, 2011.

Fairfield, J.D. *The Public and Its Possibilities: Triumphs and Tragedies in the American City*. Philadelphia, PA: Temple University Press, 2010.

Ferguson, N. *The Square and the Tower: Networks, Hierarchies and the Struggle for Global Power*. London: Allen Lane, 2017.

Filloux, F. Monday Note blog. Available at: https://mondaynote.com

Fletcher, R. and Nielsen, R.K. 'Is social media use associated with more or less diverse news use?' Oxford: Reuters Institute for the Study of Journalism, 25 November 2016.

Gillmor, D. *We the Media*. California: O'Reilly Media, 2004. Available at: http://www.authorama.com/book/we-the-media.html

Goodale, J. *Fighting for the Press: The Inside Story of the Pentagon Papers and Other Battles*. New York, NY: CUNY Journalism Press, 2013.

Grafton, A. *The Footnote: A Curious History*. Cambridge, MA: Harvard University, 1997.

Greenwald, G. *No Place to Hide*. London: Hamish Hamilton, 2014.

Grossman, L.K. *The Electronic Republic*. London: Penguin Books, 1995.

Grueskin, B., Seave, A. and Graves, L. *The Story So Far: What We Know About the Business of Digital Journalism*. New York: Columbia School of Journalism, 2011.

Hagel, J. and Singer, M. *Net Worth: Shaping Markets When Customers Make the Rules*. Boston, MA: Harvard Business School Press, 1999.

Hare, D. and Brenton, H. *Pravda: A Fleet Street Comedy*. London: Bloomsbury, 1985.

Hendriks, P. *Newspapers: A Lost Cause*. Amsterdam: University of Amsterdam, 1999.

Hirsch, F. and Gordon, D. *Newspaper Money: Fleet Street and the Search for an Affluent Reader*. London: Hutchinson, 1975.

Hooper, D. *Official Secrets: The Use and Abuse of the Act*. London: Secker & Warburg, 1987.

Jarvis, J. *Gutenberg the Geek*. Kindle Single Edition, 2012.

Kueng, L. *Going Digital: A Roadmap for Organisation Change*. Oxford: Reuters Institute for the Study of Journalism, 2017.

Leigh, D. and Harding, L. *WikiLeaks: Inside Julian Assange's War on Secrecy*. London: Guardian Books, 2010.

Levy, D., Aslan, B. and Bironzo, D. *UK Press Coverage of the EU Referendum*. Oxford: Reuters Institute for the Study of Journalism, 2016.

Lewis, A. *Make No Law: The Sullivan Case and the First Amendment*. New York: Random House, 1991.

Lichter, R., Lichter, L. and Rothman, A. *Watching America*. New Jersey: NW Prentice-Hall Press, 1991.

Lloyd, J. *What the Media Are Doing to Our Politics*. London: Constable, 2004.

Lobban, M. 'From Seditious Libel to Unlawful Assembly: Peterloo and the Changing Face of Political Crime'. *Oxford Journal of Legal Studies*, Vol. 10 No. 3 (Autumn 1990), pp. 307–352.

Lundberg, K. *Friend or Foe? WikiLeaks and the Guardian*. New York, NY: Knight Case Studies Initiative, The Journalism School, Columbia University, 2011.

Luyendijk, J. *People Like Us: Misrepresenting the Middle East*. Berkeley, CA: Soft Skull Press, 2009. Translated by M. Hutchison.

Mair, J. and Clark, T. *Last Words?: How Can Journalism Survive the Decline of Print?* Bury St Edmunds, Suffolk: Abramis Academic Publishing, 2016.

Mair, J., Clark, T., Fowler, N., Snoddy, R. and Tait, R. (eds) *Brexit, Trump and the Media*, Bury St Edmunds, Suffolk: Abramis Academic Publishing, 2017.

Martínez, A.G. *Chaos Monkeys: Obscene Fortune and Random Failure in Silicon Valley*. London: Ebury Press, 2016.

McChesney, R.W. and Pickard, V. (eds.) *Will the Last Reporter Please Turn Out the Lights?* New York, NY: The New Press, 2011.

Meyer, P. *The Vanishing Newspaper*. Columbia, MO: University of Missouri Press, 2004

Nicholas, D., Williams, P., Martin, H. and Cole, P. *The Media and the Internet*. United Kingdom: British Library Research and Innovation Report 110, March 1998.

Ofek, E. and Richardson, M. 'DotCom Mania: The Rise and Fall of Internet Stock Prices'. *The Journal of Finance*, May 2003.

Popplewell, O. *Benchmark: Life, Laughter and the Law*. London/New York: I.B. Tauris, 2003.

Ramsay, G.N. 'How Newspapers Covered Press Regulation After Leveson'. The Media Standards Trust, September 2014.

Randall, M. *The Funny Side of the Street*. London: Bloomsbury, 1988.

Rohm, W.G. *The Murdoch Mission: The Digital Transformation of a Media Empire.* New York: John Wiley & Sons, 2002.

Sandel, M. *What Money Can't Buy.* New York: Farrar, Straus and Giroux, 2012.

Shenker, J. *The Egyptians: A Radical Story.* London: Penguin, 2016.

Shirky, C. *Here Comes Everybody.* London: Penguin Books, 2008.

Starr, P. *The Creation of the Media: Political Origins of Modern Communications.* New York: Basic Books, 2004.

Surowiecki, J. *The Wisdom of Crowds: Why the Many are Smarter than the Few and How Collective Wisdom Shapes Business, Economies, Societies and Nations.* New York: Doubleday, 2004.

Tapscott, D. and Williams, A.D. *Wikinomics: How Mass Collaboration Changes Everything.* Old Saybrook, CT: Tantor Media, 2006.

Walmsley, R. *Peterloo: The Case Reopened.* Manchester: Manchester University Press, 1969.

Ward, S.J.A. *The Invention of Journalism Ethics: The Path to Objectivity and Beyond.* Montreal: McGill–Queen's University Press, 2006.

Williams, R. *Culture and Society.* London: Chatto & Windus, 1958.

Acknowledgements

Professional musicians have long debated how much difference a conductor makes to the playing of an orchestra. They can wave their hands in the air all they like: the band plays on. Comparisons are sometimes made with newspapers. Who needs editors?

I hope, if nothing else, this book shows the multiple ways in which a news organisation is a collective enterprise. So my first thanks ought to go to the hundreds of former colleagues who shared some, most or all of this journey with me. This is especially true of the book's two dedicatees – Lindsay Mackie and Georgina Henry. I met both through the *Guardian*. One became my wife, the other my deputy. Both were first-rate journalists and I learned a very great deal from them. George was with me every single step of the way from 1995 until her untimely and cruel death in 2014. Lindsay had read the *Guardian* since the age of ten before joining it as a reporter. No one had, or has, a truer sense of its purpose and values.

Beyond this heartfelt collective thank-you, how to single out some colleagues without offending others? My apologies in advance for the inevitably selective nature of this list. I can't record thanks for every significant conversation about journalism or technology over the years: they happened on an almost daily basis, in the newsrooms, over lunch, in pubs and at conferences. But there are some friends and colleagues I'd like to mention.

From my early days as a trainee there are some former workmates I must remember for the common sense about journalism they knocked into me: especially Jock Gillespie, Chris Elliott, Chris South, Crawford Gillan, Peter Wells and the late John Gaskell. Chris Elliott was kind enough to read an early draft of this manuscript, as was, most helpfully, Tif Loehnis. In my early days at the *Guardian* I was lucky enough to be mentored by Peter Cole, then news editor, and David McKie, deputy editor. Peter Preston was convinced that I might have a modest talent for editing long before I did. He remained an encouraging guide and constructive critic. Ian Mayes, who has been writing his own elegant and comprehensive history of the modern *Guardian*, was a wise colleague and guide for a reporter trying to learn how to edit.

Aside from George I had, over 20 years, other wonderfully able deputies in Ian Katz (now running programmes at C4); Paul Johnson; Kath Viner, my successor as editor; and Janine Gibson, who went on to edit Buzzfeed UK. What a team of brilliantly talented editors to work alongside and to learn from. I relied – more, I fear, than was sometimes good for her – on executive editor Sheila Fitzsimons, who had astonishing organisational skills as well as being numerate, human, centred . . . and generally lovely.

I leant heavily on people who were much more digitally clued-up than me. Among them are some extremely clever digital thinkers who later fanned out to run things at Amazon, Sky, Columbia University, Condé Nast, Twitter and elsewhere. They included Simon Waldman, Wolfgang Blau, Emily Bell and Tony Ageh. I should add – and thank – so many more who taught me so much about the new digital frontiers. Here are a few, some of whom turned up for a beer during the writing of this book, to recall some of the highs and lows of the journey: Nick Passmore, Michael Brunton-Spall, Azeem Azhar, Sean Clarke, Theresa Malone, Tony Gill, David Blishen, Dan Catt, Matt McAlister, Neil McIntosh, Harold Frayman, David Rowan, Lloyd Shepherd, Sheila Pulham, Subhajit Banerjee, Shannon Maher, Tara Herman, Kate le Ruez, Aidan Geary, James Ball, Amanda Michel, Bobbie Johnson, Aron Pilhofer, Gabe Dance, Anthony Sullivan, Luke Hoyland, Chris Moran, Tanya Cordrey, Graham Tackley, Joanna Geary, Simon Rogers, Helen

Dagley, Jemima Kiss, Duncan Clark, Mary Hamilton, Tom Happold, Meg Pickard and Alberto Nardelli.

And then there were the other external digital thinkers I came across in many contexts, all of whom tutored me in ways big and small. They include Jay Rosen, Clay Shirky, Jeff Jarvis, Dan Gillmor, Peter Barron, Madhav Chinnappa, Rasmus Kleis Nielsen, Louis Rossetto, Frederic Filloux, Nicholas Negroponte, Ricken Patel, Richard Gingras, Ethan Zuckerman, Jonathan Zittrain, Melissa Bell, Yochai Benkler, Craig Newmark and Eric Schmidt.

We were, over 20 years, seldom out of legal hot water and I came to depend on a good many of m'learned friends. The best of them were not only hugely resourceful in finding ways to publish – rather than (as some lawyers prefer) not publish – but were passionate about defending freedom of expression. So, thank you Geraldine Proudler, Andrew Caldecott, Nick Stadlen, Gill Phillips, Nuala Cosgrove, Siobhain Butterworth, Zoe Norden, Jan Clements, Harry Boggis-Rolfe, George Carman, Heather Rogers, Michael Tugendhat, Mark Stephens, David Sherborne, David Schultz, Gavin Millar, Jennifer McDermott, Sarah Davis, Tamsin Allen, Ken Macdonald, Geoffrey Robertson, Ben Wizner, Shami Chakrabarti, Alex Bailin, Philippe Sands, Keir Starmer and many more, including the teams at English PEN, Article IX, Hacked Off, Big Brother Watch, Privacy International, Liberty and the Committee to Protect Journalists. Alex Wade read the manuscript of this book.

Hugo Young and Liz Forgan were wise owls at the helm of the Scott Trust. For as long as it has existed, the Trust had been led by people who had been – or still were – *Guardian* journalists. For an editor to be able to turn to such experienced and supportive colleagues for advice was a terrific help. I was very happy to have recruited sage heads like Ole Jacob Sunde, Vivian Schiller and Stuart Proffitt to the Trust. It was also important to me that descendants of C.P. Scott, Martin and Jonathan, were still active and incredibly understanding members of the Trust. Tall, lanky and erudite like their great-grandfather, they were truly part of the *Guardian*'s DNA.

The commercial leadership of the paper and division were, almost without exception, the closest of colleagues. I should particularly mention Jim Markwick, Caroline Marland, Bob Phillis, Amelia Fawcett,

Jeremy Bullmore, Paul Myners, Bob Gavron, Carolyn McCall, Tim Brooks, Andrew Miller, Marc Sands, Paul Naismith, Darren Singer, Brent Hoberman, Adam Freeman, Stuart Taylor, John Paton, Shaun Williams, Jo Murray, Camilla Nicholls, Derek Gannon, Joe Clark, Richard Furness, Eamonn Store, David Pemsel, Alan Hudson, Stella Beaumont, Dave Kirwan, Pippa Prior, Gennady Kolker, Caroline Little, Helen Bird, Nick Hewat, Steve Folwell, Ronan Dunne, Simon Fox, David Magliano, Chris Wade, Ian McClelland, Nick Castro, David Brook, Dave Boxall, Neil Berkett, Claire Enders, Douglas McCabe, Olly Purnell and Tony Danker. Graeme Wood was an exemplary philanthropist. I have been supported better than I deserved by Pauline Willis, Doreen Pallier, Helen Walmsley-Johnson, Keren Levy, Janet Wardell, Carla Betts and Casey Charlesworth.

Then there have been numerous conversations over the years with journalists – internal and external – who have helped shape my idea of the job we do and of the digital environment beyond. None of them, of course, bears any responsibility for my views, but I learned from our discussions. Thank you Robert McCrum, David Leigh, Jonathan Freedland, Jonathan Shainin, Mark Damazer, Joanna Coles, Jocelyn Targett, Mayank Banerjee, Will Hutton, Bob Silvers, Joel Simon, Paul Chadwick, Dan Roberts, Monique Villa, Wendy Berliner, Charlotte Higgins, Martin Chulov, Anthony Lewis, Tom Rosenstiel, Hannah Jane Parkinson, Henry Porter, Paul Lewis, Jill Abramson, Natalie Nougayrède, Javier Moreno, Alex Breuer, Glenn Greenwald, Lis Ribbans, Joris Luyendijk, Ewen MacAskill, Richard Norton-Taylor, Dean Baquet, Richard Lambert, Marty Baron, Ghaith Abdul-Ahad, Ian Black, Tom Clark, Polly Curtis, Stuart Millar, Peter Wolodarski, Mike Kinsley, Michael Tomasky, Harry Evans, Lionel Barber, Charlie Rose, John Mulholland, Martin Kettle, Paul Dacre, Gary Younge, Dan Sabbagh, Adam Gabbatt, Samantha Booth, Lisa O'Carroll, Arthur Sulzberger Jr, Ben Ferguson, Helen Boaden, Michael White, Patrick Wintour, Matt Wells, Paul Webster, Ronan Bennett, Carl Bernstein, John Hooper, Shaun Walker, Jon Henley, Charles Ferguson, Steve Hewlett, Sarah Lyall, N. Ram, Mark Scott, Merope Mills, Ian Sample, Sarah Boseley, Luke Harding, Bill McKibben, Marina Hyde,

ACKNOWLEDGEMENTS

James Randerson, Roy Greenslade, Alok Jha, Andrew Sparrow, Max Hastings, Stewart Steven, Simon Kelner, Simon Jenkins, Julian Borger, Amelia Gentleman, Madeleine Bunting, Murray Armstrong, Simon Hattenstone, Andrew Brown, David Carr, Jon Snow, Olena Prytula, Sevgil Musaieva-Borovyk, Kjersti Løken Stavrum, Bella Mackie, Roger Alton, Nesrine Malik, Clare Margetson, Dominic Ponsford, Nick Davies, Ian Cobain, Rob Evans, Emma Howard, Nick Hopkins, Paul Murphy, John Mullin, Felix Salmon, Georg Mascolo, Mathias Müller von Blumencron, Julia Finch, Maggie O'Kane, Ed Pilkington, Harriet Sherwood, Brian MacArthur, Julian Glover, David Folkenflik, Louise Roug, Jan Thompson, Ben Clissitt, Mark Porter, Ben Fenton, Dominic Young, Polly Toynbee, John-Allan Namu, Joseph Odindo, William Pike, Aditya Chakrabortty, Anne Perkins, Peter Taylor, Bill Keller, Frances Stead Sellers, Denis Foreman, Lenore Taylor, David Remnick, George Brock, Charlie Beckett, Ian Hargreaves, Mark Thompson, Lloyd Embley, Maya Wolfe-Robinson, Jamie Wilson, Richard Sambrook, Jim Brady, Paul Foot, Stephen Engelberg, Paul Steiger, Laura Poitras, Jean Seaton, Hugh Muir, Mathew Ingram, Damian Tambini, Sarah Ellison, Eleanor Randolph, Martin Moore, Jane Martinson, Andrew Marr, Charles Moore, Steve Bell, Alexander Chancellor, Jacob Weisberg, Kerry Paterson, Sidney Blumenthal, Michael Jackson, Nabeelah Shabbir, Frank Schirrmacher, Ian Mayes, Ed Vulliamy, David Rose, Laurence Topham, David Yellond, Guy Rolnik, Malcolm Turnbull, Peter Baron, Brian Cathcart and too many more to thank here.

In Oxford, a group of academics, including some connected with the Reuters Institute (RISJ), have held regular and fruitful discussions on the responsibilities and regulation of social media. They include David Levy, Heidi Taksdal Skjeseth and other fellows at the RISJ, Steve Ansolabehere, Alexandra Borchardt, Timothy Garton Ash, Meera Selva, Philip Howard, Campbell Brown, John Lloyd, Kate O'Regan, Michael Parks, James Painter, Nigel Shadbolt, Nick Newman, Lucy Küng, Patrick Walker and Geert Linnebank.

Rebecca Ashton, Iva Gavanski, Hugo Ewald, Sarah Farooqui and Miriam Stewart assisted with bits of research. Philippa Mole, archivist at the *Guardian*, was unfailingly helpful. Brendan O'Grady patiently dealt with requests for information and clarification about the *Guardian* today. Marilyn Anderson was a punctilious transcriber.

Jamie Byng and Simon Thorogood at Canongate and Alex Starr at Farrar, Straus and Giroux have been meticulous, encouraging and sensitive editors. Thank you, Octavia Reeve, Lorraine McCann, Leila Cruickshank and Vicki Rutherford, for eagle-eyed attention to the text. My agents, Rebecca Carter and Lyn Nesbit, have been endlessly supportive and wise. Jenny Fry, Jeff Seroy and their teams have helped bring the book to wider attention.

Most of the (numerous) people who helped me on the *Telegraph* chapter felt unable to speak publicly, mostly for contractual reasons. But thank you, anyway, for taking time to share your experience. And thanks, Peter Oborne, for agreeing to talk – on the record. Hugh Grant, Steve Coogan, Peter Jukes, Graham Johnson, Sienna Miller, Evan Harris and others involved in the long battle to establish the truth about phone hacking deserve some kind of a medal for walking towards the gunfire.

Finally, editing can all too easily become an all-consuming obsession. It was two years after stepping down before my adrenalin levels subsided and normal-ish sleep patterns resumed. I've already thanked Lindsay as well as Bella, our elder daughter, who was writing her own excellent first book in parallel with this one: I should also thank Lizzie, our second daughter, who very sensibly veered away from journalism and whose ever-acute external perspectives on news (and life) I've always relied on. Then there were the amateur musicians – Susanna Eastburn, Clive Coen, Richard Sennett, Tif Loehnis, Mark Prescott and Martin Prendergast – who did their part for my sanity by including me in their chamber music. Lisa Jardine was always a fascinating stimulater of new thoughts about journalism, as was Ed Miliband, occasional Hampstead Heath walking partner, whose intelligence and decency always provoked new ways of seeing things.

Alan Rusbridger
May 2018
London, Oxford, La Foce, Blockley

Notes

Introduction

1. Arendt, H. *The Origins of Totalitarianism; see Bibliography*
2. Politico, 19 February 2017
3. *Economist*, 23 June 2017
4. *Times of Israel*/Jewish Telegraphic Agency, 25 February 2017; Cnaan Liphshiz
5. *Times of Israel*, 7 June 2016; Lisa Klug
6. YouTube, 12 December 2016; Ami Horowitz
7. Mainstream media, or traditional forms of mass communication, viewed collectively.
8. *Aftonbladet*, 20 February 2017
9. *New York Times*, 20 February 2017
10. Bloomberg, 20 April 2017
11. The UK Independence Party (UKIP), a right-wing populist party that successfully campaigned for Britain to leave the European Union.
12. *Independent*, 21 February 2017
13. Twitter, 17 December 2017, 12.25 p.m.; @PeterSweden7
14. Twitter, 7 August 2016, 8.44 a.m.; @PeterSweden7
15. Twitter, 14 October 2016, 3.21 a.m.; @PeterSweden7
16. petersweden.com
17. Zack Beauchamp, on Vox, noted how Steve Bannon's website had published an 'enormous number of pieces' about the alleged migrant rape crisis in Sweden.

18. *Sydsvenska*, 20 December 2017

19. *The Local*, 13 February 2018

20. BBC, *Reality Check*, 24 February 2017

21. Not all billionaires were the same. The new publisher of the *New York Times*, A.G. Sulzberger, spoke of his family's ownership of the *New York Times* in terms which C.P. Scott, who edited the *Guardian* for 57 years and ended up owning it, would have recognised: 'One of the things it allows you to do is to build towards a longer time horizon. To make bets that pay off in decades or even generations, rather than this quarter or this year. And, when I look at all the decisions that my father, Arthur, made over the years, the one that was the most important was never to cut back on the size or ambition of our newsroom. Ultimately, that wasn't just good for our journalism; it was really good for our business. And it's what's left us in such a strong position today.' (*New Yorker* interview, 22 December 2017)

1 Not Bowling Alone

1. (1887–1976) Lancashire artist, known for his 'matchstick men' figures populating industrial landscapes.

2. (1929–2011) Pulitzer prize-winning columnist and broadcaster.

2 More Than a Business

1. Haslam Mills, W. *The Manchester Guardian: A Century of History*, 1921

2. Ayerst, D. *Guardian, Biography of a Newspaper*, 1936, p. 492

3. Ayerst, *Guardian,* p. 493

4. From the C.P. Scott essay 'On Journalism', printed in the *Manchester Guardian*, 5 May 1921. Reprinted in Scott, C.P. *The Making of the Manchester Guardian*, Frederick Muller, 1946

5. (1938–2018) Editor of the *Guardian* 1975–95.

6. In 1984, Fleet Street enjoyed a brief bonanza when virtually all national papers cashed in on historic holdings in the news agency Reuters. The *Guardian*'s share of the windfall from the flotation of Reuters, which had previously been a trust, was £26 million. As the media commentator Roy Greenslade put it, 'owners had discovered a gold mine'. For Rupert Murdoch, says Greenslade, it was 'just

the kind of fillip' he needed to plot a radical transformation of production in Fleet Street – sweeping away the entire hot-metal production methods of newspapers and replacing them with computerised typesetting.

7. The 1986 battle between the print unions and Rupert Murdoch over his new production plant in East London.

8. By 2017 the league table was more or less the same in order, but the numbers were drastically different. The *Financial Times*'s sales in the UK were around 65,000. The *Guardian* was selling 156,000 – roughly what it had sold in the mid -'50s. The *Telegraph* was selling 472,000, the *Mirror* 724,000, the *Daily Mail* 1.5 million and the *Sun* 1.6 million.

9. Czech-born businessman and media proprietor who died in mysterious circumstances when he fell off his yacht in 1991.

3 The New World

1. Negroponte, N. *Being Digital*. New York: Alfred A. Knopf, 1995

2. 'Thanks, Gutenberg – But We're Too Pressed for Time to Read', *Observer*, 27 January 2008

3. The *LA Times*, by comparison had 21 newsroom people on its digital operation. The *San Jose Mercury* had 16 on staff, plus nine freelancers.

4. The *New York Times* regained significant control over its archive in December 1994.

5. Scott had previously been MD, Marketing, Planning and Research. He left the *New York Times* in 1995 and is currently running a website in West Hollywood.

6. In fact it would be 13 years before the first Amazon Kindle. The first-generation iPad was launched in 2010 – 16 years later.

7. 'The Death of the Cyberflâneur', *New York Times*, 4 February 2012

4 Editor

1. Hamilton ended up out of politics and bankrupt – though he returned some 20 years later in another incarnation representing the UK Independence Party, UKIP, in the Welsh Assembly.

2. He was, we later learned, receiving treatment for the prostate cancer that was to kill him six years later.

3. The so-called reverse burden of truth was a feature of the 1996 libel action launched by holocaust-denying historian David Irving. The defendant, Deborah Lipstadt, had to risk $3 million to prove the essence of the claims against Irving. The judge, Mr Justice Gray (who had been Aitken's QC), summed up the position: 'Defamatory words are presumed under English law to be untrue.' The case was the centrepiece of the 2017 film *Denial*, starring Rachel Weisz as Lipstadt.

4. Max Hastings, as editor of the *Telegraph* and then the *Evening Standard*, was notably supportive. The *Spectator* was almost obsessively hostile.

5. In 2018 prices.

6. Gray later told Carman's son, Dominic: 'It was the biggest surprise I'd had in a courtroom. I was absolutely staggered. He was unbelievably plausible, and I never would have conceived that anyone would take the gamble he took. He didn't need to sue.'

7. Aitken, J. *Pride and Perjury*; *see Bibliography*

8. His legal bill would be close to £2 million. He eventually sold his Lord North Street house for £2.1 million in 2001, and his constituency home, owned by a Panamanian company, for around £500,000.

5 Shedding Power

1. 'Newspapers try to cover everything because they used to have to be all things to all people in their markets. So they had their own reporters replicate the work of other reporters elsewhere so they could say that they did it under their own bylines as a matter of pride and propriety. It's the way things were done . . . But in the age of the link, this is clearly inefficient and unnecessary. You can link to the stories that someone else did and to the rest of the world. And if you do that, it allows you to reallocate your dwindling resources to what matters, which in most cases should be local coverage.' – Buzzmachine blog, 22 February 2007

2. First produced at the Almeida Theatre, London, in June 2017.

3. (1929–2000) Editor of the *Sun* 1969–72 and 1975–81.

4. (b. 1946) Editor of the *Sun* 1981–94.

5. Chippendale, P. and Horrie, C. *Stick It Up Your Punter: The Rise and Fall of the Sun*; *see Bibliography*

6. (1919–99) Editor of the *Daily Mail* 1963–66; Randall, M. *The Funny Side of the Street*. London: Bloomsbury, 1988

7. Contrast with descriptions of *Daily Mail* morning conferences in Adrian Addison's recent book, *Mail Men* (*see Bibliography*): 'Dacre takes all conferences from behind his very large oak desk in his huge office. It's very plush and chintzy, a bit like a hotel room. Posh, thick beige carpet, curtains, flat screen telly, lots of sofas . . . Stories are printed out for him to read, on paper.' After an initial meeting of senior editors, the news editor and picture editor join in and the meeting 'usually descends into Dacre having a go at the news editor for all the stories he thinks the paper missed or didn't cover well'.

8. 'I take it for granted . . . that my readers know more than I do – and this is a liberating, not threatening, fact of journalistic life.' Gillmor, D., *We the Media*; *see Bibliography*

9. Four readers' editors later, the system is now firmly embedded in the *Guardian* and *Observer*. Elsewhere, the story has been more patchy. As newsroom economics have become more pressed, some organisations in America have got rid of the equivalent figure – sometimes called ombudsman or public editor. Some frankly admitted they were too costly; others argued that social media now held newspapers to account. Conversely, the BBC – hit by a highly critical report of its journalism by Lord Hutton in 2004 – created a role not dissimilar to an ombudsman in print.

6 Guardian . . . Unlimited

1. (b. 1967) Ian Katz had joined the *Guardian* to edit a Young Guardian page in 1990. He was a reporter, New York correspondent and editor of G2 before ending up as deputy editor. He left the *Guardian* in 2013 to become editor of the BBC current affairs programme, *Newsnight*. He was a candidate for *Guardian* editor in 2015. In late 2017 it was announced he would be C4's director of programmes.

2. (b. 1957) Neville Brody had designed *The Face* and *Arena* magazines. He subsequently carried out redesigns for the BBC and the *Times*.

3. The deputy internet editor, Simon Waldman, claims to have suggested the name, based on his father's Manchester shop, Fabrix Unlimited.

4. To bridge the gulf between the two newsrooms we offered cut-price deals on Macs for use at home, with instructions on how to connect them via a dial-up service.

5. *Guardian*, 23 January 1999; Ian Mayes
6. *Guardian*, 23 October 1999; Ian Mayes

7 The Conversation

1. Hagel, J. and Singer, M. *Net Worth*; *see Bibliography*
2. Ofek, E. and Richardson, M. 'DotCom Mania'; *see Bibliography*
3. Both were eventually poached to starrier things. Simon became group product director for Lovefilm and then director of product research for Sky; and Emily became the first director of the Tow Center for Digital Journalism at Columbia Journalism School.
4. Rohm, W.G. *The Murdoch Mission*; *see Bibliography*
5. Rohm, W.G. *The Murdoch Mission*; *see Bibliography*, p. 240
6. A Primary Care Trust in the UK National Health Service.
7. Available at: https://helenblackman.wordpress.com/2011/02/27/ode-to-gut-or-the-death-of-a-talkboard/
8. A serious legal problem led to the site being closed down in February 2011. By then the main forum for discussion on the *Guardian* was on Comment is Free, where there was much more active moderation.
9. The Audit Bureau of Circulations (ABC) measured newspaper sales each month – including sales at full price or 'bulk sales' for the benefit of advertising agencies and their clients.
10. The *Express* circulation in 2017 was 392,000. By March 2018 its full-price sale was 318,000.
11. An old-fashioned newspaper war broke out between Desmond and the proprietor of the *Daily Mail*, Lord Rothermere. The *Mail* unwisely decided to use its normal attack methods and snoop out Desmond's private life. Desmond responded by looking into Rothermere's private life. A truce was rapidly arranged. The *Express*, by then selling 364,000 copies a day, was resold to Trinity Mirror in early 2018.
12. Brown, C. 'State of the American Newspaper'; *see Bibliography*
13. The *Financial Times* started to charge in 2002.
14. Filloux, F. Monday Note; *see Bibliography*

8 Global

1. Goldman, W. *Adventures in the Screen Trade: A Personal View of Hollywood*. London: MacDonald & Co, 1984: 'Nobody knows anything . . . Not one person in the entire motion picture field knows for a certainty what's going to work. Every time out it's a guess and, if you're lucky, an educated one.'

2. About 30,000 in 2005.

3. Research showed that, even in 2002, only 16 per cent of students saw a broadsheet newspaper in any given week against 42 per cent looking at the internet every day.

4. Alan Mutter, 2009; available at: http://newsosaur.blogspot.co.uk/2009/02/mission-possible-charging-for-content.html

5. Arrese, Á. 'From Gratis to Paywalls', *Journalism Studies*, Vol. 17 No. 8 (2016), pp. 1051–1067

6. Sullivan retired from blogging 15 years later after experimenting with a standalone website charging $20 a year as well as moving his blog for a while to the *Atlantic Monthly*.

9 Format Wars

1. Editor 1938–56

2. We also had two health correspondents, one of whom, Sarah Boseley, had been covering the patch for years and who was infinitely careful – avoiding the bewildering scares, fads, miracle cures and pharma-boostering that passed for medical coverage in some quarters. We also gave a column, Bad Science, to a 29-year-old medical doctor and academic, Ben Goldacre, who for ten years eviscerated and ridiculed the misuse of science and statistics by journalists – as well as politicians, drugs companies and quacks. His column won few friends in Fleet Street: his filleting of some science journalism was often toe-curlingly embarrassing. The medical correspondents hated it; the public loved it. His first book, based on his columns, sold half a million copies and was published in 18 countries.

3. All significant decisions were scrutinised by three boards – the (divisional) Guardian News and Media Board; the (overall) Guardian Media Group and the Scott Trust.

4. The main building was eventually demolished in 2017.

5. (b. 1957) His previous career included work at the *Observer* magazine, deputy sports editor at the *Independent,* and *Daily Mail* magazine editor.

6. Available at: http://ajrarchive.org/article.asp?id=4223

7. It wasn't even clear that we could physically produce the papers in a viable form on the clapped out, mainly black-and-white presses we were using in London and Manchester. The maximum tabloid pagination we could print straight was 160 pages. We could pre-print some sections and combine them – with the additional complication that you could mechanically insert sections inside each other in Manchester, not in London. To have a multiple section paper in the South involved paying newsagents to hand-insert each copy.

   We toyed with the idea of publishing the jobs sections separately. We looked into attaching insertion machinery in London (not possible, we found), or purchasing staplers to stop the papers falling apart (ditto: you could only stitch 40 pages at a time). I became an expert in press configurations, listening intently as the production director explained how we could just about produce a tabloid with two folders, with one book of 40 tabloid pages that could be run on one machine, with the rest of the paper produced in three separate 'books', with the first tabloid then inserted back into the other three books. We could print 'collect' – two books of 48 pages, with the presses running slower. To get above 112 pages we'd need to do two runs and insert one into another to produce a Russian doll of a paper, with a three- or four-section book. That way we could at least print 212 pages to accommodate the advertising. Stapling individual sections looked very doubtful.

8. Walker, C. 'Small Times, Bad Times', *British Journalism Review*, Vol. 16 No. 2, (2005)

9. Stead Sellers, F. 'Embracing Change', *American Journalism Review*, 2006

10. The *Times* front page, 19 April 2012

11. By June 2017 the *Metro* had overtaken the *Sun* in terms of average weekday copies – 1,479,775 copies a day.

12. One of our leader writers, Malcolm Dean, took part in these discussions and later went on to write a book about this intersection between the people who did things – whether policymakers or executives – and those of us simply writing about them. He eventually produced seven case studies, spread across a wide spectrum: penal policy, drug reform, asylum legislation, child poverty,

health and social care, vocational education and housing. Dean identified what he termed the 'seven deadly sins' of journalism: distortion, group think, too adversarial, dumbing down, too readily duped, more interested in politics than policy and, worst of all, concentration on the negative. 'Add them together,' he concluded, 'and it is no wonder the public have become disillusioned with politics and policy-making.' (Dean, M. *Democracy Under Attack*; *See Bibliography*)

13. Foley, M. 'Sound Bites: Rethinking the Circulation of Speech from Fragment to Fetish', *Rhetoric and Public Affairs*, Vol. 15 No. 4 (2012), pp. 613–22

14. 'The Path Back to Trust, Truth and Integrity', extract in the *Guardian*, 16 January 2005

15. The *Telegraph* had earmarked £100 million to £150 million for new presses. Associated had set aside £231 million to get 100 per cent colour by the end of 2007.

16. The size was web width: 1260mm; cut-off: 470mm.

17. There was little formal press commentary at the time. One of the most prominent commentators, Stephen Glover, subsequently wrote critically of the Berliner. But at the time he applauded our moves. 'This [the Berliner format] would be a better solution than dashing into the market with an inadequate tabloid. Mr Rusbridger may be playing a long game.' (24 April 2004) And: 'It seems to me probable that Rusbridger has made the right decision. The *Independent* went tabloid out of desperation. It was a last throw of the dice which has worked out better than almost anyone could have hoped. The position of the *Guardian* was different. It did not find itself in the same dire straits as the *Independent*. Moreover, bulging as it does with classified advertising dropped into its lap by HMG, it could not have adopted the tabloid form without being disagreeably chunky. If Mr Rusbridger had agreed two years ago to take his newspaper tabloid, it might have enjoyed the same kind of circulation lift as the *Independent* has done. But where would it have led? . . . All in all, this looks to me very far from the mess that Mr Rusbridger's critics claim it to be.' (3 July 2004)

18. There was complete agreement between editorial and commercial – the managing director of the *Guardian*, Carolyn McCall (now Dame Carolyn McCall, CEO of EasyJet), and Paul Myners, the chair of GMG, who later, as Lord Myners, went on to chair Marks & Spencer and the Trustees of the Tate, and was to be at the centre of the Treasury's successful attempts to shore up the

British banking system after the world economic crash of 2008/9. The project was significantly led by Paul Johnson, deputy editor, and executive editor Sheila Fitzsimons, along with directors of production, operations and print, Joe Clark, Derek Gannon and Dave Kirwan. Our in-house art director, Mark Porter, was to design the new paper. The presses were built by MAN Roland. The typography also involved Christian Schwartz and Paul Barnes, who cut a new Egyptian face for both headlines and text.

19. In 2017 the *Times* was still giving away 82,000 copies a day in so-called 'bulk' sales. The *Guardian* abandoned them in August 2009.

20. Within seven years (2009) the *Independent* had been bought by former KGB agent Alexander Lebedev and his son Evgeny for £1. By 2016 it was selling just 55,000 copies a day and the Russians quietly closed down the printed newspaper. The *i* – a cheaper digest of the mother paper – was sold to Johnson Press for £24 million.

11 The Future Is Mutual

1. There are those who think we invented the form, at least in mainstream news and sport.

2. Rob Smyth, Sean Ingle, Mike Adamson and James Dart.

3. Created in September 2005 by the web gurus Tim O'Reilly and John Battelle.

4. By 2017 it was reported to have 315 million members and more than 500 million reviews.

5. In December 2017 a *Vice* writer, Oobah Butler, succeeded in getting a fake restaurant to the number one London ranking on TripAdvisor. To prove a point.

6. 'The trouble with travel in Freebieland', *Independent*, 28 August 2000; Simon Calder

7. But even the *Independent* had, by then, 'relaxed' its policy because its expanded coverage was unaffordable: 'the only way the figures could add up was to accept some free facilities from the travel industry'; i.e. the *Independent* had joined virtually everyone else in Freebieland.

8. An idea shamelessly borrowed – with attribution – from *Slate* magazine, which had been blogging the Bible. Its author, David Plotz, described that experiment as the most rewarding journalistic year of his life, which resulted in more than 10,000 emails.

9. 'Blogging the Qur'an', *Guardian*, 7 January 2008; Ziauddin Sardar

10. Journalist, novelist, former *Vanity Fair* UK editor and a campaigner on civil liberties.

11. 'tl;dr, abbrev.: "too long didn't read": used as a dismissive response to a lengthy online post, or to introduce a summary of a lengthy post.' – Oxford Dictionaries blog, August 2013

12. Levin had been a columnist for the *Times* in the late twentieth century – and had had a long relationship with the young Arianna Huffington. Utley was a much revered blind political columnist for the *Telegraph*.

13. The *New York Times* innovation report in 2014 reported the *Huffington Post*'s US audience to be 32 million in August 2013, reaching a high of 40 million in November that year (against 33 million for the *New York Times*).

12 The Money Question

1. By 2017 it was 42,000 and the new owners had started a weekly free newspaper.

2. Local World's net worth was £13.7 million in 2015.

3. The same was happening all over. Newspapers believed they owned the classified advertising market. Johnston Press, which had expanded on a tide of debt in the 1990s, stated in its 2007 annual report: 'We expect our newspapers to continue to be the main source of promotional and marketing activity for the majority of estate agents.' As the media academic Keith Perch noted: 'They were wrong. In the previous 12 months, JP had taken £80m in revenue for property advertising. In 2014, it took just £22.5m. In the same period, Rightmove had gone from zero revenue to more than £167m (Rightmove Plc 2014). Another online property site, Zoopla, which did not launch until 2008 (Zoopla Plc 2015), has seen its revenues grow to more than £80m (Zoopla Plc 2014). In the eight years after Zoopla launched, the two internet-only businesses grew online revenues to £247m between them.' Quoted in Mair, J. and Clark, T. *Last Words?*; *see Bibliography*

4. Williams, F. *Dangerous Estate: The Anatomy of Newspapers*. London: Longmans Green & Co, 1957

5. Starr, P. 'Goodbye to the Age of Newspapers (Hello to a New Era of Corruption)', *New Republic*, 4 March 2009

6. Hirsch, F. and Gordon, D. *Newspaper Money: Fleet Street and the Search for an Affluent Reader*. London: Hutchinson, 1975. Hirsch was Professor of International Studies at Warwick University, David Gordon went on to chair the *Economist*.

7. It was an entirely different challenge on the tabloids, where social class mattered less: 'readers are weighed rather than counted'.

13 Bee Information

1. Clay Shirky, 'Newspapers and Thinking the Unthinkable', 13 March 2009. Available at: http://www.shirky.com/weblog/2009/03/newspapers-and-think-ing-the-unthinkable/
2. (b. 1984) Mark Zuckerberg is founder, chairman and CEO of Facebook.
3. Murdoch had also splurged $650 million on IGN, a video-game company, in 2005. He sold it six years later. He also bought Scout.com, which, as Scout Media, filed for Chapter 11 bankruptcy in December 2016; and Propertyfinder.com, which he sold four years later. He also started Globrix, another property search firm. It failed. The point is not to highlight his failures, but to show that even the smartest, most commercially minded brains in media were blundering around splashing vast sums of money on things that didn't work.
4. Shirky, C. *Here Comes Everybody*; *See Bibliography*
5. 'However Much Is in Your Facebook, It Ain't a New Google', *Observer*, 22 July 2007; John Naughton
6. *Guardian*, 20 October 2007; Andrew Clark
7. Twitter's audience – though vast compared with most mainstream media companies – was a relatively modest 330 million monthly active users in early 2018.
8. 'Twitter Has Lost a Staggering Amount of Money', *Time* magazine, 29 February 2016
9. 'Classified Advertising in Print and Online', *Enders Analysis*, November 2006
10. 'Improving the Daily Telegraph's Internet News Service' (16pp), 16 November 2006; Andrew Sparrow

14 Creaking at the Seams

1. See the *Economist* on *Le Monde*'s new owners, 28 June 2010.
2. One of the architects of that transition was Andrew Miller, its CFO, who later became CEO of GMG.
3. One person watching us closely was Lord Rothermere, proprietor of the *Daily Mail*, who had exactly the same dilemma. He told Newsworks' Shift conference

in 2013: 'We started seeing a lot of traffic from the US and we didn't know how to monetise it, so it was a bit irritating to be honest with you in the beginning . . . I remember reading an interview with [*Guardian* editor] Rusbridger, and he was talking about making the *Guardian* "a global newspaper" and I thought "actually, that's a pretty cool idea". So I started talking to Paul [Dacre] and co. and said "Why don't we follow the traffic? Why don't we put some people into California – into LA?" And that worked. Then they said we really want to be in New York, that's the centre, that's the place to be for news journalism. So we started building a team in New York. And it's just continued to grow, we just followed our success if you like. It's really that simple'. (Quoted in Addison, *Mail Men*; *see Bibliography*)

4. Dixon had been hired by a Newcastle-based developer, Peter Millican, who wanted a concert hall in the basement which he would run. He got it.

5. Anderson, C. *The Long Tail*; *see Bibliography*

6. The logistical genius behind this was Sheila Fitzsimons, who – as well as being strategically acute and a proper human being – could do numbers and operations. All newspapers need their version of Sheila, who, because she never got a byline, would be unknown to any *Guardian* reader.

7. First on the *Observer*, more latterly on the *Guardian*.

8. In December 2010 a judge said he was 'astonished' at claims that BAE Systems had not acted corruptly when its executives made illicit payments.

9. Timothy Evans was pardoned in 1966, 16 years after his execution.

10. Evans highlighted the plight of 370 known victims of the drug Thalidomide, which caused major birth deformities in babies. They eventually secured £2.5 million in compensation – ten times what they were originally offered. The story is told in the 2016 film *Attacking the Devil*.

11. Thankfully, there remain pockets of good investigative reporting. In Britain assorted national newspapers have delved into child-abuse rings; MPs' extravagance; athletes and doping; the murder of Stephen Lawrence; tax avoidance and more. But – judging annual awards in memory of the late Paul Foot (1937– 2004), a great reporter for *Private Eye* and the *Guardian* – Ian Hislop (*Eye* editor) and I noticed the same, small (and diminishing) pool of reporters entering their work each year.

12. Richard Ingrams (b. 1937) and Ian Hislop (b. 1960), editors of *Private Eye* from 1962 to the present day.

15 Crash

1. The savage effects of the recession were monitored by former *Washington Post* editor Len Downie and Columbia professor Michael Schudson, in their joint study on how to rebuild the industry: 'The Reconstruction of American Journalism', *Columbia Journalism Review*, November/December 2009.

2. Hinton, L. 'They're Stealing Our Lifeblood', *British Journalism Review*, September 2009

3. McCabe, D. 'Will Consumers Pay for Online News?', *Enders Analysis*, 27 May 2009

4. (b. 1937) Later British ambassador to Washington.

5. Quoted in 'Why Didn't the City Journalists See the Financial Crisis Coming?', *Observer*, 12 October 2008; James Robinson

6. Tesco sued three Thai critics for libel. The company dropped one action after two years. Another was settled after an apology. The criminal libel suit against a former MP, Jit Siratranont, was dismissed by a court in June 2009.

7. A longer account of this action was published in the *New York Review of Books*, 15 January 2009.

8. Tesco employed expensive City PR firms during the action. It emerged that GMG itself had used a tax avoidance mechanism. This was not welcome news, since it opened us to the charge of hypocrisy. Two of our own reporters investigated it (*Guardian*, 3 May 2008). And then I asked *Private Eye*'s tax investigator, Richard Brooks, to write about it on our website. He found little to object to in one above-board use of tax relief intended by parliament. But he added: 'More debatable is the transaction to acquire Emap in a joint venture with Apax, which was structured to avoid stamp duty. GMG says the technique was explicitly accepted by HMRC. Others might think any step to avoid a tax by putting it through the Cayman Islands counts as tax avoidance, no matter how resigned the taxman is to it' (2 February 2009).

   The truth was that if newspapers could not write about tax avoidance unless they themselves were clean then the subject would not be covered at all. The fact we wrote about it was, if you like, a further separation of editorial and commercial. But I was unhappy at GMG's use of offshore structures and probably should have said so at the time.

9. One result of the Tesco action was that a 2013 reform of England and Wales's libel laws made it more difficult for companies to sue for libel. A company now had to show it had suffered or was likely to suffer serious harm because of a defamatory statement. It would only be able to do that if it could show it had suffered, or was likely to suffer, serious financial harm. That would have made it very difficult for Tesco to go to law.

10. Martínez, A. García *Chaos Monkeys*; *see Bibliography*. Described as 'a remarkably learned book' by Jonathan A. Knee, professor of Professional Practice at Columbia Business School, *New York Times*, 28 June 2016.

16 Phone Hacking

1. Davies, N. *Flat Earth News*; *see Bibliography*

2. 'Riots, Terrorism etc.', *London Review of Books*, 6 March 2008; John Lanchester

3. A memorably dismissive column was penned by Stephen Glover in the *Independent* that Sunday. Nick Davies, he wrote scornfully, 'was the sort of journalist who can find a scandal in a jar of tadpoles'.

4. In the end the PCC's dismal report turned out to be the organisation's suicide note. Stig Abell, now editor of the *Times Literary Supplement*, but at the time deputy director of the regulator, has since revealed that an early draft of the report was personally critical of me. 'I begged for [the personal criticism] to be removed. It was, but to little avail. The PCC was on the wrong side of history, and was therefore soon to be consigned to it.' (Abell, S. *How Britain Really Works*. London: John Murray, 2018)

5. News Corporation owned 39 per cent of BSkyB. If the company succeeded in its bid for the remaining 61 per cent, it cleared the way to integrate it with other companies such as Sky Deutschland and Sky Italia. Most other newspaper groups, as well as the BBC, C4 and British Telecom, opposed the takeover, arguing that it would have 'serious and far-reaching consequences for media plurality'.

6. 'Tabloid Hack Attack on Royals, and Beyond', *New York Times*, 1 September 2010; Don Van Natta Jr, Jo Becker and Graham Bowley

7. The Labour politicians Tom Watson, Chris Bryant and Paul Farrelly were among the MPs who risked much to pursue the issue.

8. A joint byline: Nick Davies and Amelia Hill.

9. The story also said – in the seventh paragraph – that voicemail messages had been deleted by *News of the World* journalists, giving false hope to Milly's parents that she might still be alive. A subsequent police inquiry found that there were, indeed, missing messages, but that it was impossible to ascertain whether they had been manually deleted. The doubts raised about this sentence were later seized on by opponents of the resultant Leveson Inquiry to suggest that the outrage over the story was falsely based. The head of the inquiry, Lord Justice Leveson, dismissed this line of attack. 'It is sufficient for present purposes to state that the main thrust of the article published in the *Guardian* on 4 July 2011, that Milly Dowler's voicemail was hacked into by *NoW* journalists, was correct. As the Dowlers explained in their witness statement, they received substantial compensation from News International (NI) to mark the egregious conduct of their employees. Even if that conduct did not embrace causing the "false hope moment", its characterisation as egregious remains apposite . . . in the light of all the circumstances, had [the story] been couched in more cautious or less certain terms it may not have been capable of criticism at all. It certainly did not justify the attack that followed: I am certainly not criticising it or the paper. Nor, as I pointed out on 4 December 2011, does the *Guardian*'s error in any way undermine the reasons for setting up, or the work of, this Inquiry, despite what some have suggested. The fact remains that the *NoW* hacked the phone of a dead schoolgirl called Milly Dowler. The revelation of that story rightly shocked the public conscience in a way that other stories of phone hacking may not have, but it also gave momentum to growing calls for light to be shed on an unethical and unlawful practice of which there were literally thousands of victims. In that context, whether or not *NoW* journalists had caused the "false hope" moment is almost irrelevant.'

10. Hinton, L. *The Bootle Boy: An Untidy Life in News*. London: Scribe Publications, 2018

11. *Guardian*, 21 May 2015

12. *Guardian*, 5 February 2018

13. *Press Gazette*, 8 May 2015

14. Greg Miskiw, Neville Thurlbeck, James Weatherup and Ian Edmondson.

15. Glenn Mulcaire, reporters Dan Evans and Clive Goodman, and another executive, Jules Stenson.

16. Davies, N. *Hack Attack*; *see Bibliography*

17. *Daily Mail*, 6 September 2014

18. The bid ran into regulatory hurdles and was then overtaken when Disney and then Comcast made rival bids for parts of Murdoch's empire.

17 Let Us Pay?

1. Starr, P. *The Creation of the Media*; *see Bibliography*

2. 'Goodbye to the Age of Newspapers (Hello to a New Era of Corruption)', *New Republic*, 4 March 2009; Paul Starr

3. Quoted in 'Newspapers Last Bastion Against Political Corruption'; Oliver Burkeman, *Guardian*, 27 March 2009

4. A reasoned case for the power of 'open information' had been advanced in 2004 by the author James Surowiecki in his book *The Wisdom of Crowds*; *see Bibliography*.

5. An inquest found he had been unlawfully killed. The policeman who struck him was found not guilty after the jury deliberated for four days. He was dismissed from the police for 'gross misconduct' towards Tomlinson, and for using 'excessive and unlawful force'.

6. Three G4S security guards were cleared of his manslaughter in 2014. Deportation escorts were subsequently trained in safer restraint methods.

7. The *Guardian* teamed up with the London School of Economics to examine the causes and effects of the riots, in an empirical study supported by the Open Society and the Joseph Rowntree Foundation.

8. 'Rocket Man', *New Yorker*, 25 November 2013; Patrick Radden Keefe

9. Fletcher, R. and Nielsen, R.K. 'Is social media use associated with more or less diverse news use?'; *see Bibliography*

10. Cobain, I. *Cruel Britannia: A Secret History of Torture*. London: Portobello Books, 2012

11. *Guardian*, 10 May 2018

12. *Not on the Label* (2004); *Eat Your Heart Out* (2008)

13. Later a book, *Undercover* (2014), published by Guardian Faber.

14. A human crush at Sheffield Wednesday's football stadium on 15 April 1989 during a semi-final between Liverpool and Nottingham Forest, in which 96 fans died and 766 were injured. Police initially blamed fans for causing the crush.

In 2016 an inquest found the victims had been unlawfully killed following police failures.

15. The in-house team included Siobhain Butterworth, Nuala Cosgrove, Gillian Phillips, Jan Clements, Zoe Norden and Harry Boggis Rolfe. As external lawyers and counsel we frequently used Geraldine Proudler, Andrew Caldecott, Gavin Millar, George Carman and – in one notable libel trial – Nick Stadlen.

16. Ghaith continued to get into trouble. In March 2011 I had to fly to Tripoli – on the eve of Allied air strikes – to help extricate him from jail.

17. This had begun to change in Germany, with Springer AG adopting a paywall model for *Die Welt* and *Bild* in December 2009. In France some papers launched new plans to charge for online news. New tablet editions marked a change of strategies in Italy and Spain.

18. Brown, C. 'State of the American Newspaper. FEAR.COM; (*see Bibliography*. 'By the end of the decade, the general consensus in the world of the press was that free online news content would attract massive readerships, whose accumulated attention could be sold efficiently to advertisers.' Alves, R. 'The Future of Online Journalism: Mediamorphosis or Mediacide', *info*, Vol. 3 No. 1 (2001), pp. 63–72)

19. Arresse, Ángel, 'From Gratis to Paywalls', *Journalism Studies*, Vol. 17 No. 8, (2016), pp. 1051–1067

20. One problem with evaluating the economics of paywalls remains the opacity of much of the data. In November 2011 a *Forbes* article claimed *Newsday* had in fact achieved growth to 112,486 daily digital copies. But it transpired that only 935 of these were true paid copies.

21. Hewlett presented the show for nine years until his untimely death in 2017.

22. The *Guardian/Observer* editorial budget was now nearer £70 million.

23. It did. Gledhill left the *Times* in May 2014, when the paper axed the position of full-time religious affairs correspondent.

24. Hirsch and Gordon, *see Bibliography*

25. Office of National Statistics

26. We were not alone: 'hardly 15 per cent of media companies'' managers thought that charging for digital news content would be a significant source of income, according to a study carried out in 2010 by the Pew Research Center's Project for Excellence in Journalism: *Paying for Digital Content*. Washington, DC: Pew Center, 2010

27. 'Let Us Pay', *London Review of Books*, 16 December 2010; John Lanchester

28. The chances of a Spotify model for news working were dismissed by the digital commentator Frederic Filloux. For him, the maths simply didn't work – and he assumed that, in time, Apple and other digital giants would move into 'soft' areas of the news business such as entertainment, lifestyle and sport. This would leave the legacy news players with the 'hard' (i.e. unprofitable) areas to themselves. (Monday Note, 5 March 2018)

29. The new owners of the *Independent* and *Evening Standard* had turned the latter into a freesheet.

30. 'Willingness to Pay for News Online', Boston Consulting Group, November 2009

31. They did: Buzzfeed, *Vice*, Politico and many more specialist services.

32. And still no one knows. Eight years after that debate with Witherow the *Times* continues to charge and the *Guardian* – three years after I stepped down – continues to be free. Both sides continue to insist they have the right models. I subscribe to both titles online. The lure for me to take out a *Times* subscription was that, in return for paying £312 over a year, they would give me a Nespresso coffee machine worth £170. Even assuming the *Times* got the machines for far less than that – and threw in some native advertising on the side – it looked as if the paper was having to throw considerable bait to acquire and retain subscribers.

33. *New Yorker*, 15 February 2013; Tim Wu

34. We were lucky to have some brilliant digital brains working for us. Commercially, we had just lost Carolyn McCall, who had gone off to run EasyJet and, subsequently ITV. She and I had worked incredibly closely and harmoniously: she was to be replaced first by Tim Brooks, who went on to run the *British Medical Journal*, and then by Andrew Miller, an amiable Scottish accountant who had overseen the transition from print to digital of *AutoTrader*. Miller is now managing director at Terra Firma Capital Partners.

35. Gorwa, R. 'Digging Up Facts About Fake News: The Computational Propaganda Project', Oxford Internet Project, 7 August 2017

36. Edelman Trust Barometer, 2018: 63 per cent did not know how to tell good journalism from rumour or falsehood. 59 per cent agreed with the statement 'I am not sure what is true and what is not'.

37. A good summary can be found at http://schugurensky.faculty.asu.edu/moments

/1922lippdew.html and at https://theelectricagora.com/2015/10/02/lippmann-and-dewey-debating-democracy-in-age-of-the-metropolis/

38. Chomsky placed Lippmann in a tradition of thought about indoctrination that led to Edward Bernays, the 'father of spin', who settled for the phrase 'the engineering of consent'.

39. McChesney, R. and Pickard, V. (eds) *Will the Last Reporter Please Turn Out the Lights*; *see Bibliography*

40. Gove, M. *Financial Times*, 3 June 2016

41. The 2018 Edelman Trust Barometer found 61 per cent of people willing to trust an academic expert; 54 per cent trusted 'a person like yourself'; 39 per cent trusted a journalist. This showed a decline in trust for peers and (maybe stimulated by the 'Trump Bump') an uptick in trust for journalists.

18 Open and Shut

1. There may be reporters (not TV anchors or commentators) with more Twitter followers, but they are few and far between.

2. (b. 1983) A former NSA employee, who was the source of multiple documents disclosing the extent of surveillance by the NSA, GCHQ and other intelligence agencies.

3. Luyendijk, J. *People Like Us*; *see Bibliography*

4. *Guardian*, 30 November 2010; Stephen Moss

5. *NRC Handelsblad*

6. *Swimming with Sharks*, in English (Guardian Faber, 2015); *Dit kan niet waar zijn*, in Dutch.

7. Luyendijk even published his fee at the foot of his columns.

8. Mo Mowlam (1949–2005) was then a Cabinet minister heading the government's anti-drugs campaign. She admitted that she had smoked cannabis as a student.

9. A good introduction to the early days of Ophan, co-created by Graham Tackley, can be found by Abigail Edge at journalism.co.uk, 2 December 2014.

10. 'What I Learned from Seven Years as the *Guardian*'s Audience Editor', Medium, 23 November 2016; Chris Moran

11. A very high proportion of the 512,000 teachers in the UK.

12. Theartsdesk.com had started in 2009 with a team of critics, many of whom had

been laid off by national newspapers. In 2013 the *Independent on Sunday* became the first national paper to get rid of all its critics.

13. Q&A, *Guardian*, 9 December 2017; Peter Bradshaw

14. Tapscott, D and Williams, A.D. *Wikinomics*; *see Bibliography*

15. David Cameron, House of Commons, 13 July 2011

16. The UK media regulator. In its report, 'Public Opinion on the BBC and BBC News' (2017), Sky News scored 5 per cent. The *Guardian* and *Financial Times* 2 per cent.

17. Rosen became an adviser to the Netherlands-based De Correspondent as it sought, in 2018, to open a US operation.

18. Pemsel had a background in advertising and media marketing. He joined the *Guardian* as CMO in 2011 before assuming wider commercial responsibilities. As deputy CEO he ran the US operation, was responsible for all commercial revenues and ran the Membership scheme, including the idea of having a central London centre for events. He became CEO in July 2015.

19. The film scooped up numerous awards at the 2012 Cannes Lions festival – the annual jamboree of international 'creativity'. It was written by David Kolbusz and directed by Ringan Ledwidge.

20. Keith, S. 'Sinking Subs and Collapsing Copy Desks', conference paper, New Brunswick, NJ: Rutgers University, September 2009

21. He published a book about the revolution: Shenker, J. *The Egyptians*; *see Bibliography*.

19 The Gatekeepers

1. It was released as *The Fifth Estate*, starring Benedict Cumberbatch as Assange, in October 2013. David Thewlis played Nick Davies, and Peter Capaldi was a rather convincing Alan Rusbridger.

2. 'The Man Who Spilled the Secrets', *Vanity Fair* Hive, February 2011; Sarah Ellison

3. The bulk of the work was done by Harold Frayman, a former *Observer* sub-editor who had started messing around with computers in middle age and ended up as systems editor.

4. Quoted in Lundberg, K. *Friend or Foe?*; *see Bibliography*

5. The Swedish prosecutors dropped the rape investigation in May 2017.

6. The effect of the Pentagon Papers Supreme Court judgment was that the government would have to demonstrate direct, immediate and irreparable damage to the state before the courts would restrict or prevent publication.

7. Twitter, 29 May 2015, 12.44 p.m.; @wikileaks

8. 'Ghosting: Julian Assange', *London Review of Books*, 6 March 2014; Andrew O'Hagan

9. James Clapper, the former Director of National Intelligence, told Raffi Khatchadourian of the *New Yorker*: 'It was done by a cutout, which of course afforded Assange plausible deniability.' ('Julian Assange: A Man Without a Country', *New Yorker*, 21 August 2017)

10. 'Julian Assange: A Man Without a Country', *New Yorker*, 21 August 2017

11. Interview with Ian Katz, editor of *Newsnight*, BBC Two, 15 December 2016

12. 'Free' in the sense of available rather than at no cost.

13. These reports allege Trump has deep ties to Russia, 10 January 2017

14. 'A Veteran Spy Has Given the FBI Information Alleging a Russian Operation to Cultivate Donald Trump', *Mother Jones*, 31 October 2016; David Corn

15. Statement to the House of Commons, 13 July 2011

16. A league table of the most complained-of titles was compiled by Hacked Off in 2013.

17. A statement released on behalf of the group showed how the group agreed to the majority of Leveson's main recommendations: 'The editors of all national newspapers met today and unanimously agreed to start putting in place the broad proposals – save the statutory underpinning – for the independent self-regulatory system laid out by Lord Justice Leveson.'

18. Through control by the Privy Council.

19. An MST/YouGov poll in November 2012 showed that 90 per cent of *Guardian* readers (and 81 per cent of *Daily Mail* readers) wanted an independent regulator 'established by law'.

20. Ramsay, G.N. 'How Newspapers Covered Press Regulation After Leveson'; *see Bibliography*

21. This was out of step with their readers, at least half of whom approved of the proposed regulatory system.

22. *Guardian*, 18 January 2018

23. 'I Was Nothing More Than a Common Thief', *Guardian*, 7 March 2018; Dan Sabbagh and Ewen MacAskill

24. When the *Financial Times*'s editor, Lionel Barber, was awarded the Legion D'Honneur in August 2016 a *Daily Mail* editorial went into meltdown, branding him a 'weapons grade social climber and name-dropper extraordinaire'. An in-house columnist, Stephen Glover, sneered at the *FT* as being 'to most of us a peripheral newspaper'. He described the paper's coverage of Brexit as 'one-sided and hysterical' and with a 'decreasing sense of allegiance to this country'.

25. In the course of our own libel battles I had come across Anthony Lewis's 1992 book *Make No Law* (*see Bibliography*). It was there that I learned, rather late in the day, about *New York Times* v Sullivan – the ringing Supreme Court judgment by Mr Justice Brennan which – forgive my crude summary – essentially gives American journalists the right to be wrong. It acknowledges that journalism about matters of high public importance ought to be protected, not chilled; that journalists can and do make honest mistakes; and that the First Amendment – 'Congress shall make no law abridging the freedom of speech or of the press' – is a rock on which to defend free expression. So, unless a claimant can prove 'actual malice', a public figure is unable to recover damages for libel in America. In the UK there was some, but not much, interest in developing a public interest defence to libel along the lines of Sullivan. That would assume that there was an agreed idea of the public interest. Article 10 protects 'Freedom of expression . . . this right shall include freedom to hold opinions and to receive and impart information and ideas, without interference by public authority and regardless of frontiers'. It has successfully been used by several newspaper groups to defend press freedom and protect journalists' sources.

26. In September 2009, following sustained legal action and journalistic coverage, Trafigura agreed to pay more than £30 million in compensation and legal costs to 30,000 inhabitants of Abidjan in Ivory Coast, for 'flu-like symptoms' they might have suffered following the dumping. The oil traders continued to deny that the waste could have caused serious or fatal injuries. (*Guardian*, 12 October 2009)

27. The UK newspaper industry actually asked for this third factor to be included in the Human Rights Act. 'Under its second chairman, Lord Wakeham, the PCC lobbied for the press to be exempt from Article 8 of the European Convention on Human Rights which guarantees the right to respect for private life. Having failed in that respect, Wakeham negotiated with the Home Secretary Jack Straw to add a new section 12 to the Human Rights Act 1998 designed to tip

the balance of power towards the press in any trade-off between privacy and free speech.' 'History repeated as IP50 morphs into the PCC', The International Forum for Responsible Media Blog, 25 October 2016; Steven Barnett

28. The full judgment is at http://www.bailii.org/ew/cases/EWHC/QB/2011/1192.html

29. The full judgment is at http://www.bailii.org/ew/cases/EWHC/QB/2011/1308.html

30. 'Revealed: Staggering Number of Celebs Who Have Banned You from Reading About Their Sleazy Antics', *Sun*, 6 May 2016

31. Things were to change a few years later when claimant lawyers began to make extensive and creative use of data protection legislation to close down reporting.

20 Members?

1. A.P. Wadsworth, editor 1944–56; Alastair Hetherington, editor 1956–75.

2. Organised, inspiringly, by a columnist, Madeleine Bunting.

3. The most up to date NRS PADD figures we had at the time pointed up how drastically the subscriber model curtailed the reach of a news organisation. More than half of the *Guardian*'s and *Telegraph*'s readers were by 2012 based purely online compared with just 6 per cent on the *Times*, which charged for access.

4. 'We have grown our digital revenues, and we are achieving strong growth in membership, subscriptions and contributions,' said the GMG chief executive, David Pemsel, who was paid £706,000 last year. 'More people are paying for *Guardian* journalism than ever before. This is helping to build a strong foundation from which we will continue to invest in some of the most trusted journalism in the world.' (*Guardian*, 25 July 2017)

5. *Press Gazette*, 7 December 2017

6. 'How the *Guardian* Found 800,000 Paying Readers', *The Drum*, 26 October 2017; Ian Burrell

7. By March 2017 they claimed 56,000 members.

8. Medium, 1 December 2015

9. Quoted in 'The Antidote to Scale', *The Drum*, 2 February 2017; Cameron Clark

10. 'Optimizing for Trust', Medium, 13 April 2018; Jay Rosen

11. Another European start-up, Mediapart, was created in 2008 with 60,000 or so subscribers producing a budget of €500,000 in 2011. It takes no advertising.

12. Grueskin, B., Seave, A. and Graves, L. 'The Story So Far: What We Know About the Business of Digital Journalism'; *see Bibliography*

13. By 2016 Times Newspapers said it employed just 459 full-time employees, all editorial. All other costs were off the books. Henry Mance in the *FT* commented in December 2014: 'on a pre-tax basis the titles are likely to still be loss making. It is also unclear how News Corp allocates corporate costs – such as its new London headquarters next to the Shard skyscraper, and payments for the rights to sports highlights'. Associated Newspapers – a not dissimilar company – employed 1,900 people in 2014. For comparison, the *Telegraph* employed 660 editorial and production staff in 2017. The *New York Times* newsroom was around 1,450 and the *Washington Post*'s around 750.

14. A transformation team was put in place across editorial and commercial to make the changes happen more quickly. It was led by Sheila Fitzsimons, an Irish former teacher and economics graduate who was one of the rare people in the building who combined numeracy with logistical genius; strategic clear-sightedness with empathy. She had been hugely involved in the Berliner presses; in dealing with technology; in merging operations before moving building, and much more.

15. Lewis went on to work for Rupert Murdoch, first in the aftermath of phone hacking on the British titles and then as CEO of Dow Jones.

16. Statement by Murdoch MacLennan, *Telegraph*, CEO, 26 Novemeber 2009.

21 The Trophy Newspaper

1. The phrase was coined by the *Telegraph*'s much loved former editor Bill Deedes, to describe a story so gripping that it could lead to a distracted breakfast accident.

2. Quoyed in Hastings. Max, *Editor, An Inside Story of Newspapers*. London: Pan Macmillan, 2012.

3. 'Britain's Billionaire Barclay Twins Use Stealth to Amass Empire', Bloomberg, 29 November 2004; Simon Clark and Erik Schatzker

4. *Guardian*, 4 July 2018.

5. King left the *Telegraph* in 2017 to become managing director of Exterion Media.

6. MacLennan stepped down as CEO in 2017, taking a role as deputy chairman of Telegraph Media, which he relinquished the following year. He was replaced as CEO by Nick Hugh, former European vice-president of Yahoo.

PP. 301–316

22 Do You Love Your Country?

1. (1725–97) Libertine, libertarian, journalist, MP, agitator. Arrested and charged with sedition and treason. Fled to Paris. Supported by the mob on his return. Jailed, but re-elected. Reformed the reporting of parliament.

2. The British equivalent of the NSA, the Government Communications Headquarters.

3. The full transcript is published at www.parliament.uk in the Home Affairs committee minutes of evidence. https//publications.parliament.uk/pn/cm201314/cmselect/cmhaff/c23i-iv/c23101.htm

4. My father had been employed in the Northern Rhodesian education service.

5. The eventual report of the Home Affairs select committee made no criticism of the *Guardian*. It noted that British civil servants and intelligence chiefs had refused to give evidence. 'In contrast Mr Rusbridger came before us and provided open and transparent evidence.'

6. Four years later the British police confirmed they were still investigating journalists who had worked on the story. The inquiry was codenamed Operation Curable (*The Intercept*, 29 November 2017; Ryan Gallagher).

7. (b. 1964) Her film about Snowden and our reporting, *Citizenfour*, premiered in October 2014. It went on to win an Oscar as best documentary feature.

8. Greenwald, G. *No Place to Hide*; *see Bibliography*.

9. Twitter, 6 June 2013, 2.39 a.m.; @algore

10. 'Australian Spy Agencies Targeted Indonesian President's Mobile Phone', *Guardian*, 18 November 2013

11. The Panopticon was a building and system of all-seeing control imagined by the philosopher Jeremy Bentham in the late eighteenth century.

12. The story of Ellsberg and the Pentagon Papers was first made into a feature film, *The Most Dangerous Man in America*, in 2009. Steven Spielberg's *The Post* (2017) emphasised the parallel role of the *Washington Post* under Ben Bradlee and Katharine Graham.

13. His book, *No Place to Hide* (*see Bibliography*), speaks of his 'contempt for the process . . . the government should not be a collaborative editorial partner with newspapers in deciding what gets published'

14. Clegg, N. *Politics: Between the Extremes*; *see Bibliography*

418

15. 'NSA and GCHQ Target Tor Network That Protects Anonymity of Web Users', *Guardian*, 4 October 2013

16. 'Why the NSA's Attacks on the Internet Must Be Made Public', *Guardian*, 4 October 2013

17. In May 2017 it was reported that one leaked NSA tool, an exploit of Microsoft Windows called EternalBlue, had been used to rapidly spread a ransomware variant called WannaCry across the world. The ransomware hit UK hospitals hard, with multiple sources reporting closures of entire wards. (*Forbes*, 12 May 2017; Thomas Fox-Brewster)

18. The respective homes of MI6, MI5 and GCHQ.

19. 'The Detention of David Miranda Was an Unlawful Use of the Terrorism Act', *Guardian*, 21 August 2013

20. Editor 2011–13; he now works in PR.

21. *Independent*, 13 October 2013

22. *Daily Mail*, 10 January 2015,

23. Hooper, D. *Official Secrets*; *see Bibliography*

24. It was this decision that led Snowden to avoid the *New York Times* when trying to find a home for his own material.

25. Quoted in Goodale, J. *Fighting for the Press*, 2013

26. 'Protection of Official Data: A Consultation Paper', *The Law Commission*, 2017

27. *Newsweek*, 26 April 2016

28. Twitter, 25 April 2016, 5.02 p.m.; @Snowden

29. A good summary of the key findings was published by ACLU on 20 December 2013.

30. Presidential Policy Directive – Signals Intelligence Activities, 17 January 2014

31. 'Obama Outlines Calibrated Curbs on Phone Spying', *New York Times*, 17 January 2014

32. *Guardian*, 6 February 2015

33. *New York Times*, 7 May 2015

34. NBC News, 2 June 2015

35. The Investigatory Powers Tribunal revealed that GCHQ had spied illegally on Amnesty International. It did not give any details of what information GCHQ obtainedabout Amnesty, what was done with it or how long it was held for. *Guardian*, 2 July 2015

36. *The Intercept*, 6 October 2015

37. CNN, 31 May 2016

38. *Irish Times*, 4 October 2016

39. Set up in 1975 to study government intelligence activities, and chaired by Idaho Senator Frank Church.

40. https://www.brennancenter.org/sites/default/files/news/Snowden_memo.pdf

41. *Guardian*, 8 September 2017

42. *Guardian* 21 December 2016

43. *Daily Mail*, 18 June 2013

44. *Daily Mail*, 4 July 2013

45. *Daily Mail*, 1 August 2013

46. *Daily Mail*, 10 October 2013; Douglas Murray

47. *Daily Mail*, 10 October 2013; Stephen Glover

48. 'Paul Dacre, that nice man who edits the *Daily Mail*, has become famous in recent times for "double-cunting": a colleague, usually male, will be ticked off via a thunderous, compound deployment of the Old Frisian. "You call that a good cunting headline, you cunt?" might be a typical start to the afternoon.' (*London Review of Books*, 1 June 2017; Andrew O'Hagan)

49. *Guardian*, 11 October 2013

50. *Guardian*, 12 September 2013. A month later, giving evidence to the Home Affairs select committee, he said the damage 'was more serious than I think I at least was inclined to infer . . . at the more sophisticated end of the terrorism spectrum, there will be, at the very least, relief that there is greater certainty about where the risk lies for them.'

51. *New York Times*, 11 June 2013

52. Home Affairs select committee, 24 January 2014

53. Australia, Canada, New Zealand, the United Kingdom and the United States.

54. Wisconsin congressman since 1979 district. Chaired the House Judiciary Subcommittee on Crime, Terrorism, Homeland Security and Investigations and was a primary author of the USA Patriot Act. (*Guardian*, 9 June 2013)

55. *The Intercept*, 29 Novemeber 2017

56. Regardless of cost, it was not clear whether the police had taken due consideration of Crown Prosecution Service Guidelines published in September 2012 advised that – even (as with the Official Secrets Act) there was no public interest defence – prosecutors should not proceed without weighing whether a criminal case was required in the public interest.

6. (b. 1947) Founder of online travel site Wotif, and the Global Mail – a not-for-profit journalism website which closed in 2014.

7. Nielsen, June 2015. It ranked the 6th most popular news website in Australia.

8. By mid-2017 there were more than 150 non-profit journalistic enterprises in the US, which has more enlightened tax breaks for journalism than the UK.

9. See Chapter 21.

10. Currently based in New York as head of curation at Twitter.

11. Blau later became vice president (digital) for Condé Nast, while Pilhofer took the James B. Steele Chair in Journalism Innovation, Temple University, Minnesota.

12. (b. 1980) Arthur Gregg Sulzberger announced he would succeed his father as publisher in December 2017.

13. (b. 1967) A weekly columnist. Former US correspondent; broadcaster and author of non-fiction books and (as 'Sam Bourne') racy thrillers. He edited the Opinion section of the *Guardian* until 2016.

14. Politico Europe – jointly founded by the *Economist* and Axel Springer – was launched in April 2015.

15. Video views rose from 10 million per month in 2014 (26 per cent of them off the *Guardian* platform) to 30 million per month in 2015 (67 per cent off the *Guardian* platform).

16. The commercial team's aim in 2013/14 was to reach up to $40 million of US revenue in three years.

17. Nigel Morris, CEO of Aegis Media Americas, and John Paton, CEO of Digital First Media. The board also included Neil Berkett, former CEO of Virgin Media; Ronan Dunne, CEO Telefonica UK; Brent Hoberman, the founder of LastMinute.com; and Amelia Fawcett, the head of Morgan Stanley's European division, responsible for $6.7 billion.

18. A term coined by James Collins and Jerry Porras in their 1994 book *Built to Last: Successful Habits of Visionary Companies*.

19. The commercial team was, under Andrew Miller's and David Pemsel's leadership, putting together a mix of revenue streams to sustain the *Guardian* into the future. Copy sales were still a crucial, if declining, cash generator. Digital advertising was growing healthily. But all the sums depended mainly on Pemsel's predictions about digital advertising's continued growth. GMG in 2015 reduced its operating loss to £17.6 million, driven by a strong commercial performance

at the *Guardian* and at Top Right Group. The Scott Trust endowment stood at more than £1 billion once we realised all remaining assets. The GMG Board's assumption was therefore that the *Guardian* could sustain losses of up to £15 million a year without compromising the overall endowment.

It wasn't a huge cushion, but it certainly made a difference. We had been near the brink after the post-Lehmann recession. But we had – just about – charted our way back. By the time Andrew Miller, CEO, stepped down in early 2015, Berkett was sounding as though the worst was over. The organisation was 'in very strong health . . . 2014 was the year we secured the financial future of the *Guardian*' (GNM Press office, 10 December 2014). His deputy, Pemsel, took over in June and pronounced the paper 'financially secure'.

Henry Mance, in the *FT*, wrote of GMG's finances on 17 June 2015: 'If the investment fund were to generate returns of 4 per cent a year, that could sustain the newspaper's current losses indefinitely.' The overall optimism turned out to be considerably over-cooked. We all knew we – like 90 per cent of the press – were walking a tightrope. But no one internally was raising any significant red flags in spring 2015.

20. 'Digital News Report', Oxford: Reuters Institute for the Study of Journalism, 2016

21. eMarketer, 21 September 2017

22. My successor, Kath Viner, would later write to readers (in March 2017) claiming that 'for every new advertising dollar spent in the US, 99 cents is now taken up by Facebook and Google'.

23. 'Expect a Bloodbath in Media Within the Next Year', Digiday, 20 May 2016

24. Between November 2014 and July 2015, GMG, Berkett and Pemsel issued seven public statements praising the *Guardian*'s commercial success and officially predicting growing digital revenues and flat underlying losses in the year ahead.

25. Viner and Pemsel briefing to staff, 25 January 2016.

26. No strategy would – still – stay the same for long. Pemsel was proud that the *Guardian* had been the only publisher to be a launch partner for all of Facebook's Instant articles, Google DNI and Apple News. But within a year the *Guardian* pulled out of Facebook Instant (which loaded more quickly, but kept readers within the Facebook app) and Apple News. But it found that Google's AMP (accelerated mobile pages) was generating 60 per cent of its mobile pages.

27. Two and a half years after Andrew Miller and I stood down, the *Guardian* had

cut its costs significantly in response to declining ad revenues across all news-papers. But the essential business model remained the same. In October 2017 the new MD, David Pemsel, who had been commercial director under Miller – running America and membership as part of his portfolio – announced that 300,000 members were now making monthly payments. On top of that there were 200,000 subscribers across print and digital and 300,000 individual dona-tions. He said the US and Australian operations remained central to GMG's strategy (*The Drum*, 26 October, 2017). In a message to readers on the same day, Viner emphasised: 'We haven't put up a paywall. Instead, we want to remain a strong, progressive force that is open for all.'

28. 'Guardian on Track to Break Even As Company Halves Its Losses', *Guardian*, 25 April 2018

29. The BBC was, for instance, criticised in October 2017 for 'balancing' the views of scientists with erroneous opinions from former UK Chancellor, Lord Lawson, who has no apparent scientific training.

30. Breitbart, 20 March 2017

31. Breitbart, 27 February 2017

32. More encouraging was the *New York Times*'s appointment of a climate editor and team in 2017 after previously scaling back their coverage.

33. *The Star*, 18 September 2017. Jennifer Good is an associate professor of Communication, Popular Culture and Film at Brock University, Canada.

34. We'd both been awarded a Right Livelihood prize, sometimes called the 'alter-native Nobel'.

35. 'Global Warming's Terrifying New Math', *Rolling Stone*, 19 July 2012

36. We made 13 episodes, titled 'The Biggest Story in the World', narrated by Aleks Krotoski and produced by Francesca Panetta. The campaign was spearheaded by James Randerson, a former science correspondent. Emma Howard, Ricken Patel and Amanda Michel brought campaigning experience, and Alex Breuer oversaw design.

37. *Financial Times*, 15 December 2017

Epilogue

1. Kueng, L. 'Going Digital: A Roadmap for Organisational Change' *see Bibliography*

2. Reuters Institute for the Study of Journalism, 'Digital News Report', 2017

3. Monday Note, 15 January 2018

4. Editorial, 17 March 2017

5. 'Building Global Community', 16 February 2017

6. 'I ask myself what the paper stood for when first I knew it, what it has stood for since and stands for now. A newspaper has two sides to it. It is a business, like any other, and has to pay in the material sense in order to live. But it is much more than a business; it is an institution; it reflects and it influences the life of a whole community; it may affect even wider destinies. It is, in its way, an instrument of government. It plays on the minds and consciences of men. It may educate, stimulate, assist, or it may do the opposite. It has, therefore, a moral as well as a material existence, and its character and influence are in the main determined by the balance of these two forces. It may make profit or power its first object, or it may conceive itself as fulfilling a higher and more exacting function. I think I may honestly say that, from the day of its foundation, there has not been much doubt as to which way the balance tipped so far as regards the conduct of the paper whose fine tradition I inherited and which I have had the honour to serve through all my working life. Had it not been so, personally I could not have served it.' C.P. Scott essay 'On Journalism', printed in the *Manchester Guardian*, 5 May 1921. Reprinted in Scott, C.P. *The Making of the Manchester Guardian*, Frederick Muller, 1946

7. Preface to the US edition of Haslam Mills's study of the *Manchester Guardian*'s first 100 years.

8. A 430,000-square-foot campus with a nine-acre rooftop park opened in March 2015.

9. (b. 1969) Previously worked at the *Telegraph* and is a novelist.

10. *CNN*, 27 March 2018

11. The British libertarian website Guido Fawkes responded by pointing out that the *Guardian*'s own privacy policy revealed that the paper also collected data from users' accounts, along with their friends (29 March 2018).

12. Twitter, 21 March 2018, 8.59 p.m.; @fchollet

13. Katharine Graham (1917–2001), publisher and/or chair of the *Washington Post* 1963–91.

14. 'Don't Regulate Facebook', *Washington Post*, 26 March 2018

15. Levy, D., Aslan, B. and Bironzo, D. 'UK Press Coverage of the EU Referendum'; *see Bibliography*

16. During the campaign itself, Reuters found, 56 per cent of all coverage was devoted to personalities and the campaign itself, and only 42 per cent on the arguments.

17. Journalists at his papers had, incidentally, not had a pay rise since 2008.

18. The habit of newspapers becoming part of the machinery of politics was also reflected in a £30,000 Information Commission fine against the *Telegraph* for sending thousands of emails on general election day 2015, urging readers to vote Conservative.

19. Moore, M. and Ramsay, G.N. 'Brexit and Discrimination in the UK Press'. Essay in *Brexit, Trump and the Media*; *see Bibliography*

20. Whittow, H. 'The Daily Express and Brexit'. Essay in *Brexit, Trump and the Media*; *see Bibliography*

21. Highlighted in the *Economist* Daily Chart, 22 June 2016

22. Brussels correspondent of *Libération* and blogs at Coulisses de Bruxelle; *Guardian*, 15 July 2016

23. *Daily Mail*, 4 November 2016. The writer of the piece, James Slack, was later appointed the prime minister's spokesman.

24. *Daily Mail*, 19 April 2017

25. Theresa May distanced herself from the headline: 'Absolutely not, politics and democracy are about, of course, people having different opinions, different views' (*Today* programme, BBC Radio 4, 19 April 2017)

26. *Telegraph*, 17 November 2017

27. *Daily Mail*, 14 December 2017

28. But the Dewey idea of the informed citizen relied on enough people wanting to be informed – or to feel it was worth the trouble of informing themselves because it might have some effect. I asked Ian Dunt, the (pro-Remain) editor of Politics.co.uk why more news organisations had not gone for a more balanced, factual, approach. 'Oh we tried that,' he said, 'and literally almost no one read it. They don't read about fishing quotas or aviation tariffs, however vital they are. But if you write about Boris Johnson, everyone will read it.'

29. Gillmor, D. *We the Media*; *see Bibliography*

30. Archived at https://politicalscrapbook.net/2017/07/

31. *Sun,* 31 October 2017

32. Twitter, 31 October 2017, 3.15 p.m.; @BarristerSecret

33. *Daily Mail*, 15 December 2017; Larisa Brown

34. Twitter, 14 December 2017, 11.55 p.m.; @AdamWagner1

35. PressThink, 28 December 2016

36. The new publisher of the *New York Times*, A.G. Sulzberger, acknowledged that the 'Trump Bump' had added 'hundreds of thousands' of new readers (*New Yorker*, 22 December 2017). The interviewer, David Remnick, cautioned that the *Washington Post* was studying the converse effect: when Trump stopped being president would the audience slacken?

37. Quoted in Fairfield, J.D. *The Public and Its Possibilities*. Temple University Press, 2010

38. 'How the Post Office Made America', *New York Times*, 8 February 2013

39. Sandel, M. *What Money Can't Buy*; *see Bibliography*

40. The term 'subsidiariat' was coined by Paul Dacre in a 2008 speech to the Society of Editors conference in Bristol: 'those media outlets who cannot connect with enough readers to be commercially viable, and whose views and journalism are only sustained by huge cross-subsidy from profitable parts of their owners' empires or by tax payers' money . . . in most cases – [subsidy] ultimately perverts everything it touches. In the media, it produces a distorting prism, actually incentivising its recipients to operate in splendid isolationism, far removed from the real world that the great majority of readers and listeners have to live in.'

41. In May 2017, 70 per cent of Americans were using Facebook several times a day (53 per cent) or about once a day (17 per cent). Instagram and Snapchat scored around the same as ABC News (Morning Consult National Tracking poll).

42. The scheme was welcomed by the UK *Press Gazette*, which nevertheless likened it to 'using a sticking plaster to fix a severed limb' (3 February 2017).

43. *Financial Times*, 11 October 2017; Tim Harford

44. 'The False Prophecy of Hyperconnection', Council on Foreign Relations, 9 July 2017

45. IPSO website, July 2018 FAQs.

46. Around 40 per cent of Britons and Americans now have some form of college degree and have been schooled in being sceptical about sources.

47. Grafton, A. *The Footnote: A Curious History*; *see Bibliography*

48. 'Want to Attract More Readers? Try Listening to Them', *New York Times*, 9 July 2016; Liz Spayd (public editor)

49. Benjamin, A. and Benjamin, B. *A World Without Bees*; *see Bibliography*

Index

BSkyB 32, 188, 192, 196, 407n
Buckingham Palace 183
B.UK Limited 287
bulk sales 69, 70, 96, 126, 164, 342, 398n, 402n
Bunting, Madeleine 115, 116, 273
Bush, President George W. 321
Butler report (2004) 90
Buzzfeed xviii, 123, 226, 227, 254–6, 346
Byrne, Gabriel 353

Cable, Vince (MP) 332
Cadwalladr, Carole 357–8
Cairns, Colonel Douglas 320
Calder, Simon 110
Cambridge Analytica (CA) 346, 357–8
Cambridge Evening News (CEN) (newspaper) 1, 4–9, 11, 12, 13
Cameron, Prime Minister David 71, 183, 188, 191–2, 256–7, 263, 294
Campbell, W. Joseph 30
Canary Wharf 77, 88, 155
Canonbury 158
Carlson, Tucker xi–xii
Carman, George (QC) 36, 38, 39–42, 395n
Carney, Mark 353
Carter, Graydon 90
Carter-Ruck lawyers 175
Carvin, Andy 202
Catch Me If You Can (film) 196
Caulfield, Mr Justice 321
Cecil, Lord Robert 21
censorship 118, 222, 368
CERN 81
challenge 51, 53, 221, 325
Champaign News Gazette (newspaper) 70, 208
Channel 4 (TV) 264, 358
Chaos Monkeys (Martínez) 178–9, 345
Chapman, Jessica 191

charity 273
Charles, Prince 353
Chartbeat 228
Chehadé, Fadi 333
Chernin, Peter 75
Chicago Online 28
Chicago Sun-Times (newspaper) 270
Chicago Tribune (newspaper) 28, 125
China 205, 247, 313, 316
Chippendale, Peter 49
Chomsky, Noam 128, 218
Churchill, Prime Minister Sir Winston 292, 320, 328
'churnalism' 181, 182
CIA 205
CiF (Comment is Free) 112–23, 215
CiF Belief 115, 402n
circulation 22–3, 69–71, 148–54 passim, 210, 283, 292, 395n
bulk sales 69, 70, 96, 126, 164, 342, 398n, 402n
decline 74, 83, 89, 92, 342
gains 32, 46, 86, 211
international 44, 72–3, 76, 152, 348
citizen journalists (stringers) 7, 112
Citizen Kane (film) 286
City of London 224
City University of New York (CUNY) 45
Clapper, James 308, 323
Claridge's hotel 78, 288–9
classified material 245, 248, 310
Clegg, Nick (MP) 156, 188, 316, 318
Clerkenwell 84
'click-through rate' (CTR) 177
clickbait 217, 336–7
climate change xviii, 113, 205, 226, 337, 348–51, 351–3, 359, 372, 424n
Clinton, President Bill 30, 59, 205, 225

Clinton, Hillary 204, 205, 244, 251, 255–6
Clooney, George 197
Cobain, Ian 206
Cobbet, William 265
Code of Practice 298
Cole, Peter 15
Colao, Vittori 333
colour 58, 59, 95, 170, 251, 401n
Colvin, Marie 378
Comey, James 251
Committee of Imperial Defence (UK) 320
Committee to Protect Journalists (CPJ) 370, 421n
'commodity news' 61
Common Purpose 262
complexity 80, 82, 91, 93
composing room 2–3, 11
ComScore 336, 421n
concentration camps 20
Conn, David 206
consent 307
Conservative Party xx, 36, 43, 82, 184, 282, 283–5, 294, 299, 301, 316, 320, 366
content management system 58, 153–4
convergence 25
Coogan, Steve 190
Cook, Tim 333
Corn, David 256
correction 221, 374–6
corruption 16, 35, 160–1, 186, 198, 280, 330
Coulson, Andy 78–9, 183, 187–91, 194
Cox, Jo (MP) 364–5
Craigslist 30, 125
The Creation of the Media (Starr) 198
cricket 106
Crossman, Richard 321
crowdfunding 273
crowdsourcing 17, 203, 204, 223, 232, 250
Crown Prosecution Service 190, 420

INDEX

Mowlam, Mo (MP) 225,
412n
MPs 35, 71, 186, 196, 203,
301–3, 307, 326, 364
MSN 75
Mubenga, Jimmy 201, 202
Mugabe, President Robert
280
Mulcaire, Glenn 190, 191,
194
Mumsnet 69
Murdoch, James 184, 196,
236, 263, 300
Murdoch, Rupert xii–xiii,
xxiii, 11, 22, 31–2, 48,
84–5, 134, 136, 164,
184–97 passim, 211, 241,
282, 339, 346, 394–5n
Murdoch, Wendi 65
Murdoch empire 21, 32, 65,
78–9, 85, 97, 150–1,
185–6, 196, 209–11,
236–7, 263, 276, 337,
362, 404n
Murray, Douglas 327
Murray, Scott 103–4, 106
Murrow, Edward R. 197
Muslims xiii–xiv, xvi–xvii,
114–15, 205
Mutter, Alan 76
mutualisation 111, 122, 273
Myners, Paul 151, 163
MySpace xxiii, 97, 134–6,
145

National Security Agency
(NSA) 301, 303–5, 308,
310, 314, 317, 321, 323,
324, 332
National Theatre 229
National Union of Journalists 10, 260
Naughton, John 26
NCND policy (never
confirm nor deny)
314–15
Negroponte, Nicholas 25
Netherlands, Queen of the
223
netiquette 68

Netscape 24, 30
Neuberger, Lord 308
Nevin, Charles 60
New Republic (magazine) 153
New Statesman (magazine)
10, 76, 123, 194, 262
New York Observer (news-
paper) 283
New York offices 228,
305–6, 316
New York Post (newspaper)
110
New York Times v. Sullivan
case (1964) 174
New Yorker (magazine) 255,
351, 369
Newland, Martin 292
Newmark, Craig 124–5
Newmarket Road
(Cambridge) 4, 7, 9
News Corporation 65, 75,
137, 188, 192–4, 338,
407n
News Digital Media 65
News Group Newspapers
(NGN) 190, 192, 362
News International (NI) 65,
78, 95, 183–5, 187,
190–2, 196, 264, 334,
408n
News Network 65
Newsday.com 208
Newseum (US) 244
Newsnight (TV) 240
Newspaper Money (Hirsch/
Gordon) 128
Newsworks' Shift confer-
ence 404–5n
NHS 119
Nielsen NetRatings 75
1984 (Orwell) x
Nixon, President Richard
310–11, 320, 322, 358
North Africa xi, xxi
North Briton (newspaper) 301
North Korea 247
Northcliffe, Lord 339
Northcliffe Media 126
'Not Invented Here' (NIH)
resentment 232

Nottingham Evening Post
(newspaper) 11
Nougayrède, Natalie 344

Obama, President Barack
205, 255, 304, 308, 323,
324
Ofcom 137, 196, 236
Official Secrets Act (OSA)
320, 321
Official Secrets (Hooper) 321
O'Hagan, Andrew 248
oil companies 206, 352, 354
O'Kane, Maggie 206
Old Bailey 22, 191, 196, 331
Oliver, Craig 313, 315
Omidyar, Pierre 339
On Demand 67
'On Journalism' (Scott essay)
19, 394n, 425n
Open Democracy 123, 279,
280
Open Weekend (2012) 270,
377
Operation Weeting 190
O'Reilly, Tony 85
'original sin' 76
Orphan 226–8
Orwell, George x, 128, 236,
306, 323
Osborne, Peter 279–82, 291,
293, 297–8
Oscars 304
ownership model 218
Oxford University xxii

Pacino, Al 197
page views 227
Panopticon 310, 358, 418n
Panorama (TV) 286
Paris climate talks 351, 354
Parker, Andrew 333
Paton, John 127
Patriot Act (2001) 324, 333
PayPal 140
paywalls 75, 126–7, 133, 164,
180, 198, 211–13, 236,
347, 348, 409n
'hard' 208–10, 215
metred 213, 216

INDEX

Peake, Maxine 353

Pearson & Co 65, 150

Pemsel, David 239, 275, 345, 348, 413n, 416n, 422–4n

Pentagon 246, 310, 319, 322, 330, 331

People Like Us (Luyendijk) 222

Perch, Keith 403n

Perettu, Jonah 347

Periscope 204

perjury 42–3

Permira Advisers Ltd 288

Peterloo Massacre 16–18, 201, 242

Petraeus, General David 325

Pfauth, Ernst-Jan 274

PFE (Proudly Found Elsewhere) 232

philanthropy 337–9

Philby, Kim 321

Piano, Renzo 125

Pilhofer, Aron 340, 422n

Plastic Logic 165

Plender, John 354

podcasts 352, 424n

Podemos xxi

Podesta emails 251, 253

Poitras, Laura 303–5, 310, 315, 318

police 6, 35, 183–207 *passim*, 257, 258, 302–3, 328, 333, 409–10n, 418n, 420n

political subsidy 128

Politico 123

Politics.co.uk 123

Popbitch 104

Popplewell, Sir Oliver 38–9, 41–2

Porter, Henry 116

Post Office Act (US 1792) 370

Pound, Ezra 4

power 99–100

Prescott, John (MP) 183

Press Acquisitions Ltd 287

Press Association 22, 42

Press Complaints Commission (PCC) 184, 187, 193, 257, 258, 265, 407n

Press Holdings Ltd 287

Preston, Peter 20, 21, 24, 30, 31, 36, 42, 167

price war 32, 85

Price Waterhouse Cooper 75

Pride and Perjury (Aitken) 43

The Printing Press as an Agent of Change (Eisenstein) 198

printing presses 2, 3, 6, 8, 9, 11, 46, 95

prisons 43, 49, 81, 99, 159, 171, 187–8, 194, 200, 247, 284, 303

privacy 309

Private Eye (magazine) 162, 174, 279, 281, 282, 299, 372, 406n

private investigators 183, 187–8, 190, 193, 195, 263–4

private sector 308

Proctor & Gamble 232

Prodigy Internet Service 26

Product Development Unit (PDU) 24, 26, 46, 56

Professional Footballers' Association 183

proportionality 309

ProPublica 312–13, 315

Proudler, Gerald 36, 38, 40–1, 42

public goods 198–9, 272

public interest 173, 176, 250, 261–7 *passim*, 285, 302–7 *passim*, 317–22 *passim*, 332, 333–5, 359, 370–1, 415n, 420n

Public Library of Science (PLoS) 234

public service 15–16, 19, 21, 92, 109, 151, 153, 161, 218, 226–36 *passim*, 325, 332, 334

public space 116, 125, 282, 370

'publicness' 373

'purchase driver' 177

Putnam, Robert 7

pyjama injunction 206

Qantas 110

Qatar 206, 288–9, 338

Quatremer, Jean 363

Qur'an 115–16

R_2 153

Raines, Howell 91

Randall, Mike 49–50

rape xii–xvii, 245, 393n

Rath, Matthias 206–7

Ray Street offices 46, 57, 59, 60

'reach before revenue' model 28–9, 32, 64, 76, 144, 152, 336, 344, 347

readers 109

   American 72–3, 76, 133, 152, 348

   knowledge 111, 203, 222, 223, 274, 365

   letters 17, 49, 54, 66, 78, 107, 117, 175, 353

   readers' editor 51–4, 215, 397n

   response 106–7, 108–11, 111–13, 138, 146, 219

   talkboards 66–9, 72, 112, 118, 398n

   see also circulation

Reading Football Club 150

Real Networks 137

Reckless, Mark (MP) 302–3

Reddit xiv, 69, 120, 204

Redford, Robert 12, 197

Reds (film) 197

Rees, Jonathan 187–8, 189, 192

referendum (UK 2016) 129, 361–4

regulation 257–61, 263, 358, 374

Regulatory Funding Council 298

Reid, Harry 255

religious stories 210

rendition, Gibson report on 308

Reuters 22, 105, 134, 212, 394n

   Institute for the Study of Journalism (RISJ) xxii, 346, 355, 362, 372